Southwest China
Off The Beaten Track

K. Mark Stevens
and
George E. Wehrfritz

edited by
Paddy Booz

PASSPORT BOOKS

Trade Imprint of National Textbook Company
Lincolnwood, Illinois U.S.A.

Southwest China
Off The Beaten Track

K. Mark Stevens
and
George E. Wehrfritz

edited by
Paddy Booz

PASSPORT BOOKS
NTC/Contemporary Publishing Company
Lincolnwood, Illinois USA

Acknowledgements

Many thanks to the following friends, relations, fellow travelers and comrades who helped and encouraged us during the creation of this book:

Jane Smith and Diana (taitai) Garrett, our parents, the Publisher and staff of China Guides Series, Thupten Leckpel, Ganzi buddies, His Holiness the Dalai Lama, Catherine (dag) Fitzpatrick, Losang Chungsa, Professor Donald Gibbs, Mrs. Loretta Li, the Dai family, May Holdsworth, Judy Bonavia, Brian Schwartz, Dave Econome, Dave Thompson, Dreux Montgomery, Chas McKhann, Li Suk Woon, Paddy Booz, Elisabeth Booz, Ted Moise, John Dolfin, Yang Shengming, the doctor in Ganzi, Annapurna Exploration, Wyztze Bakker, Da Bian, the Happy Bachelors of Derong, Siu Wor Co., Mary-Louise Hardy, Barry and May, Ingrid Morejohn, Sam (a real good guy), James Ng, Professor Bai Yiliang, Ray and Diane Brooks, Scott Klimo and, finally, the Gonganju officials of Southwest China for the direction they gave our research.

K. Mark Stevens graduated from the University of California, Davis with a Bachelor's degree in Economics and Chinese Language. His first taste of China came in 1982 while studying Mandarin in Taiwan. Mark became the general manager of KDVS radio station in California before leaving the job market to travel widely in remote areas of China. These travels ultimately led to this book. He is currently based in Taiwan and works as a free-lance photographer and journalist.

George E. Wehrfritz came to Asia in 1983 as a language student at the Chinese University of Hong Kong. He spent his holidays trekking in China, venturing as far as Inner Mongolia, Kashgar and the wild mountains of western Sichuan. After graduating from the University of California, Davis, in 1985, George returned to China to research and co-author *Southwest China Off The Beaten Track*. He now works and studies Chinese in Taiwan.

Preface

We researched *Southwest China Off The Beaten Track* at a time when independent travelers in China were enjoying freedoms unprecedented since 1949. With good equipment, a certain proficiency in Chinese and a healthy disrespect for political boundaries, we ventured out almost at will, confronting Gonganju (Public Security Bureau) officials only when we approached international boundaries, war zones or large military bases. From monasteries high in the mountains of Kham, the ancient kingdom of eastern Tibet, to tiny hamlets in the Miao minority backcountry of Guizhou, to tropical towns on Vietnam's border, we hitchhiked, bussed and walked for six months during the winter of 1985–86. After that we studied and worked in Taiwan, transcribing our notes and soliciting publishers in our spare time. China Guides Series accepted our guidebook proposal in the summer, and we soon found ourselves back on the trail again, this time traveling separately to speed up the research.

We have tried to make *Southwest China Off The Beaten Track* the most detailed traveler's reference book on China. It covers nearly 100 cities, towns and villages, with 69 maps labeled in Chinese characters, English and pinyin romanization. We focus on 'hard' information and organize it into a logical form, with extensive, specific presentation of bus and train schedules and the practical realities of hitchhiking and trekking in isolated areas. A specially designed Chinese phrasebook, unlike any other, enables non-Chinese travelers to get whatever they need as they retrace our journeys or venture far beyond the places we went.

We started this project with the intention of writing a comprehensive guidebook. In the end, factors such as time, money, physical exhaustion and the immense size and diversity of Southwest China made this goal impossible. We did, however, make every effort to visit personally every town, temple, park, hot spring, nunnery, bus station, hotel, mosque, pagoda, mountain, cesuo, monastery and monument mentioned in this book. We give full credit in the text for information gathered from other people. Rumors are acknowledged as such.

We welcome enthusiastically any comments, corrections, critiques, new additions and maps, or even a few words of praise.

Happy trails,
The Authors
Taibei

c/o China Guides Series
20 Hollywood Road, 3/F
Central, Hong Kong

Contents

Maps

Legend for Maps

B	Bank	银行	Yinhang
(H)	Hotel	旅馆	Luguan
P	Post Office	邮电局	Youdianju
R	Restaurant	餐馆	Canguan
☙	Teahouse	茶馆	Chaguan
🏛	Cinema	电影院	Dianyingyuan
田	Department Store	百货商店	Baihuo Shangdian
▬▬▬	Railroad	铁路	Tielu
═══	Road	公路	Gonglu
- - - -	Trail	小路	Xiaolu
··········	Ferry	轮渡	Lundu
～	River	河流	Heliu
⬭	Lake	湖泊	Hubo
▲	Mountain	山峯	Shanfeng

Basic Information

Money

Two types of currency are used in China today: *renminbi* (Rmb), the standard currency for all of China, and *waihuijuan* (FEC), known as Foreign Exchange Certificates and issued to foreigners. Rmb are issued in 10, 5, 2, and 1 *yuan* (Chinese dollar) notes; 5, 2, and 1 *jiao* (dime) notes; 5, 2, and 1 *fen* (cent) notes and 5, 2, and 1 *fen* coins. FEC are issued in 100, 50, 10, 5, and 1 *yuan* notes; and 5 and 1 *jiao* notes. In conversation, *yuan* are commonly referred to as *kuai*, *jiao* are called *mao* and *fen* are always called *fen*. Rmb *yuan* and *jiao* notes have denominations written in arabic numerals while *fen* notes are only in Chinese characters. 5 *fen* notes have a drawing of a ship (five people to sail a ship), 2 *fen* has a plane (two people to fly a plane) and 1 *fen* a truck (one person to drive a truck).

The Bank of China (*Zhongguo Yinhang*), located at border crossings, most tourist hotels and CITS offices scattered throughout larger towns, will convert commonly accepted international currencies, traveler's checks and even major credit cards into FEC. The exchange rate is approximately US$1 = FEC 3.8. An exchange receipt is necessary for changing FEC back into foreign currency when leaving China. FEC is required by all major tourist hotels, some taxis, China International Travel Service (CITS), the national airline (CAAC), Friendship Stores, some trains, and a few tourist restaurants. Rmb is the standard currency for all other goods and services in China. Occasionally, in remote areas, people do not recognize FEC and refuse to accept it.

Officially, FEC 1 is equal in value to Rmb 1. However, imported or specialized goods can only be obtained by local Chinese if they pay in FEC, thus highlighting the true relative value of the currencies. This is best revealed by the current black market exchange rate. In 1986 rates were as high as FEC 1 = Rmb 1.70. Today the average rate hovers around FEC 1 = Rmb 1.50. In order to travel cheaply, you should spend as much Rmb as possible while using FEC only when necessary. It is not illegal for foreigners to have and spend Rmb. Keep in mind that you will not be able to change unused Rmb back into foreign currency when leaving China.

Some workers, especially on trains, try to charge FEC so they can switch it themselves for Rmb. We found it best to not even carry FEC in our wallet. Do not feel obligated to pay in FEC if no one can make change. That means never using FEC if your change will be in Rmb. We always kept a FEC 100 note (which is higher than the average monthly wage) stashed away for this purpose. However, travelers should not get angry when forced to pay in FEC in properly designated places. Look at it as a game; you win a few rounds and you lose a few.

Do not worry about finding the black market — it will find you. The cities of Guangzhou (Canton), Yangshuo, Guilin, Kunming, Dali and Chengdu all have thriving black markets, and foreigners are often hounded with cries of 'change money, change money'. Try to bargain for a better rate and never change more than one or two hundred FEC at one time or you might be short-changed. Always count the money first and then hand over the FEC. Everything is so open the Gonganju (Public Security Bureau) obviously knows what is occuring but does not care. The black market usually only accepts

FEC or Hong Kong dollars. If you have British pounds, for example, first exchange them at the bank for FEC and then on the black market for Rmb.

Costs

Travel in China is as cheap or as expensive as you want to make it. Posh tourists spend FEC 380 (US$ 100) per day to be spoon-fed China's exotic wonders. Veteran budget travelers adept at hitchhiking, camping and bargaining can go a month on the same money. We spent 16 months in China researching this book and our expenses, including telexes, international phone calls, flights and an occasional soft sleeper on the trains, were around US$ 200 per month. We did our share of hitchhiking, trekking and camping as well; these kept our costs down.

People on a really strict budget can expect to spend US$ 3 (Rmb 15) per day on food and lodging, and less in remote areas. Transportation is also cheap. Our travels through the Southwest via Guangzhou, Wuzhou, Yangshuo, Liuzhou, Guiyang, Kunming, Chengdu, Chongqing and the Yangzi River cost, altogether, just under Rmb 250, riding mostly hard sleeper on trains and taking local buses. Tourist price for the same will cost about FEC 315.

Off-the-beaten-track travelers invariably spend considerably less than those in major tourist cities. Consider a 30-day trip from Chengdu to Maowen, Barkam, Songpan, Huanglongsi, Jiuzhaigou, Nanping, Pingwu and back to Chengdu. The trip requires seven full-day bus rides at Rmb 8 per day, 30 nights lodging at Rmb 5 per night and 30 days of food at Rmb 5 per day. You can do the entire trip for Rmb 356 (approximately US$ 75).

Spending a little more than the minimum in China can greatly increase the comfort of your trip. Occasionally take a soft sleeper on the trains; every once in a while hire taxis instead of always taking the local bus; have a drink or a meal in a big tourist hotel; move out of the dorms and into a single room for a few nights; treat yourself to a ten-course Chinese banquet; drink a coke (or, even better, Chinese Tian Fu natural cola); take a comfortable mini-bus instead of the slower, jolting local ones; even fly instead of enduring a three-day hard seat train ride. Take it easy from time to time and avoid turning yourself into a nerve-frazzled lunatic just because you do not want to spend a little extra for an upgraded ticket on the train or a quiet place to sleep.

Itineraries

Most budget travelers visit China for a few weeks or months and try to cover as much ground as possible. This is fine if you enjoy spending one third of your time on trains or buses, another third purchasing tickets or finding hotels and the final third in a collection of remarkably similar large cities. The angry, rude, nerve-shattered travelers you meet at the youth hostel in Guangzhou as they leave China exemplify the results of these tactics.

On recent research trips we encountered a surprisingly large number of travelers who were returning to China. Most got burned out several years ago on lengthy all-China trips. Now they are back, taking what our publisher calls the 'Daoist (Taoist) approach' to travel. They visit relatively few places but spend their time extensively exploring and appreciating these areas. Decisions about where to visit are often based on the availability of train, bus or boat tickets. Unburdened by preconceived itineraries, they are patient and flexible. Their experiences collectively are invaluable, their message to fellow travelers clear: the less you base your itinerary on the dream of a no-holds-barred comprehensive China trip and the more you regionalize (Southwest China) or localize (western Guizhou Province) your travel plans, the more special and meaningful your trip will be.

The most common itinerary is the circular route around Southwest China that passes through Guangzhou, Wuzhou, Yangshuo, Guilin, Guiyang, Kunming, Chengdu, Chongqing (Chungking) and the Yangzi River Gorges. Most points along this route have interesting side trips that range in duration from a few days to a few weeks.

From Wuzhou there are boats or buses to Guiping, Guixian or Nanning along the Xijiang River. From Nanning buses lead to Beihai, where boat connections to Hainan Island are numerous.

From Guilin it is easy to take a bus tour of the recently opened Longsheng Various Nationalities Autonomous County, and then on to the Sanjiang Dong and Rongshui Miao Nationality Autonomous Counties before linking up with the rail line in Liuzhou.

From Guiyang you can travel east on a loop through Kaili, Shibing and Zhenyuan, or west to Anshun, Huangguoshu Waterfall and Liupanshui before heading to Kunming.

From Kunming travel south to Xishuangbanna or west to Dali and Lijiang before linking up with the Kunming-Chengdu rail line at Jinjiang.

From Chengdu there is a circular bus route to Maowen, Barkam, Songpan, Huanglongsi, Jiuzhaigou, Nanping, and then back to Chengdu. The route links up with the Chengdu-Xian rail line in Guangyuan or Jiangyou.

From Chongqing the riverboat trip down the Yangzi River can easily be broken at any number of interesting towns.

Always remember that even the most popular tourist spots can be stepping off points to nearby villages that are fascinating in themselves and rarely visited by Westerners.

The above itineraries are only the most obvious. You are limited solely by your imagination, time constraints and budget.

Things to take

Travelers invariably take more than they need to China. To an overburdened traveler, every hotel change or trip to a new area is a hardship because, even in large cities, the most convenient form of transportation is often by foot. Bring what you can comfortably carry for a few kilometers or expect backaches and other trouble. Backpacks are highly recommended as they are easy to carry and fit into irregular spaces on buses and trains. External frame backpacks are easily snagged or even broken, and internal frame packs are more convenient for storage when traveling. A day-pack is extremely useful as well.

We consider the following list of equipment necessary for travelers to China. Many items, especially inexpensive, durable clothing, are available in China from department stores and tourist hotels.

Clothing Fashion has come alive in China, or so says the television news, but you need not be concerned with the craze. Most people in China wash their clothes by hand and probably own a wardrobe smaller than the one stuffed in your backpack. Adhering to local norms is quite easy in the land of unisex soldier suits.

While most Chinese people do not wear shorts, it is acceptable for Westerners to do so, especially the longer Bermuda style. Wear conservative swimwear, and not Speedos or bikinis, when swimming. Women who go braless or wear revealing Western clothing may be openly stared at by Chinese men, and though these stares may seem rude, such dress is considered really indecent in China. Let common sense and discretion be your guides for dressing.

Two or three shirts or blouses and one or two pairs of pants are all you need. It is good to bring one nice shirt you can wear to a club or fancy dinner, though even this is not essential.

Shoes Good shoes or hiking boots are difficult to find in China, especially in large sizes. Estimate what type of traveling you will be doing and plan accordingly.

Toiletries China makes its own brands of most toiletries, but some items differ significantly from their Western counterparts (such as green, wax-like shampoo in a jar or large, brown, rough sheets of toilet paper). If you are particular, bring enough shampoo, tampons, make-up, toothpaste and razor blades to last through your trip.

First-aid kit A small travel kit will do. There is a good chance you will need bandages, aspirin, antibiotic ointment, gauze pads, elastic bandages, mosquito repellant, diarrhoea medicine and perhaps a cycle of antibiotics.

Sleeping bags Sleeping bags are recommended in colder areas, such as Ganzi or Jiuzhaigou, and are necessary when trekking or camping out. A sleeping pad is also a good item for campers.

Earplugs A pair of earplugs is useful when traveling on noisy buses or trains or sleeping in thin-walled hotels.

English-Chinese dictionary and maps Our phrasebook is good, but it cannot possibly cover everything. The Commercial Press publishes an excellent travel dictionary with both Chinese characters and pinyin romanization entitled the *Concise English-Chinese Dictionary*. It is available in Hong Kong and quite inexpensive. Our maps are not as detailed as some printed in China, so trailblazers might get stuck without adequate information. The Cartographic Publishing House prints a map entitled *Map of the People's Republic of China*. This map is in characters and pinyin, so you can say the name of the city as well as point to it.

Visas

Not so long ago the gates of the Middle Kingdom were closed tight against the rest of the world and only a select few were able to penetrate the "bamboo curtain". In 1977 carefully supervised group tours were initiated, and four years later the first individual visas were granted.

Today, tourism is flourishing and individual visas are a routine matter. Guidelines for issuing individual visas vary from place to place and can change overnight. In Western countries, individual visas granted by consular offices can take anywhere from a few days to a few months. Some entry ports in China, like Beijing and Shenzhen, grant visas on the spot. Contact Chinese consulates for up-to-date information. The only requirements are a completed application form, two recent passport photos and a processing fee. Visas are issued for either 30 or 90 days (specify on the application form) and are valid from the date of issue, not from the date of entry. Visa extensions of up to a total of six months are routine within China. Hong Kong has always been the easiest place to get a Chinese visa, and one can be obtained in as quickly as five hours. Look under the Visas to China heading in the Hong Kong section.

Health

In China, foreigners who fall ill will be given the best doctors and care available. It is not uncommon to be personally examined for a minor complaint by the chief resident. Many doctors, especially those in the hinterland, enjoy contact with foreigners and often want to practise their English.

Hospital standards are probably equivalent to those of the US during the 1950s. Conditions are generally clean and sanitary but do not yet match Western standards. Communication difficulties and unfamiliar Chinese methods of treatment may be intimidating at first, but remember the doctors are trying their best to help you. Chances are good that if you are really ill, you will be put on the next plane to Hong Kong.

A positive aspect of Chinese health care is its incredibly low cost. One traveler suffering from altitude sickness was given several housecalls, oxygen, injections and a physical examination for just Rmb 14.

Preparation No shots or vaccines are required before coming to China. Some doctors recommend a gamma globulin injection and some people feel safer having cholera, tetanus and typhoid shots, but these are up to individual preference. If planning a trip to Xishuangbanna or other areas up near the borders of Burma, Vietnam or Laos, consider taking malaria tablets. Get advice from a doctor or pharmacist on the treatment of diarrhoea and common viral infections; these are the two most common health problems for travelers.

Altitude and health In northern Yunnan and western Sichuan, because of the high altitude, travelers with anaemia or pre-existing heart or lung problems should consult a doctor before even thinking about a visit. Most people, once they are acclimatized, rarely suffer more than mild discomfort from the altitude. But enough travelers have had trouble, especially on the road to Tibet, so approach the problems of altitude seriously.

Acclimatization is the adjustment of the human body to the diminished supply of oxygen at high altitudes. Bone marrow produces quantities of extra, new red blood cells to take oxygen from the air in amounts needed for good health, a process which may take several days. Mountain sickness (also called altitude sickness) is caused by an insufficient flow of oxygen to the brain and other vital organs. It can affect anybody above 3,000 meters.

Each person has a different tolerance for altitude which has nothing to do with age, sex or state of fitness. One person will get a headache at 3,400 meters, another not until 5,000 meters. The symptoms of mountain sickness include headache, nausea and shortness of breath, singly or together. In nearly all cases, rest and 2 aspirins will relieve the discomfort. However, the serious — sometimes fatal — conditions of pulmonary and cerebral edema also begin with these same symptoms. If a headache does not respond to aspirin and a good night's rest, or if a dry cough with frothy sputum develops, or if there are any signs of severe lethargy or poor coordination, get to a hospital at once. Better yet, descend as quickly as possible. A lower altitude is the surest cure.

Over-exertion seems to contribute to mountain sickness and dehydration may be a predisposing factor. Sensible precautions should include:

— Stick to a schedule of mild activity and rest for the first two days.
— Drink plenty of fluids. Three to five liters a day are recommended to maintain a clear, copious urine.
— Don't smoke. If you are a chronic smoker, keep it to a minimum.
— Avoid sedatives such as sleeping medicine or tranquilizers. They tend to depress respiration and limit oxygen intake.
— Diamox (acetazolamide), a mild diuretic which stimultes oxygen intake, is used by doctors of the Himalayan Rescue Association in Kathmandu for climbers making sudden ascents. This is a prescription drug that may help to forestall discomfort for people known to be susceptible to mountain sickness. Consult a doctor.

It is not unusual to wake up at night at high altitudes gasping for breath. Don't panic! This complaint, known as "periodic breathing", is normally quite harmless, caused by a change in the control of breathing within the brain while you sleep. Normal breathing can be quickly re-established by relaxation, rhythmic deep-breathing, and the understanding that there is nothing to worry about.

Lodging

Accommodations in China range from first-class, Western-style hotels to filthy, rat infested earthen floor rooms with three cots tossed in. All open areas have hotels designated to accept foreigners, though smaller towns that seldom receive Western visitors rely on guesthouses built for government officials. In big cities, the cheaper hostels where most Chinese travelers stay almost always turn away foreigners. Don't blame the staff for this rule; it comes from on high. If you do manage to check into such a hostel, the Gonganju (Public Security Bureau) might try to move you to a more comfortable hotel that presents a better image to foreigners. At popular tourist destinations, dormitory beds range between Rmb 5−10 and double rooms from Rmb 10−20. Double rooms with a private bathroom cost an additional Rmb 5−10. In more obscure places, the cheapest bed might cost as little as Rmb 0.50, and suites only Rmb 5.

To find a hotel, ask fellow travelers for up-to-date information. Our lodging information is comprehensive within each section of this book, but things change quickly. If you reach a town we do not cover and have no idea where to spend the night, use the phrasebook to find a hotel. Small towns and villages often have only one hotel.

Many hotels, especially in the larger cities, only accept FEC from foreign guests. Such hotels normally post a sign to this effect; if they don't you are under no obligation to pay FEC. Hotel prices are usually non-negotiable, but bargaining takes place over the type of room or bed you want. Hotel workers generally assume that you want the best bed or room in the hotel. Patient, polite (and often repeated) requests for a dorm bed, a bed in a three-bed room (pay for one bed, not the whole room), or a private room without an attached bathroom, usually work. Even in new hotels there are often older wings with reasonably priced rooms. Keep old receipts to show hotel workers if you feel you are being overcharged. Remember that patience and persistence will get you a bed, but loud, angry outbursts will almost certainly ruin any chance you have for success.

Dorms and large rooms tend to be noisy — people come and go at all hours. Light sleepers may want to bring a pair of earplugs and eyeshades. Even private rooms can be loud because televisions are usually played by other guests at full volume until late at night.

Chinese standards of cleanliness do not match Western levels, especially in cheaper places. Most hotels are cleaned daily, but sheets are usually changed only after a guest leaves, and sometimes only after a week. Many rural hotels have only bedcovers that are never changed and become unbelievably dirty. If you stay in expensive Western-style hotels, the level of cleanliness and service is usually quite high.

There are four main types of hotels in China. Though they vary from city to city, here is a general description of what to expect from each.

Lushe Privately run, these are the smallest, cheapest hotels in China. They are always spartan and cater to Chinese travelers, mainly truck drivers and bus passengers, who spend just one night and leave early the next day.

Zhaodaisuo These are government guesthouses located near government offices in most small cities. They are often the only place a foreigner can stay.

Binguan Reserved for high level cadres, Hong Kong Chinese, and Westerners, *binguans* are often luxurious and expensive.

Fandian These can be anything from a rat trap to a luxury hotel. *Fandian* covers the whole range of hotels and hostels, and also means "restaurant" in Chinese.

Food and drink

Chinese cooking ranks among the best in the world, although what you find in China may differ from Chinese food cooked in the West. Basic meals include several dishes such as stir-fried vegetables, thinly sliced meats and watery soups accompanied by either rice or noodles. Regional variations of Chinese cooking are huge, and in the Southwest three provincial styles of cooking dominate — Cantonese, Sichuanese and Yunnanese.

Cantonese is the most famous. It features a wide variety of meats (including snake, eel, pigeon, turtle and dog) and an abundance of fresh vegetables and fish cooked in a variety of sauces. Cantonese cuisine is known for *dim sum*, steamed pastries, dumplings and meat-filled rolls served with tea. Cantonese food is most common in Guangxi and Guangdong. Sichuan cuisine, renowned for its abundant use of chili peppers, features *huoguo* firepot, noodle dishes and an assortment of spicy fried dishes that can burn the mouth of an unwary traveler in Sichuan and Guizhou. Yunnan cuisine is most famous for its steamed chicken and delicate rice noodles served in soup. In addition, fresh fruits, including bananas, pineapples, pears, oranges, apples, sugarcane, coconuts, and papayas are available throughout most of Southwest China. Chinese farmers use liberal quantities of insecticides and fertilizers, so peel all fruit before you eat it.

For those on a budget, Chinese food is cheap, even in many of the finest restaurants. Most people find Rmb 5–10 a day is more than adequate for good food. Good restaurants in China have banquet rooms for tourists and cadres, and more basic dining rooms for the masses. These cheaper sections, usually near the entrance on the ground floor, offer the same food as in the banquet rooms for a fraction of the cost. Even on special occasions, gourmet meals can be had for Rmb 10–15. The best restaurants are the easiest to find as they are usually the most crowded, and you often have to fight for a seat.

Chinese dining customs differ from those of the West. Guests rarely order individual portions. Instead, plates of food are set in the center of the table for everyone to share. Many Westerners who order food individually get upset because everyone at the table is served their order at a different time. People either eat as they are served or wait for the others and eat cold food. In Chinese kitchens, whole meals are cooked in one wok, and groups of people dining together expect a constant flow of dishes rather than everything being served at once. Western-style silverware is usually unavailable, so bring your own if chopsticks are beyond your ability. Travelers worried about sanitation should carry their own chopsticks.

Vegetarians in China face a challenging time. While Chinese people consume very little meat, it is present in small quantities in most dishes, and the cooking oil is often pork fat. Do not dispair, for China also has some of the best vegetarian cooking in the world. Most Buddhist and Daoist (Taoist) temples serve vegetarian food, and Hui (Muslim) restaurants serve some meatless dishes cooked in vegetable oil. Some travelers bring their own vegetable oil to restaurants, and cooks will often try to prepare special vegetarian dishes. For protein, doufu (tofu, or beancurd), an invention of China, can be found practically everywhere. We sought out vegetarian restaurants and have included them in the text.

In China, drink only water that has been either boiled or sterilised. Untreated water, with the possible exception of run-off found high in the mountains, will surely make you sick. Most people have no trouble because boiled water is widely available, usually in thermoses, for the ubiquitous Chinese tea. Although we are confident contaminated water never made us ill, lightweight, portable water purification filters are a practical way to be absolutely sure of your water supply. Bottled water can be purchased in many places, though it is quite expensive.

Chinese beer is exceedingly cheap and usually excellent, but be careful to clean the dirty bottle mouths. Bottled soft drinks, including some imported from the West, can be found nearly everywhere and are safe to drink. It is hard to find something cold to drink in China. There are very few refrigerators, and most are rarely used to keep drinks cold. Many shop owners will refrigerate drinks only after you tell them to, which means waiting a few hours for a cold beer or soda.

Since China began allowing limited free enterprise, food has improved enormously. Street vendors and family-run restaurants serve good food, stay open until late at night, and make an effort to please their customers. Sometimes cooks will prepare special meals for you if you make arrangements ahead of time. Always set the price in advance. Private establishments are out to make money so foreign friends can be grossly overcharged. Sometimes you will be charged a slightly higher price in lieu of grain ration coupons. Hotel food is generally overpriced and inferior to what is available on the streets. Hotel restaurants often feature Western-style breakfasts (Rmb 5−10), and some have good Western food to satisfy that occasional craving. From experience we believe that the chances of getting ill from unsanitary food are about the same no matter where you dine — even in expensive hotel restaurants.

Most guidebooks recommend restaurants in every city they cover. When too many foreigners flock to a restaurant, prices quickly rise, portions shrink in size, English menus replace Chinese ones and the local character of the restaurant vanishes. Therefore, whenever possible, we mention streets or neighborhoods with a selection of restaurants, leaving you to choose the most appealing one. We also put restaurants on our maps as geographic reference points, whether they are good or not.

Ordering food can be difficult if you do not speak Chinese, but it is never impossible. Use the phrasebook to order dishes and give instructions on how you want them prepared. Seek out the recommendations of fellow travelers, because their information is the most up-to-date. Some of the best restaurants we found in China were recommended by non-Chinese speaking travelers with a flair for sniffing out good food.

China International Travel Service

China International Travel Service (CITS) is the official Chinese tourist organization, providing guides, vehicles, interpreters, ticketing, hotel reservations, foreign currency exchange and travel information. If you have the money, CITS is glad to arrange just about anything, including visits to closed areas. Unfortunately, the staff are often incompetent, surly, uninformed about the surrounding area and weak in English skills.

All tickets purchased through CITS will be charged in FEC, at tourist prices, with a small service charge. For the budget traveler it is cheaper, and often easier, to buy tickets directly. But in certain cases, CITS is very useful. For example, it has a quota of tickets that may be sold out elsewhere. Also, if you are on a side trip out of town for a week and unable to purchase advance tickets the day they go on sale, CITS will take payment in advance and purchase the ticket for you.

Meiyou

meiyou (沒有): not have; there is not; be without

Meiyou will probably be the first word you learn in China. At hotels, on trains and at restaurants workers will, with surprising consistency, use it to answer your requests, no matter how reasonable or appropriate they seem to you. Before long you will have mastered the use of it yourself: *meiyou* FEC, *meiyou* travel permit, etc.

Travelers in China hate *meiyou* because they understand it as a negative reply to a direct question. Experienced travelers teach *meiyou* to new arrivals, lamenting the horrible experiences the phrase has brought them, warning of deceitful workers who infuriate visitors for nothing more than the joy of denying an available service.

Except in the minds of the most paranoid travelers, no conspiracy exists to deny visitors anything. Rather, the vision of China as the land of *meiyou* stems from an inadequate understanding of what the word can mean. For example, a Swedish woman asked for a hard sleeper berth on a train, and the answer she received from the train worker was *meiyou*. The train worker always answers this way to the first request for hard sleeper berths, regardless of how many are available. In this way, people who can afford soft sleeper berths are compelled to buy them, people on short trips are discouraged from taking a sleeper, and

Trains

Trains will linger in the mind of any visitor to China, either as a unique cultural experience, more open and spontaneous than encounters in China's cities, or as a hellish nightmare. You will determine the quality of the experience by your travel schedule and, most importantly, by your attitude.

The cheapest tickets on Chinese trains are for hard seats (*ying zuo*). It takes little imagination to understand this class of ticket: hard benches facing tiny tables with a small aisle running down the middle of the car. The Chinese masses travel this way, packed in with luggage, vegetables and animals fresh from the farms, amidst clouds of cigarette smoke. Babies wail like sirens in the standing-room-only cars, while all-night card games and English lessons are interrupted only for a quick trip to the toilet or a bite to eat. Overhead the intercom blares: 'Comrades, do not allow your children to relieve themselves except in designated areas.'

Some hard seat rides are not this lively; others are much worse. This is the real China, stripped of stereotypes and propaganda, so make the most of the unique opportunity to befriend a family returning from a trip, a student off to university or a worker out to see the world. Some hard seat rides are trying, even repulsive, but others are the source of wonderful stories, friendships and spur-of-the-moment detours to previously unknown destinations.

Short trips are usually the best, while 33 sleepless hours in a smoky, oxygen-starved car stuffed to three times its intended capacity taxes even the best sense of humor.

Tickets for soft seats (*ruan zuo*) are rare in Southwest China. Soft seat compartments are more comfortable and much less crowded than hard seat

---

people with special connections, such as politicians and soldiers, are given ample time to claim a berth before they are all sold out. The Swedish woman, however, immediately assumed there were no hard sleeper berths available. Unable to contain her frustration in the face of a long, hard-seat train ride, she raised her voice and shouted, "In China, everything is *meiyou!*" The train worker, not knowing why the woman was so angry, concluded that any available berths should go to someone less rude and impatient.

Travelers frequently encounter *meiyou* when requesting dormitory beds in a hotel. In cities the beds may well be sold out, but in small towns the answer is often given so 'foreign friends' will stay in nicer, more comfortable rooms. Proving to the hotel workers that you are accustomed to dorms in China (old hotel receipts will do the trick) is usually enough to get you the cheap bed. On the other hand, any unpleasant reaction to *meiyou* will only entrench the workers behind their original statement, even if there are dozens of empty dorm beds.

The preceding are but two examples of the wide-ranging uses of *meiyou* in China. People using it can have anything in mind, from 'don't have' to 'come back later when we are less busy', from 'maybe, depending on who you are' to 'we don't have it now, but we may in a little while'. Remember that, in all cases where *meiyou* means something other than an emphatic 'don't have', there is a chance of getting what you want. Do not get upset and never give the person you are dealing with a reason to refuse you.

cars, though they can become nearly as smoky. Passengers must have reserved seat tickets to enter soft seat compartments, so travelers need not worry about losing their places. On some trains, a four-person soft sleeper compartment may be sold to six people at soft seat prices.

Hard sleeper (*ying wo*) is the best choice for budget travelers. This class avoids the overcrowding of hard seat cars and still affords the opportunity of meeting many interesting people. Hard sleeper cars have 18 rows of triple-bunk beds, with fold out seats near each aisle window. Most Chinese on trains feel free of normal restraints and will candidly discuss politics, sex, religion, economics and other taboo subjects. These rides are relaxing and of genuine cultural value.

To Chinese travelers, the bottom bunks are the most desirable even though they are slightly more expensive. They become communal seats from early morning until lights out at night so you could well be awakened at 7:00 with a card game in session at your feet. Most Chinese travelers will gladly switch to the bottom bunk if you ask them. The middle bunk is good for looking out the window or watching life inside the train. The upper bunk, though cramped, is usually quite dark and a good place for travelers in need of sleep.

Soft sleepers (*ruan wo*) are for political heavyweights, rich businessmen, blue-haired tourists, and the occasional travelers who want some ease for a change. These enclosed compartments, each with four soft beds, a potted plant and delicate lace, seem oddly out of place in proletarian China. It is worth trying a soft sleeper once, especially if the alternative is a long stint in a hard seat compartment. At the tourist price, however, it is nearly as cheap to fly. A soft sleep berth is almost always available, so you can usually find a bed if things get desperate.

The dining car forms a barrier between the hard seat and the sleeper cars. There are set dining hours, but meal times vary from train to train. The food is adequate though rarely very good. Meals cost about Rmb 2 each. The best time to eat is toward the end of a meal period when cooks are much more willing to make something special. After the meal you can sit in the dining car for an hour or two sipping beer. On some trains hard seat passengers are barred from the dining car and, instead, served boxed meals by workers plying the aisles with carts.

Buying tickets

Train ticket prices are calculated according to both the distance and speed of a train. As a rough guide, take the cost of a slow train hard seat ticket as the base price, add 20% for an express train (*zhi kuai*), and 40% for a fast express train (*te kuai*). Add 75% to the base price for a soft seat, 80% for a hard sleeper, and 205% for a soft sleeper. For example, a 500-kilometer trip with hard sleeper by fast express train is Rmb 8.50 (hard seat) + (Rmb 8.50 × Rmb 0.40) fast express + (Rmb 8.50 × Rmb 0.80) hard sleeper, or Rmb 18.70. Too easy? You still have to consider the difference between local and tourist price. With the exception of foreign students studying in China and foreign employees within the country, all foreigners in principle are required to pay tourist prices for tickets in FEC. To compute the tourist price add 70% to the total ticket cost. Consequently, our 500-kilometer trip jumps from Rmb 18.70 to FEC 32.60. In fact, few foreigners are forced to pay tourist prices for every ticket they buy, and often, in less popular tourist destinations, train station workers do not realize there is a tourist price. The Chinese government claims tourist prices are higher because transportation is subsidized for locals. If you complain about prices to train workers, keep in mind that foreigners often get the first chance to upgrade tickets, have access to special waiting rooms in train stations and are often taken to the front of the line when purchasing train tickets.

Hard seat tickets are the easiest to buy. They never sell out, so it makes no difference if you purchase them days in advance or minutes before departure. Only large stations sell reserved seats, so it is often a mad fight to get on a train before all available seats are filled up. Do not be polite; jump in like everybody else.

Sleeper tickets usually go on sale three days before departure. Finding out exactly when and where tickets are sold can be quite difficult because tickets for each train line are sold at different times and often advance tickets are sold at booking offices rather than train stations. Fellow travelers are the best source of information. Once you know when and where tickets are sold, all you have to do is show up early and fight your way to the front of the line before too many people cut in on you and buy all the tickets. By buying tickets directly, even with all this hassle, you only pay the local price in Rmb. Some travelers opt for tickets supplied by China International Travel Service (CITS). Though more convenient, these are always more expensive and require FEC. Whenever you buy your ticket, always make sure the Chinese characters match your intended destination. Too many unsuspecting travelers have been rudely awakened in the middle of the night to learn they must leave their bed because they were sold a ticket to a city far short of their destination.

Even if you are at the train station minutes before departure with only a hard seat ticket, do not give up hope for a bed. If there is a special waiting room for hard and soft sleeper ticket holders, go there and ask the railroad workers to help you. If this fails, befriend a foreign traveler who purchased a berth ticket in advance. If you can get on the train together, tell the workers that your traveling companion bought the last sleeper ticket and that you still need one. This will usually get you a bed. Even if there are no beds, they might allow you to sit in the sleeper car rather than move to the hard seat section. If you find no one to befriend and end up in the hard seat section of the train, work towards the hard seat car nearest the dining car. Here you will find a desk where tickets are upgraded to hard and soft sleepers. Workers will offer you a soft sleeper first, and only consider giving you a hard sleeper after you have turned down the more expensive bed (politely) several times. If there are no beds, try a few minutes later or ask if you can reserve a bed that will be vacated at a future stop.

Some trains have a few extra sleeper cars reserved for train workers. Although tickets are not formally sold for these cars, foreigners can usually get a bed on one of them. On several occasions we ended up being served tea and snacks by six curious train workers in a pristine, hardwood sleeper coach.

Black market tickets are turning up in China's big cities, most notably Guilin. Local touts try hard to sell tickets for the local price if you pay in FEC. Initially this may appear to be a good deal, until a wise train worker asks for your student identification and makes you upgrade to the tourist price. When this happens, do not get angry at the workers; they are only doing their job.

Above all, when buying a train ticket in China remember that strategy and patience are everything. A single outburst of rage can ruin the positive effects of a five-hour wait. Workers often vengefully pass by a rude passenger to give a ticket to one more patient and friendly, even when the perpetrator is a high-level cadre or a foreigner. Trains in China always depart with a few empty berths, no matter what other travelers may say, so never give up.

Buses

Travelers must rely heavily on bus travel in Southwest China because of the limited number of rail lines. They soon come to know there is no such thing as a typical bus or bus trip. Comfortable, modern Polish coaches travel the 400 kilometers from Kunming to Dali in one day and express buses from Guangzhou reach Guilin in 20 hours. But old Chinese buses, with holes in the floorboards and few windows remaining, may take 12 hours to cover the 180-kilometer trip from Xiangcheng to Derong — if the transmission doesn't drop out. In western Sichuan, buses seldom go beyond second gear and covering 200 kilometers a day is a feat, while air-conditioned Japanese coaches in Guangxi routinely drive twice that distance in less time.

All buses, no matter how clean when they start, will invariably arrive covered with sunflower seeds, fruit peels, paper, dust, mud and vomit. It is not uncommon to see the same three people who vomited in the aisle all morning consume a plate of fried noodles with a bottle of beer at lunch only to start vomiting once again back on board the moving bus. All bus drivers seem to have strong bladders, so stops are infrequent. Go whenever the bus stops and don't be shy about asking the driver to pull over and let you run out into a field to relieve yourself.

For a full day trip, put your luggage in the storage area (usually on the roof), grab a snack for the road and go. For shorter trips, bring your luggage on board. Also do this if you are getting off before the end of the line; drivers do not like to get luggage down from the roof before they have reached the terminus. On multi-day trips, more preparation is necessary. In China, all luggage stowed on the roof of the bus stays until the final destination, even if it is three days away. Take a small day pack loaded with your camera, toothbrush, soap, cards and snacks. Do not fear for your luggage on the roof; theft from the cargo area of buses is almost unheard of. Be prudent, though, and keep all valuables with you. Drivers sometimes want foreigners to keep their luggage with them on the bus. This is always a hassle as the bus is invariably overloaded and your luggage gets crushed. To protect your backpack, you have to carry it on your lap for the whole trip. Sitting on a sleeping bag cushions the bumps and jolts, increases leg room and insulates against the drafts coming through the holes in the floor. Multi-day trips require no hotel hunting because drivers always stop at a hotel in the evening. Be sure to find out what time the bus is leaving the next day.

Long bus tours need to be planned in advance. For example, it is possible to take buses from Chengdu to Dege, on the Tibetan border, but no one bus goes the whole way. You must change buses at an intermediate destination. Find out how far you can travel on one ticket, ride to that place and then continue the process, stage by stage, until you reach your destination. If at any point a ticket seller says 'meiyou', try to ascertain whether no buses go to your destination or whether tickets are simply sold out. Also, as a rule, few bus companies will sell tickets to destinations more than two or three days away, but be assured that if a road exists, there will be at least one bus a week.

Finally, buses that leave on odd days depart on either the 31st or first of the month, but not on both.

Bus ticket prices vary little in Southwest China. Tickets for regular buses cost about Rmb 8 each for a full day's 200-kilometer bus ride.

Boats

Boats in China are often the easiest, cheapest, and most relaxing way to travel. Some unforgettable times are had while looking out the window or resting on the deck of a Chinese river boat. Boats range in size from glorified single deck barges in Guangxi to luxury tour boats that ply the Yangzi River between Chongqing and Wuhan. There are also hovercrafts and hydrofoils serving some routes. Most boats are slow and routes quite long; many trips take 24 hours or more to complete.

All boats have several classes of berths. The cheapest are usually below deck and often crowded, hot and stuffy. Medium-priced berths frequently have windows and are pleasant. On larger boats, the most expensive berths can be quite luxurious.

Food on board has improved in the last two years, though it is still basic. Plan ahead by bringing dry noodles and snacks. Drinking water is pumped straight from the muddy, polluted rivers and boiled, so you may want to bring bottled water.

Boats, like trains, are a good way to strike up friendships and meet interesting Chinese, unencumbered and away from their normal constraints.

Air Travel

China's national airline, the Civil Aviation Administration of China (CAAC), has planes ranging from new Boeing 747s to creaky Soviet turbo-props complete with folding chairs to accommodate overbookings. The airline has a deservedly bad reputation, but, when time is short, it is convenient and sometimes necessary to hop on a plane for another city or province. Service extends to 10 cities in the Southwest and to dozens of destinations throughout China and the world.

Although CAAC charges FEC, rates for internal flights are competitive with those throughout Asia. International flights on CAAC are more expensive. Purchasing tickets yourself is relatively easy; just fill out the English form that is available in all airline offices for a nominal fee of Rmb 0.10. Schedules in English for the whole country are usually available as well. Tickets to a particular destination go on sale anywhere from three to seven days in advance. If a flight is sold out, try the afternoon before departure and you may be sold a seat reserved for special cases. Also, CITS has a daily allocation and will purchase tickets for a small fee. Service and food on board are not up to international standards, so you may want to bring a snack.

A word of warning: flights are routinely cancelled because of bad weather, scheduling problems or mechanical reasons. CAAC assumes no responsibility for cancellations and will not provide accommodations or meals to stranded travelers.

Below is a list of the ten cities in Southwest China that have CAAC air service, and the destinations from each city.

Chengdu has flights to: Beijing, Changsha, Chongqing, Guangzhou, Guilin, Guiyang, Hefei, Hong Kong, Kunming, Lanzhou, Lhasa, Nanjing,

Shanghai, Shenyang, Wuhan, Xi'an and Xichang.
Chongqing has flights to: Beijing, Changsha, Chengdu, Guangzhou, Guilin, Guiyang, Kunming, Nanjing, Shanghai, Xiamen and Xi'an.
Guilin has flights to: Guangzhou, Guiyang, Hangzhou, Hong Kong, Nanjing, Nanning, Shanghai, Xiamen and Xi'an.
Guiyang has flights to: Beijing, Changsha, Chengdu, Chongqing, Guangzhou, Guilin, Kunming and Shanghai.
Kunming has flights to: Baoshan, Beijing, Changsha, Chengdu, Chongqing, Guangzhou, Guilin, Guiyang, Hong Kong, Nanning, Shanghai, Simao and Xi'an. There is also periodic service to Rangoon and Bangkok.
Nanning has flights to: Beihai, Beijing, Guangzhou, Guilin and Kunming.
Liuzhou has flights to: Guangzhou.
Simao has flights to: Kunming.
Baoshan has flights to: Kunming.
Xichang has flights to: Chengdu.

Hitchhiking

Impossible a few years ago, hitchhiking has developed into the preferred mode of transport for travelers serious about visiting remote areas. Anywhere there is a road you can usually find a ride on cargo trucks, and such movements are difficult to trace. Trailblazing with truck drivers is easy: eat where they eat and stay where they stay.

If you plan on hitchhiking extensively in China, travel as lightly as possible. Drivers will hesitate to pick up passengers with more luggage than will fit in the truck cab. This is especially true in western Sichuan where goods are always bundled in canvas for protection against severe weather and drivers are unwilling to untie their cargo to make room. Groups of more than two will find it harder to get rides because cabs only hold three or four people. In addition, drivers are reluctant to allow passengers to ride in the back of trucks, especially during cold weather. People have frozen to death this way.

Drivers may or may not want money. Rmb 5 a day seems fair.

Stories abound of drivers picking up travelers, feeding them and paying for lodging during the entire trip. Drivers are well-off by Chinese standards, but keep the next traveler in mind and do not exploit a good thing by being stingy. Most drivers chain-smoke, so packs of Western cigarettes are always appreciated, as are photos of the journey sent later to their home addresses. Try to give drivers something special as payment for their hospitality.

When hitchhiking, it is important to have both a good map and familiarity with the route. Some truck drivers do not realize that you will be happy to travel with them part way to your destination. Have them point to their terminus on a map and then you point to where you would like to accompany them.

If you want to explore some sights en route, plan on stopping for a few days before finding another truck. Many people have made the overland trip from Chengdu to Lhasa, but most have missed the incredible monasteries, markets and village life along the way because they spent every waking hour of their two-week journey in a truck. Try to tell the driver realistically how far you want to travel with him; he may be offended if you say Lhasa but get off at Dege.

The traditional thumb signal does not work in China. Get out in the road and wave your arms in the air. The sooner a driver sees you are a foreigner, the better chance you have of getting a ride. These truck drivers are bored driving 29 days a month, and you are a welcome break in the monotony.

Bicycles

Bicycles in China are one-speed, steel-frame workhorses designed to carry people, animals and furniture. It is fortunate they are slow because the brakes never work very well. Bicycle rental shops are appearing everywhere, and open areas that do not yet have them soon will. Bicycles allow you to set your own schedule and detour to interesting areas at a moment's notice. A passport or security deposit is required for bicycle rental and the hourly or daily rate should be set before leaving the shop. In cities bicycles must be parked in designated areas, where they will be looked after by attendants who collect a Rmb 0.05 fee. Theft is widespread so be careful with your bicycle.

Touring by bike in China is a new and largely untried method of transportation. The few travelers who have used Chinese bikes for multi-day tours have not gotten far before giving up. Roads in China are too rough and the gearing on Chinese bicycles is so high that you will be forced to walk up most hills. If you bring a mountain bike (and spare parts) from America or Europe, every city, town or village in China becomes accessible. Taking bicycles on boats and buses in China seems to be no problem, but the freight cost on trains is expensive.

An American on a round-the-world cycling tour spent almost three months on his bike in China with little trouble. On the other hand, a woman from Montana had her mountain bike confiscated and was then deported after a series of bad encounters with Gonganju (Public Security Bureau) officers in southern Yunnan Province. To avoid such trouble, arrange an official letter of permission from provincial or local Gonganju offices. It is wise to heed official warnings and turn back if told not to continue. Store your bicycle and rely on local transportation in sensitive areas if you are determined to carry on.

Camping

Not many travelers in China camp out. This is strange considering the assortment of depressingly similar budget hotels most individual travelers end up in. In all but the coldest places of Southwest China, camping is ideal for most of the year. In our opinion, the additional weight of sleeping bags and tents or ground covers is a small price to pay for freedom from dependency on local hotels. Some of the most spectacular sites in the Southwest are in remote areas, accessible only by trail, so camping becomes essential.

Gonganju (Public Security Bureau)

Gonganju is a Chinese term that means Public Security Bureau. English speakers in China refer to it by this name, or PSB, but its true function is that of traffic police, FBI and KGB (judge, jury, executioner?) all rolled into one. Most travelers will have very little contact with the Gonganju. Heavy-handed tactics against foreigners are rare and usually reserved for reporters and other public critics of China's democratic dictatorship.

Gonganju officials should never be bribed. In China, bribery may get you into serious trouble.

Visa extensions Entry visas are usually extended by the Foreign Affairs section (*waishike*) of the Gonganju, but policy varies from place to place. Officials in all large cities and some smaller ones have the authority to extend visas. If one office will not extend your visa, try again later. If that fails, try in the next city on your itinerary. People with expired visas receive a lecture and a FEC 10 fine. Extensions are generally for one month and cost FEC 5. You can usually obtain three extensions on an original three-month visa, giving you six months in China. Some Foreign Affairs offices are more lenient than others. Ask around.

Open and closed areas In 1987 China had 436 cities and areas officially open to foreign tourists. Foreign visitors can travel freely to these places and stay as long as their visas remain valid. Any area off of this list is closed. Foreigners are not allowed to visit these places except under special conditions.

Officially, areas are closed because of inadequate transportation, limited health care, substandard hotels and dangerous conditions. We found that factors such as poverty, proximity to an international border or an indigenous population's historical resistance to Chinese domination were also relevant reasons for an area to be closed.

Foreign tourists are not allowed to visit, and in many cases even pass through, closed areas. Usually you can make day trips from an open area to a closed one, as long as you spend the night back in an open city. The only official way to visit a closed area is by obtaining an Aliens' Travel Permit from the Gonganju. Usually no one will issue this permit unless you have a written invitation from a sponsoring organization in China. However, by paying enough money, China International Travel Service (CITS) will cut through red tape and escort you to just about anywhere you wish to go.

Most foreigners who visit closed areas without permission eventually encounter problems with the Gonganju. This is no big deal (even fun once or twice), but you must remember some essential points.

First, do not get mad until you have lost all hope of a satisfactory solution, as this will ruin any chance for a compromise.

Second, try to determine from its actions why the Gonganju has business with you. If officials show up at your hotel room and want to see passports they might only want to record your presence. They might also want to know where you have come from and when you are leaving. If they have not brought along an English interpreter to inform you to be on the next bus back to an open area, then you can probably stay for a few days. Any subsequent visits will only be to hasten your departure. If you are ordered onto the next bus, claim to be too sick or too tired to travel. This ploy may get you a day or two in town. A closed city is often small enough to be seen in just a day anyway.

Third, be clear about what the Gonganju wants you to do. If the authorities suggest you return to an open area but do not specify when you should leave, you have tacit permission to visit where you want, provided you leave soon and do not mention any names further down the road. Forced escorts back to open areas are rare, arrests and deportation even more unlikely. You will never be arrested or deported for going into a closed area if you have not already been caught and warned to leave. If the Gonganju puts you on a bus back to an open area, you leave town and then get off the bus and return to where you were caught, you are simply inviting a serious confrontation.

26

Many places in China are officially closed, but in practice no one cares. Hundreds of travelers often pass through a city before it finally makes its way onto the open list. Word of mouth is the best way to obtain this kind of information.

Occasionally, officials do not know that an area has been opened and will hinder your efforts to visit. Chinese from Hong Kong, Macao and Taiwan, as well as many Overseas Chinese, are allowed to travel freely throughout China.

The Gonganju follows trends instead of setting them. Widespread disregard for Aliens' Travel Permits for several years rendered them virtually useless. The more travelers of today disregard political boundaries, the quicker closed areas will open for all to see.

Open Areas

The following cities and areas are officially open to foreign tourists. Check with the Gonganju (Public Security Bureau) in any large city for the latest information on open areas.

Guangxi	Wuzhou	Lijiang	Guangyuan
Beihai	Xing'an	Menghai	Jiang'an
Beiliu	Yulin	Qujing	Leshan
Binyang	**Guizhou**	Simao	Luzhou
Guilin	Anshun	Tonghai	Maowen
Guiping	Guiyang	Yuxi	Mianyang
Guixian	Huangguoshu	**Sichuan**	Nanchong
Hepu	Kaili	Barkam	Nanping
Jinxiu	Liupanshui	(Ma'erkang)	Neijiang
Lingshan	Qingzhen	Changning	Songpan
Liuzhou	Shibing	Chengdu	Wanxian
Long'an	Zhenyuan	Chongqing	Wushan
Longsheng	Zunyi	Deyang	Wuxi
Luchuan	**Yunnan**	Dukou	Xichang
Nanning	Chuxiong	Fengdu	Xingwen
Qinzhou	Dali	Fengjie	Yibin
Rongshui	Jinghong	Fuling	Yunyang
Rongxian	Kunming	Gongxian	Zhongxian
Sanjiang			Zigong

Entertainment

Nightlife in China may not be as exciting as in other Asian countries, but it can be fun and rewarding nonetheless. Chinese discos and nightclubs have emerged in every major city and in many smaller ones. Usually featuring a live band and occasionally even dancing, these clubs are good places to share first-hand in Chinese popular culture. Chinese opera, though hard to find, can provide a fascinating evening. Invite your new Chinese friends to a night out. In return, ask them to make the arrangements and take over as cultural guides. The best tickets in the house rarely cost more than Rmb 0.40. The same is true for movies, plays, concerts, ballets, variety stage shows, gymnastics, sports and martial arts exhibitions.

In some cities, magicians, storytellers, strongmen, musicians and other street performers entertain for donations in teahouses, night markets, and public squares or parks. In small towns or villages, particularly in minority areas, locals gather periodically for singing contests, indigenously produced plays or other community activities. If you are lucky enough to be invited to such an event, do not pass up the chance.

Crime

The crime rate in China is extremely low, making it one of the safest places in the world for travelers. Cases of violent crimes against Westerners are practically unheard of, perhaps because the perpetrators would face the firing squad if apprehended.

Anyone who stays in China for any length of time, however, will meet or hear about someone who has had something stolen. A major threat of theft in China is posed by other travelers. They rob in the crowded hostels and, once gone, are virtually impossible to track down. Hotel staff are not entirely innocent, either. Lock your belongings in a private room or take your camera and other valuables with you, even when going to the toilet or shower. In large cities gangs of young Chinese snatch cameras and wallets from unsuspecting foreigners in crowds or on city buses during rush hour. Bag-slashing also occurs. The best prevention against theft is a money-belt for traveler's checks, cash, passports and credit cards. Wear it *inside your clothing*.

If you do have something stolen and want to report it, visit the Gonganju. Security officers are reluctant to admit that Chinese people steal, so attempts to report a theft may be resisted. You may be questioned about unrelated events and asked to repeat your story to many different people. Do not give up or leave until a theft report is written and you have a copy for future claims.

Smoking

For the non-smoking traveler, China seems to be a nation of men who do nothing but smoke. There is no concept of non-smoking areas, or even the notion that cigarette smoke bothers some people. Restaurants, buses, trains, planes and hotels are often filled with enough side-stream smoke to kill a horse. For Chinese people, offering someone a cigarette is a standard act of courtesy, like pouring a cup of tea. If you accept a smoke, be prepared to smoke for the rest of the day or night because 'polite' people will go to any extreme to see that you accept all subsequent cigarettes offered.

Non-smokers should be prepared to endure the carcinogenic clouds with patience rather than try to change the habits of an entire country.

Toilets

There are few Western-style 'sit' toilets in China. Squat toilets are the norm, as in most Asian countries, and for good or ill you will need to get used to them.

Public toilets consist of rows of holes to squat over. These are sometimes separated by a low wall, which provides the only privacy. Some are quite breezy and nice, while others are festering cesspits that send even the rats running.

Bring your own toilet paper or use newspaper, cigarette packs, or scraps of tissue, like the locals. In more remote areas, toilet paper and even newspapers are unavailable, so stock up or suffer the consequences.

Getting There From Hong Kong

The cheapest and most convenient way for many independent travelers to enter China is through Hong Kong. This avoids the hassle of getting visas in America, Australia or Europe and the expense of a flight directly to China. Cut-rate flights to Hong Kong are numerous, and visa procedures in Hong Kong are simple no matter what travel agents say. In addition, a smart shopper can outfit himself for a trip to China cheaper in Hong Kong than in most Western countries. Below is a rundown of useful information about Hong Kong to help travelers prepare for their trip to China. All prices in this section are quoted in Hong Kong dollars. The exchange rate when we wrote this was approximately US$ 1 = HK$ 7.8.

Lodging
Chung King Mansions
40 Nathan Road
Kowloon, Hong Kong
Chung King Mansions is a complex of five 16-storey blocks connected on the ground by a large shopping arcade. Within this maze of buildings are countless guesthouses and hostels where prices range from HK$20 for dorm beds and HK$50 for private rooms to HK$200 for large rooms with private bath, television, refrigerator and air-conditioning. Most of the guesthouses are reasonably safe, though theft is common enough to warrant caution. Always lock your door and take your valuables with you, even when going to the phone or bathroom. Some people are put off by the dirty hallways, smelly stairwells and long waits for the elevators. A and B blocks, the most popular with foreign travelers, are the worst in these respects.

Many of the people who live and work in Chung King Mansions are Indian, Pakistani or African. Shunned by the Hong Kong Chinese, they have chosen to live together in one large, multi-ethnic community. The blocks are filled with excellent, inexpensive restaurants serving Indian, Pakistani and Chinese food.

Travellers' Hostel
Block A, 16th Floor
Chung King Mansions
40 Nathan Road
Kowloon, Hong Kong
tel. 3-687710, 3-682505
Dormitory HK$20; double room HK$50
All rooms share communal bathrooms, kitchens, steel lockers, a lounge, a television and a canteen.

Travellers' Friendship House
Block B, 6th floor
Chung King Mansions
40 Nathan Road
Kowloon, Hong Kong

The Garden Hostel
F4 Mirador Mansion
3rd Floor, 58 Nathan Road
Kowloon, Hong Kong

tel. 3-7218567

Just up Nathan Road from Chung King Mansions, The Garden Hostel offers similar services at competitive prices.

Visas to China

Visas can be obtained directly from the Visa Office of the Ministry of Foreign Affairs of the People's Republic of China in Hong Kong:

China Resources Building
26 Harbour Road
6th Floor
Wanchai, Hong Kong
tel. 5-744163

Requirements are a valid passport, two recent photos, a completed application form (available at the office), and a HK$40 processing fee. Visas take one to three days to process.

For a fee, most travel agents have a rush service, and can obtain a visa in as little as five hours.

Travel agents

Cheap air tickets are commonly available in Hong Kong. When using a Hong Kong travel agency, be sure it is a member of the Hong Kong Tourist Association and has a travel agent's license. Insist on a written record of all deposits, balances, refunds, dates, destinations and services rendered. Most agencies offer China visas, but visas obtained directly are cheaper. We found the following to be cheap and reliable agencies:

Hong Kong Student Travel
8th Floor, Tai Sang Bank Building
130 Des Voeux Road
Central, Hong Kong
tel. 5-414841

Phoenix Services Agency
6th Floor, Hanford House
221D Nathan Road
Kowloon, Hong Kong
tel. 3-7227378, 3-7233006

Shoestring Travel
Flat A, 4th Floor, Alpha House
27–33 Nathan Raod
Kowloon, Hong Kong
tel. 3-7232306

Time Travel Services
Block A, 16th Floor
Chung King Mansions
40 Nathan Road
Kowloon, Hong Kong
tel. 3-7239993, 3-687710

Traveller Services
Room 704, Metropole Building
57 Peking Road
Kowloon, Hong Kong

tel. 3-674127

China Travel Service (HK) Ltd.
1st Floor, Alpha House
27 Nathan Road
Kowloon, Hong Kong
tel. 3-7219826, 3-7211331
China Travel Service (CTS) is not a bargain travel agency but occasionally has tickets when everyone else is sold out. The office has limited information on transportation and destinations in China.

Shopping

Hong Kong is famous as a shopper's paradise, but due to changing foreign exchange rates many products are no longer cheaper here than in North America or Europe. Fixed prices are rare, so bargain everywhere except in major department stores. It makes sense to shop away from the main streets, especially Nathan Road in Tsim Sha Tsui. Prices are generally much lower in the areas of Mongkok and Yau Ma Tei.

Walkmans, recorders and camera equipment The neighborhood in Mongkok district, along Argyle Street between Nathan Road and the Mongkok railway station on Fu Yuen Street, has a large number of shops with cheap, posted prices. A visit here first can help determine approximate prices before your actual bargaining begins. Most shops have warranties and the original boxes for all equipment.

Take an ample supply of batteries, especially camera batteries, for the trip.

Used Camera Equipment There are several shops with a wide selection of inexpensive, used camera equipment at 16 Kimberly Road, Champagne Court, Block B, next to the Miramar Hotel in Tsim Sha Tsui, Kowloon. Shoot a roll of film before going to China to test the equipment.

Chinese Products Stores A wide range of Chinese export products and manufactured goods can be found in Hong Kong, often cheaper than in China. Browse here before going to China to get an idea of prices and availability of useful items:

Yue Hwa Chinese Product Stores
301–309 Nathan Road, Kowloon (main store)
54–64 Nathan Road, Kowloon (branch)
143–161 Nathan Road, Kowloon (Park Lane branch)

Chung Kiu Chinese Product Store
12 Peking Road, Kowloon
47 Shan Tung Street, Kowloon
528–534 Nathan Road, Kowloon

China Products
31 Yee Wo Street
Causeway Bay, Hong Kong
tel. 5-8908321

Tai Wah Emporium
92–104 Queen's Road Central, Hong Kong
tel. 5-241051

Camping Equipment Items such as stoves, mess kits, first-aid kits, compasses, water containers, as well as low-quality tents and sleeping bags are inexpensive in Hong Kong. Chinese-made down sleeping bags, though slightly heavy, are fully adequate and quite cheap. Karrimor and Lowe backpacks can be as much as 25−50% cheaper than in the United States. The selection of good, high-quality equipment, such as gortex and poly-propylene products, boots, down sleeping bags and water purification systems, is both expensive and limited.

Perfect Corporation Limited
132−134 Austin Road
Kowloon
tel. 3-672873

Tai Chung Sporting Goods Company
71−73 Fa Yuen Street
Mongkok, Kowloon
tel. 3-963968

Mountain Services·
56 Morrison Hill Road
Happy Valley, Hong Kong
tel. 5-733313

Eyeglasses Hong Kong is one of the best places in the world for good, cheap eyeglasses, contact lenses and supplies. Fast service from highly qualified opticians is the norm. Check the phone book for addresses.

Getting to China

By boat

Night boat There are two night boats that ply the waters of the Pearl River between Hong Kong and Guangzhou (Canton). Modern and clean, both of these boats have a restaurant, bar, nightclub and comfortable observation decks. Spend a full day in Hong Kong, have a good night's sleep on the boat, and be through customs and out on the streets of Guangzhou by 8:00 the following morning.

The *Xing Hu* departs on even days, and the *Tian Hu* on odd days. There are no departures on the 31st of each month. Departure time is at 21:00. Plan on being at customs by 19:00. The ships depart from Tai Kok Tsui Ferry Pier, Kowloon.

Direct ticket purchase:
Chu Kong Shipping Company Limited
3 Shanghai Street, Kowloon
tel. 3-671162

class	direct purchase (HK$)	travel agents (HK$)
cabin (two people)	170	210
cabin (four people)	155	175
dormitory	90	110
seat	60	80

Hoverferry to Guangzhou (Canton) A daily hoverferry service also operates from Tai Kok Tsui Ferry Pier, Kowloon, to Guangzhou. Several boats make the three-hour trip every morning. Tickets are HK$ 140 (travel agents charge

$ 160). There are also boats to Macao and Shekou.

Direct ticket purchase:
HYFCO Travel Agency Limited
1st Floor, Jordan Road Ferry Pier
Kowloon
tel. 3-7805257, 3-305257
or

Booth No. 1, Tai Kok Tsui Ferry Pier
Tai Kok Tsui, Kowloon
tel. 3-905528

Ship, hydrofoil and jetfoil service to Macao, Zhuhai, Shekou, Hainan Island
and Shanghai can be purchased directly from:

Far East Hydrofoil Company
200 Connaught Road Central
Basement and 2nd Floor
Shun Tak Centre, Hong Kong,
tel. 5-8593333, 5-8593288.

By train

Express train Trains depart from Kowloon (Hung Hom) Station several times
daily and arrive three hours later at the Guangzhou Huochezhan Railway
Station. Tickets purchased directly are HK$ 135 – 140 while travel agents
charge HK$ 190.

Direct ticket purchase:
Kowloon Railway Station
Hung Hom, Kowloon
tel. 3-646321
or

China Railway Services (HK) Limited
41 Chatham Road
Kowloon
tel. 3-7214543

Local train Kowloon-Canton Railway (KCR) trains depart Kowloon (Hung
Hom) Station for the Lo Wu border station every 20 minutes. Trains begin
running at 07:00 and take 35 minutes to reach the border. Economy class is
HK$ 14.50; first class is HK$ 29.

The border closes at 22:00. On arrival at Lo Wu, first go through Hong
Kong immigration, then cross the Lo Wu Bridge to the clearly marked
Chinese immigration section for foreigners. The exit on the Chinese side leads
directly to the train station where tickets to Guangzhou are purchased. You
can also leave the station, enter a large parking lot and catch a mini-bus to
Guangzhou.

Several trains depart daily from Shenzhen for the three-and-a-half hour trip
to Guangzhou. Tickets are approximately FEC 12 for hard seat and FEC 24
for soft seat.

By air

The following companies offer direct air service from Hong Kong to
Guangzhou, Guilin, Kunming and Chengdu, as well as to other points

throughout China:

Cathay Pacific Airways Limited
5th Floor, Swire House
9 Connaught Road Central
Hong Kong
tel. 5-7698111

Civil Aviation Administration of China (CAAC)
504 Gloucester Tower, The Landmark
Des Voeux Road, Central, Hong Kong
tel. 5-216416

Dragonair
19th Floor, Wheelock House
20 Pedder Street, Hong Kong
tel. 5-8105105

Customs and immigration

Entering China these days has become a mere formality. All travelers must complete a customs declaration form, listing the valuables they are bringing in, including watches, jewellery, radios, cameras and tape recorders. When exiting China, travelers must present a copy of this form and be prepared to account for all items to make sure they have not been sold on the black market. Losing your declaration form may cost you FEC 50.

Art objects and antiques obtained in China are closely scrutinized. Antiques should carry a seal showing that they were bought in an official shop. Contemporary art objects should be accompanied by a receipt. Souvenirs bought on the street are usually allowed to pass, but customs officials have been known to confiscate jewelry if they consider that a tourist has purchased 'too much'.

Guangzhou (Canton)

Unless you fly from Hong Kong to Guilin, Chengdu or Kunming, or arrive from another point inside China, you will have to pass through Guangzhou on your way to or from the Southwest. It is beyond the scope of our book to describe Guangzhou in detail, but we have listed basic travel information below.

Lodging

Guangzhou Youth Hostel
2 Shamian Si Jie, Guangzhou
tel. 884298, 889251

Located across the street from the expensive White Swan Hotel, the Guangzhou Youth Hostel, also known as the Black Duck, has dormitory beds for FEC 8 and FEC 10. If all rooms are full, the staff will set up a cot in the hall. The hostel has hot showers and a snack shop/bar. Nearby are dozens of small restaurants serving a wide range of food.

Transportation

Guangzhou Huochezhan Train Station
Trains depart daily to all parts of China, including the Southwest. In addition, there are direct trains to Hong Kong and local trains to Shenzhen, where you can cross the border and take a KCR train to Kowloon. Keep in mind that the

Shenzhen border closes at 4 pm.

Dashatou Matou Pier
Riverboats, though slower than express buses, are the most relaxing way to reach Southwest China. Boats to Wuzhou depart daily at 12.30, 14:00, 16:00 and 17:00; the trip takes 18 hours. There are also boats to Guiping, Guixian, Nanning and Liuzhou.

Take the 12:30 boat to Wuzhou if you want to connect with buses onward from Wuzhou immediately after your arrival. Combination boat-bus tickets to Yangshuo or Guilin are sold in Guangzhou, and bus tickets are sold on the boat or in Wuzhou.

Guangzhou Qiche Keyunzhan Bus Station
This bus station, located just west of the train station, offers express buses to five cities in Southwest China. Buses drive day and night, making them the fastest mode of surface transport into Southwest China.

destination	distance (kms)	transit time	departure	ticket window	cost (Rmb)
Liuzhou 柳州	705	20 hrs	8:15	11	25.60
Guilin/Yangshuo 桂林，阳朔	723	20 hrs	8:30	11	23.70
Wuzhou 梧州	315	10 hrs	7:15	11	10.10
Nanning 南宁	751	20 hrs	9:00	12	23.60

Zhoutouju Matou Pier
There are nightly boats that leave for Hong Kong from Guangzhou. The *Xing Hu* departs on odd days and the *Tian Hu* on even days. There are no departures on the 31st of the month. Departure time is 21:00; immigration opens at 19:00. You can change unused FEC back into foreign currency at the pier's Bank of China office.

class	cost (FEC)	
	Xing Hu	Tian Hu
VIP suite	175	158
special class	56	49
cabin (four people)	44	35
dormitory	28	28
seat	18	no seats

CAAC The CAAC airline office just east of the train station has a multitude of flights serving the entire country. Flights leave Guangzhou for the Southwestern cities of Chengdu, Chongqing, Guilin, Guiyang, Liuzhou, Kunming and Nanning.

CITS The CITS office is located between the train station and CAAC.

Local Transportation The crowded public bus system leaves much to be desired. You often have to transfer once or twice to reach your destiination. Bicycles are a practical and enjoyable mode of transportation because Guangzhou is so flat. Taxi service is the best in China and superior to Hong Kong. Taxi fares are cheap; the majority of destinations can be reached for under FEC 10.

Tickets The White Swan Hotel, Dong Feng Hotel and China Hotel all offer a ticketing service far superior to that of CITS.

The Minority Nationalities and Autonomous Regions

The four provinces of Southwest China form a vast area, nearly as large as Alaska in surface area, sharing borders with three countries and seven other provinces and regions. The geographic and human make-up is extremely complex, not the mono-dimensional, gray place stereotyped by many outsiders.

The Han Chinese (the name Han comes from China's first long-lasting, unified empire, 206 BC−220 AD) are by far the most important nationality in China, comprising 94 per cent of the population, but 55 other nationalities, the 'minorities', occupy over 60 per cent of the land, much of it in strategic areas. The Chinese have always realized the significance of these people, who from time to time have made their presence known with a vengeance. Nomads in the north, indefatigable Tibetans in the west and a host of lesser nations on the periphery have chipped away at China whenever it showed vulnerability. Two great dynasties, the Yuan (Mongol) and Qing (Manchu), proved the ascendancy of non-Chinese people at critical moments in history.

The Southwest has 33 minority groups, more than half of the country's total. Special administrative areas have been established where one or more of these groups is heavily concentrated or outnumbers the Han Chinese. These areas may be huge, as in the case of Guangxi, which is known as an autonomous region (*diqu*). Autonomous prefectures (*zhou*) and counties (*xian*) are the more common units of delineation, but these too may be vast in size.

Autonomous areas exist in principle to give the minority people some self-governing power and independence. Some officials are drawn from the local population and policies are designed with local conditions in mind to preserve and enhance the indigenous culture. Schools are often taught exclusively in the local language. In the Ganzi Tibetan Autonomous Prefecture, for example, religious freedom is guaranteed, Tibetans are exempt from the national one-child policy, official government signs are in both Chinese and Tibetan script, and a number of Gonganju members and cadres are native Tibetan. These rights and policies exist on paper, but whether they are actually implemented is not always clear. The application of policies varies considerably from region to region and from minority group to minority group.

Guangxi Zhuang Autonomous Region 广西壮族自治区

The Guangxi Zhuang Autonomous Region consists of a large basin surrounded on all sides by mountains. It is bordered on the south by the Beibu Gulf and Vietnam, on the east by Guangdong, on the north by Hunan and Guizhou, and on the west by Yunnan. The most famous mountain region, centered around Guilin, is known for its exotic karst pinnacles and spires, sink-holes and caverns, picturesque hills and subterranean streams. The vast flatland at the center of the province is a major grain and sugar cane producing area. The Pearl River system, with tributaries throughout Guangxi, flows east past Wuzhou into Guangdong Province and on to the South China Sea near Hong Kong.

As in Yunnan, Chinese inroads into Guangxi came relatively late. The Qin Dynasty (221–207 BC) first established Chinese control and set up a trade route linking the Pearl River network with that of the Yangzi River to the north. But subsequent governments found the border regions difficult to control. During the 11th century, a powerful Zhuang state sprang up in Guangxi and went so far as to lay siege to Canton.

During the Qing Dynasty (1644–1911), population pressures and corrupt leadership fueled rebellion throughout China. The most famous uprising, the Taiping Rebellion, began in Jintiancun, a village in Guangxi Province, in 1847. The Taiping Heavenly Kingdom (Taiping Tianguo) consumed most of southern China before it was crushed in 1864 by combined Qing and European forces. The latter half of the 19th century brought an influx of foreign traders and missionaries to Guangxi. Western businessmen set up offices in the trading cities of Wuzhou, Guiping, Guixian, Liuzhou, Nanning and Baise. Churches were built and stores filled up with European goods.

The collapse of the Qing Dynasty in 1911 threw Guangxi into chaos. Warlords grabbed power wherever they could before the Nationalist government came in to restore order in the 1920s. Japanese armies sent the Nationalists fleeing west in 1938 and occupied half of Guangxi during the war, reducing beautiful, ancient cities to rubble.

Guangxi was officially changed from a province to a Zhuang Nationality Autonomous Region in 1958 in a symbolic effort to integrate its 12 million Zhuang people into the country. Other nationalities in the region include the Yao, Miao, Dong, Mulao, Maonan, Hui, Yi and Gin.

Today, Guangxi is still primarily agricultural. Only 2.4 of its 35 million people are employed in industrial work. A mild climate allows two, and sometimes three, crops per year. Farm products include rice, maize, sweet potatoes, wheat, beans, sugar cane, peanuts and tobacco. Fruits are a specialty of the region and they abound in local markets. Industry in Guangxi consists mainly of mining and processing raw materials, and newly discovered petroleum deposits in the Beibu Gulf promise to fuel further industrial development.

Guangxi has a subtropical monsoon climate featuring long summers, warm winters, high humidity, plentiful rainfall and frequent storms (including typhoons) in summer and autumn. The average annual temperature is 17°C in the north and 23°C in the south.

Wuzhou 梧州

The area around Wuzhou has been settled since the Qin Dynasty (221–207 BC) and the town itself was founded in 621 AD. Wuzhou is known as the 'Gateway to Guangxi' because of its proximity to the Guangdong border.

An age-old trading city, Wuzhou attracted many European traders as they expanded their river commerce. The British opened Wuzhou to foreign trade in 1897, and soon began a regular shipping service from Hong Kong, past Wuzhou, to Nanning. By 1930, Wuzhou had a British consulate, numerous foreign trading companies and an American hospital.

Today, Wuzhou is a small industrial city that still retains many colorful street markets selling produce, birds in cages, jade and handicrafts. Though there are no spectacular sights in town, travelers can easily spend a day or two exploring the lively streets before making the connection to Guiping, Guilin, Yangshuo or Guangzhou.

Things to do

There is much to see on the streets of Wuzhou. Near the river, the markets are filled with goods from as far away as Hong Kong and Yunnan Province. The alleyways off Dazhong Lu or Baiyun Lu sell exotic animals, including pangolins and many types of snakes. In summer, a large public swimming and diving area on the Guijiang River is open, with three diving platforms, a place to swim laps and another where you can just float in the refreshing water.

Western Bamboo Temple (Xizhusi) 西竹寺

This temple, under repair since 1983, has just recently re-opened. More than 20 nuns live here, and the head teacher is an 80-year-old monk from Zhejiang Province. Morning devotions begin at 4 am. The nuns run an excellent vegetarian restaurant; portions are quite large, so start out with only one dish per person. The temple is about a half-hour walk from the boat dock through nice old neighborhoods, and affords a fine view of town.

Beishan Gongyuan Park 北山公园

The park has a memorial to Dr Sun Yat-sen, father of the Chinese Republic, but it is closed much of the time. The rest of the park is mundane and the zoo has only a few pathetic looking animals in small cages.

Hebin Gongyuan Park 河滨公园

The trail to Hebin Gongyuan winds up a brush-covered, tree-shaded hill to a peak just above the confluence of the Guijiang and Xijiang Rivers. The park has a wonderful flower garden and a large collection of dwarf trees and miniature rock gardens. A viewing platform offers the best view of the two rivers and Wuzhou.

White Cloud Mountain Scenic Area (Baiyunshan Fengjingqu) 白云山风景区

This nature area in the mountains northeast of town is an undeveloped park filled with lush vegetation and steep hills. The walk from town takes about an hour and passes through some of the oldest neighborhoods in Wuzhou.

Jinpingshan Ta Pagoda 锦屏山塔

Completed in 1824, this pagoda is still in fine shape even though it has never been restored. The central stairway looks safe, but the doors are bolted shut and the caretaker seldom climbs the mountain to the site. Nevertheless, the view from the pagoda and the walk from the ferryboat make the trip worthwhile. To get there, cross the Xijiang River on the ferryboat from Wuzhou

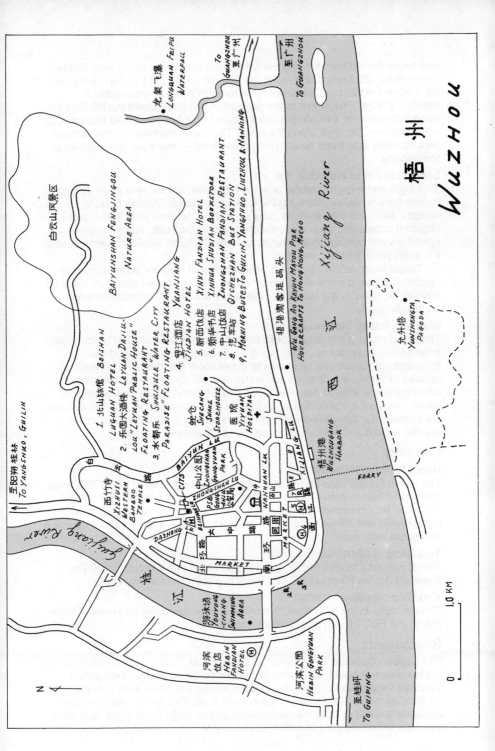

梧州 *Wuzhou*

桂江 *Guijiang River*

西江 *Xijiang River*

允外塔 YUANSHENGTA PAGODA

至广州 To GUANGZHOU

至广州 To GUANGZHOU

龙泉飞瀑 LONGQUAN FEIPU WATERFALL

白云山风景区 BAIYUNSHAN FENGJINGQU NATURE AREA

北山 BEISHAN

至阳朔桂林 To YANGSHUO, GUILIN

西竹寺 YIZHUSI WESTERN BAMBOO TEMPLE

白云路 BAIYUN LU

中山公园 ZHONGSHAN GONGYUAN PARK

蛇仓 SNAKE STOREHOUSE

医院 YIYUAN HOSPITAL

梧港澳客运码头 WU GANG AO KEYUN MATOU PIER HOVERCRAFTS TO HONG KONG, MACAO

梧州港 WUZHOUGANG HARBOR

FERRY

至桂坪 To GUIPING

河滨公园 HEBIN GONGYUAN PARK

河滨饭店 HEBIN FANDIAN HOTEL

游泳场 YOUYONG CHANG SWIMMING AREA

中山路 ZHONGSHAN LU

南环路 NANHUAN LU

西江路 XIJIANG LU

大中路 DAZHONG LU

北环路 BEIHUAN LU

CITS

MARKET

MARKET

1. 北山旅馆 LUGUAN HOTEL
2. 乐园大酒楼 LEYUAN DAJIU- LOU "LEYUAN PUBLIC HOUSE" FLOATING RESTAURANT
3. 水都乐 SHUIDULE "WATER CITY" PARADISE "FLOATING RESTAURANT"
4. 鸳江酒店 YUANJIANG JIUDIAN HOTEL
5. 新西饭店 XINXI FANDIAN HOTEL
6. 新华书店 XINHUA SHUDIAN BOOKSTORE
7. 中山饭店 ZHONGSHAN FANDIAN RESTAURANT
8. 汽车站 QICHEZHAN BUS STATION
9. MORNING BUSES TO GUILIN, YANGSHUO, LIUZHOU & NANNING

N

0   1.0 KM

and follow the dirt road leading away from the river at the boat ramp. Follow this road for 100 meters and make the first left onto a dirt trail that climbs the hill. Follow the trail past gravesites and through bamboo groves until it reaches a ridge. Follow this to the pagoda. A trail leads down the hill from the pagoda to the river, providing a quick return route, but if you take this trail both ways you miss the walk along the ridge. The round trip from Wuzhou should take no more than three hours. Bring some food — there are picnic tables at the pagoda.

Longquan Feipu Waterfall 龙泉飞瀑

This eight-meter-high waterfall is not spectacular, but the hike there through a narrow farming valley offers a good look at traditional Chinese farming villages. Men and draft animals plow small plots, women plant seed, repair irrigation canals and cook while children play in the bush. You can easily spend several hours in this picturesque area. In warm weather, swim in one of the small pools near the waterfall.

To get there, follow Xijiang Lu eastward out of town for 30 minutes until opposite an island in the river. Here you will find a wide dirt road that leads up the narrow valley to the falls. The walk takes another 30 minutes once you are on this dirt road.

Shecang Snake Storehouse 蛇仓

This storehouse is the largest of its kind in Southwest China and holds snakes to be sold to Guangzhou, Hong Kong or overseas clients. Among the thousands of snakes are two types of cobra (both found locally), several species of vipers, tree snakes and water snakes. By luck, we were allowed into the viewing area to see poisonous snakes being filmed for a television show. The area is not designed for tourists, and hordes of visiting Westerners will probably be turned away. For awhile at least, it should be possible to wander around the area, viewing the myriad snakes in wire cages.

Lodging

Hebin Fandian Hotel 河宾饭店

The Hebin Fandian sits above the Guijiang River just west of town. This large, clean hotel has so many rooms it is never full. Beds in a four-bed room are FEC 5.50 with communal toilet and shower. Double rooms are FEC 14 with a private toilet and shower. There is a restaurant at the hotel. The boat dock is a 15-minute walk away.

Yuanjiang Jiudian Hotel 鸳江酒店

This Overseas Chinese hotel has all the comforts of a Western hotel. The cheapest double room is FEC 18. There is a restaurant at the hotel.

Xinxi Fandian Hotel 新西饭店

Though close to the boat dock, this place is dirty, run-down and noisy. Double rooms are FEC 21 with private toilet and shower.

Restaurants

The **Leyuan Dajiulou** (乐园大酒楼) and **Shuidule** (水都乐) are interesting floating restaurants with both budget and higher priced dining areas. **Zhongshan Fandian Restaurant** (中山饭店), located across the street from the bus station on Zhongshan Lu, has delicious Cantonese food. The dining room near the entrance is cheaper than the nicer rooms further back. Even in the best room, travelers should be able to stuff themselves for Rmb 3 per person.

Transportation

Bus tickets can be purchased at the Wuzhou Qichezhan Bus Station, at the Wuzhou Boat Ticket Office or on the boat from Guangzhou. Every morning English-speaking workers meet the boat from Guangzhou to help travelers buy bus tickets and direct them to the proper buses. Local buses are cheaper than the Japanese buses that meet the boat from Guangzhou, but they are slower and less comfortable. Tickets must be purchased in advance at the bus station, and workers may not want to sell you the cheap tickets.

Riverboat tickets are sold on the right side of the Wuzhou Boat Ticket Office, and hovercraft tickets are sold on the left side. Riverboats depart from the nearby wharf but hovercrafts leave from the Wuzhou-Hong Kong Pier on Xijiang Lu, located 15 minutes away by foot from the ticket office.

Wuzhou Qichezhan Bus Station 梧州汽车站

destination	departure	arrival	cost (Rmb)
Yangshuo 阳朔	07:00	15.30	16.00
Guilin 桂林	07:00	16.30	16.00
Nanning 南宁	06.10	16:00	20.00
Liuzhou 柳州	06:00	19:00	20.00

Wuzhou Gang Keyunzhan Riverboat Station 梧州客运站

destination	departure	cost (Rmb)
Liuzhou 柳州	19:00	13.00
Guiping 桂平	18:00	5.30
Nanning 南宁	18:00	14.90
Guangzhou 广州	19:00,19:30,20:00	10.50
Hong Kong 香港 (hovercraft, odd days only)	19.30	FEC 70 or HK$ 150

Yangshuo 阳朔

The karst landscape around Yangshuo has been famous for millennia. Today the beauty of the area, known to surpass even that of Guilin, has made the Lijiang River cruise the most oversubscribed tourist trip in China.

Yangshuo is either the best or worst destination in China, depending on what you think travel should be. Two hundred or more travelers stay in Yangshuo every night and as many as 60 tour buses arrive by 10:00 with groups from Guilin. The town is simply overrun by tourists.

Five years ago, the main street was slow-paced and cozy, but today gift shops and restaurants dominate this street, having long since bought out the less profitable stores. Every restaurant in town has an English menu, an English-speaking staff and serves both Western and Chinese food. By foreign standards the prices are cheap but locals complain because many of them can no longer afford to eat at restaurants.

The entrepreneurs who built the local tourist industry have made it one of the easiest places in China to get to and enjoy. If you do not speak a word of Chinese, have no guidebook or phrasebook, no maps and no experience buying a ticket or using money in a foreign country, all you have to do is get on the boat in Guangzhou and you are taken care of. You are met at the

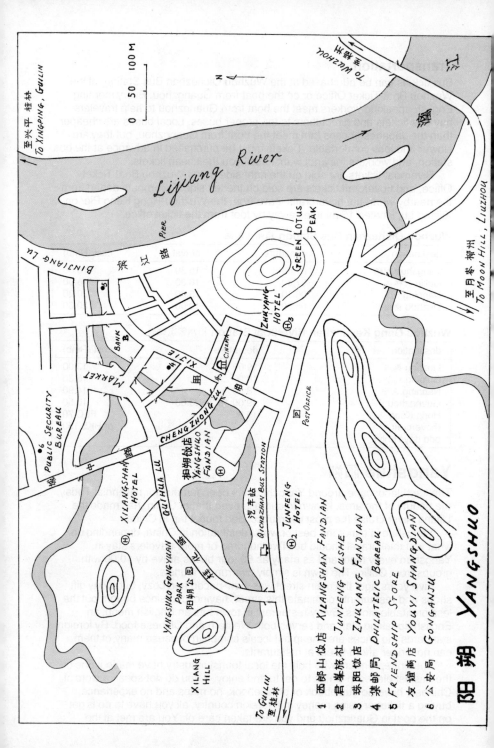

阳朔 **YANGSHUO**

1 西郎山饭店 **XILANGSHAN FANDIAN**
2 君峰旅社 **JUNFENG LÜSHE**
3 珠阳饭店 **ZHUYANG FANDIAN**
4 集邮局 **PHILATELIC BUREAU**
5 友谊商店 **YOUYI SHANGDIAN**
6 公安局 **GONGANJU**

Lijiang River

至兴平 桂林
To XINGPING, GUILIN

至月亮山 柳州
To MOON HILL, LIUZHOU

To WUZHOU 至梧州

PIER

BINJIANG LU 宾江路

GREEN LOTUS PEAK

ZHUYANG HOTEL H₃

CINEMA

XIJIE 西街

BANK B

MARKET

PUBLIC SECURITY BUREAU 6

CHENGZHONG LU 城中路

XILANGSHAN HOTEL H₁

GUIHUA LU 桂花路

YANGSHUO GONGYUAN PARK 阳朔公园

XILANG HILL 西郎山

To GUILIN 至桂林

相朔饭店 **YANGSHUO FANDIAN** H

汽车站 **QICHEZHAN BUS STATION**

JUNFENG HOTEL H₂

POST OFFICE

FRIENDSHIP STORE

N

0 50 100 M

42

Wuzhou boat dock by workers who put you on the bus to Yangshuo and give you the business cards of local hotels. You get off the bus in Yangshuo and have only to decide which hotel to stay at (all have English-speaking staff) and which restaurant to eat at. When you want to leave, workers at the hotel will, for a small premium, buy you a bus or train ticket. You are free to spend your days exploring not-so-traditional villages, swimming at the local swimming hole or trading travel stories with any of your 200 new friends.

Go to Yangshuo and try to imagine what it was like ten years ago. It was, no doubt, a magical place. If all the independent travelers were distributed roughly equally throughout Southwest China at all places that still seem magical to us Westerners, metamorphoses like that of Yangshuo would probably never occur.

Things to do

In town, visit the local market with its wide selection of fruits and vegetables. The **Yangshuo Gongyuan Park** is a quiet, pleasant place, and a climb up the hill to the pavilion on the peak offers a dramatic view of town and nearby eccentric mountains. For a swim, go to the boat dock and head downstream for a few minutes. Hot weather usually means a good crowd at the swimming hole.

To get away from town, walk or rent a bike and follow any of the dirt trails that branch off the main road through the hills. You will find many small villages that typify farming settlements in southern China.

All the hotels in town offer boat tours of the river. Some are night tours where you can go cormorant fishing with local fishermen. Hire a boat to Fuli, 45 minutes south of Yangshuo, and ride your bike back — a fun and satisfying afternoon trip.

Moon Hill 月亮山
Moon Hill is a karst peak with a giant hole in the shape of a half moon. The hill presents a perfect place for taking photos or simply viewing the wierd karst formations. The climb to the top is steep but worthwhile for the vista. Visit early to avoid the tourists bused in from Guilin.

Xingping 兴坪
Xingping is a beautiful, small town on the Lijiang River, three hours by boat downstream, with scenery even more dramatic than Yangshuo's. Very few foreigners have made this trip. You can also ride bikes to Xingping (about two hours), or take the local bus. Buses depart daily from Yangshuo at 07:00, 08:00, 08:40, 10:00, 13:00, 14:30, and 15:30. There is a small hotel in Xingping, but it may not let foreigners stay.

Lodging

Good Companion Holiday Inn (Junfeng Lushe) 君峰旅社
The Good Companion Holiday Inn is clean and comfortable. Beds range from FEC 3 in a triple room to FEC 6 in a single room. All rooms have ceiling fans and mosquito nets and share communal showers. The helpful staff speaks good English and can help arrange bus, boat, plane and train tickets. Couples may be able to rent a secluded double room in a separate house.

Zhuyang Fandian Hotel 珠阳饭店
Comparable to the Good Companion Holiday Inn, this hotel offers travel information, local tours, bike rentals, ticketing services and a beauty shop.

Beds range from FEC 4 in a four-bed room to FEC 10 in a double room with private bathroom.

Yangshuo Fandian Hotel 阳朔饭店

This place is for monied tours and generally not for individual travelers. It is extremely clean, carpeted, and has its own restaurant and bike rental. The Yangshuo branch of CITS is located here. A triple room costs FEC 6 per bed, a double costs FEC 24 and a double room with private toilet and shower is FEC 44.

Xilangshan Fandian Hotel 西郎山饭店

This old, secluded, rustic hotel attracts mainly Chinese guests. Though it is not quite as comfortable as the other hotels in town, the atmosphere makes it our favorite. Beds in a triple room are FEC 4 and double rooms with private toilet and shower are FEC 10.

Transportation

Yangshuo Qichezhan Bus Station 阳朔汽车站

destination	departure	cost (Rmb)
Guilin 桂林 (from Yangshuo bus station)	13 buses daily from 07:00−18:00	2.00
Guilin 桂林 (from Yangshuo bus stop)	5 buses daily from 10:00−16:00	2.30
Liuzhou 柳州	07:10	5.40
Wuzhou 梧州	08:00	15.00
		11.00
Xingping 兴坪	7 buses daily from 07:00−15:30	0.85

Boats

There are boats to Guilin and points in between along the Lijiang River every day. Check local hotels and restaurants for information. A boat to Yangti costs Rmb 15. From Yangti, a motorcycle-cart taxi to the main road is Rmb 3, and the bus to Guilin costs Rmb 1.10.

Guilin 桂林

Guilin is probably China's oldest tourist site. For over a thousand years painters have sought to recreate the astonishing pinnacles with pavilions clinging to their vertical cliffs and poets have used the dramatic landscape as inspiration for their work. Not surprisingly, early Western stereotypes of China were drawn from Guilin's image of mystical bread-loaf hills shrouded in mist and floating in space.

Guilin was a small village of little importance until the Qin Dynasty (221−207 BC). In 214 BC the Lingqu Canal, linking the Pearl and Yangzi river networks, established Guilin as a regional trading center that was able to monitor trade between Guangzhou and Changsha, in Hunan Province. Guilin grew in importance until, in the Ming Dynasty (1368−1644), it was made the capital of Guangxi Province, an honor it held until 1914.

When Japanese occupation forces drove the Nationalist armies from the coastline in 1936, they fled to Guilin and briefly made it China's capital before moving on to Chongqing, in Sichuan Province. During this period, a flood of affluent Chinese refugees converged on the city, swelling its population to

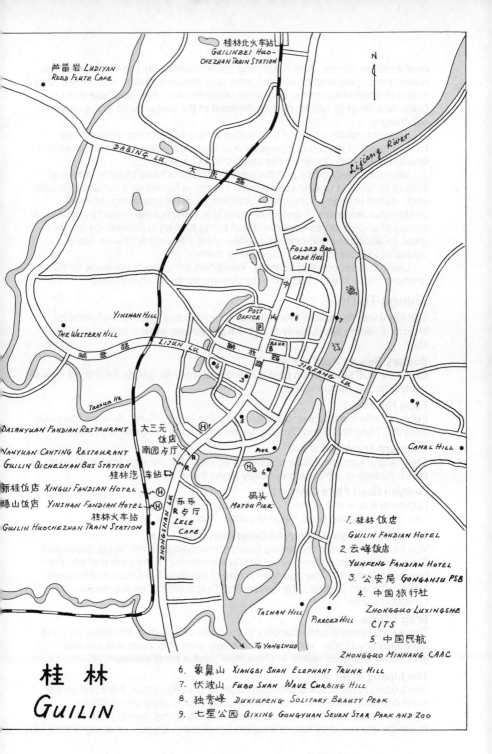

芦笛岩 LUDIYAN
REED FLUTE CAFE

桂林北火车站
GUILINBEI HUO-
CHEZHAN TRAIN STATION

N

Lijiang River

DAQING LU 大庆路

FOLDED BRO-
CADE HILL

YINSHAN HILL

THE WESTERN HILL
丽君路 LIJUN LU 解放路
POST OFFICE
BANK
JIEFANG LU

Taoxua He

DASANYUAN FANDIAN RESTAURANT 大三元饭店
NANYUAN CANTING RESTAURANT 南园厅
GUILIN QICHEZHAN BUS STATION 桂林汽车站
新桂饭店 XINGUI FANDIAN HOTEL
隐山饭店 YINSHAN FANDIAN HOTEL
桂林火车站
GUILIN HUOCHEZHAN TRAIN STATION

ZHONGSHAN LK

乐乐
R 卢厅
LELE
CAFE

PIER

CAMEL HILL

码头
MATOU PIER

TASHAN HILL
PIERCED HILL

To YANGSHUO

桂 林
GUILIN

1. 桂林饭店
GUILIN FANDIAN HOTEL
2. 云峰饭店
YUNFENG FANDIAN HOTEL
3. 公安局 GONGANJU PSB
4. 中国旅行社
ZHONGGUO LUXINGSHE
CITS
5. 中国民航
ZHONGGUO MINHANG CAAC
6. 象鼻山 XIANGBI SHAN ELEPHANT TRUNK HILL
7. 伏波山 FUBO SHAN WAVE CURBING HILL
8. 独秀峰 DUXIUFENG SOLITARY BEAUTY PEAK
9. 七星'公园 QIXING GONGYUAN SEVEN STAR PARK AND ZOO

over a million people. With a lightning-quick offensive in 1944, the Japanese routed the unprepared Nationalist army and occupied Guilin, capturing a large cache of unused weapons. In a spree of destruction, the Japanese reduced Guilin to a heap of rubble, destroying most of the monuments to the region's rich history.

From the rubble of World War II rose a new and modern Guilin, a city lacking much of its former character and elegance. Today, grey factories and apartment houses dominate the smog-darkened skyline.

New-found prosperity and the opening of China have brought droves of visitors to Guilin. For Chinese tourists, the city is famed as a romantic vacation spot, visited by many honeymoon couples. Guilin is also a stop on most foreign tour itineraries. Foreigners walking in town are harrassed by countless money changers or restaurant workers trying to drag in passers-by to buy a meal. In addition, week-long waits often greet travelers who want plane tickets or sleeper tickets on trains out of town.

Guilin is disappointing to many. Yangshuo, only two hours away by bus, is cheaper, more scenic, and more convenient for the budget traveler.

Things To Do

The ideal way to explore Guilin and the surrounding karst formations is by bicycle. Evening walks away from the main streets allow a look into Chinese life.

Solitary Beauty Peak 独秀峰
Climb the 306 stone steps past numerous stone inscriptions for a good view of the city and its surroundings.

Fubo Hill 伏波山
Fubo Hill offers a panorama of Guilin and the Lijiang River. Buddhist carvings from the Tang and Song Dynasty fill the caverns at the base of the hill.

Elephant Trunk Hill 象鼻山
This natural karst sculpture resembles an elephant drinking from the Lijiang River. Nearby is a pleasant walkway along the river.

Ludiyan Reed Flute Cave 芦笛岩
Ludidong is one of the finest caves in Southwest China. Ingeniously-named rock clusters fill the eerie, neon-lit vaults. This is not a cave to miss.

Seven Star Crags (Qixingyan Gongyuan Park) 七星岩
You can escape from the dreary Guilin surroundings in this large, green park. Save your entrance receipt in case you wander out of the park and into the bordering farmland. The zoo here is one of the nicest in China and features two overheated pandas. The Seven Star Crags are not as impressive as Ludidong Cave.

Ming Tombs 明陵
This newly opened tomb complex at the base of Yaoshan Hill dates from the Ming Dynasty (1368−1644). Set in a lovely area of fir trees, the site has impressive entrance gates, a 'Spirit Way', and a small museum.

The Lijiang River 漓江
The Lijiang River, flowing between Guilin and Yangshuo, is heralded as the most dramatic stretch of river in China. The river flows past countless limestone peaks on the five-hour downstream journey, leaving most who make the trip awed by nature's outlandish display. Equally amazing is the FEC

50 ticket price which makes this by far the most expensive river trip in China. When the river is low, buses take tourists from Guilin down river to where the boats can navigate. The trip ends in Yangshuo where buses wait to take customers back to Guilin. In the past, travelers were sometimes allowed to journey with the boats back upstream to Guilin for a fraction of the downstream cost, but as more people did this the boats became more crowded and appreciably slower. Buy your tickets at the Foreign Ticket Office at Guilin's Qichezhan Bus Station.

Tours

City tours are offered by many small companies located near the train station and on Zhongshan Lu. The Foreign Ticket Office at the train station also offers tours.

The La La Cafe, Dasanyuan Restaurant and the Nanyuan Restaurant all arrange special tours to various closed areas around Guilin. Some people have had problems, so be prudent and do not pay the full price in advance.

Farther Away

Lingqu Canal 灵渠

The Lingqu Canal is located in Xing'an, about 60 kilometers north of Guilin on the railway line. During the Qin Dynasty (221–207 BC), Emperor Qinshi Huangdi, first unifier of China, wanted a link between the Yangzi River and Guangdong Province to supply his armies. A huge block of masonry was positioned to divide the Xiangjiang River, thereby diverting water to the Lingqu Canal. The canal was kept in good repair and expanded over the years. Sections of the canal and some of its 36 former locks can still be seen. About a kilometer upstream from Xing'an are tombs honouring the three generals sent by Qinshi Huangdi to supervise construction of the canal.

We did not visit this area, but some travelers thought it an interesting day trip from Guilin. Others spent several days camping out and visiting small villages in Xing'an County.

Lodging

Guilin Fandian Hotel 桂林饭店

This is a large, drab hotel with a gift shop and restaurant. Double rooms range from FEC 15.40 with no bathroom to FEC 44 with private bathroom and air-conditioning. Dormitory beds cost FEC 5.

Xingui Fandian Hotel 新桂饭店

This is a typical budget hotel, which also has more expensive double rooms with private bathroom, television and air-conditioning. We found the hotel staff friendly and helpful. There is a restaurant at the hotel and a bike rental service. Beds in two-and three-bed rooms cost FEC 6.60.

Yishan Fandian Hotel 隐山饭店

This hotel is clean, comfortable and conveniently located between the train and bus stations. Double rooms are FEC 30. Dormitory beds cost FEC 11.50.

Yunfeng Fandian Hotel 云峰饭店

Most guests at this hotel are Chinese tourists. Although it is a bit noisy, the Yunfeng Fandian is enjoyable and has character. There is a restaurant and bike rental service. Double rooms start at FEC 12 for a room sharing communal toilet and shower. Double rooms with private bathrooms are FEC 35.

Restaurants

Restaurants line Zhongshan Lu between the train station and Jiefang Lu. All have English signs and menus, Western dishes and energetic workers on the street screaming hello and trying to get you inside. Many local restaurants serve exotic fare such as snake, dog, pigeon, snail, eel, turtle and pangolin. Some of the expensive hotels have Japanese food and Japanese-speaking staff.

Transportation

Numerous bicycle rental shops can be found along Zhongshan Lu. The basic rate is Rmb 2.50 per day or Rmb 0.40 per hour.

Guilin Huochezhan Train Station 桂林火车站

Foreigners must go to the 'ticket window for FEC' to buy tickets. Student cards will not get you a low price unless you speak some Chinese. Beware of buying a ticket from a hotel at discount; many travelers end up paying for an upgrade to tourist price once they board the train.

destination	departure
Kunming 昆明	21:55
Nanning 南宁	06:30, 07:30, 07:47, 08:34, 14:52
Guangzhou 广州	16:18
Shanghai 上海	04:21, 20:36
Beijing 北京	02:44
Zhanjiang 湛江	10:14, 18:30
Wuchang 武昌	19:30
Hengyang 衡阳	07:58, 23:38

Guilin Qichezhan Bus Station 桂林汽车站

destination	departure	cost (FEC)
Wuzhou 梧州	06:40, 06:50	13.00
	07:00	18.00
Guangzhou 广州	08:30	23.60
Changsha 长沙	06:40	26.50
Yangshuo 阳朔	07:00−18:00 (many buses daily)	2.00
Longsheng 龙胜	07:00, 07:40	3.25

Boat tickets from Wuzhou to Guangzhou are sold at the bus station. Add Rmb 10.40 to the bus ticket price for the combined cost of the bus to Wuzhou and boat to Guangzhou.

Guilin City Bus Routes

bus #1: CAAC, Bank of China, Solitary Beauty Peak, and Beizhan North Train Station.
bus #2: Fubo Hill, Lijiang Theater.
bus #3: Reed Flute Cave.
bus #11: Seven Star Crags and zoo.
buses #1,2,3,11: All serve the Guilin Huochezhan Train Station.
bus #13: Direct service from Reed Flute Cave to Seven Star Crags.

The Taiping Rebellion (1850–1864)

The Taiping Rebellion, a giant political and religious upheaval that began in Guangxi Province, shook China to its foundations. It was probably the most important event in China in the 19th century. Before being crushed, it ravaged 17 provinces, took 20 million lives and speeded the Qing Dynasty towards its downfall in 1911.

The rebellion was started by Hong Xiuquan, an unhappy candidate for the civil service in Guangxi. Hong had been influenced by Christian teachings and when he failed the civil service examinations he not only began to have visions, he declared that he was the younger brother of Jesus Christ, sent by God to reform China. Helped by a friend, he gathered a strong following among poor peasants in Guangxi and on January 1, 1851, he proclaimed a new dynasty, the Taiping Tianguo (Heavenly Kingdom of Great Peace) with himself as the Heavenly King.

The Taiping philosophy — to distribute land equally and share property according to a primitive form of communism, and to get rid of the foreign Manchu (Qing) Dynasty in Peking — attracted many famine-stricken peasants, miners and laborers. Before long there was a Taiping army with over a million totally disciplined, fanatical soldiers organized into separate divisions of men and women. Their harsh brand of Christianity called for strict worship and obedience but paid little attention to New Testament ideas of personal kindness, forgiveness or redemption. Slavery, prostitution, adultery and foot-binding were outlawed. Equality between men and women was decreed. Taiping followers did not smoke, drink, take opium or gamble and the army lived by the sternest puritanical rules.

The Taiping forces swept through Guizhou Province into the Yangzi River Valley and fought on to Nanjing, which they captured in 1853, renaming it the Heavenly Capital. Then their momentum stalled. A northern expedition failed to capture Peking, the Qing capital, while power struggles among the movement's leaders led to purges and assassinations. Hong, the Heavenly King, managed to hold on to his position.

In 1860, the Taipings tried to regain their strength by attacking Shanghai but they were turned back by an army of Western-trained mercenaries commanded by an American adventurer named Frederick Townsend Ward. Later, when Ward was mortally wounded, a British major, 'Chinese' Gordon, took over. Meanwhile, the Chinese upper class, which had been alienated by the radical, anti-Confucian ideas of the Taipings, organised their own army under an official of the Qing government. This army surrounded Nanjing, which fell in 1864. Hong Xiuquan committed suicide and almost 100,000 of his followers chose death rather than capture.

The Taiping ideals of land distribution and common ownership came a whole century before Chinese communism. Some Western-educated Taiping leaders even suggested industrialization and democracy, too. The introduction of sexual equality on such a wide scale was the first in the modern world. The Taiping Rebellion failed, but the Qing Dynasty was so weakened that it never established a firm hold over China again and the way was opened for revolution.

Elisabeth Booz

Guiping 桂平

Guiping is a sleepy town at the confluence of the Qianjiang and Yujiang Rivers. Roads here are little more than dusty trails, and locals lead a dual life of urban and rural activities. Much of the work done in town relates directly to the region's vast rural economy.

Good examples of southern Chinese crops can be seen nearby. East of town, towards the river junction, lie groves of banana trees, large sugar cane fields and occasional rice paddies cleared from the dense jungle. At the base of Xishan Mountain are terraced rice fields with tea plantations extending far up the mountainside.

Things to do

In town, the oldest neighborhoods are east of the northern wharf. Many walled compounds originally housing large gentry families still stand, unchanged since the Qing Dynasty. Just north of this old section, the rocky Qianjiang shoreline is sublime for swimming or sitting in the sun. A stroll through the Zhongshan Gongyuan Park in the morning or late afternoon is especially pleasant, for at these times old men congregate in the park toting their pet birds in wonderfully constructed bamboo cages.

Xishan Mountain 西山

This 1,000-meter peak northwest of town is Guiping's primary tourist attraction. The trail winding to the top passes small temples and pavilions set beside steep tea plantations and shady groves and traverses vertical cliffs. While the temples and pavilions are new and uninteresting, beautiful pine forests covering the upper half of the mountain and a spectacular view of Guiping and the rivers beyond make the climb worthwhile. China's oldest Buddhist nun lives on the mountain.

The walk to the top is strenuous, taking about three hours. If possible, avoid the park on weekends when thousands of noisy sightseers crowd the trail.

To get to Xishan, take the local bus from Guangchang Square or walk from town. Buses leave Guangchang at 08:00, 09:00, 11:00, 14:10, 15:45 and arrive at the base of the mountain ten minutes later to pick up passengers for the return trip.

Jintiancun Village 金田村

Jintiancun is a village 25 kilometers north of Guiping where China's largest peasant revolt, the Taiping Rebellion, began. The Taipings were led by Hong Xiuquan, a thrice-failed candidate for the imperial examinations. After experiencing fever-induced hallucinations, he declared himself to be Jesus Christ's brother. In 1851 Hong's army won its first battle over Qing soldiers, beginning a string of victories that ultimately made the rebels rulers of southern China. The Taipings fueled their rebellion with pooled resources, lived communally and were ostensibly Christian (as defined by Hong's interpretation of missionary teachings). The Taipings were only defeated after unprecedented Qing concessions of power to southern generals making them virtual warlords. The intervention of Western powers played a small part in the defeat as well.

Today, all that is left of the historic site are the remains of a large fort on a hill west of town and a few dusty weapons, coins and official documents housed in a small museum.

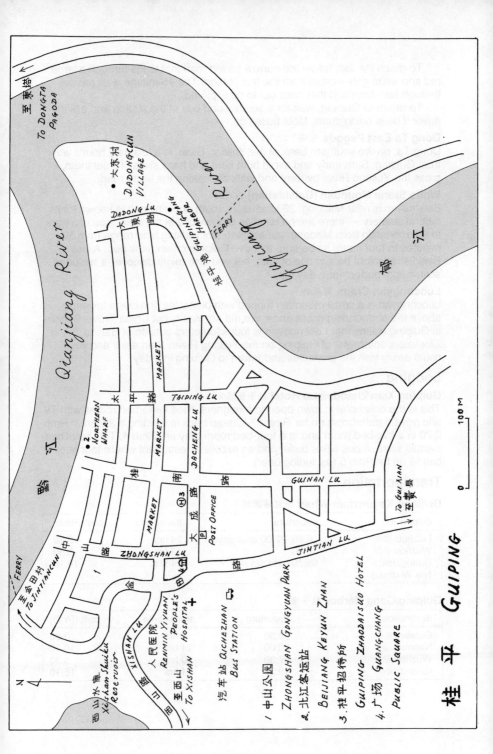

至东塔
To Dongta Pagoda

Qianjiang River

黔江

西山水库 Xishan Shuiku Reservoir

至金田村 To Jintiancun

人民医院 Renmin Yiyuan People's Hospital

至西山 To Xishan

中山路 Zhongshan Lu

西山路 Xishan Lu

金田路

大成路 Dacheng Lu

市 Post Office

汽车站 Qichezhan Bus Station

大东路 Dadong Lu

大东村 Dadongcun Village

桂平港 Guiping Harbor

FERRY

浔江 Xunjiang River

郁

北 Northern Wharf

大平路 Taiping Lu

市 Market

南路

桂南路

Guinan Lu

Jintian Lu

广场 Public Square

至贵县 To Gui Xian

N

0   100 M

桂平 GUIPING

1 中山公园
  ZHONGSHAN GONGYUAN PARK

2 北江客运站
  BEIJIANG KEYUN ZHAN

3 桂平招待所
  GUIPING ZHAODAISUO HOTEL

4 广场 广场
  GUANGCHANG
  PUBLIC SQUARE

To reach the fort, follow the narrow paved road that leads through a large red and white gate across from the bus station. The 45-minute walk passes through lush farmland that cries out to be explored.

To return to Guiping, wait for a southbound bus at the station and ask the driver if he is going there. Most buses do.

Dong Ta East Pagoda 东塔

Dong Ta, on the southern bank of the Yujiang River, is a leisurely hour's walk from Guiping. Start early and avoid both heat and hazy skies. To get there, cross the Yujiang River by ferry and walk east along the levee road.

White Stone Mountain (Baishishan) 白石山

Baishishan is near Madong, 39 kilometers south of Guiping. It is known for its natural scenery — there are no temples or pavilions in the area. You can walk to the mountain from Madong, but estimates of walking time range from 30 minutes to four hours so be sure to leave Guiping on an early bus. A visit to Baishishan might be a waste of time, but you also might discover a secluded, scenic spot perfect for a day trip.

Luocongyan Crags 罗丛岩

Luocongyan is a small mountain topped with pinnacles and crags towering above the surrounding grasslands. We did not visit it, but China Travel Service in Guiping claims that Luocongyan is four kilometers outside of Baisha, 37 kilometers southwest of Guiping on the Yujiang River. Start early and you could easily visit the pinnacles and return to Guiping in a day.

Lodging

Guiping Xian Zhaodaisuo Hotel 桂平县招待所

This is the only hotel in town open to foreigners. Nice three-bed rooms with TV and private bathrooms go for Rmb 27. Cheap beds in building #2 start at Rmb 2.70 in a five-bed room and in a four-bed room they are Rmb 4. This hotel has a small store, a bus ticket outlet and an excellent restaurant where four people can fill up for Rmb 5 (excluding beer).

Transportation

Beijiang Keyunzhan Wharf 北江客运站

destination	departure	transit time	cost (Rmb)
Liuzhou 柳州	06:00, 22:00 (odd days)	24 hrs	9.20
Wuzhou 梧州	18:00	12 hrs	5.30
Guangzhou 广州 (via Wuzhou)	05.30 (odd days)	24 hrs	16.10

Guiping Gang Harbor 桂平港

destination	departure	transit time	cost (Rmb)
Guixian 贵县	23:30	6 hrs	3.60
Nanning 南宁	20:00	24 hrs	10.40
Wuzhou 梧州	07:30	10 hrs	5.30
Guangzhou 广州	19:30	24 hrs	16.10

Guiping Qichezhan Bus Station 桂平汽车站

destination	distance (kms)	departure	cost (Rmb)
Jintian 金田	25	06.40 — 17:10 10 buses daily	0.65
Guixian 贵县	69	07:40 — 18:00 6 buses daily	1.80
Liuzhou 柳州	255	06:10, 07:25	6.65
Nanning 南宁	254	06:50	6.66
Madong 麻垌	39	10:20, 15:45	1.00
Baisha 白沙	33	06:40, 11:00, 15:40	0.85

Guixian 贵县

Traders have thrived in Guixian since the Qing Dynasty, using the Yujiang River, and later the railroads, to ship agricultural goods east to the South China Sea and west as far as Burma. Today, Guixian is a small clean city, fairly typical of many in southern China; narrow streets with Cantonese-style covered walkways lined with lively open-front shops.

Things to do

The city is small and easily explored in a day. The willow-lined lily pond in Donghu Gongyuan Park attracts older folks who come to stroll or sit in the gardens. The Diyi Zhaodaisuo Hotel rents bicycles for excursions around town and into the surrounding farmland and small farming villages.

Nanshan Mountain 南山

Nanshan is a karst hill south of town with a cave and a small museum. The cave houses several very old Buddhist sculptures and a bell cast in 1025. The small museum is a treasure trove of newly excavated objects that span Guangxi's long history. A 2,000-year-old tomb of a high official buried with his wife and 11 servants, the 500-year-old headstone of an early Ming Dynasty general, a Qing Dynasty vase decorated with paintings of all 108 brigands from the Chinese classic *Outlaws of the Marsh* and an 1,800-year-old copper battle drum are among the most interesting items. The finds have yet to be expropriated by a more prominent museum.

To reach Nanshan, ride a bike or walk south from Guixian across the Yujiang River bridge and head towards the karst hills. The bike ride takes 45 minutes and the walk two or three hours.

Lodging

Guixian Diyi Zhaodaisuo Hotel 贵县第一招待所

Though you can probably stay elsewhere, this is the only hotel officially open to foreigners. Beds start at Rmb 3 in three- or four-bed rooms. The friendly hotel clerks speak some English and are happy to help you with directions and answer your transportation questions. Bikes for hire cost Rmb 0.50 per hour. The hotel restaurant is awful, so eat elsewhere.

Guixian Fandian Hotel 贵县饭店

Beds in this large, somewhat run-down hotel start at Rmb 1.70 in a four-bed room. Double rooms go for Rmb 5.20.

Guixian Di'er Zhaodaisuo Hotel 贵县第二招待所

Of the dozen or so hotels near the train station, this appears to be the cleanest. Beds start at Rmb 2.

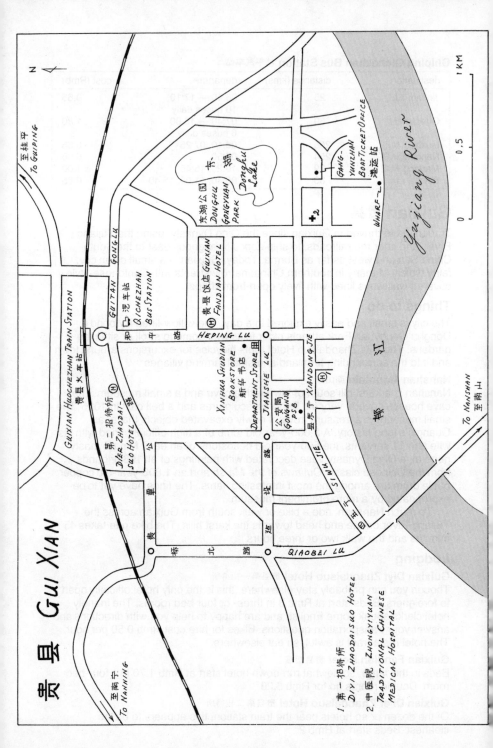

贵县 GUI XIAN

To Nanning 至南宁

To Guiping 至桂平

GUITAN GONGLU 贵滩公路

GUIXIAN HUOCHEZHAN TRAIN STATION 贵县火车站

QICHEZHAN BUS STATION 汽车站

DIER ZHAODAISUO HOTEL 第二招待所

GUIXIAN FANDIAN HOTEL 贵县饭店

HEPING LU 和平路

XINHUA SHUDIAN BOOKSTORE 新华书店

DEPARTMENT STORE 百货

JIANSHE LU 建设路

GONGANJU PSB 公安局

XIANDONG JIE 县东街

SIWU JIE 司五街

QIAOBEI LU 桥北路

DONGHU GONGYUAN PARK 东湖公园

Donghu Lake 东湖

GANG-YUNZHAN BOAT TICKET OFFICE 港运站

WHARF 码头

Yujiang River 郁江

To Nanshan 至南山

N

0   0.5   1 KM

1. 第一招待所 DIYI ZHAODAISUO HOTEL
2. 中医院 ZHONGYIYUAN TRADITIONAL CHINESE MEDICAL HOSPITAL

54

Transportation

Guixian Huochezhan Train Station 贵县火车站

destination	departure
Nanning 南宁	13:32, 02:24
Liuzhou 柳州	15:00

Guixian Qichezhan Bus Station 贵县汽车站

destination	distance (kms)	departure	cost (Rmb)
Nanning 南宁	183	06:45	5.45
Liuzhou 柳州	175	06:30	
Baise 百色	393	06:30	11.90
Guiping 桂平	69	07:00−17:20 9 buses daily	2.20
Wuzhou 梧州	315	06:45	9.45
Guangzhou 广州 (2-day trip)	566	13:00	17.60

Guixian Gangyunzhan Boat Dock 贵县港运站

destination	departure	transit time	cost (Rmb)
Nanning 南宁	03:00	18 hrs	6.80
Guangzhou 广州	13:30	30 hrs	19.70

Liuzhou 柳州

Liuzhou, in the center of Guangxi, was founded during the Tang Dynasty (618−907), but today little remains of the pre-1949 town. Massive industrialization has made Liuzhou Guangxi's largest industrial city, covering 541 square kilometers with a population of 800,000. Like big cities elsewhere in China, Liuzhou is ugly, noisy and badly polluted. The city's non-Han population is largely sinicized and only wears traditional clothing during festivals.

Liuzhou is often hot and humid, so late fall or early spring are the best times to visit. The city has excellent connections by train, bus and boat with the rest of Southwest China.

Things to do

In town, explore the day and night markets, walk along the Liujiang River to the Jiangbin Gongyuan Park or find the Dongmen Chenglou City Gate.

Fish Hill Park (Yufeng Gongyuan) 鱼峰公园

Climb Fish Hill for an unobstructed view of polluted Liuzhou. This park is the site of the Mid-Autumn Festival in Liuzhou. Fish Hill is also famous because one of China's better beers is named after it.

Dule Yan Cave 都乐岩

Although this is the most popular tourist site in Liuzhou, we found the caves, lake and park mediocre. (The caves in Guilin and Guizhou Province are far better.) Admission: Rmb 0.05, additional Rmb 1.50 for the caves. Take bus Number 9 or make the trip by bike in an hour.

Jianpanshan Gongyuan Park 箭盘山公园
There is a nice pond here and a hill with a good view of town. Take bus
Number 6.

Ma'an Gongyuan Park 马鞍公园
Right next to Yufeng Gongyuan Park, this park has a hill with yet another good
view of Liuzhou.

Liuhou Gongyuan Park 柳侯公园
Visit the tumulus of Liu Zongyuan, a famous Tang Dynasty writer, but avoid
the awful zoo in this large, uninspiring park.

Cadres

Any official, indeed anybody wielding any authority whatever in China, is called a
cadre (pronounced cah-der). He or she is generally a member of the Communist
Party. You run into cadres whenever you seek a permit, lodge a complaint or get
caught doing something you shouldn't. Most people in China take cadres as an
encumbering fact of life, while many expend great effort trying to become one
themselves.

"The cadres serve as transmission belts between the summit and the base.
They have some privileges, of course, but before reproaching them for that, we
should consider how unrewarding and dangerous their job is. They are
perpetually torn between the leaders and the led. Directives from on high are
deliberately ambiguous; in case of failure, the leaders must have a fall-back
position, while those who applied the policy are stranded and unprotected, and
can be sacrificed to the rancor of the masses. It is unfair to criticize Maoist
bureaucrats for their slowness and inertia: most often nonaction is their best
chance of survival. How could they go forward? They must set their compasses
on the Thought of Mao Tse-tung — a very mobile, shifting, and slippery pole.

"Judge for yourself. One should avoid leftism, neither should one fall into
rightism (sometimes, as in the case of Lin Biao, leftism is a rightist error), but
between those two pitfalls, the cadre will seek in vain for a 'middle way' — this
being a feudal-Confucian notion. Since the right, the left, and the center are
equally fraught with danger, the cadre may be tempted to shut his eyes and
follow the successive and contradictory instructions of the great leader without a
murmur. Another error. 'To obey blindly' is a poisonous error invented by Liu
Shaoqi in pursuit of his unmentionable project of capitalist restoration. In such a
situation, the downcast and fearful cadre has his courage renewed by daring new
watchwords: one must dare 'to swim against the current'; 'not be afraid of being
in the minority'; 'not be afraid of disgrace, even of exclusion from the party'.
However, before jumping in the water to swim against the current, the cadre
cannot but recall that 'the current of history is irresistible' and the Communist
Party that embodies it is 'grandiose and infallable'. His resolve weakens, then he
is reminded that 'rebellion is legitimate'. Ready to act now, he gets another cold
shower: 'in all circumstances, strict party dicipline should be maintained'. Whom
to believe? 'Truth is quite often the position of the minority'. This helps, but its
value is reduced by another axiom: 'the minority must always submit to the
decisions of the majority'. Should decisions be taken by a vote? Not at all, since
'respect for majority voting is a bourgeois superstition'."

Simon Leys, *Chines Shadows*, pp 119–20.

Longtan Gongyuan Park 龙潭公园

This large, relaxing country park has three ponds and a natural spring. The trip there is great on a bike.

Festivals

Mid-Autumn Festival（中秋节）Held on the 15th day of the eighth lunar month (September or early October) at Fish Hill, this Han and Zhuang festival features colorful lanterns, delicious 'moon cakes' and singing competitions in the Zhuang language.

Lodging

Liuzhou Nanjiang Fandian 柳州南江饭店

This nice, comfortable hotel is two minutes from the train station. Beds in a four-person room start at Rmb 4 and double rooms are Rmb 24. Double rooms with private toilet and shower are Rmb 32. The hotel runs two daily tours to Liuzhou's scenic sites at 08:00 and 13:00. A restaurant is located in the basement.

Liuzhou Fandian 柳州饭店

This big, ugly, inconvenient hotel caters to Hong Kong Chinese tourists. Beds in a triple room are FEC 9 each and double rooms are Rmb 32. The hotel is clean and has a coffee shop and a restaurant. CITS is located in the back of the building.

Transportation

Liuzhou Huochezhan Train Station 柳州火车站

destination	departure
Nanning 南宁	09:18, 10:23, 11:56, 13:00, 17:55
Beijing 北京	23:38
Kunming 昆明	00:47
Guilin 桂林	11:59
Zhanjiang 湛江	13:50
Guiyang 贵阳	16:35, 21:56
Wuchang 武昌	16:14
Guangzhou 广州	13:04
Maoming 茂名	20:21
Hengyang 衡阳	18:39

Liuzhou Qichezhan Bus Station 柳州汽车站

destination	departure	cost (Rmb)
Guangzhou 广州	07:00	25.10
Wuzhou 梧州	06:00, 06:15	11.45
Guilin 桂州	08:00	7.30
Yangshuo 阳朔	12:00	5.40
Beihai 北海	06:00	12.70
Guiping 桂平	06:30	7.70
Baise 百色	06:00	14.20
Nanning 南宁	06:00	7.85

Bus tickets can also be purchased from a stand in the train station, but all departures are from the bus station.

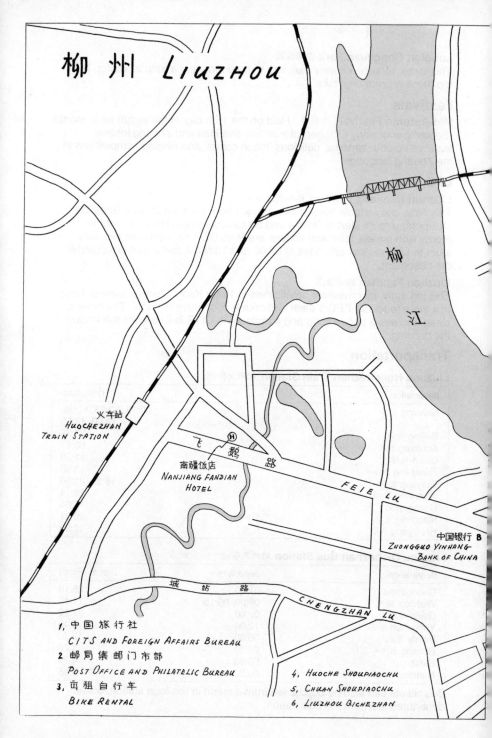

柳 州 *LIUZHOU*

柳 江

火车站
HUOCHEZHAN
TRAIN STATION

飞 鹅 路

Ⓗ
南疆饭店
NANJIANG FANDIAN
HOTEL

FEIE LU

中国银行 Ⓑ
ZHONGGUO YINHANG
BANK OF CHINA

城 站 路
CHENGZHAN LU

1, 中国旅行社
CITS AND FOREIGN AFFAIRS BUREAU

2 邮局集邮门市部
POST OFFICE AND PHILATELIC BUREAU

3, 出租自行车
BIKE RENTAL

4, *HUOCHE SHOUPIAOCHU*

5, *CHUAN SHOUPIAOCHU*

6, *LIUZHOU QICHEZHAN*

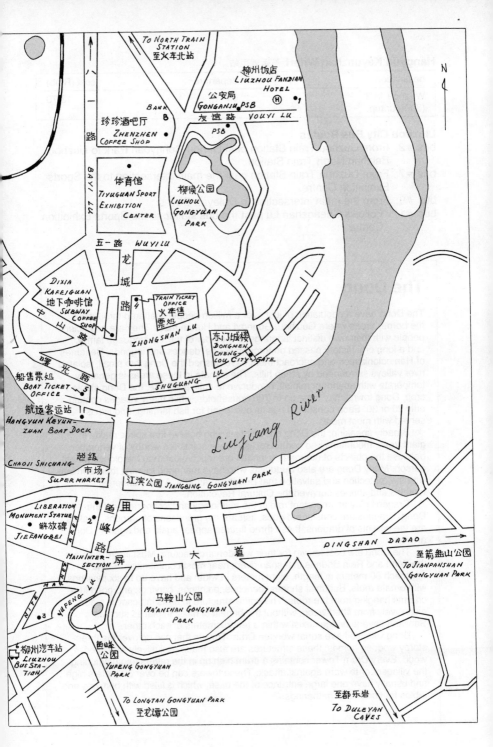

Hangyun Keyunzhan Wharf 航运客运站

destination	departure	cost (Rmb)
Wuzhou 梧州 (30-hour trip)	05:00	13.70

Liuzhou City Bus Routes

bus #2: From Liuzhou Train Station past Liuhou Gongyuan Park to Liuzhou Beizhan North Train Station.

bus #7: From Liuzhou Train Station past the main intersection to the Sports Exhibition Centre.

bus #9: From the main intersection to Duleyan Caves.

bus #11: Follows Chengzhan Lu past the bus station to the Sports Exhibition Centre.

The Dong

The Dong have a population of just over a million people scattered throughout the border areas where Guizhou, Guangxi and Hunan meet. They are an ancient people with their own distinct language, a member of the Tai language family, and a long oral history passed on through songs, dances and legends. Centuries of Han colonization and encroachment have pushed the Dong into small, isolated river valleys surrounded by steep hills. The climate in these areas is generally temperate with abundant rainfall, conducive to cultivating rice, the Dong staple crop. Dong towns may have up to 700 households, while many villages contain only 20 or 30. Each household has its own pond for fish farming, and fish is served with most meals.

Broadly speaking, the Dong are animists who believe that spirits reside in giant trees, mountains and certain rocks. These spirits are worthy of veneration because the objects of nature they inhabit are much older than the oldest, wisest person. Many Dong are also Buddhists who have managed to meld their animism with the protection and salvation that Buddhism affords. A few nunneries, temples and shrines survived the Cultural Revolution.

Dragons play an important role in the mythology and iconography of the Dong. Dragons are considered gods, fish are the grandsons of dragons, snakes are the parents of dragons; these three figures appear again and again in Dong artwork.

The Dong are best known for their wooden architecture. Most impressive are the Wind and Rain Bridges that span rivers near most communities. Some approach 80 meters in length, eight meters in width and have up to six pavilions, with ornate roofs, Buddhist shrines, benches, paintings, carvings and good luck charms hanging from the roofs. The entire structure in all its intricacy is made exclusively from fitted wood, without the benefit of nails. In places such as Sanjiang several bridges exist within a few kilometers of each other.

Dong villages have squat wooden Drum Towers that rise up over the three-storey wooden homes; these structures are also made exclusively with fitted wood. Every Drum Tower contains a drum high up in the rafters for summoning the villagers or to warn against attack. These towers can be over 30 meters high and usually have one large entrance at the base, which is filled with benches and tables for communal gatherings.

Sanjiang Dong Nationality Autonomous County 三江侗族自治县

This is the only Dong area in China open to foreigners. Sanjiang itself is a new town of 10,000 people built up around older Dong villages. It is an excellent base for exploring the county. The rainy season falls in April, May and June, with the winter months receiving the least rainfall.

Things to do

The main attraction here is the strong presence of the Dong themselves, attired in their colorful clothes, speaking their own language, all in a traditional setting. They are friendly people although communication is a problem.

Throughout the area are testaments to the Dong woodworking abilities: Wind and Rain Bridges, Drum Towers, Dong dwellings and water wheels.

Chengyang Qiao Wind and Rain Bridge 程阳桥

Locals claim this to be the most impressive Wind and Rain Bridge, so named for the protection it affords from the elements. Built in 1916, this beautiful bridge has five pavilions, three shrines and resting areas. It is over 80 meters long, eight meters wide and is made entirely of fitted wood and tiles — there are no nails. Chengyang Qiao suffered some minor damage during the Cultural Revolution but is now a protected cultural relic.

Around the bridge are fields irrigated by ingeniously crafted water wheels. Nearby, you can visit eight Dong villages of traditional three-storey wooden

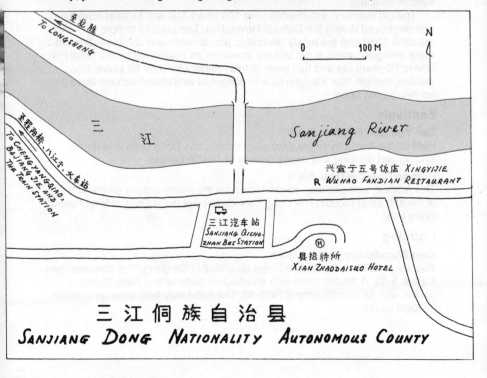

至龙胜
To LONGSHENG

三 江

Sanjiang River

0   100 M

N

To CHENGYANGQIAO,
BA JIANG JIE AND
THE TRAIN STATION

兴宜宁五号饭店 XINGYIJIE
R WUHAO FANDIAN RESTAURANT

三江汽车站
SANJIANG QICHE-
ZHAN BUS STATION

县招待所
XIAN ZHAODAISUO HOTEL

三江侗族自治县
SANJIANG DONG NATIONALITY AUTONOMOUS COUNTY

homes, each community dominated by a Drum Tower. Though the finest Drum Towers were destroyed by marauding Red Guards 20 years ago, the ones that remain are unusual, impressive structures.

A walk upstream from Chengyang Qiao will bring you to other less well-known Wind and Rain Bridges.

Bajiang Jie 八江街

A day trip by bus to the town of Bajiang Jie will bring you to the heart of another Dong community, with some Miao people mingled in. There is a small Wind and Rain Bridge here, the next village has an even more interesting Wind and Rain Bridge, and the village beyond that has a Drum Tower. It is possible to arrange bicycles, but walking in this area is also enjoyable. The last bus returns to Sanjiang at approximately 14:15.

Pingba Gulou Drum Tower 平巴鼓楼

This is said to be the most impressive Drum Tower in existence. Standing more than 50 meters high and made exclusively of fitted wood, its size and construction justify the claim, but unfortunately this tower seems anti-climactic after the long, three-hour bicycle ride to reach it. Pingba seems little different from the other ten villages along the way. We feel that spending time in villages near Bajiang Jie is a better choice than a six-hour round-trip by bike. Traffic along this road is extremely scarce so hitchhiking is not really viable.

Xianglin Si Buddhist Nunnery 香林寺

Locals will be glad to point the way to Xianglin Si, located 45-minutes by foot west of Sanjiang.

The old nunnery, established over 100 years ago and located elsewhere, was destroyed during the Cultural Revolution. The present temple was only rebuilt in 1980 and the newly decorated prayer room and shrines lack artistic merit. Religious merit is not lacking, however, as evidenced by the head nun. She is 72 years old and has been at this nunnery for over 50 years. She worries, though, that Xianglin Si is in danger of extinction because there are no new young nuns.

Festivals

San Yue San Festival 三月三

Held on the third day of the third lunar month, this Dong festival features singing and dancing and draws crowds of 10,000 people.

Dragon Boat Festival 龙船节

This festival, with exciting, colorful races on the rivers, occurs on the fifth day of the fifth lunar month. The Dong here do not celebrate Dragon Boat Festival every year.

Lodging

Xian Zhaodaisuo Hotel 县招待所

You will most likely be directed here on arrival in Sanjiang. The cheapest bed is Rmb 5.60. A double room with an attached bathroom is Rmb 20 and a double with air-conditioning is Rmb 45. The hotel may help arrange vehicles for local jaunts.

Transportation

Sanjiang Qichezhan Bus Station 三江汽车站

destination	distance (kms)	departure	cost (Rmb)
Liuzhou 柳州	202	08:00	5.50
Guilin 桂林	167	08:00	4.60
Rongshui 融水	111	06:50	3.25
Longsheng 龙胜	66	11:00	1.85
Tongdao 通道	77	07:30, 11:30	2.05
Chengyang 程阳	20	07:40, 15:00	0.65
Linxi 林溪	35	07:40, 15:00	1.10
Train Station 火车站	15	13:00, 14:00 20:30	
Bajiang Jie 八江街	20	several buses daily	

Sanjiang Huochezhan Train Station 三江火车站

There are two slow local trains daily, one to Liuzhou and one to Huaihua. The station is almost one hour by bus from Sanjiang.

If you are going to or coming from Huaihua you must take the train as there are no buses on this route. The 13:00 bus from Sanjiang to the train station will arrive in time for the train to Huaihua. If you are headed towards Liuzhou or a point in between, the bus is faster and more convenient.

Longsheng Various Nationalities Autonomous County 龙胜各族自治县

Longsheng is only 125 kilometers north of Guilin but seems to be worlds away. The dramatic karst formations around Guilin soon disappear, along with the tourists, as the road climbs into steep, forested hill country. The land is green and the air is clean and, blessedly, Longsheng has yet to be discovered by the hordes down below on the Lijiang River.

The county is home to four different minority groups, the Zhuang, Dong, Yao and Miao. A few of these hill people live in the drab town of Longsheng, but with a little time and effort you can visit their villages and tiny hamlets in the remarkable countryside.

Things to do

Titian Terraces 梯田

Longsheng County has the most astounding and impressive rice terracing in China — and perhaps the whole world. Rising almost 1000 vertical meters, the manicured landscape is the result of 18 generations of toil, the bulk of which was completed by the 11th generation. The Zhuang responsible for the terracing have lived here for over 500 years.

The grandeur of this man-made wonder deserves to be seen leisurely and at close range rather than simply glimpsed from the Guilin road. Anyone who hikes for three hours up these incredible terraces will be rewarded with a breathtaking view and an understanding of the effort and ingenuity that went into their creation. Water has been channelled to every square centimeter of land, and where farmers can no longer plough with oxen because of the steepness they work by hand. (Some terraces are so narrow they can barely fit two rows of rice.)

The terracing is best viewed from the top at either dawn or dusk, but unfortunately there are no shops, restaurants or places to stay in the upper villages. Most people will be more than satisfied with the panorama from the river at the base of the terraces. The villages here are Zhuang, with some Yao settlements farther away. The women and many of the older men wear traditional clothing, and everyone was extremely friendly though definitely surprised to see a lone backpacker sweating his way up the mountainside.

One word of warning: beware of poisonous snakes in this area. The last bus back to Longsheng leaves the bottom village of Jinjiangcun（金江村）at 15:30.

Chengbu Village 城步
Take the early morning bus from Longsheng to this Yao village and surrounding Yao hamlets for an interesting day trip. Catch the returning bus, hitchhike or walk five kilometers back towards Longsheng to Wenshui Hot Springs.

Wenshui Hot Springs 温水
The hot springs consist of three large outdoor pools. The top pool is ten meters across and over two meters deep, with a temperature of 45°C. The middle one, used for washing, is cooled somewhat by a mountain spring, and the bottom pool is for cooling off. Bring your own towel, swimming suit, soap and shampoo. Foreigners are charged Rmb 3 and can soak for an unlimited amount of time. Snacks are available but there is no restaurant.

The hot springs are a 20-minute walk from the main road, where the bus to

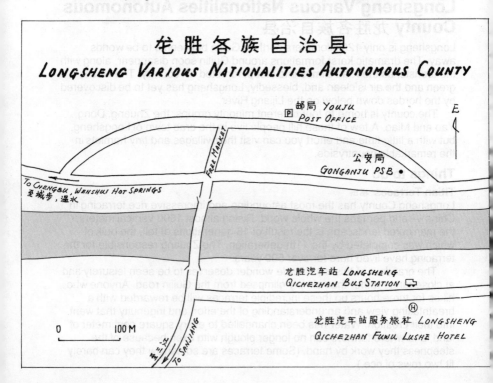

龙胜各族自治县
LONGSHENG VARIOUS NATIONALITIES AUTONOMOUS COUNTY

邮局 YOUJU
POST OFFICE

公安局
GONGANJU PSB •

FREE MARKET

To CHENGBU, WENSHUI HOT SPRINGS
至城步，温水

龙胜汽车站 LONGSHENG
QICHEZHAN BUS STATION

龙胜汽车站服务旅社 LONGSHENG
QICHEZHAN FUWU LUSHE HOTEL

0   100 M

To SANJIANG

E

and from Chengbu Village will drop you off. The last bus back to Longsheng passes by at around 15:00, so be waiting for it on the main road.

Nature Preserve 自然保护区
Longsheng County has a nature preserve, though what is there is anybody's guess since we could never get a straight answer. It should be worth exploring.

Festivals

San Yue San Festival 三月三
Held on the third day of the third lunar month, this festival is celebrated by the Zhuang, Dong, Yao and Miao. We understand the festival takes place simultaneously at many different locations throughout the county.

Lodging

Longsheng Qiche Fuwubu Lushe Hotel 龙胜汽车服务部旅社
Located directly across from the bus station, this spartan hotel has showers, communal toilets and a good restaurant. Beds in a three- or four-person room cost Rmb 1.70 and each bed in a double room is Rmb 2.

Transportation

Longsheng Qichezhan Bus Station 龙胜汽车站

destination	distance (kms)	departure	cost (Rmb)
Guilin 桂林	125	08:00, 09:30, 12:00 13:30, 14:00	3.25
Sanjiang 三江	66	07:00, 10:40	2.20
Chengbu Village 城步	38	06:40, 10:30	1.20
Wenshui Hot Springs 温水	33	06:40, 10:30	1.00
Jinjiang (terraces) 金江	20	08:00, 10:00, 14:30	

Nanning 南宁

Nanning is the capital of the Guangxi Zhuang Autonomous Region. For 1,600 years Nanning, benefiting from its strategically important position on the Yongjiang River, has had significant military and political power over China's southern frontier. Rapid post-1949 development of light industry, robbing the city of its trading-post character, has created a largely new and uninteresting city.

The Zhuang people are quite sinicized, especially near Nanning, and are hard to distinguish from the Han Chinese. Some women wear dark blue, grey or black tunics that button under the right arm and over the collarbone. Some also wear headdresses. The Zhuang language is still widely spoken in surrounding towns and villages.

The best time to visit Nanning is in late autumn or early winter. High temperatures and humidity make the rest of the year sticky and unpleasant.

Good transportation links connecting Nanning with the rest of China make it a jumping-off point for the entire province. Unfortunately many of the most interesting destinations in Guangxi are closed, making travel more difficult.

Things to do

The neighborhood between the bookstore and the Baihuo Gongsi Department Store is an exciting market area that fills every evening with hawkers and

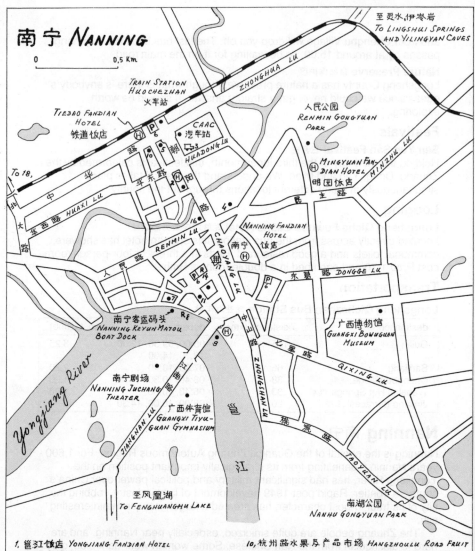

南宁 NANNING

0   0.5 Km

至灵水伊岑岩
To LINGSHUI SPRINGS
AND YILINGYAN CAVES

ZHONGHUA LU

TRAIN STATION
HUOCHEZHAN
火车站

TIEDAO FANDIAN
HOTEL
铁道饭店

CAAC
汽车站

HUADONG LU

人民公园
RENMIN GONGYUAN
PARK

MINGYUAN FAN-
DIAN HOTEL
明园饭店

MINZHU LU

To 18,

中华路 HUAXI LU

华东路

华西路

RENMIN LU

CHAOYANG LU

NANNING FANDIAN
HOTEL
饭店

南宁

主路

东葛路 DONGGE LU

南宁客运码头
NANNING KEYUN MATOU
BOAT DOCK

七星路

广西博物馆
GUANGXI BOWUGUAN
MUSEUM

QIXING LU

Yongjiang River

南宁剧场
NANNING JUCHANG
THEATER

江南路 JIANGNAN LU

邕江

南宁江

ZHONGSHAN LU

桃源路 TAOYUAN LU

广西体育馆
GUANGXI TIYU-
GUAN GYMNASIUM

至风凰湖
To FENGHUANGHU LAKE

南湖公园
NANHU GONGYUAN PARK

1. 邕江饭店 YONGJIANG FANDIAN HOTEL
2. 风凰宾馆 FENGHUANG BINGUAN PHOENIX HOTEL
3. 南宁汽车站 NANNING QICHEZHAN BUS STATION
4. 伊岑岩游览车 YILINGYAN CAVE TRAVELING BUS
   BOOKING OFFICE
5. 南宁市旅遊社 NANNINGSHI LUYOUSHE TOUR
   COMPANY
6. 邮电局 YOUDIANJU POST AND COMMUNICATIONS OFFICE
7. 南宁港客运站 NANNINGGANG KEYUNZHAN BOAT
   COMPANY
8. 龙宫大酒家 LONGGONG DAJIUJIA FLOATING
   RESTAURANT
9. 富邕阁酒家 FUYONGGE JIUJIA FLOATING
   RESTAURANT

10. 杭州路水果及产品市场 HANGZHOULU ROAD FRUIT
    AND PRODUCE MARKET
11. 当阳路食亍 DANGYANGLU RESTAURANT STREET
12. 万国酒家 WANGUO JIUJIA RESTAURANT (2ND
    FLOOR)
13. 南宁市糖果食品二厂 NANNINGSHI TANGGUO SHIPIN
    ERCHANG ICE CREAM SHOP
14. 回民饭店 MUSLIM HUIMIN FANDIAN RESTAURANT
15. 新华书店 XINHUA SHUDIAN BOOKSTORE
16. 友谊商店 YOUYI SHANGDIAN FRIENDSHIP STORE
17. 百货公司 BAIHUO GONGSI DEPARTMENT STORE
18. 西郊公园水库,民族学院 XIJIAO GONGYUAN PARK
    AND ZOO, SHUIKU RESERVOIR, MINZU XUEYUAN
    NATIONALITIES IINSTITUTE.

gawkers. There are still some older streets near the train and bus stations, as well as along the Yongjiang River.

Guangxi Bowuguan Provincial Museum 广西博物馆
The museum is a bit disappointing but worth the trip, especially for the cultural and historical photographs. Main exhibitions include: clothes and a few photographs of the 13 minority nationalities in Guangxi, a Taiping Rebellion exhibit and several temporary displays (a nice calligraphy collection when we were there). Museum hours: 08:30 – 11:30, 14:30 – 17:00; no entry after 16:00.

Nanhu Gongyuan Park 南湖公园
Nanning's nicest park features boats for rent, a fish restaurant, a monument to martyrs of the revolution, a children's amusement area, an orchid nursery, a miniature tree and rock garden, and an herb garden.

Renmin Gongyuan Park 人民公园
This verdant park has two lakes, a nine-bend bridge, swans, a restaurant, snack shops, animals in tiny cages, a running track and a swimming pool.

Xijiao Gongyuan Park and Zoo 西郊公园
This might be the worst zoo in China. Most pathetic is the lone panda struggling through the hot summers. Guangxi's heat and humidity torture the larger animals. Coincidentally, a restaurant at the zoo specializes in exotic animals (no joke). The whole complex closes at around 18:00.

Guangxi Minzu Xueyuan Nationalities Institute 广西民族学院
Representatives of Guangxi's various ethnic groups are here to learn Mandarin Chinese and train as middle school teachers. The diverse groups at this institute do not wear native dress, so they are often visually hard to distinguish from the Chinese.

Farther away

Yiling Yan Cave 伊岭岩
One of the best caves in the Southwest, Yiling Yan was discovered in 1973 and opened for viewing in 1975. Visitors must take the 1,100-meter, hour-long guided tour, conducted in either Mandarin or Cantonese. Music blasts out of hidden speakers while the guide explains the name of each garishly-lit formation. Be on the lookout for the Statue of Liberty and Two Hidden Pandas. A restaurant at the cave site sells simple food and cold drinks. The cave is open from 09:00 to 12:00 and from 14:00 to 16:00. Admission is Rmb 0.50.

To visit Yiling Yan Cave, take a bus from either Nanning or Wuming to Tengxiang. From Tengxiang it is an interesting four-kilometer walk through several secluded Zhuang farm villages to the cave. Tours to the cave run from the Nanning Tour Agency and the Yiling Cave Travelling Bus Booking Office. You can also hitchhike to or from Tengxiang with little difficulty.

Wuming and Lingshui Springs 灵水泉
This park, featuring a natural spring where visitors can swim or do laundry with the locals, is so uninteresting that it has been taken off local Chinese tours.

A majority of the population in Wuming is Zhuang, but most people dress like Han Chinese. The Zhuang villages near the Yiling Yan Cave are much more interesting. To get there, take a bus to Wuming and walk for 15 minutes through town to the spring. Buses return to Nanning every hour and also stop in Tengxiang.

Shuiku Reservoir 水库
Foreign teachers in town told us of a man-made lake where you can rent inner tubes and go swimming. During the fall, many people camp in the area. To get there, ride a bike or walk past the zoo and take the first right. This road leads to the lake, a 20-minute walk away.

Fenghuanghu Phoenix Lake 凤凰湖
Foreign teachers also recommended renting a nice, romantic place on the lake. The area is an ideal place to relax for two or three days, particularly in the autumn. To get there, take a bus from Nanning to Dawang Yan and walk the short distance to the lake.

Festivals

Dragon Boat Festival 龙船节
The Dragon Boat Festival, held on the fifth day of the fifth lunar month, brings some welcome excitement and color to Nanning. The races themselves *are* exciting, but those held in Guizhou and Yunnan are said to be more spectacular.

Lodging

Tiedao Fandian Hotel 铁道饭店
The Tiedao Fandian is a clean, conveniently located Chinese hotel about two minutes from the train station. Beds in a four-person room in the basement are Rmb 2.50. Triple rooms range in price from Rmb 4.50 to Rmb 9, double rooms

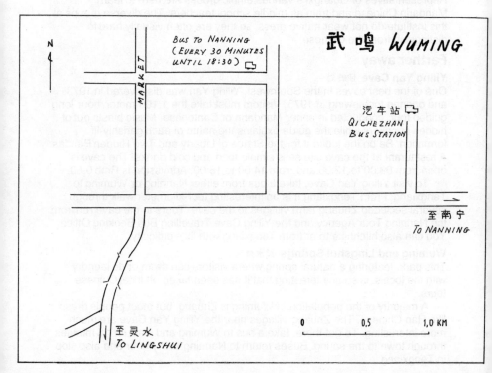

武鸣 WUMING

BUS TO NANNING
(EVERY 30 MINUTES
UNTIL 18:30)

MARKET

汽车站
QICHEZHAN
BUS STATION

至南宁
TO NANNING

N

0   0,5   1,0 KM

至灵水
TO LINGSHUI

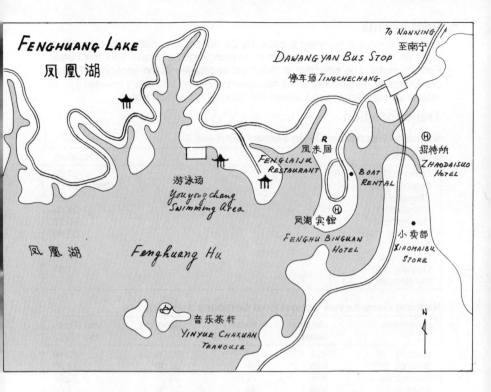

from Rmb 8.50 to Rmb 10. All rooms come with private toilet, shower and fan. Skip the restaurant on the third floor — there are plenty of places to eat across the street near the fruit market. The hotel sells bus tickets to Guangzhou, Beihai and Guiping, and you can hire bikes across the street.

Fenghuang Binguan Phoenix Hotel 凤凰宾馆
The Fenghuang Binguan is noisy and run-down but convenient, being only a few minutes' walk from the train station and a block from the bus station. Beds in a six-person room are Rmb 2.30, and Rmb 5.50 each in a double without private bathroom. Double rooms with a private toilet, shower, phone and air-conditioning cost Rmb 25. Bus tickets to Beihai, Guangzhou, Kunming and Baise are sold in the lobby.

Nanning Fandian Hotel 南宁饭店
The Nanning Fandian is a cavernous hotel used primarily for Chinese conventions. Beds in a four-person room are FEC 6 and double rooms with private toilet and shower cost FEC 40.

Yongjiang Fandian Hotel 邕江饭店
Beds in an eight-person room with toilet and shower are FEC 6. Double rooms with toilets and showers are FEC 40 each, and FEC 46 with air-conditioning. Bus tickets to Wuzhou, Guangzhou and Beihai are sold here.

Mingyuan Fandian 明园饭店
This hotel is not for the budget traveler; beds start at FEC 36.

Restaurants

The food served in Nanning is basically Cantonese. In addition to restaurants listed on the map, try the fruit market on Hangzhou Lu across from the Tiedao Fandian Hotel. The selection of fruits and vegetables is extraordinary. There are a number of excellent small restaurants nearby, and many private restaurants on Dangyang Lu near the Yongjiang Fandian Hotel.

Transportation

Nanning Huochezhan Train Station 南宁火车站

destination	departure
Guilin 桂林	07:30
Zhanjiang 湛江	06:03, 09:03
Shanghai 上海	11:55
Chongzuo 崇左	07:00
Hengyang 衡阳	10:35
Pingxiang 凭祥	09:50
Beijing 北京	19:06
Guangzhou 广州	08:00
Guiyang 贵阳 (no sleepers)	17:01

Nanning Gang Keyun Gongsi Boat Company 南宁港客运公司

destination	distance (kms)	transit time (hrs)	departure	cost (Rmb) (3rd class)
Guiping 桂平	424	19	09:00	10.40
Wuzhou 梧州	623	48	09:00	14.90
Guangzhou 广州	965	72	09:00	22.90
Baise 百色	410	48	07:00	7.00

Nanning Qichezhan Bus Station 南宁汽车站

destination	distance (kms)	departure	cost (Rmb)
Kunming 昆明	1062	06:00	30.35
Wuzhou 梧州	500	06:00	16.70
Guangzhou 广州	751	07:50	23.30
Liuzhou 柳州	264	06:30	7.85
Guiping 桂平	254	07:30	7.55
Ningming 宁明	192	07:30	5.75
Baise 百色		06:50, 07:10 07:30, 07:50	8.00
Beihai 北海		07:10, 07:30 13:30	7.65
Dawang 大王		08:00, 13:30 15:00, 16:00	1.05

Nanning Luyoushe Tour Agency 南宁旅游社

A bus to Kunming departs at 06:50 and costs Rmb 35.30. There are also buses to Wuzhou, Guangzhou and Beihai, as well as city tours. This private bus company is known to sell tickets to closed areas even if the bus station will not.

Yiling Yan Travelling Bus Booking Office 伊岭岩旅游社 has trips to Yiling Cave for Rmb 2.30. Buses depart at 09:00 and return at 13:00.

Nanning City Bus Routes

bus #4: From the Huaxi Lu — Huyang Lu intersection past Xijiao Gongyuan Park, Shuiku Reservoir, and the Nationalities Institute.

bus #5: From the train station, past the Yongjiang Hotel and beyond the Guangxi Gymnasium.

Beibu Gulf 北部湾

Beihai 北海

Pearl collecting has existed for more than 2,000 years in the 'Pearl City' of Beihai. Since the Han Dynasty, emperors and officials collected enormous amounts of pearls from this ancient port and sent trading ships as far as Malaysia, Burma and India. Beihai was an important port during the Opium Wars and today is a port of call for 67 countries. Covering 275 square kilometers, the population of Beihai is 168,000. The region is famous for magnolia trees, some of which are 30 meters high.

We never visited the Beibu Gulf. Our coverage is based on information from Brian Schwartz, other travelers and from Hong Kong tourism magazines.

Baihutou Beach

This 30-kilometer long beach is said to have the finest sand in China. Haibin Gongyuan Park and Guantou Range form part of the scenic countryside, and

The Zhuang

The Zhuang are China's largest minority group with a population of 13.5 million spread throughout Guangxi, Guangdong, Hunan, Guizhou, and Yunnan. Over 10 million Zhuang live within Guangxi, where they comprise over a third of the population. The Zhuang have lived here for more than 3,000 years and are the original inhabitants of the region. The Dong, Shui and Buyi are descendants and distant relatives of the Zhuang; they all speak related dialects within the Tai language family.

Two thousand years ago the Zhuang occupied vast areas of China, from southern Guangxi all the way north to Shandong Province. During the Qin Dynasty (221−207 BC) they were forced by the Han into mountainous regions but refused to submit to imperial rule. In the 11th century, Zhuang armies attacked Guangzhou and during the Taiping Rebellion, continuing their tradition of armed resistance against the central government, many Zhuang took part and even established 10 independent counties.

Today the Zhuang are dwellers of valleys and plains, practicing rice culture in irrigated fields with the help of water buffaloes. Most Zhuang live in raised wooden houses with a stone hearth for cooking; the first floor is used for livestock and storage while the second floor comprises the living quarters.

Most Zhuang marry young, between 20 and 22 years of age. By official government decree they can have only two children; fines of over US$500 are levied against families who exceed this quota.

The Zhuang language had no orthography until after 1949. The strange-looking script can be seen most readily in school primers and on official notices and road signs throughout Guangxi. Despite this symbol of ethnicity, today nearly all the Zhuang are sinicized and only in remote regions do they still wear traditional headdresses and hand woven clothing.

shell-carving factories, marine breeding farms and pearl processing factories are open for tourists.

Farther away

Hepu 合浦

This is another city renowned for its pearls. Sites include two pavilions, a 100-year-old wooden bridge and an ancient grave that has been excavated in the countryside to the east of town.

Qinzhou 钦州

Located on China's southern coast, fishing grounds nearby are rich with prawns, oysters, crabs and groupers. Many ancient cannon emplacements and forts are found in the area. Qinzhou was the home of Liu Yongfu, a Chinese general who, at the invitation of the Vietnamese king, twice fought and defeated French armies in the late 1800s. His tomb, Tianya Pavilion, Sanxuan Hall military fort, the museum of Feng Zicai, and 72 waterways are the important sites in this seaside town.

Wanwei, Wutou and Shanxin Islands

From Fancheng there are boats to these islands inhabited by the Gin, ethnic Vietnamese who immigrated hundreds of years ago. Primarily fishermen, they also cultivate pearl oysters, make salt and do some farming. When fishing, the Gin people walk on stilts in the shallow ocean water.

A singing festival occurs on the tenth day of the first lunar month in Wanwei and Watou, and on the eighth day of the eighth month in Shanxin. Songs are based on ancient folk tales and feature a 'Singing Brother', 'Two Singing Sisters' and a fiddle player. This fascinating, watery area is still largely closed to foreigners.

Shangsi 上思

This county seat located in the Shiwan Dashan (100,000 Hills) is the home of the Yao people. The males spend much of their time in the hills collecting herbs and spices while the females work in the fields. Yao women here use violet ribbons instead of silver as headdresses. Silver jewelry takes the form of necklaces.

Lodging

Beihai Binguan 北海宾馆
Beibuwan Dong Lu
tel. 3512

Beihai Yingbinguan Guesthouse 北海迎宾馆
Beibuwan Zhong Lu
tel. 3131

Huaqiao Fandian Overseas Chinese Hotel 华侨饭店
Jianshe Nan Lu
tel. 3038
These hotels should have cheap rooms or they can direct you to a place that does.

Transportation

Qichezhan Bus Station 汽车站

destination	departure	cost (Rmb)
Guangzhou 广州	12:00	21.85
Zhanjiang 湛江	07:30, 08:30	6.60
Nanning 南宁	07:20, 08:25	7.65
	12:00	
Wuzhou 梧州	06:00	15.30
Liuzhou 柳州	05:55	12.70

Enquire about other local buses.

Matou Dock 码头

There are boats from Beihai to Haikou on Hainan Island, Weizhou and the Xieyang Islands.

Baise 百色

Baise, the last port on the Youjiang River, lies 246 kilometers northwest of Nanning. Baise grew into a sizable trading post when Europeans recognized the need for a storage and trading area at the upper end of the vast Pearl River network. The predominantly Cantonese architecture was brought by merchants from Guangdong Province who arrived with their goods. These merchants stayed in control of local commerce until 1949. Even today, street stalls displaying Hong Kong and Guangzhou goods stand as testimony to the continuing influence of river trade in the area.

Things to do

The southernmost neighborhoods are the oldest and thus the logical places to start exploring. Many fine examples of old Cantonese architecture are to be found here. For a nice place to sit, find several tables set up in a small open area in front of the Baise Harbor Ticket Office at the end of Zhonghua Lu and make yourself at home. Observe the river traffic float by the mouth of a small tributary. For a swim, the area above the bridge northeast of town is where the local children go.

For a view of Baise, the rivers and the surrounding landscape, hike to the Deng Xiaoping Monument on the hill east of town. The monument commemorates Deng's 1929 visit to Baise to organize local resistance to the Nationalists. The monument is not special, but the fresh breeze and view make this walk worthwhile.

Yuedong Huiguan Museum 粤东会馆

This small museum commemorating Deng's 1929 visit has an interesting collection of photos and small items from the earliest days of the Chinese Communist Party. The ornate hall that houses the museum was once a temple.

Chengbihe Reservoir 澄碧河水库

Chengbihe is a clean reservoir ten kilometers north of town, and an excellent place for swimming. Miao villages are said to occupy the surrounding hills. With a sleeping bag you could easily camp out, spending several days in this isolated forest area.

Lodging

Baise Qiche Zongzhan Zhaodaisuo Hotel 百色汽车总站招待所
This clean, well-managed hotel is conveniently located behind the bus station and has two-, three- and four-bed rooms with private showers. Beds in a five-bed room are Rmb 2 and beds in a four-bed room are Rmb 3.50.

Youjiang Binguan Hotel 右江宾馆
The Youjiang Binguan has clean, comfortable double rooms with private bath and TV for Rmb 11. Bus tickets to Nanning are sold in the lobby.

Restaurants

The Shuishang Canting（水上餐厅）is a floating restaurant that serves good Cantonese food 24 hours a day. The atmosphere on the river is unbeatable, but prices are a little expensive, so bargain. This place is managed by two worldly businessmen from Guangzhou who know about the outrageous prices travelers sometimes pay for food.

Transportation

Yunnan Sheng Wenshan Zhou Qiche Lianying Gongsi (bus to Yunnan)
云南省文山州汽车联营运输公司

destination	distance (kms)	departure	cost (Rmb)
Kunming 昆明 (2-day trip)	795	05:40	22.00

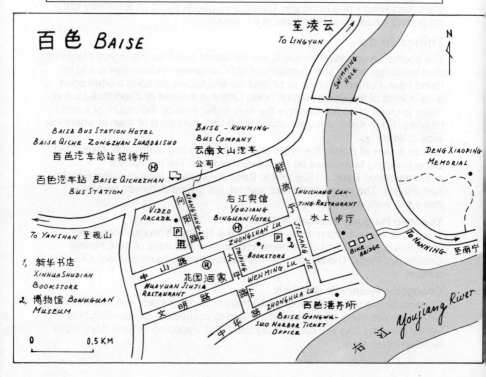

Baise Qichezhan Bus Station 百色汽车站

destination	distance (kms)	departure	cost (Rmb)
Nanning 南宁	227	06:50–15:00 Six buses daily	8.00
Guixian 贵县	393	06:30	11.60
Wenshan 文山		05:30	11.80
Xingyi 兴义		06:50	11.65
Lingyun 凌云	100	06:30, 07:00 11:20, 11:25	3.15

Baise Gang Harbor 百色港

Boat service to Nanning: check to make sure the 07:00 departure time is still valid. The Youjiang River winds its way through karst hill regions above Nanning that are not visible from the road. Beds for this relaxing, 24-hour trip are about Rmb 8.

Lingyun 凌云

Lingyun is a small town 100 kilometers north of Baise beyond a high range of mountains traversed by a single-lane dirt road. Miao and Zhuang villages, clearly visible from the road, grip the mountainsides precariously above terraced paddies and pasturelands. Closer to Lingyun, karst formations dominate the landscape and the limestone-tinted water of a vast river network, subterranean in places, flows between jutting crags, ever deepening the valleys to expose once submerged caves.

Lingyun sits in the shade of a deep valley beside a clean, fast-flowing river. It grew from a village after the completion of the road and the opening of the nearby cement factory. The attraction of the area is the dramatic karst landscape, which humbles the best of Guilin or Yangshou, without hordes of sightseers.

Lingyun is not officially open to foreigners. If you want to visit the mountains and caves, do so swiftly and carefully because you will not likely be allowed to stay for more than a day.

Things to do

Shuiyuan Dong Cave 水源洞

The cave appears today as it might have several hundred years ago, with Buddhist statues, notably one of *Guanyin*, and a series of steles decorating a large cavern at the entrance where several small shrines stand. Light reflected by the ripples of a small stream emerging from the depths of the mountain shoot across the cavern. Modern times have brought only a string of ten-watt lightbulbs at 25-meter intervals. With its Buddhas, muddy floors, dripping stalactite ceilings and bats, the Shuiyuan Dong Cave is a genuine and impressive site, far from the garish, overcrowded grottoes found throughout the Southwest. The stream flowing from the cave towards town is crystal-clear and wonderful for swimming.

The walk to this cave takes 30 minutes from Lingyun. The road over the second bridge is a little quicker, but the trail through the fields is more enjoyable.

Dashan Dong Cave 大山洞

This cave, being prepared at present for tourism, is said to be much larger than Shuiyuan Dong and comparable in size to the large caves in Guilin. Dashan Dong is about an hour north by foot of Shuiyuan Dong Cave. Confirm its location in Lingyun before heading off.

Lodging

The main street in town is lined with small *lushe* (旅社) hotels. Pick one that looks good to you; they are all spartan but very cheap.

Transportation

Lingyun Qichezhan Bus Station 凌云汽车站

destination	distance (kms)	departure	cost (Rmb)
Baise 百色	100	06:30, 07:00 11:00, 11:25	3.15

If you leave Baise on the 06:30 bus, you will arrive in Lingyun between 10:30 and 11:00. Walk straight to the caves, avoiding an encounter with the Gonganju until after 11:25. You will then be assured of one day in Lingyun before being sent back to Baise on a bus the next morning.

Hitchhiking

Cargo trucks on the journey from Baise to Lingyun are often empty in order to pick up concrete from the nearby factory. They often go back with two empty passenger seats, so hitching is easy. Get out on the road in Baise early and avoid taking the bus.

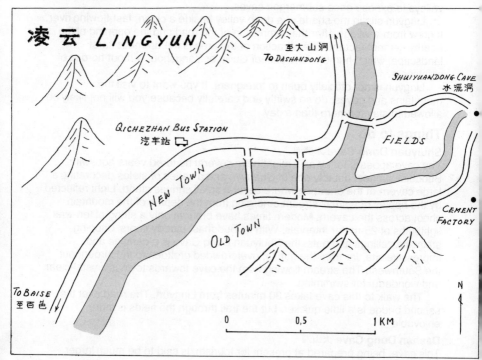

Other Places in Guangxi

Rongshui Miao Nationality Autonomous County 融水苗族自治县
This county is less than 100 kilometers away from Liuzhou on the rail line.

Jinxiu Yao Nationality Autonomous County 金秀瑶族自治县
This county may be the best place to visit these interesting people. Located approximately 150 kilometers from Liuzhou and 125 kilometers from Yangshuo, the hills are peopled almost exclusively by the Yao.

Guizhou Province 贵州

The poor conditions of Guizhou are summed up in an old Chinese saying: In Guizhou you will never see three consecutive days of sunshine, three taels of silver, or three *mou* of flat land. Isolated throughout its history, Guizhou may still be the least travelled province in China. It covers more than 170,000 square kilometers, 80% of which is made up of rugged mountains. Despite extensive terracing, only 12% of the land is cultivated. Karst and limestone formations are found in many areas, often accompanied by caverns and underground streams.

Guizhou remained on the outer fringe of the Chinese Empire until fairly recent times. Emperors of the Han Dynasty set up heavily fortified outposts there over 2,000 years ago, traces of which still exist at Zhenyuan. The Miao, the largest and most powerful minority in the region, fought the Chinese bitterly in the 18th century before finally submitting to domination. In the 19th century, soon after the Taiping Rebellion, the Miao tried to regain their independence, but were once again crushed.

Of the 28 million inhabitants, more than six million belong to ten minority groups, including Miao, Buyi, Dong, Hui and Yi. Encroaching settlement by Han Chinese has slowly forced most of the minorities to move into rocky, inaccessible and infertile mountains. Today the autonomous regions and counties that make up one-third of Guizhou Province are among its poorest areas.

There is an eight- to ten-month growing season that allows two harvests a year. The main crop is rice, followed by maize, potatoes and chili peppers. While relatively undeveloped, Guizhou is rich in mineral resources.

Guizhou has a humid, sub-tropical monsoonal climate, with warm winters, mild summers and unclear seasonal contrasts. It has an average annual temperature of 15–17°C and the yearly rainfall averages 900–1,500 mm. It has more overcast days than any other part of the country. Guiyang, the capital, can count on 220 cloudy days a year.

Guiyang 贵阳

Guiyang, with a population close to one million, is the capital of Guizhou Province. This clean, modern city, is the capital of China's most unexplored, unknown and misunderstood province. Guiyang has taken merciless criticism from previous guidebook writers who clearly never ventured beyond the train station. Part city and part village, with modern convention centers and apartment blocks interspersed among family-owned restaurants and aging cobblestone alleyways filled with magicians and street vendors, Guiyang escapes characterization, leaving visitors impressed by the richness of life and looking for excuses to spend a few extra days.

Chinese Buddhist temples and a Confucian pavilion, Buyi and Miao people passing by in traditional dress, all add to the cultural diversity of the city.

Opened in 1985, Guiyang is still a secret and rarely visited. Because of its temperate climate, this 'Second Spring City' is enjoyable year round but you had better bring a raincoat.

Things to do

Take a walk. The neighborhoods around the department store are interesting, as is the store itself which offers a great selection of goods ranging from modern factory commodities to hand-made *batik*. For a trip out of town, visit Huaxi, 17 kilometers away.

For English brochures and updated information about Guiyang or Guizhou Province, stop at the Guiyang CITS office. The English-speaking staff are competent, friendly and try their best to make up for the poor reputation most CITS offices deserve.

Qianling Gongyuan Park 黔灵公园

This is one of the few parks in China that no traveler should miss. Shrubbery, large fir and maple trees, rolling hills and lush greenery make this 300-hectare park a joy to wander in. The main attraction here is the Confucian Temple, a large complex of buildings set amidst beautiful gardens. Built in 1673 by the monk Chisong, it was the center of Chan (Zen) Buddhism in Guiyang before the Confucian metamorphosis.

There is a Buddhist temple here as well which serves vegetarian meals on weekends and holidays.

Nearby is a small cave where Zhang Xueliang, the young marshal, was imprisoned after his involvement in Chiang Kai-shek's kidnapping during the Xi'an Incident of 1936. There is also a poorly kept zoo with two pandas, a large lake, bumper cars, and a roller skating rink.

You would probably have no trouble camping on one of the hills a few kilometers away.

Jueyuan Ni'an Fojiao Fandian Buddhist Nunnery and Restaurant
觉园尼庵佛教饭店

What is most interesting here is not the crude shrines the nuns have constructed, but the nuns themselves. There were over a hundred of them at the Baonian Temple before it was turned into a granary in 1952. The nuns have outlasted the temple, survived the Cultural Revolution and are now thriving. On occasion, they have an all-day prayer celebration, which foreigners are welcome to observe. These friendly nuns are a living example of Buddhism's survival in China. The restaurant the nuns run serves delicious, inexpensive vegetarian food.

Nanjiao Gongyuan Park 南郊公园

The attraction here is a cave with colored neon lights, piped-in music, a guide, and artificial subterranean pools traversed by the anti-climactic '100-Step Bridge' near the exit. The 30-minute tour costs foreigners Rmb 2. This cave is not special and only worth a trip if you have no chance to see some of the better caverns that dot the Southwest. Take bus #7 to its terminus and walk for 20 minutes to the park.

Jiaxiu Lou Pavilion 甲秀楼

This Ming-Dynasty pavilion, built to exhort young Guiyang scholars, now houses an antique furniture exhibit.

Qianming Si Temple 黔明寺

Qianming Si Temple, founded in 1614, was badly damaged during the Cultural Revolution but has been largely reconstructed. At present, faint revolutionary slogans are still visible above the main gate. In 1949 there were over 100 monks here; today there are eight.

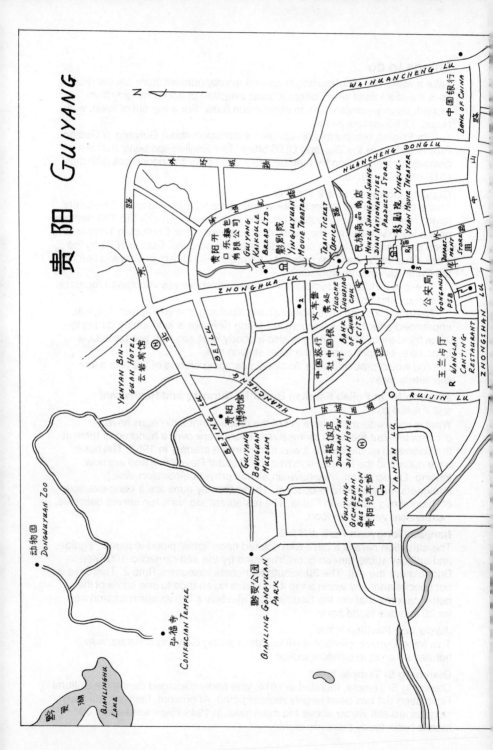

貴阳 GUIYANG

WAIHUANCHENG LU

中国银行
BANK OF CHINA

HUANGCHENG DONGLU

外环城北路

民族商品商店
MINZU SHANGPIN SHANG-
DIAN NATIONALITIES
PRODUCTS STORE

影剧院 YINGJIA-
YUAN MOVIE THEATER

贵阳开口乐糖包有限公司
GUIYANG KAIKOULE BREAD LTD.

影剧院 YING-JIAYUAN
MOVIE THEATER

火车票售处
TRAIN TICKET
OFFICE

ZHONGHUA LU

R DEPARTMENT STORE

公安局
GONGANJU
PSB

ZHONGSHAN LU

火车售票处
HUOCHE SHOUPIAO
CHU

中国旅行社
中国银行
BANK OF CHINA & CITS

2

王兰�厅
R WANGLAN
CANTING
RESTAURANT

YUNYAN BIN-
GUAN HOTEL 云岩宾馆 ⒣

BEIJING LU

HUANCHAN LU

贵阳博物馆
GUIYANG
BOWUGUAN
MUSEUM

筑花饭店
DUJUAN FAN-
DIAN HOTEL ⒣

RUIJIN LU

YAN'AN LU

动物园
DONGWUYUAN ZOO

弘福寺
CONFUCIAN TEMPLE

贵阳汽车站
GUIYANG
QICHEZHAN
BUS STATION

黔灵公园
QIANLING GONGYUAN
PARK

黔灵湖
QIANLINGHU
LAKE

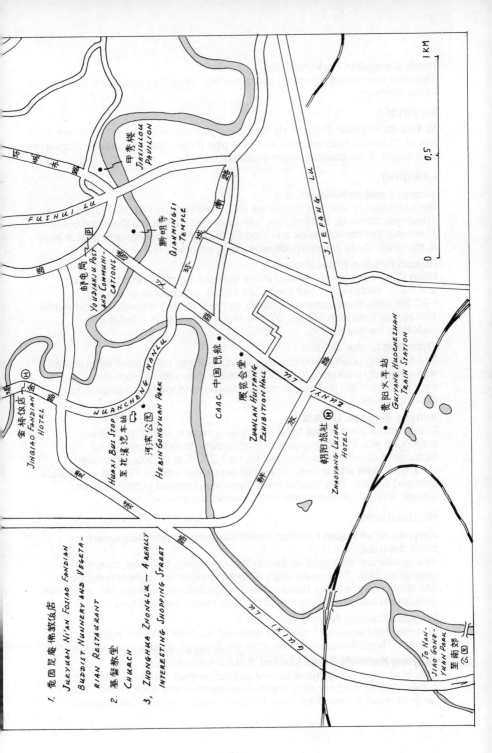

1. 觉园尼庵佛教饭店
   JUEYUAN NI'AN FOTIAO FANDIAN
   BUDDIST NUNNERY AND VEGETA-
   RIAN RESTAURANT

2. 基督教堂
   CHURCH

3. ZHONGHUA ZHONGLU — A REALLY
   INTERESTING SHOPPING STREET

FUSHUI LU

JIAXIULOU PAVILION

甲秀楼

邮电局
YOUDIANJU POST-
AND COMMUNI-
CATIONS

QIANMINGSI TEMPLE
黔明寺

JIEFANG LU

JINBAO FANDIAN HOTEL
金桥饭店

HUANCHENG NANLU

HUAXI BUS STOP 花溪汽车站

HEBIN GONGYUAN PARK
河滨公园

CAAC 中国民航

展览会堂
ZHANLAN HUITANG
EXHIBITION HALL

NANLU

朝阳旅社
ZHAOYANG LÜSHE HOTEL

GUIYANG HUOCHEZHAN TRAIN STATION
贵阳火车站

GAIXI LU

To NAN-
JIAO GONG-
YUAN PARK
至南郊公园

Hebin Gongyuan Park 河滨公园

This park has no distinguishing characteristics other than occasional dancing in the evenings.

Festivals

Si Yue Ba Festival 四月八节 Held on the eighth day of the fourth lunar month, this Miao festival features flute and wind pipe music, dancing and the singing of love songs. Participants number 30,000 or more.

Lodging

Jinqiao Fandian Hotel 金桥饭店

Beds in three- or four-bed rooms are FEC 8 with communal toilet and shower. Three-bed rooms on the first floor with toilet and shower are the same price. There is a taxi service, telex and long distance phone service and a restaurant at the hotel. There is renovation work going on (late 1987).

Dujuan Fandian Hotel 杜鹃饭店

Hong Kong tourists usually stay in this big hotel equipped with a restaurant and disco. Beds in four-bed rooms are FEC 8, and double rooms are FEC 30. Both share communal toilets and an excellent shower. Double rooms with private bath start at FEC 40. The Dujuan Fandian is a two-minute walk from the bus station.

Zhaoyang Lushe 朝阳旅社

The only thing positive you can say about this filthy, rat-infested hotel staffed with unfriendly workers is that it is next to the train station. Beds range in price from FEC 2 to FEC 9. The communal showers and toilets are disgusting. Don't stay here.

Yunyan Binguan 云岩宾馆

This is an old government hotel set inside a secure, walled, park-like compound with beautiful grounds. Red carpets, friendly workers and restaurants abound. The cheapest bed is FEC 15 in a double room with communal toilet and shower. The most expensive room is FEC 80 with private bath and kitchen. This hotel is great if you are prepared to go a little over budget. A new high-rise tourist hotel is under construction here.

Restaurants

Jueyuan Ni'an Fojiao Fandian Buddhist Nunnery and Restaurant 觉园尼庵佛敎饭店

This restaurant, managed by Buddhist nuns, serves delicious, inexpensive vegetarian food. They make eight different kinds of *doufu* (beancurd) daily. The latest news is that a Buddhist library has been set up here. We hope it will reincarnate back into being one of the best restaurants in China.

Wanglan Canting Restaurant 玉兰餐厅

This nice little restaurant has cold beer and will cook food the way you request. To get there, walk north from the Jinqiao Fandian.

Guiyang Kaikoule Bread Limited 贵阳开口乐面包有限公司

This is an excellent Chinese bakery and coffee shop with freshly brewed coffee, donuts, coconut rolls, cream-filled pastries and good bread. Order to go or sit down in one of the three booths to enjoy the fresh baked goods.

Transportation

Guiyang Huochezhan Train Station 贵阳火车站

destination	departure
Kunming 昆明	05:23, 15:39, 19:40, 21:28
Beijing 北京	17:00, 22:58
Shanghai 上海	10:37, 19:47
Chongqing 重庆	05:52, 09:60, 18:31, 22:24
Chengdu 成都	07:40, 16:40
Guangzhou 广州	20:27
Nanning 南宁	09:00
Chengdu 成都	16:40
Huaihua 怀化	06:56
Liuzhou 柳州	13:15
Chongqing 重庆	07:10

Times are not set but trains #402, 150, 152, 192 and 254 go to Kaili and Zhenyuan.

Guiyang Qichezhan Bus Station 贵阳汽车站

Long-distance tickets are to the left, local tickets to the right.

destination	departure	cost (Rmb)
Kaili 凯里	07:20, 07:40	8.50
Zunyi 遵义	08:40, 11:00	9.30
Qianxi 黔西	07:40, 11:00, 12:00	5.60
Anshun 安顺	06:30–10:00 (several buses)	6.60
Longgong 龙宫	07:00	7.70
Huangping 黄平	07:40	8.60
Tongren 铜仁	07:00	15.40
Shibing 施秉	07:20	10.10
Zhijin 织金	08:00, 08:20, 08:40	6.90

Local bus

destination	departure	cost (Rmb)
Hongfenghu 红枫湖 (Red Maple Lake)	08:00, 16:00	0.60

Guiyang City Bus Routes

bus #1 and bus #2: A 45-minute trip beginning at the train station, bus #1 goes counter-clockwise and bus #2 goes clockwise in a circular route around Guiyang, passing CAAC, Hebin Gongyuan Park, Jinqiao Fandian Hotel, the bus station, Qianling Gongyuan Park, Yunyan Binguan Hotel, main department store, main post office, and back to the train station.

bus #3: Follows Rui'an Lu.

bus #5: Follows Zhongshan Lu to Guixi Lu and the stop for Nanjiao Gongyuan Park.

bus #8: Follows the length of Zhonghua Lu.

Huaxi 花溪

17 kilometers from Guiyang, Huaxi is a small Buyi Nationality town surrounded by karst hills. It is a colorful little town famous for its park, but the largest crowds come from far and wide to witness several Buyi festivals held anually that frequently attract over 10,000 visitors. Guiyang University is located nearby.

Things to do

After wandering around town, walk through the countryside and into one of the many Buyi villages nearby. Camping in the countryside around town is ideal.

Huaxi Gongyuan Park 花溪公园
Called 'A Flower on the Guizhou Plateau', this park has a small river gently flowing through it and is backed by karst hills. Except when crowded on Sundays and holidays, Huaxi Gongyuan Park is relaxing and enjoyable. Picturesque Buyi hamlets border the park.

Festivals

Tiaochang Festival 跳场节
Held on the ninth day of the first lunar month, this Miao festival features dancing to reed pipe music. Thousands of people attend.

Tiaodixi Festival
Held on the 15th day of the first lunar month, this Buyi festival is a memorial ceremony for village ancestors. Participants number 20,000.

Liu Yue Liu Festival 六月六
Held on the sixth day of the sixth lunar month, this Buyi festival features singing and a song competition based on who can sing the fastest. Participants number 10,000.

Lodging

Huaxi Jiulou Hotel 花溪酒楼
This hotel, across from the main entrance to Huaxi Gongyuan Park, is reasonably clean and comfortable. Beds in a four-bed room are Rmb 5 and double rooms are Rmb 20. Eat at the hotel restaurant or at any of the others near the bus station.

Huaxi Binguan Hotel 花溪宾馆
Located inside Huaxi Gongyuan Park, this exceptionally good hotel is expensive. Rooms start at FEC 80.

Transportation

There are frequent buses to Guiyang from 06:30 to 19:00. Tickets are Rmb 0.50 and the trip takes 30 minutes.

Kaili 凯里

Kaili was once a sleepy little Miao village, but post-1949 development has changed it into a dirty industrial Chinese town. People in Miao dress are still visible, especially at the Sunday market or on festival days, and traditional Miao villages stand on the outskirts of town. The streets in Kaili are filled with vendors, charlatans performing 'magic tricks', herbal medicine men, and even a muscle man selling 'secret' formulas. The government is trying with great effort to turn Kaili into a Miao and Dong tourist area to attract big-spending tourist groups. It has just completed a comfortable tourist hotel and now plans to construct a new park with a zoo.

For the individual traveler, Kaili is unique because of its proximity to many of China's most secluded Dong and Miao areas.

Things to do

There is an outdoor market where you can watch evening street performances. During the daytime there is a large group of Miao women in their traditional clothing selling produce.

Gu Lou Drum Tower 鼓楼

This Dong Nationality Drum Tower was made entirely of wood — no metal nails were used. Two brothers assisted by 30 workers labored for six months in 1985 to build it. Although much of the artwork on the tower appears as an afterthought, and the string of colored lights on the roof is gaudy, the tower itself is impressive. Villagers gather beneath the tower for town meetings and young people meet there for singing and dancing. In winter, fires are built beneath the center of the tower for warmth.

Xiangle Shan Mountain, site of the Hill Climbing Festival, is visible from the drum tower.

Bage Ta Pagoda 八阁塔

This Chinese pagoda is a pleasant 30-minute walk from the traffic circle at the center of town.

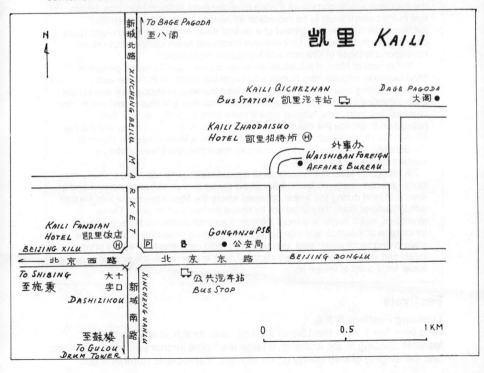

The Miao

The Miao are among the most numerous and diverse of China's minority nationalities, spread throughout southern China and Southeast Asia and differing physically and linguistically to such a degree that identification is often difficult. In China, they now number over 3.6 million, with 2.6 million in Guizhou Province alone.

Today's Miao are descendants of a mountain people known for their vigor, pride, stamina and love of freedom. Originally, they were hunters and gatherers who also practiced slash and burn agriculture, planting millet and buckwheat with primitive digging sticks on newly cleared mountain slopes. Groups living at higher elevations raised livestock and used wool.

Their dispersal throughout Southeast Asia and southern China was due in large part to their agricultural system, which required new fields to be cleared every five to ten years as old ones lost their fertility. Anthropologists have noted that Miao migrations followed mountain ranges rather than river valleys, suggesting that their need for virgin mountain slopes charted their migrations. In more recent times, their virgin forests depleted, the Miao have adopted the terrace farming techniques of the Yao, building elaborate terrace networks covering whole mountains, irrigated by canals and pipes of linked bamboo poles.

The Miao's ancient history is both fascinating and mysterious. Though no written records of the event exist, an arctic migration myth passed down through the ages tells of an exodus from a central Asian homeland to an arctic zone and then south to a more moderate climate. Though the first Chinese records of the Miao place them in Hunan Province at the end of the Song Dynasty, legends of the migration are so consistent among even the most isolated Miao populations that many believe them to be records of an historic event. Some scientific evidence corroborates the legend of a central Asian homeland. Miao blood types differ greatly from southern Chinese and Southeast Asian samples but closely correspond to those of Chinese and Mongolian populations.

In the face of Mongol advances south during the Yuan Dynasty, groups of Miao began to migrate from Hunan southwest into Guizhou Province and beyond, fighting indigenous populations along the way. In successive waves, the Miao extended themselves west into Yunnan Province and Burma and south into Guangxi and Indochina, leaving behind more sedentary elements of their population to terrace the mountains. Among the largest groups today are the Red Miao in the Hunan-Guizhou border region, the Black Miao in eastern Guizhou, the Blue Miao in central Guizhou, and both the White and Flowery Miao in western Guizhou and Yunnan.

A traditional Miao home consists of a small rectangular structure built of either stone or wood at ground level. A fire at the center serves as both a kitchen and a source of heat during the winter. In areas where the Miao have come into contact with Zhuang or Buyi, they often opt for raised homes built on piles. These structures, much larger and more intricate than their traditional homes, provide for storage of livestock and farm implements below a raised living area. Large grain drying racks adorn such villages. In all Miao settlements, markets bring locals and visitors together every six to 12 days and serve as the economic and social focal point of village life.

Festivals

Lusheng Festival 芦笙会

Held from the 11th to the 15th of the first lunar month, this Miao festival features dancing to the *lusheng*, a large reed-pipe instrument. Music, dancing and the singing of love songs go on all night. Participants number 5,000.

Second Lusheng Festival 芦笙会
Held from the 16th to the 18th of the first lunar month, this Miao festival is a continuation of the Lusheng Festival. Activities include dancing to traditional drum music, horse racing and bull fighting. Participants number around 30,000.

Drum Day 翻鼓节
Held on the 13th day of the second lunar month, this traditional Miao festival features music played on wooden and brass drums and reed pipes. Participants number 10,000.

Lusheng Day 芦笙节
Held from the 19th to the 21st of the third lunar month, this traditional Miao festival features dancing to traditional music, horse racing and bull fighting. Participants number 5,000.

Horse Racing Day 跑马节
Held during the fifth day of the fifth lunar month, this Miao festival features horse races and young people singing love songs. Participants number 1,000.

Eat New Rice Day 吃新节
Held on the second day of the sixth lunar month, this Miao festival celebrates the harvest by eating newly threshed rice. Participants number 10,000.

Hill Climbing Day 爬坡节
Held on the 19th day of the sixth lunar month, this traditional Miao festival is held on Xiangle Shan Mountain near Kaili. The festival is like a large picnic and many groups of young people sing, dance and play reed-pipe music. Participants number around 30,000.

Eat New Rice Day 吃新节
Held on the fifth day of the seventh lunar month, this festival is similar to the one held a month earlier. It is celebrated by people whose harvest comes later. The Miao assemble together to celebrate a fruitful harvest by eating new rice. Participants number 20,000.

Mid-July Festival 七月半节
Held on the 13th day of the seventh lunar month, this Miao festival features dancing to reed-pipe music, horse racing and bull fighting. This festival is large, with participants numbering 20,000.

Lusheng Day 芦笙节
Held on the 21st day of the seventh lunar month, this traditional Miao festival features many types of wind instruments. Young men and women sing love songs and there are horse races. Participants number 10,000.

Chongyang Day 重阳节
Held during the ninth day of the ninth lunar month, this Miao festival features pipe and drum music, bull fighting and horse racing.

Miao Nationality New Year 苗年
Held on the first four days of the tenth lunar month, this new year's celebration features singing, dancing, drum and pipe music, bull fighting and horse racing. This is the largest annual festival held in Kaili with over 50,000 participants.

Lodging

Kaili Zhaodaisuo Hotel 凯里招待所
This comfortable new hotel was built primarily for foreigners. The hotel is

staffed by Miao and Dong women who wear native dress and perform for groups of tourists. Double rooms are FEC 20 or FEC 24 with private bathrooms. There is a dining room at the hotel and a tourist desk that will rent you a car and driver with interpreter for the day.

Kaili Fandian Hotel 凯里饭店
This Chinese hotel seems eager to attract foreign guests, and the staff is friendly and helpful. Beds in six-or seven-bed rooms are Rmb 1 and beds in a four-bed room are Rmb 1.50. Double rooms are Rmb 8. All prices include a shower ticket.

Transportation

No official bicycle rental services exist yet, but both hotels in town may be able to help arrange something.

Kaili Qichezhan Bus Station 凯里汽车站

destination	departure	cost (Rmb)
Guiyang 贵阳	07:00, 07:30	5.40
Congjiang 从江	06:30	7.10
Zhenyuan 镇远	07:00	4.20
Shibing 施秉	13:00	3.10
Rongjiang 榕江	07:00, 07:30	4.80
Liping 黎平	06:30, 12:00	7.60
Huangping 黄平	07:00, 07:30, 14:00	2.20
Taijiang 台江	16:00	1.50

Kaili Huochezhan Train Station 凯里火车站
The bus to the train station leaves from the main traffic circle regularly between 05:30 and 20:00 and costs Rmb 0.15.

destination	departure
Kunming 昆明	14:38
Beijing 北京	03:33, 21:23
Guiyang 贵阳	05:07, 13:22, 16:27
Chongqing 重庆	00:52
Shanghai 上海	15:34, 00:16
Huaihua 怀化	12:37
Chengdu 成都	02:35
Guangzhou 广州	01:23

Huangping 黄平

A Miao center between Kaili and Shibing, this town with active street markets is not strictly open but can be visited as a day trip. Foreigners are allowed to go to Huangping for festivals.

Festivals

Hill Climbing Day 爬坡节
Held on the 27th day of the third lunar month, this Miao festival features a huge outdoor picnic and the singing of love songs between young men and women. The participants in this festival number around 20,000.

Si Yue Ba 四月八
Held on the eighth day of the fourth lunar month, this Miao and Han festival

features reed-pipe music, horse races and bird exhibitions. The participants in this festival number 15,000.

Chongan Meeting 重安镇集会
Held on the 26th day of the fifth lunar month, this Miao festival features the singing of love songs between young men and women, reed-pipe music and horse races. The participants of this festival number 15,000.

Lusheng Festival 芦笙节
Held on the 27th day of the ninth lunar month, this Miao festival features bull fighting and horse races. The participants of this festival number around 40,000.

Shibing 施秉

Shibing is a small Miao town surrounded by terraced hills, with Miao hamlets and fields within easy walking distance. Traditional dress, including elaborate headdresses and jewelry on the women, is common in this area.

Although Shibing has been open since 1986, months can go by without a foreign traveler passing through. Anyone who does so is stared at, followed and talked about. People kept asking us if we were Russian. To really create a stir, hike into a surrounding village.

Things to do
Every fifth day of the month there is a large street market with about 1,000 people from the surrounding villages. Many act as if they have never seen a

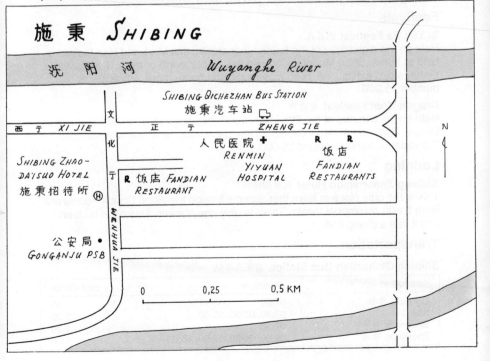

foreigner before. They all come in native dress, but not in their fine holiday attire. On non-market days, there are about 50 Miao people lined up selling products. The market is along the main street between the small department store and the traffic circle, and extends to the government hotel.

People wash clothes or swim on the banks of the Wuyanghe River. Inner tubing and fishing are fun here. Locals were pulling out large fish that weighed more than a kilo each.

Walk south out of town. In half an hour you can be in tiny Miao hamlets which are seldom visited by even Chinese. We were welcomed, taken in and fed before our hosts would let us leave. Camp in the hills south of town by the river.

Wuyanghe River Cruise 舞阳河

The Wuyanghe River meanders through dramatic karst formations as it flows east towards Hunan Province. The five-hour river cruise passes through this scenery, stopping frequently so Chinese tourists can position themselves on the bow of the boat for portraits. The best scene is the *kongquan kaiping*, a double-tipped rock formation that extends above a sheer cliff. Tickets for the boat trip are sold at the Shibing Zhaodaisuo Hotel.

Feiyun Dong Cave 飞运洞

This is the oldest Buddhist temple in Guizhou Province, now inactive with little remaining except an ornate gate. The freshly restored, repainted buildings are empty. The large cave chamber is not much better. The cave lies 20 kilometers outside Shibing, towards Kaili. There is no local transportation serving the site. If you want to go, you will have to hitchhike.

Festivals

Si Yue Ba Festival 四月八

Held on the eighth day of the fourth lunar month, this Miao and Han festival is held at Yuntai Shan Mountain, 30 minutes by bus north of town. The festival features bird exhibitions, reed-pipe music and horse races. Participants number 15,000.

Dragon Boat Festival 龙船节

Held on the fifth day of the fifth lunar month, this large Miao festival features Dragon Boat races, bird exhibitions, reed pipe music and horse races. Participants number around 25,000.

Lodging

Shibing Zhaodaisuo Hotel 施秉招待所

This is the only place in town that accepts foreign travelers. Double rooms are Rmb 5 with communal toilets. There is only one shower. This hotel is clean and it has a dining hall.

Transportation

Shibing Qichezhan Bus Station 施秉汽车站

destination	departure	cost (Rmb)
Guiyang 贵阳	07:20	7.40
Kaili 凯里	07:00, 07:30, 09:00	3.60
Shuangjin 双井	07:30	1.20
Zhenyuan 镇远	09:00, 09:30, 12:00, 16:00	1.30

There are buses to the train station at 12:00 and 13:30. Tickets cost Rmb 0.50 and the trip takes 30 minutes. There are better train connections at Kaili and Zhenyuan.

Zhenyuan 镇远

Zhenyuan, situated on the south bank of the Wujiang River, is on the road from Guiyang to Hunan Province. Founded during the Yuan Dynasty (1279–1368) as a southern imperial outpost, Zhenyuan is now a new town with few old neighborhoods. Maoism certainly left its mark here. Slogans such as 'Mao Zedong Thought for Ten Thousand Years' are still on many walls and we even saw an old man wearing a Mao button. Although Zhenyuan is a Miao and Dong area, neither group is much in evidence even during festivals. Most historical sites in town were ruined during the Cultural Revolution and those that remain are newly repaired, freshly painted buildings with nothing inside.

Things to do

Explore the town and the surrounding Miao villages that fill the terraced valley.

Zhongyuan Dong Cave 中元洞
Zhongyuan Dong is an 850-square-meter cave with three entrances. The Buddhist temple attached to the cave appears attractive from the outside, but the inside is just an empty shell. Many niches which once contained shrines are now empty. A large one near the toilet has been filled in with concrete. The monks were said to have moved to Emei Shan Mountain in Sichuan Province after 1949.

Qinglong Dong Cave 青龙洞
Serious repairs and reconstruction are still going on at this Daoist temple. Though the cave is not yet officially open, you can enter through the front gate. Not much is left but the shell of this once magnificent complex. Qinglong Dong and Zhongyuan Dong are situated next to each other, an anomaly because Buddhist and Daoist holy sites were usually kept far apart.

Sigong Dian Four Palaces Temple 四宫殿
This Buddhist temple was built in 1887. The temple halls are being renovated though no shrines or images exist yet. Follow the winding alleys up the hill beyond the town to reach Sigong Si Temple. The view of Zhenyuan from the temple is beautiful.

Gucheng Wall 古城
This ancient wall was built about 2,000 years ago, a contemporary of the famous Great Wall. Though it has never been restored, you can still walk along it for quite a distance. There are farms and a graveyard nearby. The view of the city, the surrounding hills, the temples and Wenbi Ta Pagoda is good. The walk from Zhenyuan to the wall takes about an hour. Walk past Sigong Si Temple and head for a large power pole up the hill to the right.

Wenbi Ta Pagoda 文辟塔
Unlike many pagodas in China, Wenbi Ta Pagoda, dilapidated and overgrown with vegetation, has never been restored. Even though the pagoda is closed, the walk up past peasant huts and the view are both worthwhile.

Rong Dong Cave 溶洞
Rong Dong is a natural cave: no colored lights, piped in music, stairs, cement

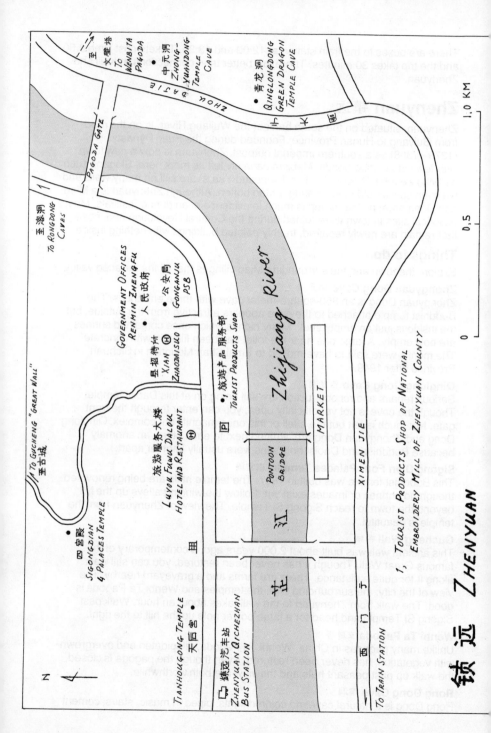

镇远 ZHENYUAN

1, TOURIST PRODUCTS SHOP OF NATIONAL
EMBROIDERY MILL OF ZHENYUAN COUNTY

Zhijiang River

To Train Station

XIMEN JIE

MARKET

PONTOON
BRIDGE

江

西

门

街

ZHENYUAN QICHEZHAN
BUS STATION
镇远汽车站

TIANHOUGONG TEMPLE
天后宫

SIGONGDIAN
4 PALACES TEMPLE
四宫殿

TO GUCHENG "GREAT WALL"
至古城

LUYOU FAWU DALOU
HOTEL AND RESTAURANT
旅游服务大楼

XIAN
ZHAODAISUO
县招待所

GONG'ANJU
PSB
公安局

GOVERNMENT OFFICES
RENMIN ZHENGFU
人民政府

TOURIST PRODUCTS SHOP
旅游产品 服务部

TO RONGDONG
CAVES
至溶洞

PAGODA GATE

To WENBITA
PAGODA
文笔塔
至

ZHONG-
YUANDONG
TEMPLE
CAVE
中元洞

QINGLONGDONG
GREEN DRAGON
TEMPLE CAVE
青龙洞

N

0   0,5   1,0 KM

passageways or handrails. It is muddy, water is always dripping and there are standing pools everywhere. Sometimes there is no electricity in the cave. We were guided through by three children with two candles and a flashlight. Several hundred metres beyond the string of ten-watt lightbulbs is a low passageway that you must crawl through before it opens into a large chamber. The caretaker might be pursuaded to take you into this chamber. Some of the passageways are less than a meter high so watch your head. Do not wear good clothes; you will certainly get muddy inside the cave. Bargain on the entrance fee.

The cave is four kilometers out of town along a flat road perfect for bicycles, if you can find some in town. The walk to the cave takes about an hour. Follow the road to the 'four-kilometer' marker, cross the stone bridge and follow the dirt road to the left.

Festivals

San Yue San 三月三
Held on the third day of the third lunar month, this Dong and Miao festival features the 'offering basket' courtship ritual, drum dancing and love songs. Participants number 10,000.

Dragon Boat Festival 龙船节
Held on the fifth day of the fifth lunar month, this Han festival features Dragon Boat races. Having participated in this festival, we recommend celebrating the Dragon Boat elsewhere. Participants number more than 40,000.

Singing Festival 踩歌堂
Held on the sixth day of the sixth lunar month, this Miao festival features singing and a 'fastest song' competition.

Lodging

Zhenyuan Zhaodaisuo Hotel 镇远招待所
Triple rooms are Rmb 12, double rooms are Rmb 12 and single rooms range from Rmb 9 to Rmb 12. Double rooms come complete with a large bed, couch and chair. There are no showers and all rooms share communal toilets. There is a restaurant in the hotel.

Luyou Fuwu Dalou Tourist Service Hotel 旅游服务大楼
The cheapest bed here is Rmb 4.50 and nice triple rooms are Rmb 10.50. There are communal toilets and no showers. There is a restaurant on the ground floor.

Transportation

Zhenyuan Huochezhan Train Station 镇远火车站
The train station is a 30-minute walk from the hotels; there is no local bus. Taking buses to small towns in the area is easier than taking the train.

destination	departure
Guiyang 贵阳	02:33, 10:50, 13:27
Beijing 北京	23:35
Shanghai 上海	02:39, 17:40
Chongqing 重庆	22:36
Huaihua 怀化	15:37
Chengdu 成都	23:40
Guangzhou 广州	03:33

Local train #524 goes to 13 small towns. However, the train station at each stop may be 30 minutes away from town.

Zhenyuan Qichezhan Bus Station 镇远汽车站

destination	departure	cost (Rmb)
Kaili 凯里	07:00	4.90
Tianzhu 天柱	07:00	3.80
Shibing 施秉	16:00	3.30
Mahao 马号	07:30	1.30

Gu

1. legendary poisonous insect
2. poison, venom, harm
3. bewitch, enchant

According to Han Chinese popular belief, many women from the hilltribes of Southwest China were witches. Certain members of the Zhuang, Yao, Dong, Buyi and most notably the Miao nationalities made a drug from *gu*, which was added to tea and given to unsuspecting victims. After ingesting the drug, the victim was compelled to receive doses of the *gu* antidote at regular intervals, usually between three and 12 months, or face an excruciating death. It was this cycle of dependency on the antidote that 'bewitched' and enslaved.

The victim (always a man), on learning of his predicament, was then told what specific conditions and tasks he must fulfill. *Gu* was often used to snare a lover or censure errant husbands. The power of the poison was also used politically to bring outsiders into the clan; enemy chieftains or Chinese officials could be forced, under pain of death, to protect and serve the controlling clan. In the days before roads entered the remote border regions of these tribes, an official might travel for months from his home in China and, once poisoned, never be able to return.

For centuries, fear of *gu* inhibited contact and understanding between and within different ethnic groups.

Shidong 施洞

Shidong, a small Miao village of 6,000 people set in a terraced valley, offers travelers a good chance to spend some time with the local people and learn about their rural life. Except during harvest times, the Miao people in Shidong wear colorful traditional clothing. Local women wear a long silver pin in their hair and some wear headdresses. Older women have centimeter-sized holes in their earlobes from wearing heavy silver earrings. Every sixth day has a market, with colorful villagers flooding into town to do business. Although Shidong has a few concrete structures, the town is comprised mainly of traditional Miao wooden houses and stores.

The Qingshuijiang River separates Shidong from Mahao, a small Miao village accessible by ferry.

Shidong is officially closed, but we got travel permits from the Kaili Gonganju. If you show up without permits, especially after the bus leaves, you will probably be allowed to stay.

Things to do

There is nothing to do in Shidong except explore the town and the surrounding countryside. If you visit on market day or during a festival, things will be lively.

Festivals

Lantern Festival 元宵节
Held on the 15th day of the first lunar month, the Miao Lantern Festival features a variety of colorful lanterns, including long dragon lanterns. The participants in this festival number around 10,000.

Eat Sister's Rice Festival 吃姐妹饭
Held from the 15th to the 17th of the third lunar month, this Miao festival is a time for walking in the hills, playing drums and singing love songs. Participants number 3,000.

Dragon Boat Day 龙船节
Held on the 27th day of the fifth lunar month, this Miao festival features Dragon Boat races, horse races and dancing to traditional drum music. Participants number more than 25,000.

Lodging

Shidong Zhaodaisuo Hotel 施洞招待所
Beds in a four-person room are Rmb 2. Double rooms are Rmb 8 and come with a desk and chair. All rooms share communal toilets and showers. The restaurant serves decent food at Rmb 1 per meal. There are two small

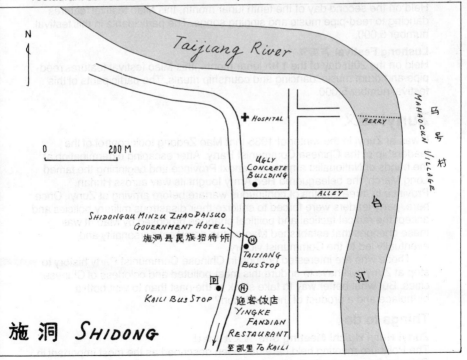

施洞 SHIDONG

restaurants on the road near the theater.

Transportation

The bus to Kaili leaves at 07:00 from the post office. Buy your ticket the day before from the bus driver between 17:00 and 19:00. The bus to Taijiang leaves at 10:00 from the hotel. The Zhenyuan bus leaves at 08:30 from Mahao village across the river.

Leishan 雷山

Leishan is a Miao town south of Kaili on the road towards the Rongjiang River. It is a closed town that can be visited, with care, as a day trip, though foreigners are allowed to view the festivals.

Festivals

Lusheng Festival 芦笙节

Held on the 24th day of the tenth lunar month, this Miao festival features reed-pipe and brass drum music, dancing, and the offering of embroidered belts as a courtship ritual. The participants in this festival number 10,000.

Eat New Rice Day 吃新节

Held on the 16th day of the eighth lunar month, this Miao festival features the singing of love songs, dancing, bull fights and horse races. The participants in this festival number 10,000.

Miao New Year 苗年

Held on the second day of the tenth lunar month, this Miao festival features dancing to reed-pipe music and singing songs. The participants in this festival number 5,000.

Lusheng Festival 芦笙节

Held on the 20th day of the 11th lunar month, this Miao festival features reed-pipe and drum music, dancing and courtship rituals. The participants of this festival number 5,000.

Zunyi 遵义

It was at Zunyi in the winter of 1935 that Mao Zedong took control of the leadership of the Chinese Communist Party. After escaping extermination at the hands of Nationalist armies in Jiangxi Province and beginning the famed Long March, the beleaguered Red Army fought its way across Hunan Province in three months of continuous warfare before arriving at Zunyi. Once here, party leaders were forced to criticize their disastrous military policies and accept the radical tactical and political changes proposed by Mao. It was these changes that established Mao as the dominant personality and eventually led to the Communist victory.

Those who are interested enough in Chinese Communist Party history to stop at Zunyi will have to endure this most polluted and colorless of Chinese cities. But what better way to take stock of the past than to visit both a birthplace and a product of the revolution?

Things to do

Zunyi Huiyi Huizhi Meeting Site 遵义会议会址

The Politburo meeting held here has been described as the most important in Chinese Communist Party history. Mao, disgraced and seemingly powerless only three months before, rose to power in Zunyi and changed the course of the revolution. The meeting ended with the signing of the Zunyi Resolution, a 14-point document criticizing past errors and advocating fundamental tactical changes.

The meeting rooms and living quarters where the dramatic events took place have been restored and are open for viewing. During the Cultural Revolution the meeting hall was a Maoist shrine visited by hundreds of thousands of Red Guards. There is a large collection of memorabilia.

Excerpts from the Zunyi Resolution

'We should not engage the enemy in a decisive battle in whch we have no confidence to win because we have neither discovered nor created the enemy's weakness. We should use our second forces — guerrilla units, armed masses, independent battalions and regiments — and a part of the main forces of the Red Army, to confuse and bait the enemy.'

'It must be realized that the civil war in China is not a short, but a long, protracted war.'

'The Party has bravely exposed its own mistakes. It has educated itself through them and learnt how to lead the revolutionary war more efficiently towards victory. After the exposure of mistakes, the Party, instead of being weakened, actually becomes stronger.'

The Long March, Dick Wilson

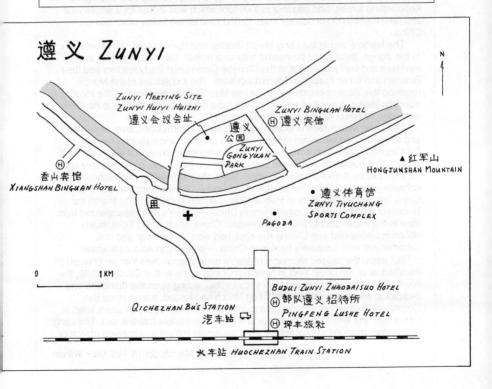

遵义 ZUNYI

ZUNYI MEETING SITE
ZUNYI HUIYI HUIZHI
遵义会议会址

遵义
公园
ZUNYI
GONGYUAN
PARK

ZUNYI BINGUAN HOTEL
Ⓗ 遵义宾馆

Ⓗ
香山宾馆
XIANGSHAN BINGUAN HOTEL

▲ 红军山
HONGJUNSHAN MOUNTAIN

遵义体育馆
ZUNYI TIYUCHANG
SPORTS COMPLEX

PAGODA

N

0   1 KM

BUDUI ZUNYI ZHAODAISUO HOTEL
Ⓗ 部队遵义招待所
PINGFENG LUSHE HOTEL
Ⓗ 坪丰旅社

QICHEZHAN BUS STATION
汽车站

火车站 HUOCHEZHAN TRAIN STATION

The site is open weekdays from 08:30 to 18:00 and on Sunday from 10:00 to 18:00.

Hongjun Shan Mountain 红军山

A long flight of stairs leads up the mountain to a large concrete memorial with four giant faces and murals of PLA soldiers in action below a giant hammer and sickle. Nearby are two mass graves filled with dead soldiers.

Zunyi Gongyuan Park 遵义公园

The Zunyi Gongyuan Park is boring, but it does have a nice rose garden and an old MiG aircraft. The road from town to the park passes through an old neighborhood with a lively market.

Lodging

Pingfeng Lushe Hotel 坪丰旅社

This spartan hotel near the train station is convenient and cheap, but very noisy. Beds in a four-bed room start at Rmb 1.50, double rooms are Rmb 6.

The Long March

On October 16, 1934, about 100,000 Chinese Communist men and women set out on the most extraordinary march in human history. Abandoning their soviet base (as large as Belgium) in the south-central province of Jiangxi (Kiangsi), they burst through the stranglehold of their enemy, Chiang Kai-shek's Nationalist or Kuomintang forces, and began a trek on foot which was to last for a whole year and take them 6,000 circuitous miles (9,600 kilometres) to the other end of China.

The leaders began the Long March divided and demoralized. The evacuation of the Jiangxi base could be viewed only as a defeat, owed in large part to the mistakes and bad judgement of the Chinese Communist Party leaders and their Russian and other European Marxist advisers. The exigencies of the March resolved this dissension; during its course Mao Zedong emerged as the most powerful leader, a position which, though it did not allow him always to have his own way, he never afterwards entirely forfeited.

The Long March led the Communists through 11 provinces, over raging rivers and snow-capped mountain ranges, through swamps and forests. They had to fight against Nationalist armies as well as the troops of provincial warlords, local bandits and hostile tribesmen. At one point where water was unknown they could survive only by drinking their own urine. Soon after they began their odyssey, the collapse of most of the other scattered Communist bases in various parts of China left on the shoulders of Mao and his colleagues on the Long March the burden of the survival of Communism in China. As Mao's men disappeared from view in the impenetrable interior of Western China, abutting on Tibet, many observers assumed that Chiang Kai-shek had won his civil war and that Communism was decisively beaten in China — possibly in Asia as a whole.

But when the ragged remnants of Mao's band approached Yan'an (Yenan) in the shadow of the Great Wall in Northern China, at the end of October 1935, the tide had unexpectedly turned. Mao's leadership, acting upon the discipline and dedication which the rigors of the Long March had forged, transformed the Communist movement into the driving force which succeeded, 14 years later, in taking over the entire country and pushing the Nationalists into the sea. The Long March thus changed in character from a desperate retreat to a prelude of victory.

The Long March, pp 14–15, Dick Wilson

Zunyi Bingdui Zhaodaisuo Army Guesthouse 遵义兵队招待所
The hotel staff believes this hotel is below standard for foreign travelers so
they might not let you stay here. We found the hotel rather nice. Beds in a
four-bed room start at Rmb 2.50 and triple rooms are Rmb 10. All rooms have
a toilet and sink and share a communal shower. There is a restaurant at the
hotel.

Zunyi Binguan Guesthouse 遵义宾馆
This hotel, set inside a large walled compound, is both good and expensive.
Double rooms start at Rmb 20 and come with a private toilet and shower.
Public Security is located at the hotel. The restaurant here is very expensive.

Transportation

Zunyi Huochezhan Train Station 遵义火车站

destination	departure
Shanghai 上海	06:46
Chongqing 重庆	02:26, 09:59, 13:32
Guangzhou 广州	16:00
Chengdu 成都	11:58, 21:17
Kunming 昆明	00:32
Guiyang 贵阳	04:45, 16:54

The Buyi

The Buyi share a common ancestry with many of China's minority nationalities,
including the Dai, Zhuang and Dong. Their roots may extend to the Longshan
and Shang, two pre-Chinese civilizations dating back to neolithic times. The
original home of these civilizations was central China and their representatives
settled as far north and east as Hebei and Shandong. As with the Miao, the first
written record of the Buyi places them in Hunan Province at the end of the Song
Dynasty. They also entered Southwest China under pressure from advancing
Mongol armies at the beginning of the Yuan Dynasty.

The ancestors of the Buyi have always been valley dwellers, adept at
cultivating rice in irrigated fields with the help of draft animals. Their homes, large
dwellings built above the ground on piles, have changed little over time. Such
homes have even been adopted by some Miao groups who prefer them to their
traditional structures. Buyi farmers grow corn, cabbage, sweet potatoes and other
vegetables in addition to rice, their staple.

Today, the Buyi are best known for their fine batik work. Traditionally, batik
was produced during the winter when the fields needed little tending. The batik
process begins with beeswax, extracted from a hive and heated. The liquid wax
is applied to undyed cloth with metal spoons and other specially shaped
instruments with spouts and bamboo handles. Dots, lines, figures and shapes of
various sizes make up the overall pattern, and once the wax has hardened the
cloth is soaked in indigo dye and set aside to dry. Later, hot water is used to
remove the wax, revealing the final design. Batik is used to make child carriers,
children's clothing, borders for skirts and aprons, and to line embroidered
wedding jackets. Traditional designs of flowers arranged in rows or large spirals
are still common, though mass production spurred by tourism has introduced
non-traditional motifs and products.

destination	distance (kms)	departure	cost (Rmb)
Guiyang 贵阳	163	07:20, 08:20	5.20
Yuqing 余庆	188	07:00, 08:00	6.70
Wuchuan 武昌	200	07:00, 08:00	6.40
Weng'an 翁安	162	07:40	5.20

Check for buses going to Tongren and Anshun.

Anshun 安顺

Anshun deserves more attention from travelers than it gets. The city is a maze of narrow streets and alleyways lined with timber structures and the surrounding countryside is composed of lush valleys, perennially green, separated by jutting karst crags pock-marked with caves. Foreign tourists tend to view Anshun as an unavoidable delay, a convenient but uninteresting jump-off point for the Longgong and Daji Dong caves or the Huangguoshu waterfalls. Anshun, as Guiyang, suffers from an undeservedly bad reputation.

Anshun is an old town, with a history going back 600 years to the early Ming Dynasty. In the 19th century, it grew rich from the brisk opium trade with British merchants. At that time, European goods were a common sight in the markets. Recently the town has blossomed into a regional manufacturing center and is Guizhou's sixth largest city with a population of over 200,000.

Western Guizhou is the home of many different Miao sub-groups. The Buyi, often difficult to distinguish from the Miao, are also widely scattered throughout this area.

Things to do

Get a feel for the town by walking through it. There are, as in all parts of China, new workers' apartments, cavernous government offices and dull, utilitarian buildings, but efforts to preserve the old town's flavor by dispersing the new, ugly projects away from the center have left many older neighborhoods intact. Zhonghua Lu, with rows of open-front two-story timber buildings housing stores, restaurants, barber shops and private homes, is perhaps the most interesting place to start. For a taste of Anshun's past, visit either of the two pagodas. Just north of the White Pagoda, a 21-meter high structure built in 1362, is a crumbling temple.

The area's primary attractions are the countless minority villages spread out for hundreds of kilometers in fertile valleys beneath karst peaks. If you are short of time, a glimpse of these villages during the trip to the Longgong Caves or Huangguoshu Waterfall will have to do. If you have a day, get on the main road to Guiyang early in the morning and hitch a ride eastward by bus or truck. The entire 105-kilometer trip between Anshun and Guiyang reveals a spectacular Miao and Buyi wonderland, so it matters little where you decide to get off and explore. Be back on the main road by 15:00 for a sure ride to either Anshun or Guiyang. With proper camping gear you can easily stay for an extended period in the isolated areas of Guizhou.

Farther away

Huangguoshu Waterfall 黄果树大瀑布

Huangguoshu (Yellow Fruit Tree) is China's largest waterfall. The 67-meter fall is impressive year round, but in the late spring, summer or early fall the

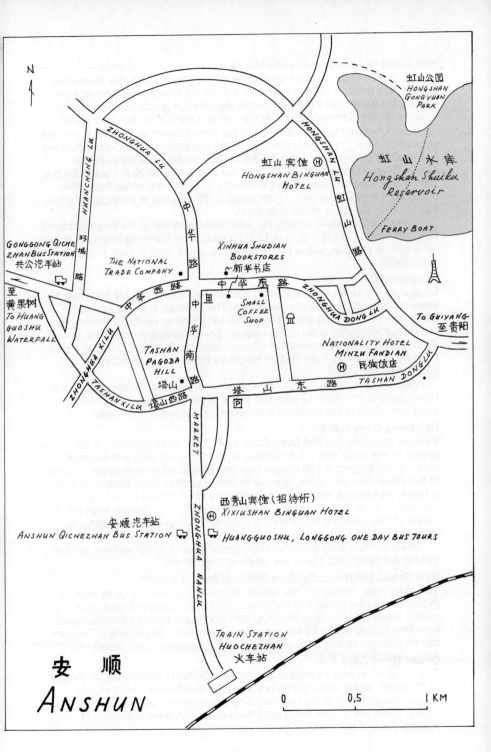

虹山公园
HONGSHAN GONGYUAN PARK

虹山宾馆 Ⓗ
HONGSHAN BINGUAN HOTEL

虹山水库
HONGSHAN SHUIKU RESERVOIR

FERRY BOAT

GONGGONG QICHE ZHAN BUS STATION
共公汽车站

THE NATIONAL TRADE COMPANY

XINHUA SHUDIAN BOOKSTORES
~新华书店

To HUANG GUOSHU WATERFALL
至 黄果树

SMALL COFFEE SHOP

ZHONGHUA DONG LU

To GUIYANG
至 贵阳

TASHAN PAGODA HILL
塔山

NATIONALITY HOTEL
MINZU FANDIAN
Ⓗ 民族饭店

TASHAN DONG LU
塔 山 东 路

XIXIUSHAN BINGUAN HOTEL
西秀山宾馆（招待所）

ANSHUN QICHEZHAN BUS STATION
安顺汽车站

HUANGGUOSHU, LONGGONG ONE DAY BUS TOURS

TRAIN STATION
HUOCHEZHAN
火车站

安 顺
ANSHUN

0   0.5   1 KM

N

river swells and separate jets of water merge into a curtain of white water veiled in mist. A path which crosses behind the falls is slippery and very dangerous at peak flow periods, but the view from behind the wall of water tempts most tourists to take the risk. The park below the falls is a good place for a picnic lunch or, in the summer, to bask in the sun and swim in the ice-cold water.

You can make Huangguoshu a day trip from Anshun, or you can spend the night at the falls. For the day trip, take a one-day mini-bus tour, which includes a stop at Longgong, from either the Minzu Nationality Hotel (Rmb 6), the Xishan Binguan Hotel (Rmb 5) or meet the bus before 08:30 in front of the bus station on Zhonghua Nan Lu. For a two-day trip, take one of the three daily buses from the bus station to Huangguoshu. Either hotel at Huangguoshu can help you buy tickets to return to Anshun.

There are two hotels serving the area. Double rooms at the **Huangguoshu Binguan Hotel**（黄果树宾馆）are FEC 30 each. The **Tianxing Binguan Hotel** （天星宾馆）is cheaper, with a bed in a triple room for Rmb 5. Both hotels have restaurants.

Longgong Caves 龙宫
Longgong, the Dragon Palace, is a 15-kilometer series of nearly 100 caverns weaving through 20 separate mountains. The caverns, both dry and water-filled, range in size from small, tunnel-like passages to vaults 20 meters high lit by small 'skylights' open to the outside. Some caves are accessible by foot, but the most dramatic water-filled caverns must be viewed from boats. The most popular route is from Tianchi Heavenly Pond to Bangyun Clam Crag, 1,800 metres away.

Visit the caves on a day tour from Anshun or Guiyang (buses also stop at Huangguoshu Waterfall) or take one of the three local buses which run daily to Longgong. Stay at the small hotel at the caves. Beds are very cheap.

Daji Dong Cave 打鸡洞
By most accounts, the Daji Dong Cave near Zhijin Shan Mountain is the largest in the world. The cave complex is 13 kilometers long and boasts 47 caverns; the biggest is 150 meters high and almost 200 meters wide. The top of this cave, said one visitor, is covered with countless large stalactites, and is barely visible. In summer, the air inside the cave, cooled by underground streams, is quite chilly. The most spectacular section is reported to be the Forest of Pagodas in a Monastery, a collection of caverns filled with squat, pagoda-like stalagmites.

There are four daily buses to Zhijin Shan, three at 07:00 and one at 12:30. Tickets are Rmb 3.30. There are hotels at Zhijin Shan.

Baili Dujian Lin Rhododendron National Park 百里杜鹃林
This large park, covering 1,800 square kilometers, is famous for its vast rhododendron fields that turn the mountains into a rainbow of color each spring. Flowers bloom from March to May and many summer flowers bloom from May to July over a 50-kilometre area that covers two counties. The park can be reached by bus from either Guiyang or Anshun.

Chuan Dong Cave 穿洞
This small cave, only 18 meters long, is an important neolithic site. At the time of discovery, stone and bone tools littered the floor below animal murals. Human bones found at the site, including a complete skull, are believed to be 10,000 years old. Chuan Dong is 18 kilometers northwest of Anshun at Puding. Several buses make the trip daily.

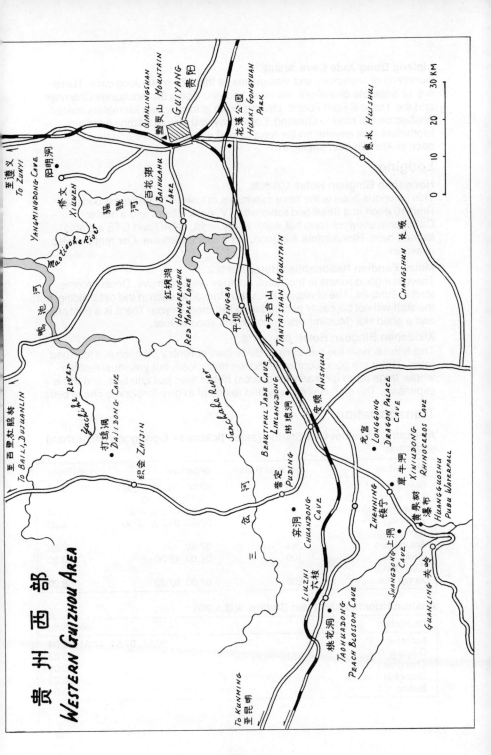

贵州西部 WESTERN GUIZHOU AREA

GIANLINGSHAN MOUNTAIN 黔灵山 GUIYANG 贵阳

黔灵山公园 QIANLINGSHAN PARK

花溪公园 HUAXI GONGYUAN PARK

百花湖 BAIHUAHU Lake

至遵义 To Zunyi

阳明洞 YANGMINGDONG Cave

修文 XIUWEN

猫跳河 Maotiaohe River

惠水 HUISHUI

鸭池河 Yachihe River

至百里杜鹃林 To BAILI, DUJUANLIN

红枫湖 HONGFENGHU Red Maple Lake

平坝 PINGBA

天台山 TIANTAISHAN Mountain

长顺 CHANGSHUN

三岔河 Sanchahe River

打鸡洞 DAIIDONG CAVE

织金 ZHIJIN

六枝 LIUZHI

穿洞 CHUANDONG CAVE

普定 PUDING

琳琅洞 LIMLANGDONG BEAUTIFUL JADE CAVE

安顺 ANSHUN

龙宫 LONGGONG DRAGON PALACE CAVE

犀牛洞 XINIUDONG RHINOCEROS CAVE

镇宁 ZHENNING

黄果树瀑布 HUANGGUOSHU PUBU WATERFALL

上洞 SHANGDONG CAVE

关岭 GUANLING

桃花洞 TAOHUADONG PEACH BLOSSOM CAVE

至昆明 To KUNMING

30 KM
20
10
0

Linlang Dong Jade Cave 琳琅洞

Hundreds of stalactites and stalagmites fill this 478-meter long cave. There are 12 separate chambers, the most beautiful being the Antiquities Chamber and the Tropical Rain Forest. Linlang Dong is located ten kilometers east of Anshun on the road to Guiyang. Locals say you should hitchhike the ten kilometers, ask anyone on the road to lead you to the cave and then walk back to Anshun after seeing it.

Lodging

Hongshan Binguan Hotel 虹山宾馆

This luxurious hotel is the most expensive in town. The cheapest beds are Rmb 10 each in a three-bed room with TV, desk, chairs and a heater. Communal showers have hot water every night. CAAC and CTS are also located here. Restaurants are good, but a little expensive. Car rental is also available.

Minzu Fandian Nationalities Hotel 民族饭店

There are good rooms in this hotel, but they are expensive. Double rooms start at Rmb 24. The cheapest beds are Rmb 3.50 each in the old building, but the staff will not be easily persuaded to sell them to you. There is a post office and a good Hui (Muslim) restaurant on the second floor.

Xixiushan Binguan Hotel 西秀山宾馆

This hotel is near the bus station. Beds start at Rmb 2.50 each in a four-bed room. There are good dorms behind the main hotel, but you must rent the whole, large room (primarily for groups) rather than just one bed, and this is expensive. The staff is unfriendly and reluctant to give foreigners cheap beds.

Transportation

Anshun Qichezhan Bus Station (same tickets as Gonggong Qichezhan) 安顺汽车站

destination	distance (kms)	departure	cost (Rmb)
Guiyang 贵阳	105	07:00, 08:00, 12:00 13:30(2), 15:30	3.40
Huangguoshu 黄果树	46	07:00, 07:20, 12:00	1.50
Zhenning 镇宁 (Longgong)（龙宫）	31	07:00, 07:20, 12:00	1.00
Anlong 安龙	244	07:40	7.80
Zhijin 织金 (Daji Dong)	100	07:00, 12:30	3.30
Xingyi 兴义	256	07:00, 07:20	8.20

Anshun Huochezhan Train Station 安顺火车站

destination	departure
Kunming 昆明	00:21, 07:51, 17:51, 22:04
Guiyang 贵阳	05:23
Chongqing 重庆	20:00
Shanghai 上海	08:28
Beijing 北京	20:54

Liupanshui 六盘水

Liupanshui is a small city set amidst a stunning karst landscape. The quality of your time here depends primarily on when you arrive. In spring, summer or fall, accessibility to surrounding villages and nearby karst areas is good, making exploration an enjoyable exercise. In winter and early spring, the rains come and the damp clouds never rise far above the ground. You cannot reach nearby villages through the ankle-deep mud, and if you could, the cloud cover would be there masking the view.

Things to do

In town, the area around the Zhongshan Fandian Hotel is the liveliest. For a good panorama of town, hike to the top of the hill at Zhongshan Gongyuan Park.

Shuigang Steel Plant 水钢

Shuigang, employing over 20,000 workers, is Guizhou's largest steel plant. It works in cooperation with West German companies, importing used equipment and sending engineers to Germany for training. The steel plant, completed over 20 years ago, has been such a large source of jobs in western Guizhou that local labor has long since been depleted. Men and women now come from other parts of China to fill vacant positions. The plant, composed of four large factories and dozens of small buildings, is crisscrossed by public roads lined with apartments. There is a cave and a park on the factory grounds.

It is worth investing a day at Shuigang, walking around the factory area, observing workers pouring molten metal or photographing the archaic factory in the fog.

Lodging

Zhongshan Fandian Hotel 钟山饭店

Beds in a five-bed room in this large, well-kept hotel are Rmb 5 each. Double rooms without bathrooms cost Rmb 16, with bathrooms Rmb 20. To reach the hotel, take bus #1.

Lushe hotels 旅社

If you arrive in Liupanshui too late to make the trip to the Zhongshan Fandian Hotel, you will have to stay at one of several *lushe* hotels near the train station. They usually send representatives to meet the late train and escort guests to their hotels.

Restaurants

The private restaurants along Wenhua Lu north of Zhongshan Jie serve a variety of dumplings, noodles and rice dishes.

Transportation

Shuicheng Qichezhan Bus Station 水城汽车站

destination	distance (kms)	departure	cost (Rmb)
Weining 威宁	79	07:30, 12:00	2.60
Zhaotong 昭通	201	07:00, 07:20, 07:30	6.50
Bijie 毕节	204	07:20	7.70
Nayong 纳雍	97	07:20	3.70
Panxian 盘县	204	06:40, 07:20, 07:30	7.40

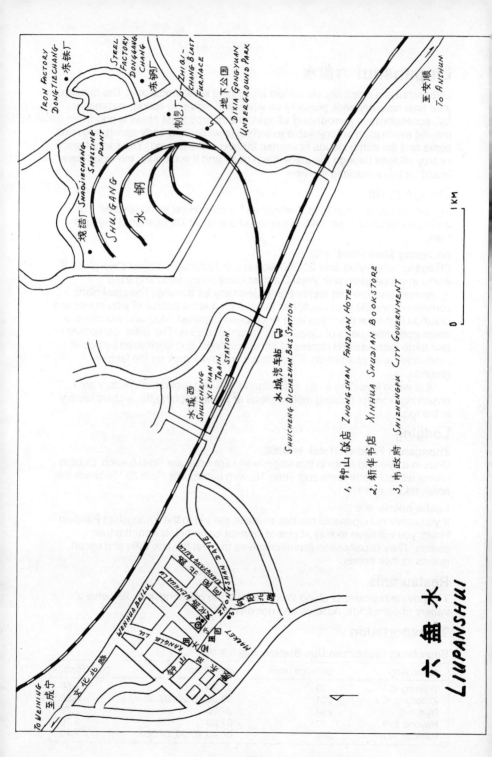

六盘水
LIUPANSHUI

1, 钟山饭店 ZHONGSHAN FANDIAN HOTEL
2, 新华书店 XINHUA SHUDIAN BOOKSTORE
3, 市政府 SHIZHENGFU CITY GOVERNMENT

水城汽车站 SHUICHENG QICHEZHAN BUS STATION

水城西 SHUICHENG XIZHAN Train Station

Iron Factory DONGTIECHANG 冻铁厂

STEEL FACTORY DONGGANGCHANG 冻钢厂

ZHIGI-CHANG BLAST FURNACE 制钢厂

DIXIA GONGYUAN UNDERGROUND PARK 地下公园

SHAOJIECHANG SMELTING PLANT 烧结厂

SHUIGANG 水钢

WENHUA BEILU 文化北路

YANGGUANG DADAO 阳光大道

WENHUA LU 文化路

KANGLE LU 康乐路

MARKET 市场

至威宁 To WEINING

至成宁 To WEINING

至安顺 To ANSHUN

1 KM

0

106

destination	departure
Kunming 昆明	02:01, 11:53, 21:49
Beijing 北京	17:36
Shanghai 上海	05:19
Chongqing 重庆	16:35

The Dahua Miao and the Mission

Historically, the Miao of Weining, known as the Dahua or Big Flowery Miao, occupied the lowest rung on the multi-ethnic social ladder. By the late Qing Dynasty, most Miao people were landless laborers, virtual slaves of landed Yi or Chinese proprietors.

'They were treated as slaves, and in former years no Lolo (Yi) would have sat down for a meal at the same table with a Miao. The feudal lord mounted his horse from the back of a stooping Miao. Out of this oppressed state the Miao submitted to the teachings of Christianity with veritable fanaticism when the first missionaries appeared among them around the turn of the century. They submitted to baptism by the thousands and took their conversion very seriously. They allowed themselves to be talked into giving up their old customs. Music, dance, festivals, which in the case of the Miao were always connected with ancient traditional recitations, were abolished. The use of tobacco and wine was given up, not to mention numerous "superstitious" customs at death, birth, and in the event of sickness. The relationship between young men and girls, which, to be sure, was often rather free, was thoroughly reformed.

'Out of some traditional symbols and designs that had been preserved in ornamental patterns of their clothing, Samuel Pollard created a Dahua Miao script. He arranged for a printing press to be established in Japan, which made it possible for bibles and hymnals to be distributed among the Miao soon thereafter. This, their own script, was the object of great pride among the Miao. Only if one realizes what it means in rural China to be able to read and write can one appreciate this pride. The Communists, in their endeavor to provide the languages of the non-Chinese people of China with their own writing, exhibited great interest in the Pollard script. Among the Miao this writing had become quite popular. In Shimenkan, north of the city of Weining, very close to the Yunnan border, a Dahua mission center was established with a very good school. Talented Miao could then continue their educational training at the mission school in Zhaotong (Chao-tong). It was furthermore made possible for a few to study at the West China Union University in Chengdu. Among these there later were teachers, two physicians, and a sociologist.

'In this manner, within two generations, the Dahua Miao almost became the sustainers of culture in Guizhou. The Communists immediately placed educated Dahua Miao into leading positions involving the organizing and administration of minorities.'

The Ta-Hua Miao of Kweichow Province, 1954, Inez de Beauclair

Weining 威宁

The difference between Weining and the rest of Guizhou Province seems astounding. Only 79 kilometers from Liupanshui, Weining shares little of its climate or geography; the countryside is dominated by Caohai (Grass Sea), a large, shallow lake in the process of becoming a meadow. The wide valley around the lake, formerly Caohai's lake bed, is surrounded by low mountains barely visible in the distance. In Weining, the people spend the dry, mild winters outside enjoying the sun while much of Guizhou Province is mired in mud.

One look at the colorfully dressed people on Weining's streets will tell you why the area has been designated a Miao, Hui, Yi Nationality Autonomous County. Nearly everyone you see is either a Miao or Hui, with an occasional Yi down from the hills to trade. The daily street markets, rivalling Dali's famous markets (see page 149) in diversity of people, dominate town life, filling the roads with lines of vehicles stranded in a sea of people.

The Hui (Muslims), a group present all over Southwest China, play a visible role in Weining community life. This might be the best place in the Southwest to see them.

Things to do

Walk the streets and find the oldest neighborhoods in town east of the main road.

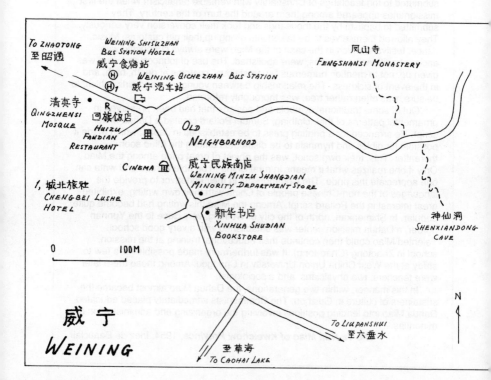

Caohai Grass Sea 草海

This shallow, grass-filled lake surrounded by peat bogs is Weining's prime attraction. Around the lake is a wildlife sanctuary established to preserve the many species of endangered birds that nest in the area. We saw herons, cranes, several species of duck and flamingos (we think). Hawks and falcons soar above the bogs in search of small rodents.

To get to the lake and surrounding bogs, walk southward out of town and take the large dirt road branching off to the right. The lake is visible from the south of town so finding the road is easy. Ten minutes down this dirt road will bring you near the bogs. Parallel canals have been cut into them allowing small boats to navigate. If there are fishermen in the area, try to ride with them. If not, walk out on a levee until you run out of solid ground. You should be able to get well into the bog on foot before becoming mired.

To approach the actual lake, stay on the dirt road for about an hour until it passes close to the shore.

Fengshan Si Monastery 风山寺

This badly razed Buddhist monastery sits in a pine grove on a hill east of town. At one time there were over 200 monks in Weining, but none remain today to tend this burned-out shell. Save for two large steles, no cultural relics remain. However, the government has not abandoned this monastery — the site was officially protected in 1982 and stacks of bricks near the main gate signal impending restoration.

Climb the hill for a beautiful sunset view of the town.

Shenxian Dong Cave 神仙洞

This cave lies in the hills east of Weining. It rests behind the foundation of a completely destroyed monastery that was once associated with Fengshan Si Monastery. The cave is not large, but contains unusual statues of Guanyin, the Goddess of Mercy, and a monkey carved from stalagmites hundreds of years ago. Mineral deposits from dripping water make the figures now look fat.

The foundation of the old monastery affords a magnificent view of town and Caohai and would be an ideal campsite if you bring your own water.

Weining Qingzhen Si Mosque 威宁清真寺

This turquoise mosque on the main road at the northern edge of town is the best place to meet local Muslims. The caretakers are friendly and will give visitors a tour of the mosque.

Lodging

Weining Shisuzhan Hostel 威宁食宿站

This hotel is reasonably clean and comfortable. Beds start at Rmb 3.

Chengbei Lushe 城北旅社

Next to the bus station, beds here are Rmb 1.50 each. The staff may be reluctant about renting to foreign friends.

Restaurants

The two Hui (Muslim) restaurants near the mosque serve a selection of vegetarian food in addition to steak and roast beef.

Transportation

Weining Qichezhan Bus Station 威宁汽車站

destination	distance (kms)	departure
Bijie 毕节	171	07:00
Xuanwei 宣威	177	07:00
Zhaotong 昭通	122	07:00
Shuicheng 水城 (Liupanshui)	79	07:00, 07:30, 13:00
Hezhang 赫章	76	12:00
Niuzhazi	81	10:00

Bus departures are half-an-hour later from October to April.

The Hui

Many people find it surprising to discover Muslims in nearly every part of China. Known as the Hui, these followers of Islam first came to China as sea merchants within 50 years of the death of Muhammad (632). They soon adopted Chinese family names as well as the Chinese language, and spread throughout the southern part of the country, living as traders in urban ghettos and along important transport routes.

The second wave of Muslims came to China by land, from Turkestan, in the 10th century. Today, most of China's seven million Hui still live in the northern and western parts of the country.

Nevertheless, the four provinces of the Southwest have considerable numbers of Hui, descendants of the third important infusion of Muslims. In the 13th century, Kublai Khan conquered China and established the Yuan Dynasty with the help of tough Muslim mercenaries from Persia and Central Asia. He sent these troops to the Southwest, mostly to Yunnan, to keep them out of mischief far from the capital of Peking, but also to repopulate the area after the terrible wars.

In the Southwest today, every major city has a Hui community, with its special markets, restaurants and mosques. Kunming alone has 40,000 Muslims and five active mosques.

The Hui are considered a minority nationality because of their religion. Otherwise, for all intents and purposes, they are racially, linguistically and culturally Chinese. Some Hui read the Koran in Arabic and attend mosque on Friday, but in religious matters most of them practice little of the Islamic faith. An abhorrence and strict avoidance of pork is the one tangible and universal mark of their belief.

Patrick Booz

Yunnan Province 云南

Yunnan Province, whose name means 'South of the Clouds', is China's southwest border area. Historically, Yunnan was populated mainly by non-Han Chinese ethnic groups, and even today 24 different minority groups make up a third of its total population.

Evidence of Yunnan's pre-historic populations is scant, though a fascinating discovery made by geologists surveying for a railroad in 1964 proves the region to be among the oldest inhabited areas in China. Two humanoid teeth belonging to *Homo erectus* were found at Yuanmou among fossils of long-extinct mammals. Paleontologists now believe that Yuanmou Man predates the more famous Peking Man. In 1955, archeologists uncovered tombs from a sophisticated Bronze Age culture at the south end of Dianchi Lake. Known as the kingdom of Dian, this ancient society practised slavery, advanced forms of agriculture, and an animist religion with a cult of bulls.

In the broad scope of Chinese civilization, Yunnan is among China's newest acquisitions. In 339 BC, the first Chinese inroads to the region, then known as Dian, were partly successful until the victorious Chinese commander, finding his return to China proper blocked by rival Chinese armies, declared himself the King of Dian. His descendants ruled for 200 years, adopting local customs and intermarrying with the "southwestern barbarians" they had once sought to subdue.

During the eighth century, the Kingdom of Nanzhao was formed from six small states in the west of the province. For 400 years, its rulers, the Bai and Yi nationalities, controlled Yunnan. Though they were influenced culturally by the neighboring Tang Dynasty, they lived beside the Chinese as equals, making treaties and protecting their vital interests with capable armies.

In the 13th century, Mongol invaders from Central Asia ended Bai rule in Yunnan, establishing Chinese authority in the region (even though they were not themselves Chinese). Chinese control, though challenged periodically by rebellions, has continued up to the present.

The 20th century brought rapid change to Yunnan Province. After China's last emperor was overthrown in 1911, large numbers of Han Chinese settlers ventured to the Southwest. When Japanese forces occupied much of China, completely cutting off the Nationalist government from the coast, officials, affluent Chinese families, and intellectuals moved to Kunming, Yunnan's capital, transforming this sleepy frontier town into a modern city. Airfields and roads, most notably one to Burma, were built to facilitate greater resistance to Japanese occupation armies. Since 1949, economic and medical advances have brought widespread development to Yunnan, though government policies have periodically treated the region's non-Han populations with indifference or contempt.

Geographically, Yunnan occupies two distinct regions. The Yunnan-Guizhou Plateau dominates the eastern half of the province, higher to the west and lower to the southeast. This limestone plateau features karst formations, with characteristic caves, subterranean streams, and an unusual Stone Forest. Western Yunnan is a region of high mountains running in long ranges from north to south. The Salween, Mekong and Yangzi Rivers parallel each other in spectactularly deep trenches separated by 6,000 meter snow peaks.

The complicated terrain gives rise to three different climatic regions within the province. It is temperate in the mountain valleys of the north and west, sub-tropical on the plateau, and tropical in the southern hills. Generally, the climate is characterized by small seasonal changes within each geographic area. Average temperatures range from 7°C in the northwest to over 22°C in the Yuanjiang River valley in the southeast. There is a sharp contrast between wet and dry seasons. Abundant rainfall during the wet season accounts for 83% of the yearly total. The monsoon begins in May and ends in October, though rain is only heavy during July, August and September, and even then there is some sunshine nearly every day.

Yunnan's wide range of geographic and climatic conditions accounts for an extraordinary diversity of plant and animal life. The province contains fully half of all species of flora and fauna in China.

Kunming 昆明

Kunming has stood at its present location for more than a thousand years. Marco Polo, visiting in the 13th century, judged it a "very great and noble city". At that time it was called Yacheng, meaning Duck City. Dianchi Lake was bigger by several miles then and the city's waterfront was ideal for raising ducks. Later it became known as Yunnanfu (Yunnan City) but has been called Kunming for the past 50 years.

Through most of its history, Kunming was considered a remote backwater of the empire, since it took three months to reach from Peking. But development was spurred in 1910 by the building of a railroad to Hanoi and, three decades later, by the flight of many professional and intellectual Chinese to Kunming from the Japanese-occupied eastern seaboard. Expansion continued under the Communist government and Kunming has become an important manufacturing center with a population fast approaching two million.

Things to do

Kunming is known as 'Spring City' because of its mild climate. The pleasant weather is best enjoyed on foot or on a bike. For a walk, the old neighborhoods around Green Lake Park offer a charming alternative to the wide, busy, main streets. For a bike ride, head south from town for ten kilometers to Haigeng Gongyuan Park on the northern shore of Dianchi Lake for a picnic by the water and a close-up view of the Western Hill. The road between Kunming and Haigeng goes through typical farming villages and serene countryside, adding to the pleasure of the trip.

Between bicycle trips and walks in the city, many travelers pass the time at the Nanlaisheng Kafei Mianbao Dian Coffee and Bread Shop at 299 Jinbi Lu where excellent Vietnamese coffee is served with freshly baked bread. Chinese patrons range from factory workers to retired professors, who like to practice their English with foreigners. Many money-changers also operate out of this coffeehouse.

One block north on Nanqiang Jie is found an interesting teahouse frequented by old men who come to play cards, smoke their pipes and tell stories. Go early in the afternoon to get a good seat. A larger teahouse, the Jingxing Wenyi Chashi, on Jinxing Jie just north of the Kunming Department

112

Store, features storytellers and other informal entertainers daily.

Green Lake Park (Cuihu Gongyuan) 翠湖公园

Beautiful flower gardens and a group of five lakes crisscrossed with tree-lined causeways comprise this park. In winter, the shallow lakes are sometimes drained and the grassy lakebeds used for soccer games. A carnival-style freak show or an occasional informal opera performance add life to a weekend visit.

Yuantong Hill 圆通山

Yuantong Hill is the site of the Yuantong Si Temple, a park with fine trees and flowers, and the zoo. The temple, by far the oldest in Kunming, dates to the Tang Dynasty. Its halls are in good condition and the surrounding gardens are beautiful. The zoo, on top of the hill above the temple, is one of the best in China, and has several pandas. If you like zoos, see it.

Tiger in Kunming

A tiger killed two people and injured three others on Wednesday morning in the city of Kunming, Yunnan Province, then was shot to death by police after it roamed the city for more than six hours, the Shanghai Evening News reported yesterday.

The tiger was first spotted about 06:30 by Li Deming, a worker at the Yunnan Tyre Repair Factory, who was doing his exercises.

He was knocked to the ground by the tiger, which sprang from behind tall grass.

After a fierce scuffle with the tiger, Li got free. Li's face and both shoulders were badly cut by the animal's paws. He was able to get to his factory, where he reported the attack. Police immediately started a search of the city.

But it wasn't until well after noon that the tiger was reported attacking another victim. It bit to death a farmer cutting grass in the field and another farmer transporting manure to the field, the paper reported. The tiger also injured two people walking on the streets. According to the paper, the tiger jumped onto the highway and ran toward a crowd of people as police rushed to the scene. They surrounded the tiger, in an attempt to catch it alive, but were forced to open fire as the tiger pounced toward them.

According to the paper, the tiger did not come from any of the city's zoos or animal research institutes. Investigation is under way to find out where the animal came from.

The China Daily, December 8, 1986

Tang Dynasty Pagodas 东寺塔，西寺塔

These may be the only pagodas you will see sitting amidst brick apartment blocks, rundown workers' neighborhoods and factories. Located in the southern part of town, the pagodas house several families, chickens, dogs and garbage. As historical and architectural monuments they are extremely rare and valuable. They are also the oldest structures in Kunming.

Kunming Culture Center 市工人文化宫

On the central square sits the new, modern Kunming Cultural Center. The patio area out front with the large fountains is a good place to meet people. Entertainment changes frequently; check for posters advertising upcoming events near the entrance. For a few *mao*, you can ride the elevator to the rooftop observation platform for a beautiful view of the whole city.

Qingzhen Si Mosques 清眞寺

'At least five mosques serve Kunming's 40,000-strong Muslim

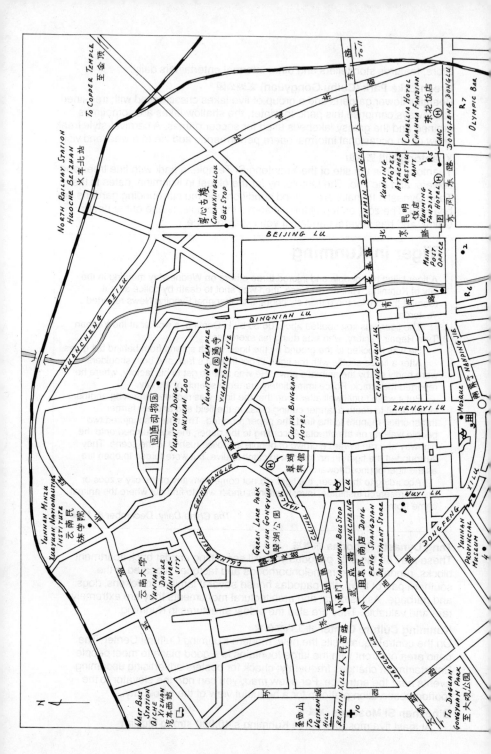

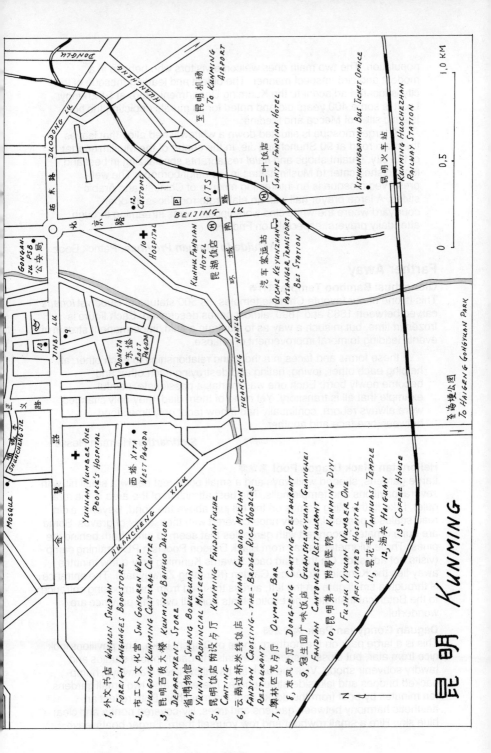

昆明 KUNMING

1, 外文书店 WAIWEN SHUDIAN
  FOREIGN LANGUAGES BOOKSTORE
2, 市工人文化宫 SHI GONGREN WEN-
  HUAGONG KUNMING CULTURAL CENTER
3, 昆明百货大楼 KUNMING BAIHUO DALOU
  DEPARTMENT STORE
4, 省博物馆 SHENG BOWUGUAN
  YUNNAN PROVINCIAL MUSEUM
5, 昆明饭店 KUNMING FANDIAN FUSHE
  KUNMING FANDIAN FANDIAN FUSHE
6, 云南过桥米线饭店 YUNNAN GUOQIAO MIXIAN
  FANDIAN CROSSING-THE-BRIDGE RICE NOODLES
  RESTAURANT
7, 奥林匹克厅分厅 OLYMPIC BAR
8, 东风厅分厅 DONGFENG CANTING RESTAURANT
9, 冠生园广味饭店 GUANSHENGYUAN GUANGWEI
  FANDIAN CANTONESE RESTAURANT
10, 昆明第一附属医院 KUNMING DIYI
  FUSHU YIYUAN NUMBER ONE
  AFFILIATED HOSPITAL
11, 昙花寺 TANHUASI TEMPLE
12, 海埂 HAIGENG
13, COFFEE HOUSE

MOSQUE
宣威街 XUANWEI JIE
金碧路 JINBI LU
西塔 XITA WEST PAGODA
环城西路 HUANCHENG XILU
环城南路 HUANCHENG NANLU
YUNNAN NUMBER ONE PEOPLE'S HOSPITAL
东塔 DONGTA EAST PAGODA
GONGANJU PS局 公安局
柏东路 DUGDONG LU
黄河路 HUANGHENG
北京路 BEIJING LU
公安局 GONGANJU PS局
正义路 ZHENGYI LU
管城街 GUANCHENGJIE
昆华饭店 KUNHUA FANDIAN HOTEL
H 南城 HOSPITAL
CUSTOMS
CITS
三叶饭店 SANYE HOTEL
汽车客运站 QICHE KEYANZHAN□ PASSANGER TRANSPORT BUS STATION
至昆明机场 To KUNMING Airport
昆明火车站 KUNMING HUOCHEZHAN RAILWAY STATION
西双版纳汽车票 XISHUANGBANNA BUS TICKET OFFICE
至海埂公园 To HAIGENG GONGYUAN PARK

0   0.5   1.0 KM

N

population. The two main ones welcome visitors who behave in a modest and circumspect manner. The oldest and leading mosque of the city is located adjacent to the Kunming Department Store at 51 Zhengyi Lu. It is some 400 years old and noted for its murals depicting the holy Islamic sites of Mecca and Medina.

'A larger mosque is situated down a whitewashed alley that leaves the main road at 90 Shuncheng Jie, in the center of the Muslim quarter of the city. Quaint shops and *halal* restaurants specializing in beef and lamb dishes cater to Muslim tastes in the neighborhood. The well-preserved mosque is an interesting mixture of Chinese and Arabic styles. A large prayer hall with an elaborate roof faces an open courtyard where the white clad worshippers come streaming through after daily prayers, especially on Fridays.'

A Guide to Yunnan Province, Patrick Booz

Farther Away

Qiongzhusi Bamboo Temple 筇竹寺
This is one of our favorite Chinese temples. Its 500 statues of Buddhist *lohans* carved between 1883 and 1890, almost defies description. Each figure is frozen in time, but in such a way as to illustrate a fluid, impermanent stream of events leading to moral improvement or relapse.

'. . . these forms and faces in a thousand relationships to each other, all helping each other, loving, hating and destroying each other and become newly born. Each one was mortal, a passionate, painful example that all is transitory. Yet none of them died, they only changed, were always reborn, continually had a new face: only time stood between one face and another.'

Siddhartha, Herman Hesse

Heilongtan Black Dragon Pool 黑龙潭
Large gardens, shaded walkways and a small pond rest below a small hill with several pavilions and temple halls. The best attraction of the area is the rural quiet. Hike to the Ming Tombs on the hill just above the pond. Beyond, a dirt road scales a peaceful, breezy ridge covered with thousands of graves. Some are quite ornate, decorated with gargoyles that seem to jump from behind the pines. Three kilometers away from Black Dragon Pool is a PLA training camp (visits not advised). On the road back towards Kunming only a few minutes away lies the Kunming Botanical Garden (Kunming Zhiwuyuan). The entrance is through a small gate on the left, across the road from the imposing entrance to the Botanical Institute. The exotic plants from all over the province are wonderful.

Daguan Gongyuan Park 大观公园
This is a large park on the northern shore of Dianchi Lake. The pavilions look nice from afar, but closer inspection reveals the gaudy photo studios and tawdry souvenir shops. Visit the park for its willow-lined walkways, hump-backed bridges and lakeside atmosphere. There are also two small gardens ten minutes by boat from the docks near the main hall. Both reflect an aesthetic harmony between gardens and trees, lily-covered ponds and clear blue sky. Hire a small rowboat and row yourself there. Larger boats leave

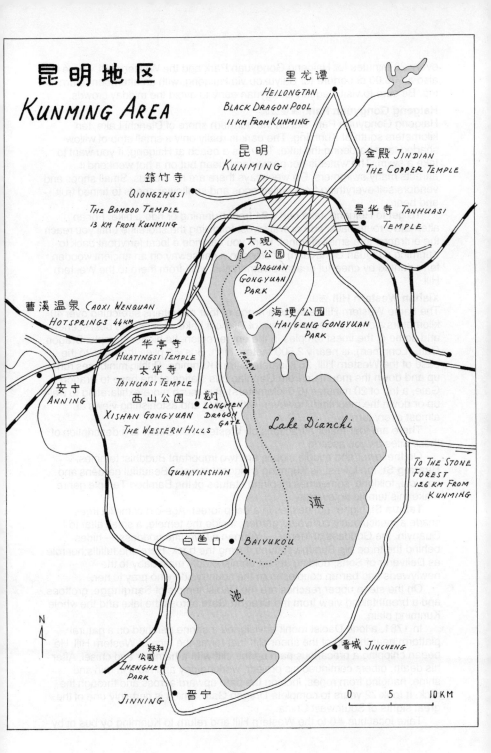

昆明地区
KUNMING AREA

黑龙潭
HEILONGTAN
BLACK DRAGON POOL
11 KM FROM KUNMING

昆明
KUNMING

金殿 JINDIAN
THE COPPER TEMPLE

筇竹寺
QIONGZHUSI
THE BAMBOO TEMPLE
13 KM FROM KUNMING

昙华寺 TANHUASI
TEMPLE

大观
公园
DAGUAN
GONGYUAN
PARK

曹溪温泉 CAOXI WENQUAN
HOTSPRINGS 44 KM

海埂公园
HAIGENG GONGYUAN
PARK

华亭寺
HUATINGSI TEMPLE
太华寺
TAIHUASI TEMPLE
西山公园
XISHAN GONGYUAN
THE WESTERN HILLS

龙门
LONGMEN
DRAGON
GATE

安宁
ANNING

Lake Dianchi

滇

GUANYINSHAN

TO THE STONE
FOREST
126 KM FROM
KUNMING

白鱼口 BAIYUKOU

池

N

郑和
公园
ZHENGHE
PARK

晋城 JINCHENG

0   5   10KM

晋宁
JINNING

every 20 minutes for Haigeng Gongyuan Park and the Western Hill. There is also an 08:00 departure for Baiyukou via Haigeng, with an afternoon return trip. Be sure to visit Daguan Gongyuan early to avoid the midday crowds.

Haigeng Gongyuan Park 海埂公园

Haigeng Gongyuan Park sits on the northern shore of Dianchi Lake, ten kilometers south of Kunming. The park is really only a small strip of willow-shaded land bordering the lake. There is a beach at Haigeng, if you want to take a swim. The water is not particularly clean but on a hot weekend it attracts many swimmers. On weekdays there are no crowds. Small shops and vendors sell everything from boiled eggs and sunflower seeds to tinned fruit and beer.

To get to Heigeng, take bus #24 from Kunming or ride a bike. For an alternative route back, ride or walk west following the shoreline until you reach the entrance to a small channel. Here you can ride a local ferryboat back to Kunming (Daguan Gongyuan) or cross to a causeway on an ancient wooden ferry punted by cheerful peasant women and walk from there to the Western Hill.

Xishan Western Hill 西山

The name Western Hill refers to a range of four mountains stretching over 40 kilometers along the western shore of Dianchi Lake. It offers the best scenery and some of the finest temples in the entire region. Its highest temple, Dragon Gate (Longmen), is nearly 2,500 meters high. Bus #6 plies the route to the base of the Western Hill, 26 kilometers from Kunming. Public minibuses run up and down the mountain from Gaoqiao bus station at the base to Dragon Gate, a trip of 20 minutes (6.5 kilometers). It is much more exhilarating to walk up or down the mountain, however, with sights and astonishing views at almost every turn.

There are four major attractions on Western Hill. Below is a description of these sites as you ascend.

On the lower and middle slopes are two important Buddhist temples. **Huating Si**, the lowest, is Kunming's biggest temple. Beautiful gardens and comical, folkloric, sometimes inspiring statues of the Bamboo Temple genre make this temple noteworthy.

Taihua Si, higher up, nestles in a deep forest. Age-old camellia trees shade a meticulously cultivated garden. Inside the temple, a small altar to Guanyin, the Goddess of Mercy — Yunnan's favourite goddess — hides behind the three big Buddha statues, facing the back. Here she fulfills her role as Deliverer of Sons, holding out an unmistakably male baby to the newlyweds and barren couples from the countryside who pray to her.

On the steep upper reaches are the Daoist temple of **Sanqingge**, grottoes, and a breathtaking view from the **Dragon Gate** across the lake and the whole Kunming plain.

In 1781, a lone Daoist monk envisioned a shrine perched on a natural platform near the top of the sheer cliff that forms the face of Western Hill. He began chipping a precarious path up the cliff with a hammer and chisel. After his death, others continued his project, working day and night in rain and shine, hanging from ropes, inching the path upward across and through the rock. It took 72 years to complete Dragon Gate, which is certainly one of the great sights of Southwest China.

Take local bus #6 to the Western Hill and return to Kunming by bus or by boat via Daguan Park. Board the boat at the end of the long spit extending into the lake at the base of the hill. The last boat leaves at 17:00, the last bus at 18:00.

Caoxi Si Temple and Hotsprings 曹溪寺

Bring your swim suits to Caoxi so you can rent a bath and relax in bubbling luxury. The temple, on the hill above the hotsprings, has several dozen unique statues, old steles, an intricate sundial and weather vane as well as the usual first-rate garden. Located 42 kilometers from Kunming near the town of Anning, the hotsprings can be reached by bus #18 or you may want to join a local tour group. For a change of pace, stay at the **Wenquan Binguan Hotel** ﹙溫泉宾馆﹚at the hotsprings. Beds are Rmb 6 each in a four-person room.

Jindian Copper Temple 金殿

One thing worse than a razed temple is one that has been hastily reconstructed to accommodate tourists in search of 'sites'. Make the forests, mountain breezes and pathways beneath traditional 'Heavenly Gates' the aim of your visit, not the awful buildings and plaster of paris 'antiquities'.

The original Copper Temple, at the top of the temple complex, was established in the early 17th century to honor the Daoist hero-god Zishi who was supposed to live at the northern extremity of the universe. In Chinese it is still known as the Golden Temple because, when first built, the burnished copper gleamed like gold.

Tanhua Si Temple 昙花寺

The attraction of Tanhua Si is the large park area with shade trees and covered pavilions. This place is a bit off the tourist track and a good place to go for some relaxation.

Lodging

Kunming Fandian Hotel 昆明饭店

Most tourists to Kunming stay here, an excellent place to exchange information and travelers' tales. Dorm beds in the main, highrise building are FEC 10 per night. Dorms are heated and comfortable, but can get noisy during peak periods. The old four-storey building also has dorms, but the hotel staff seems reluctant to rent them. This hotel has everything: CITS booking in the lobby; post office, mail, telephone and telex services; snack bar, disco and a good restaurant; gift shops; barber shop and beauty parlor; bike rental (outrageous at FEC 2 per hour); and taxi booking. Most services can be used even if you stay at a cheaper hotel.

Kunhu Fandian Hotel 昆湖饭店

This hotel has the cheapest beds in Kunming at Rmb 4 per night. This clean, spartan hotel is usually quite pleasant, but at times phone calls and noises, accentuated by the echoing hallway, can keep you up most of the night. Sometimes the toilets are clean, but other times the stalls back up with smelly piles of human waste. Equally inconsistent is the hot water heater, and the staff, though sometimes friendly, can be surprisingly rude. The service desk in the lobby sells bus tickets to Dali, the Stone Forest, and to local sites.

Sanye Fandian Three Leaf Hotel 三叶饭店

This renovated Chinese hotel is the newest place open to foreigners in Kunming. Beds in the second and fifth floor dorms are Rmb 5 each, and we found them much better than the dorms in the Kunhu Hotel. Double rooms with bathrooms start at Rmb 32. There is good laundry service and bike rental just outside the front door. The train station is a five-minute walk away.

Green Lake Hotel (Cuihu Binguan) 翠湖宾馆

The Green Lake, Kunming's closest approximation to a first-class hotel, was completely renovated and modernised in the early 1980s. Its 172 rooms all have carpeting, air-conditioning and television. The cheapest beds are FEC 10 in a four-bed room, but these are hard to get. The hotel has all services and two nice bars.

Chahua Fandian Camellia Hotel 茶花饭店

Though not as fancy as the Kunming Hotel, this hotel has fine double and triple rooms equipped with showers and television. Double rooms start at FEC 36. There are a small number of dorm beds available for FEC 7. The hotel offers a Western breakfast in the second floor lounge which converts to a bar at night.

Restaurants

Kunming offers travelers an amazing selection of restaurants at every price level. The cheapest food in town is found at street stalls and open-air restaurants. Many family-run *shuijiao* dumpling and noodle shops on Beijing Lu near the train station serve tasty meals for less than Rmb 1. Nearby are numerous fruit vendors. On occasion, restaurants set up in the alley just north of the Kunhu Binguan and serve a wide range of stir-fried meats and vegetables. Raw ingredients are stacked on platters, so you can easily choose what you want. Set prices beforehand.

Kunming might be the best place in Southwest China to blow your budget and have a nice meal, given the variety of nice restaurants specializing in unique dishes. The following restaurants are listed according to price, from cheapest to most expensive.

Yunnan Crossing-the-Bridge Rice Noodle Restaurant (Yunnan Guoqiao Mixian Fandian) 云南过桥米线饭店

In service for over half a century, this restaurant is among the most famous in Kunming. The specialty is Crossing-the-Bridge Rice Noodles, a delicious, inexpensive meal. Arrive early; this place is always crowded.

Olympic Bar (Aolinpike Canting) 奥林匹克餐厅

The restaurant is a bit dirty and the service is sometimes slow, but the food at the Olympic Bar, both Chinese and Western, is inexpensive and consistently good. Where else can two people eat Yunnan fried cheese, Vietnamese spring rolls, German beefsteak, salad and French toast for dessert, for Rmb 3 each?

Dongfeng Canting Restaurant 东风餐厅

Steam pot chicken (*qiguoji*) is the speciality here and the reason for the restaurant's high reputation. This dish is supposed to have all sorts of healthful properties as well as being one of the most delicious local offerings.

Beijing Fandian Restaurant 北京饭店

Common and rare dishes from north China provide an alternative to the good food of Yunnan. The large menu is adroitly cooked by a team of experienced chefs.

Kunming Hotel Attached Restaurant (Kunming Fandian Fushe Canting) 昆明饭店附设餐厅

This popular restaurant is located just to the east of the Kunming Hotel. It is under separate management from the hotel and has better cooks. It is noisy and sometimes crowded but serves a large variety of good, inexpensive dishes.

Green Lake Hotel Restaurants (Cuihu Binguan Fandian) 翠湖宾馆饭店
The Green Lake Hotel is well known for its good cooking. An army of over 80 chefs specialize in all of Yunnan's most famous dishes. There are two main dining rooms and two smaller ones. Regular meals are in the area of Rmb 15 per person.

Kunming Cooking School
If there was ever an overrated and overpriced restaurant with small portions and a dirty dining room staffed by ornery workers — this is it. A peek into the kitchen reveals egalitarian China, with all male chef's and all female dish-washers. Ostensibly this school teaches students the finer points of the culinary trade. As they say, those who can't do, teach.

Local Tours
Most popular sites in the Kunming area are a good distance from town, so taking local buses to see them all could take a week or more. Most Chinese tourists opt for convenient, and only slightly more expensive, minibus tours. Excepting the Western Hill, all sites take no more than two hours to see and are well suited for combined tours. The following companies serve the Kunming area.

Kunming Tourist Bus Service (Kunming Luyou Qiche Fuwu) 昆明旅游汽车服务

tour	destination	departure	cost (Rmb)
one-day	Caoxi Hotsprings and Western Hill	07:30	4.00
one-day	Bamboo Temple, Black Dragon Pool. Tan Hua Temple, Daguan Park and Copper Temple	07:30	4.80
one-day	Stone Forest	07:00	9.50 (minibus) 7.00 (bus)

Tickets are sold at the entrance to the modern supermarket across the street from the Kunhu Hotel.

Kunming Tourist Bus Rental (Kunming Chuzu Qiche Luyou Gongsi)
昆明出租汽车旅游公司

tour	destination	departure	cost (Rmb)
one-day	Caoxi Hotsprings and Western Hills	07:00	5.00
one-day	Bamboo Temple, Black Dragon Pool, Copper Temple and Daguan Park	08:20	5.00
one-day	Stone Forest	06:50	10.00 (minibus) 7.00 (bus)
two-day	Stone Forest	08:00	10.00 (bus)

Tickets are sold just south of the railroad tracks that cross Beijing Lu, next to the Sanye Fandian Three Leaf Hotel.

Taxi Tourist Bus Company (Kunming Shi Qiche Chuzu Gongsi)
昆明市汽车出租公司

tour	destination	departure	cost (Rmb)
half-day	Western Hill	07:40	3.50
one-day	Bamboo Temple, Black Dragon Pool		
	Copper Temple and Daguan Park	08:30	4.20
one-day	Caoxi Hotsprings, Western Hill	07:30	4.20
one-day	Stone Forest	07:00	10.00 (minibus) 7.00 (bus)
two-day	Stone Forest	08:40	9.30

Car with driver costs Rmb 60 per day (extra charge after 60 kilometers).
Tickets are sold next door to the Kunhu Hotel, on Dongfeng Xi Lu across from
the Department Store, and on Dongfeng Dong Lu across from the Kunming
Hotel. They also have Dali bus and minibus tickets which depart from the
Kunhu parking lot. The Kunhu Hotel also sells tickets at a premium.

Express Buses
Two express bus routes provide alternative transportation to the Bamboo
Temple, Dragon Gate, Taihua Si Temple and Huating Si Temple. Both routes
stop at 569 Beijing Lu across from the Kunhu Hotel and at the Yunnan Hotel.
Schedules do change; latest times should be posted at the bus stop. Buses
run every 90 minutes.

Transportation

Kunming Huochezhan Train Station 昆明火车站

destination	departure
Chengdu 成都	11:50, 18:35
Chongqing 重庆	06:55
Beijing 北京	08:25
Shanghai 上海	20:20
Guilin 桂林	20:20
Liuzhou 柳州	20:20
Hengyang 衡阳	20:20
Guiyang 贵阳	06:55, 08:25, 11:55, 20:20

Kunming Nanzhan South Bus Station 昆明南站

destination	departure	cost (Rmb)
Stone Forest 石林 (one-day tour)	07:30	23.00
Stone Forest 石林	13:30	3.50
Yuanjiang 元江	08:00	8.00
Simao 思茅 (two days)	07:30	23.00
Chuxiong 楚雄	08:25, 13:30	6.10
Xiaguan 下关	07:40, 08:00, 19:30 (night bus)	15.00
Xiaguan 下关	19:30 (Hungarian bus)	19.60

Kunming Xizhan West Bus Station 昆明西站

destination	departure	cost (Rmb)
Chuxiong 楚雄	07:30	5.00
Xiaguan 下关	06:30	13.20
		(Chinese bus)
	07:30	17.20
		(Polish bus)
Dali 大理	06:30	13.50
		(Chinese bus)
	07:30	17.50
		(Polish bus)
Lijiang 丽江	07:15	19.90
(two days)		
Simao 思茅	07:15	19.10
(two days)		
Jinghong 景洪	07:15	20.80
(2 1/2 days)		

Kunming City Bus Routes

bus #1: Dongzhan East Bus Station, Toudong Lu, Jinbi Lu, Main Department Store, Green Lake Park and Hotel, Xizhan West Bus Station.

bus #2: Huochezhan Train Station, Kunhu Hotel, Donfeng Lu, Main Department Store, Wucheng Lu, Xizhan West Bus Station.

bus #3: Train station, Huancheng Xi Lu, Jinbi Lu, Zhengyi Lu, Dongfeng Lu, Beijing Lu, Beizhan North Train Station.

bus #4: Qingnian Lu (at the zoo), Foreign Language Bookstore, Nanping Jie, Dongfeng Xi Lu, Renmin Lu, Huancheng Xi Lu, Daguan Lu, Daguan Park.

bus #5: Dongzhan East Bus Station, Huancheng Dong Lu, Dongfeng Lu, Kunming Hotel, Main Department Store, Yunnan Museum, Xizhan West Bus Station.

bus #6: Dongfeng Xi Lu at Renmin Xi Lu to Western Hill.

bus #7: Xizhan West Bus Station to Bamboo Temple.

bus #9: Beizhan North Train Station, Botanical Garden, Black Dragon Pool, Longtougai Village.

bus #10: Beizhan North Train Station to Jindian Copper Temple.

bus #23: Huochezhan Train Station, Beijing Lu, Beizhan North Train Station.

bus #24: Huochezhan Train Station, Beijing Lu, Huancheng Lu, Haigeng Lu, Haigeng Park.

The Stone Forest (Shilin) 石林

'The Stone Forest is the name given to an extremely rare geological phenomenon 126 kilometers southeast of Kunming. It is not a petrified forest but 80 hectares of karst limestone pillars in fantastic shapes that, from a distance, resemble a forest. About 270 million years ago, during the Permian Period, this area was covered by water. Later, due to shifts in the earth's crust, the ocean slowly receded while the limestone sea bed rose up to form a tableland. Rain and seeping water ate away at the limestone surface. The stone eroded in different places, causing fissures to open around small pinnacles. In time, acidic rain devoured most of the limestone, leaving the huge, isolated, but densely packed stone pillars that can be seen today in the middle of Lunan County. The Stone Forest, one of the main attractions of Yunnan, is the home of the Sani people, who make up a branch of the Yi tribe.

'There are several ways to reach the Stone Forest. Tourist groups travel there by private bus, but there are also numerous public buses bound for the Stone Forest every day. The most convenient public bus leaves from the alley directly west of the Kunming Hotel. The round trip costs Rmb 10. Tickets can be bought at the travel desk of the Kunming Hotel.

'The least known but most interesting way to get to the Stone Forest is to use a combination of train and bus. Early this century, the French built a narrow-gauge railway to link their colonial capital of Hanoi, in Indochina, with Kunming. It snakes across craggy mountains and lush valleys on its way southeast to the Vietnamese border, where it now terminates. Tourists can take this charming little train to the county seat of Yiliang, two-thirds of the way to the Stone Forest, and travel the remaining 36 kilometers by bus. Yiliang's bus station is on the left side of the main road just before the chief intersection as you walk into town.

'Train #501 leaves from Kunming's Beizhan North Station at 08:35 and chugs along at barely 40 kilometers per hour, allowing you to see some of Yunnan's most pleasant countryside. Small stations are built in French style, with painted shutters and steep roofs. After crossing a high, barren mountain pass, the train makes a big curve to the left. Far below, on the right, is Yangzong Hai, a wild, blue lake about 15 kilometers from Yiliang. A strong walker might want to alight at Yangzong Hai Station, walk down the sparsely inhabited mountain to the lake shore, have a picnic, then walk to Yiliang.'

***A Guide to Yunnan Province**, Patrick Booz*

Among independent travelers, whether or not to visit the Stone Forest is a controversial subject. Some find the dramatic stone pinnacles fascinating, while others feel their grandeur is far outweighed by the fake, tourist-site atmosphere that permeates all but the remote reaches of the area. Around every turn and over every bridge you meet a group of Sani girls, able to say 'this bag beautiful' in five languages, trying to sell handicrafts to any passerby. If you plan to visit the Stone Forest in a day, it is difficult to get far enough out into the 'forest' to avoid such scenes, and the seven-hour round-trip seems to be more trouble than it is worth. On the other hand, most people we met who spent the night at the Stone Forest had a great time exploring either before or after the tourist rush.

Lodging

Shilin Binguan Hotel 石林宾馆
This hotel stands at the entrance to the Stone Forest. Beds in dorms are Rmb 10 and double rooms start at Rmb 50. The hotel has a good restaurant and offers Sani song and dance shows each evening. Cheaper beds are available at a number of *lushe* hotels near the bus station.

Qujing 曲靖

Qujing was opened to foreigners in early 1986. A small city, consisting mostly of new buildings, there are no temples or other historical sites in town, nor are there many minority people, although a few Hui and Miao can be seen on the streets.

Why is Qujing open? One answer might be commerce. What looks like a large convention center is now under construction just west of town. Another answer might be to provide a convenient break on the Kunming-Guiyang rail line. Travelers who haven't spent time in a pleasant little Chinese city often find Qujing fascinating. Qujing can also be easily combined with a visit to the Stone Forest.

Things to do

The two parks in town are both new and bare because plants have hardly taken root yet. The main street from the bus station south to Wenchang Jie is the most active market area in town. Some of the smaller streets have old buildings, but they are rapidly being swept away by blocks of new apartments.

Tiansheng Dong Cave 天生洞

Considering the number of fine caves open to tourists in Southwest China, Tiansheng Dong was a disappointment. This cave is little more than a tunnel that works its neon-colored way through the center of a small hill. Nearby are two small reservoirs nestled in parched hills where you can hire paddle boats to do circles in the ponds.

Transportation to Tiansheng Dong is inconvenient. A morning bus leaves from the city bus station at 08:30 for the one-hour trip and starts the return trip at 11:00. An afternoon bus leaves at 13:00 and starts the return journey at 15:30. The buses are always crowded and very slow.

Lodging

Qujing Zhaodaisuo Hotel 曲靖招待所

The Qujing Zhaodaisuo is the only hotel in town officially open to foreigners. However, the hotel is often filled with official delegations, forcing travelers to make other arrangements. The cheapest beds are Rmb 4 in a four-bed room. Prices go up quickly from there.

Hongyan Luguan Hotel 鸿雁旅馆

Spartan two-bed rooms are Rmb 8 in this small, clean hotel. It is near the Zhaodaisuo.

Xuantan Lushe Hotel 玄坛旅社

This place is cheap and conveniently located in front of the city bus station. Chinese travelers usually try to get a room here first.

Restaurants

The Huimin (Muslim) Fandian Restaurant 回民饭店

They serve excellent vegetarian food, in addition to big steaks for Rmb 2 each.

Transportation

Qujing Keyunzhan Bus Station 曲靖客运站

Buses to all important cities and towns in eastern and central Yunnan leave from this bus station daily. Check at the station for departure times; most

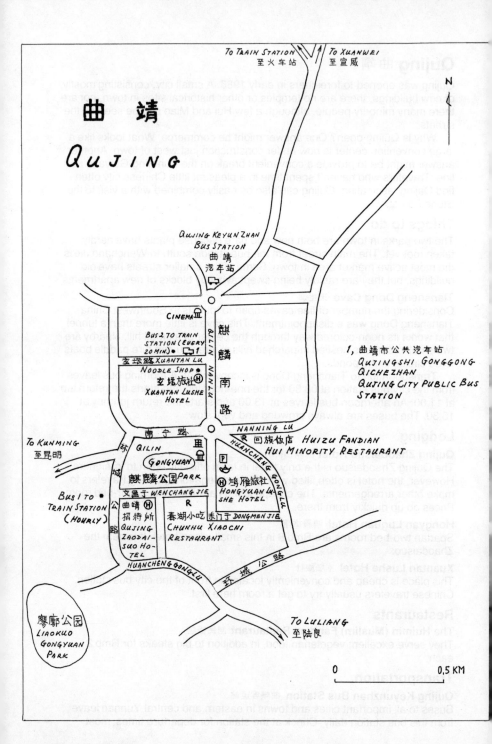

buses leave early in the morning.

Qujing Shi Gonggong Qichezhan Bus Station 曲靖市公共汽车站

destination	distance (kms)	departure	cost (Rmb)
Kunming 昆明	165	07:10−13:30 seven buses daily	4.60
Xuanwei 宣威	105	08:00,10:30 14:00,15:00	2.90
Luoping 罗平	133	07:20, 08:30	3.10
Qiubei 丘北	320	07:10	8.50
Shilin 石林 (Stone Forest)	113	12:50	3.20

Qujing Huochezhan Train Station 曲靖火车站

destination	departure
Kunming 昆明	03:30, 07:36, 10:40
Beijing 北京	12:03
Shanghai 上海	23:40
Chongqing 重庆	02:51

Yanshan 砚山

Yanshan is the overnight stopping point on the two-day bus ride from Baise in Guangxi to Kunming. The Sino-Vietnamese war has made this city a sensitive one, as it is only 100 kilometers north of the frontier. Police control is tight. If you are traveling towards Kunming on the bus, you may be able to pass through the town undetected by going directly to the **Yanshan Xian Xiangyang Lushe Hotel,** (砚山县向阳旅社) across from the bus station.

For those who want to risk exploring the town, the hill to the north with three small pavilions and a radio station is the best place to view the surroundings. If you show your camera in town, the Gonganju might find out and visit you at your hotel to demand your film.

Although they were not happy about our arrival, the Gonganju allowed us to continue our journey to Kunming. Travelers going towards Baise are likely to encounter more severe trouble. Officials do not want foreigners in closed areas that straddle provincial borders.

Xishuangbanna Dai Nationality Autonomous Region 西双版纳傣族自治州

Situated on China's frontier with Burma and Laos, Xishuangbanna is a 20,000-square-kilometer region of remote valleys between low, rounded mountains covered with dense jungle. The Mekong River (Lancangjiang) bisects Xishuangbanna, meandering through the jungles midway between its source high on the Qinghai-Tibetan Plateau and its mouth beyond Laos and Kampuchea at the southernmost tip of Vietnam. The jungles of Xishuangbanna are a biological treasure, holding one-quarter of China's fauna and nearly one-fifth of its flora.

Though much of the ancient history of the Dai people of Xishuangbanna has been lost, there are unquestionable links between them and the peoples

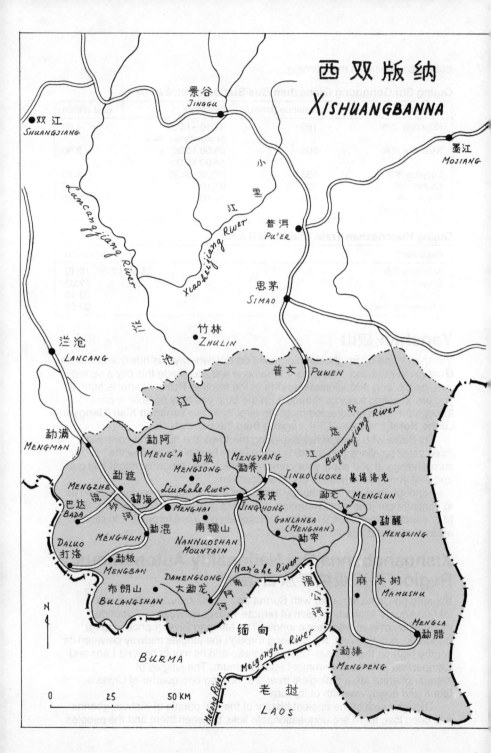

西双版纳
XISHUANGBANNA

景谷
Jinggu

双江
Shuangjiang

墨江
Mojiang

Lancangjiang River

小黑江

Xiaoheijiang River

普洱
Pu'er

思茅
Simao

兰沧
Lancang

竹林
Zhulin

普文
Puwen

Buyuanjiang River

勐满
Mengman

勐阿
Meng'a

勐松
Mengsong

勐养
Mengyang

基诺洛克
Jinuo Luoke

勐遮
Mengzhe

Liushahe River

勐仑
Menglun

巴达
Bada

勐海
Menghai

景洪
Jinghong

勐醒
Mengxing

Daluo
打洛

勐混
Menghun

南糯山
Nannuoshan Mountain

橄榄坝
Ganlanba (Menghan)
勐罕

勐板
Mengban

布朗山
Bulangshan

大勐龙
Damenglong

Nan'ahe River

麻木树
Mamushu

勐腊
Mengla

缅甸
Burma

勐捧
Mengpeng

Meilonghe River

Meilong River

老挝
Laos

0   25   50 KM

N

128

of Thailand. Tribute from Dai chieftains to the Chinese government began in the second century BC, and these records constitute the first written history of the area. For 400 years, Xishuangbanna was controlled by the independent Bai kingdoms of Nanzhao and Dali. The area became a permanent vassal of China after the fall of the Dali Kingdom in the 12th century. When the power of China's emperor weakened in the 19th century, Xishuangbanna became a pawn in a struggle between France and Britain for colonial domination. Jinghong was occupied by 500 British troops before both powers decided to leave the area a demilitarized buffer zone between French Indochina and British concerns in Burma and China.

The 20th century brought warlords and oppression to Xishuangbanna until Japan invaded China prior to World War II. Then the area was transformed into a transportation center as American cargo planes airlifted goods from India to supply China's isolated Nationalist forces. After the war and subsequent civil war, the remnants of the defeated Nationalist armies arrived in Xishuangbanna, fleeing the Communists in 1949. They escaped across the border to Burma where they eventually established small states and became dominant in Southeast Asia's drug trade.

'Liberation' of Xishuangbanna by PLA forces followed in 1950, bringing medical and economic advancement. But unstable government policies inflicted the region with periods of religious persecution, the imposition of Han Chinese language and customs, and discrimination against its ethnic groups. These tribulations alternated with periods of relative autonomy in local administration and religious freedom, such as exist today.

There are 12 of China's registered nationalities in the region, along with more recent Han Chinese settlers. They are the Dai, Hani, Yi, Hui, Miao, Zhuang, Bulang, Lahu, Wa, Yao, Jinuo and Bai. Some of these peoples live in very remote areas, but visitors to Xishuangbanna can hope to encounter at least half of them during the course of their trip. For those interested in the diverse ethnic groups of China and Southeast Asia, a visit to Xishuangbanna is imperative.

The weather in Xishuangbanna differs little from that of Thailand and Burma, with alternating dry and monsoon seasons. It is always hot and humid. Rain brings some relief, beginning in June, heaviest in August and September, and ending in October. The yearly rainfall averages 1,750 millimeters.

The Road to Xishuangbanna

The trip from Kunming to Xishuangbanna is slower, and definitely more spectacular, than the one-day trip from Kunming to Dali. The mountains along the route, though not particularly high, are so steep and numerous that the road seems to be a perpetual switchback. The road is paved but travel is slow. Terraced farms cling to the mountains where they can, and dense foliage drapes the steepest slopes with green. Near Jinghong, Xishuangbanna's capital, the vegetation becomes more tropical: large trees block out the sun, hanging vines and thick jungle conceal the contours of the land.

The bus trip to Jinghong takes two and a half days from Kunming. The trip could be completed in less time but bus schedules forbid this. You might reach Jinghong as early as 10:00 on the third day, if you are lucky.

You could easily hitchhike to Xishuangbanna in two days, provided you start early. To get a ride quickly, you must first get out of Kunming. Take the city bus #5 to its southwest terminus, transfer to a #12 county bus and ride it to its terminus. Get out on the road heading south, and you should have a ride almost immediately.

The four most likely stopping points on the route to Xishuangbanna are listed below, in order from north to south.

Eshan 峨山

This is the county seat of a small Yi Nationality Autonomous County, three hours south by bus from Kunming. Stay at the large **Eshan Lushe Hotel** on the main road in the center of town. Double rooms are Rmb 4, and cheaper beds are available in three-, four- or five-bed rooms. The restaurant on the ground floor is quite good. For a nice walk, try the streets behind the hotel heading away from the main road.

Yuanjiang 元江

This is the county seat of a Hani, Yi and Dai Nationality Autonomous County. There are several small hotels in town, so try to stay near the bus stop. If the proprietors will not let you stay, go to the **Yuanjiang Xian Zhaodaisuo Hotel** (元江县招待所) which is the hotel designated for foreigners. Beds cost Rmb 2 in a four-person room and the communal showers have hot water.

Yuanjiang is small but very active with people congregating at the park in the middle of town. The Yuanjiang River meanders gracefully past the town towards the southeast where it crosses into Vietnam and becomes the Red River, flowing through Hanoi and Haiphong before entering the Gulf of Tonkin. Those considering a trek through culturally rich, tourist-free minority areas could walk for days on trails along this river.

Mojiang 墨江

Mojiang is just a wide spot in the road in a Hani area. Stay at the **Mojiang Xian Lushe Hotel** (墨江旅社). Double rooms are Rmb 6 and beds in a four-bed room are Rmb 1.50.

Mojiang sits in the Ailao Shan Mountains above hundreds of rice terraces. These mountains, known as The Home of Clouds and Terraced Fields, are famous for their near-vertical terraced slopes, contoured by generations of Hani farmers.

Many inhabitants of this visually enchanting town are poor, even by Chinese standards. Beggars roam the main road looking for an unfinished meal or an occasional handout.

Simao 思茅

The largest town on the road to Xishuangbanna, Simao offers a wide choice of restaurants, snack bars, shops and noodle stands. Daily flights connect Simao with Kunming. Nearly everyone spends at least one night here.

There are two ways to pass a few hours in Simao. One is to go exploring on foot. The old, wooden town with cobbled alleyways and carved lintels is on a hill east of the main north-south road, living in another century from the bustling, dusty, modern thoroughfare. The other is to visit Plum River Reservoir Park (Meizihe Shuiku Gongyuan) seven kilometers southeast of Simao. Here you will find paddle boats, clean water and quiet surroundings — a good place to swim and relax.

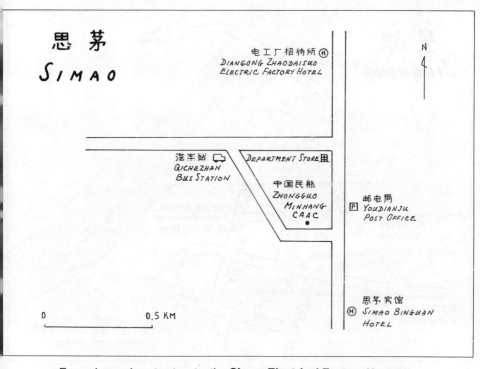

思茅
SIMAO

电工厂招待所 Ⓗ
DIANGONG ZHAODAISUO
ELECTRIC FACTORY HOTEL

汽车站 🚐
QICHEZHAN
BUS STATION

DEPARTMENT STORE ⊞

中国民航
ZHONGGUO
MINHANG
CAAC
●

邮电局
Ⓟ YOUDIANJU
POST OFFICE

N

思芽宾馆
Ⓗ SIMAO BINGUAN
HOTEL

0   0.5 KM

For a cheap place to stay, try the **Simao Electrical Factory Hostel (Simao Dian Gongchang)** (思茅电工厂) where beds are Rmb 1.50 each in a double room. More expensive accommodations can be found at the **Simao Binguan Hotel** (思茅宾馆) nearby. Most foreigners stay at the **Simao District Guesthouse (Simao Diqu Zhaodaisuo)** (思茅地区招待所) which has double rooms for Rmb 40, with private bathroom. There is a good dining room here.

Around Xishuangbanna
Jinghong 景洪

It is a good thing that Jinghong, more a modern town than a traditional village, is no longer the end of the line for foreign travelers in Xishuangbanna. It is now a convenient, central location where treks, bus or hitchhiking trips, walks or boat rides originate. The local guesthouse has a romantic bungalow atmosphere and is the ideal place to compose yourself after the bus ride from Kunming, sunbathe between walks or plan trips to villages, temples or forests in the area.

Things to do

The market in Jinghong that runs between Galan Lu and Minzu Lu might send you staggering away with the intention of never eating meat again. Flies swarm around freshly slaughtered animals warmed by the hot sun as blood and entrails flow into the open sewers. Business is competitive and bargaining lively. Avoid the butchers and make some good deals on locally

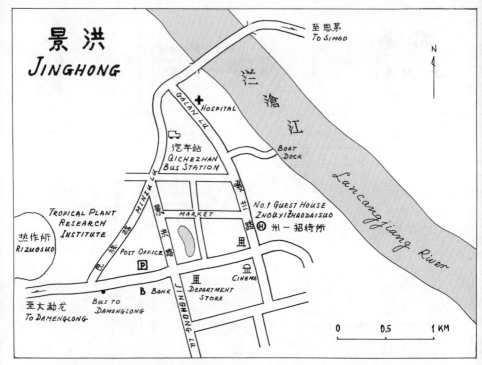

景洪
JINGHONG

至思茅
TO SIMAO

N

澜
沧
江

HOSPITAL

GALAN LU

汽车站
QICHEZHAN
BUS STATION

BOAT
DOCK

MINZHU LU

TROPICAL PLANT
RESEARCH
INSTITUTE

热作所
RIZUOSUO

MARKET

NO.1 GUEST HOUSE
ZHOUYIZHAODAISUO
州一招待所

POST OFFICE

P

B BANK

CINEMA

DEPARTMENT
STORE

JINGHONG LU

Lancangjiang River

至大勐龙
TO DAMENGLONG

BUS TO
DAMENGLONG

0   0.5   1 KM

grown fruit or custard-filled pancakes.

For a walk, either head towards the Mekong River for a refreshing swim or to any one of the villages south or west of town. Walk early or late in the day, reserving the hottest hours for a beer and a siesta at the hotel. If you like plants, visit the Tropical Plant Research Institute just west of town. Research is aimed at developing cash crops for the region, with much of the effort centering on local rubber trees. There is a large rubber plantation on the grounds of the institute.

Lodging

Diyi Zhaodaisuo Number One Guesthouse 第一招待所
This is the most popular place to stay in Jinghong. Beds in a four-bed room start at FEC 4 (though Rmb is sometimes accepted). More expensive rooms offer private balconies, toilets and showers. Avoid staying in the new concrete building; the beauty of the lush, tropical hotel compound is lost in this sterile five-storey structure. Food in the restaurant is quite good, but a bit overpriced. The restaurant does serve cold beer.

Tropical Crops Research Institute Guesthouse (Rezuosuo Binguan)
热作所宾馆
This small guesthouse located on the institute grounds offers travelers an alternative to the Number One Guesthouse. Beds in double rooms are Rmb 12 each and there is a small restaurant at the hotel.

Dai Minority House (Daizu Binguan) 傣族宾馆
This Dai hotel is officially closed to foreign guests, though a few travelers are

occasionally allowed to stay. Beds are Rmb 2.50 each. The restaurant at the hotel is said to be quite good.

Transportation

Two boats make the trip down the Mekong River to Menghan daily, one at 08:00 and one at 13:00. Tickets cost Rmb 1 and are purchased on board. If there is no fog and few passengers to be picked up along the way, the trip takes about two hours. In late spring, the level of the river drops and it becomes unnavigable. During this period, usually in late March and April, buses serve Menghan from Jinghong.

Buses run to Damenglong from the western edge of town at 90 minute intervals from 07:00—14:30 or so.

Jinghong Qichezhan Bus Station 景洪汽车站

destination	distance (kms)	departure	cost (Rmb)
Kunming 昆明	580	06:30, 07:00, 09:30	24.50
Simao 思茅	163	06:40,08:30,09:30, 10:00,13:00,15:30	5.40
Mengyang 勐养	34	07:00	1.00
Youle Shan 友乐山	53	07:00	1.50
Longpa 龙怕	71	07:00	2.10
Menghai 勐海	53	06:40,07:30,09:00, 11:30,13:30,14:00	1.50 50.00

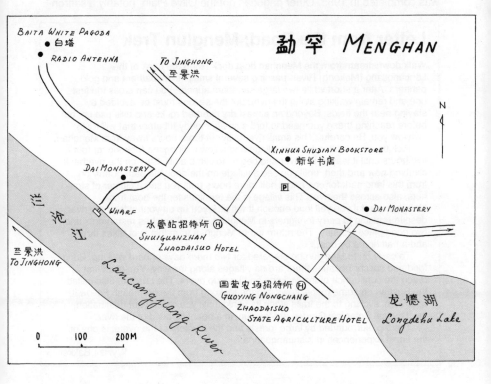

勐罕 MENGHAN

BAITA WHITE PAGODA
白塔
RADIO ANTENNA

TO JINGHONG
至景洪

N

XINHUA SHUDIAN BOOKSTORE
新华书店

DAI MONASTERY

澜沧江

兰景洪
TO JINGHONG

Lancangjiang River

DAI MONASTERY

WHARF

水电站招待所 Ⓗ
SHUIGUANZHAN ZHAODAISUO HOTEL

国营农场招待所 Ⓗ
GUOYING NONGCHANG ZHAODAISUO STATE AGRICULTURE HOTEL

龙德湖
Longdehu Lake

0   100   200M

133

Menghan 勐罕

Menghan lies at the southern terminus of the Mekong River ferryboat from Jinghong. It is a large Dai village of houses on stilts, dirt paths, temples and busy markets. There are two Dai monasteries in town, one near the boat dock and the other beside Longdehu Lake. They both house bands of young monks and appear more like forts or playhouses than pious places of worship. They are sparsely decorated with crude religious statues, but the lively monks make them worth a visit.

Traditional Dai houses comprise most of Menghan. They are raised on stilts and entered through a trap door, with bicycles, livestock, wood and furniture stored on the ground below. Their hinged walls open to capture the cool breeze and incidentally give the curious traveler a look into Dai life. Do not miss the market street filled with enthusiastic Dai, Hani and Han Chinese merchants selling fruit, vegetables and village necessities.

Ganlanba（橄榄坝）, the Olive Plain, is a large state-run farm bordering Menghan on the southeast. Plantations of fruit and rubber trees conceal several small, serene Dai villages. Explore the Olive Plain on foot by following one of the narrow shaded paths from Menghan.

On a hill overlooking the Mekong River just northwest of Menghan sits the Weijiang Baita Pagoda next to a large radio tower. Built during the 12th century, it was among the best extant Burmese-style pagodas in China until Red Guards blew it up during the Cultural Revolution. This less refined copy was completed in 1985. Other pagodas dot the Olive Plain, notably a saffron-

---

Letter from the Road: Menglun Trek

Walk downstream from the Menghan boat dock along the bank of the Lancangjiang (Mekong) River, passing several small fields, bathers and gold panners. After a short while two large sandbars appear; you can cross the first one and remain walking along the river, but the second must be avoided by staying near the fields. Beyond an almost dry riverbed rocks and hills rise up, but before reaching these you need to ford a small, muddy tributary that will try to swallow you. Be careful. This small river is about three hours away from Menghan.

Pick up a track after the next village and follow it along the Mekong for four or five hours until it leaves the river and begins to climb a hill. Stay on the riverbank, climbing now and then, until you see a village on the opposite bank. Carry on from this landmark for one and a half more hours until you see a cluster of straw huts, also across the river. This village is the terminus for the boat from Menghan, and if you yell loud enough it will pick you up on your side of the river, despite refusing to carry foreigners in Menghan. The village has restaurants and two good places to stay. The return trip to Menghan from this spot takes three and a half hours by boat.

To carry on to Menglun be prepared for two more days of hard walking. Bring food and succor because there are no villages along the way. You must first reach the confluence of the Mekong and Luosuo rivers. The Luosuo, also called the Buyuan on some maps, flows into the Mekong from the northeast. Follow it upstream, sticking to the trails along its banks until you reach your destination, the Tropical Botanical Garden at Menglun, in a beautiful bend of the river.

The trip, surrounded by large forests and the mystery of the rivers, is one of the finest experiences in Xishuangbanna.

Wyztze Bakker

colored one 90 minutes by foot southeast of town.

You could easily spend several days around Menghan exploring the banks of the Mekong River or smaller outlying villages that have little contact with foreign travelers.

Lodging

Ganlanba State Agricultural Hotel (Guoying Nongchang Zhaodaisuo)
国营农场招待所
Beds in this grubby hotel range from Rmb 1–2. Rumors of bugs and large, bold rats abound so be forewarned.

Menghan Pump Station Hotel (Shuiguanzhan Zhaodaisuo) 水管站招待所
This hotel is similar to the Agricultural Hotel in every respect.

Transportation

There are two boats daily from Menghan to Jinghong, one at 08:00 and the other at 13:00. Tickets are Rmb 1.20 each (more expensive because the return trip is upstream). Buses serve this route only in March and April when the river is too low for the riverboats. Hitchhiking along the main road that heads northwest towards Jinghong should be easy. The trip takes two to three hours.

Damenglong 大勐龙

Damenglong sits at the end of a dusty dirt road, 70 kilometers south of Jinghong and only eight kilometers from the Burma border. The road passes rice paddies, small villages, large trees and temples on its journey south. The

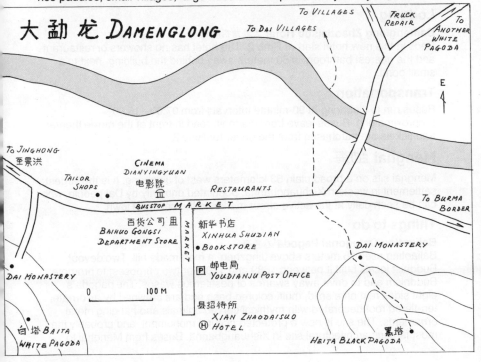

town itself is on the edge of a large farming valley, brightly colored by a diversity of crops. American cargo planes refueled at an airfield in this valley during World War II.

Damenglong is a Dai and Hani village. The small, slight Hani are recognized by their black tunics and skirts, silver jewelry and betel nut-stained teeth. Dai, Hani and Han Chinese merchants sell a variety of produce, traditional clothing and an occasional curio in a market on the main road that is larger and more cosmopolitan than those of Jinghong or Menghan.

There are three pagodas near Damenglong. The Baita（白塔）(White Pagoda), originally built in AD 1204, is perhaps the best Burmese-style pagoda left in Xishuangbanna. It is now made largely of cement, supported on two great concentric circular bases. Eight small stupas surround a taller, central spire. The Heita（黑塔）(Black Pagoda), just south of town on a hill, is a gaudy reconstruction of another Burmese-style pagoda. The view of Damenglong from the hill makes the climb worthwhile, regardless of the pagoda's inlaid mirrors, bright tiles and shoddy plaster work. On the way up the hill, the trail passes a Dai monastery filled with playful young monks, some of whom can also be seen in town smoking and shooting pool. The third pagoda lies hidden in a rubber plantation four kilometers away. To get there, follow the road southwest out of town, cross the river and go right at the fork in the road.

East of Damenglong, several large Dai and Hani villages are hidden by trees beyond the fields. Unspoiled by modern Chinese architecture, the stilt homes are shady and cool. We found the residents extremely friendly, and we were invited into a home for tea. Surprisingly, several people we met spoke a bit of English and many spoke Chinese.

Lodging

Damenglong Zhaodaisuo Hotel 大勐龙招待所
Beds in this new hotel start at Rmb 2. The hotel has no showers or restaurant and the nearest bathroom is 50 meters away behind the building, next to a small pond.

Transportation

Buses run to Jinghong at 90-minute intervals from 07:00−15:00 (approximately). Buses leave from the main road in front of the movie theater and tickets are purchased from the driver for Rmb 2.

Menghai 勐海

Menghai sits on a broad plain 53 kilometers west of Jinghong. It is the largest settlement in western Xishuangbanna, populated primarily by Dai people, who can be seen daily at the active street market in the center of town.

Things to do

Bajiaoting Octagonal Pagoda 八角亭
Bajiaoting rises 16 meters above Jingzhen, a man-made hill. Two devout Buddhist locals built it between 1689 and 1701 for two purposes: to promote Buddhism and to drive away swarms of pestiferous wasps. The pagoda's eight sides rest on a solid, multi-colored base and are crowned by an ornate, ten-tiered roof decorated with mythical carved animals and hanging metal ornaments. The site is now a protected cultural monument, and probably the most famous architectural site in Xishuangbanna. Buses from Menghai to

Jingzhen Hill depart daily at 08:30. Tickets cost Rmb 0.40.

Menghai Chachang Tea Factory 勐海茶厂
Menghai's mild climate and relatively high altitude (1400 meters) make it one of China's prime tea-growing regions. Specialties are *pu'er cha*, exported to Hong Kong, *tuo cha*, sold to France as a dietetic, and tea bricks sold to Tibet. Menghai's tea factory is now Xishuangbanna's largest industrial employer. Make arrangements to tour the factory through CITS because few travelers are allowed in unescorted.

Lodging

Menghai Xian Zhaodaisuo Hotel 勐海县招待所
Beds in this simple hotel start at Rmb 3. There are also rooms with private toilet and shower for Rmb 12. Reach the hotel by walking south for one kilometer from the main market street.

Banlacun Village 斑拉村

Banlacun is a traditional Hani village located in the hills 31 kilometers west of Jinghong. Its residents, easily recognized by their distinctive black clothing with silver ornaments and their rough, almost abrasive manner, pay little attention to foreigners in their village. Many travelers visit Banlacun, so you might have to hike further into the hills to find a village without other tourists.

Get on the bus from Jinghong to Menghai and tell the driver you want to get off at Banlacun. Tickets cost Rmb 1.

Nannuo Shan Mountain 南糯山

Nannuo Shan, the mountain home of both the Hani and Lahu minorities, sits south of the main road to Menghai, 35 kilometers west of Jinghong. To get there, take the Menghai bus to a dirt road that leads to the mountain. Tell the bus driver you want to go to Nannuo Shan; he will know where to let you off. The mountain is most famous for its King of Tea Trees. This six-meter giant of a tea tree is said to have been planted 800 years ago by ancestors of the Hani people. Scientists use the tree to support the theory that all the world's tea originated in southern Yunnan Province. The King of Tea Trees is eight kilometers south of the road at the end of a rugged track and a long flight of stairs.

Nannuo Shan is also known for its upland rice, a variety grown by Hani farmers that requires little or no irrigation. The Lahu villages in the area are found higher up the mountain beyond the tea tree and Hani villages. You can hitch a ride back to Jinghong by getting back to the main road early, or else camp on the mountain.

Mengyang 勐养

Mengyang, 34 kilometers northeast of Jinghong, is the home of the Huayao Dai, a colorful and distinct Dai subgroup. There are many villages near the town worth investigating. A spartan guesthouse on the main road has cheap beds.

Youle Shan Mountain 友乐山

Youle Shan, home of China's 12,000 Jinuo people, is a mountain area 19 kilometers southeast of Mengyang and 53 kilometers from Jinghong. Youle

Shan is the Chinese transliteration of a Jinuo name meaning 'place the Han (Chinese) cannot find'. The Jinuo occupy forty villages in the region and still practice slash-and-burn agriculture. They were only officially recognized as a distinct minority nationality in 1979, so aid to their impoverished villages is quite recent. Longpacun Village, 18 kilometers east of Youle Shan on the road to Menglun, is the site of the only remaining Jinuo clan longhouse.

Menglun 勐仑

Menglun is the easternmost settlement in Xishuangbanna open to foreigners. The town is on the north bank of the Luosuo River 110 kilometers southeast of Jinghong.

The important site in Menglun is the Tropical Botanical Garden, a research institute founded in 1958 that now boasts over 3,000 species of plants. This collection, one of the most extensive in the world, includes giant palm trees, aromatic camphor trees, mature bamboo groves, and ponds filled with enormous, boat-like lily pads. To reach the garden, cross the Luosuo River on the local ferryboat and walk to the entrance. Beyond the garden are many Dai and a few Yao villages. The territory beyond the garden is closed, but hitching or hiking and camping away from roads is possible all the same.

Chuxiong 楚雄

Chuxiong, 176 kilometers west of Kunming on the Burma Road, is the capital of the Chuxiong Yi Nationality Autonomous Region. It was opened to foreign tourists in 1986. Unfortunately, Chuxiong and its immediate vicinity are the only places that are open in this region. Unsullied Yi villages are not to be found here, but farther north in places like Dayao Xian County, still closed to foreigners.

The new section of Chuxiong is a bore, with wide, dusty streets and large, government-owned businesses. The older section of town, south of the new neighborhoods, still has many green-painted timber buildings once common in Yunnan. Small restaurants, barber shops and bakeries are numerous. The streets here are crowded and lively.

Our research trip to Chuxiong was frustrating. Though it is nominally their capital, the only Yi people we saw in town were 'professionals,' wearing matching costumes to entertain distinguished guests. Traditional Yi people, the friendly, grubby, slightly undernourished potato farmers, are elsewhere.

Things to do

Walk along Lucheng Nan Lu, the main road in the old section of town, with its diverse and colorful collection of shops. Chuxiong also has two parks; Xishan Gongyuan is the better choice.

We learned about (but did not visit) three temples that ought to be accessible from town in a day: Fayun Si (法云寺), Ziding Si (紫顶寺) and Huayan Si (华严寺). The people in the villages around these temples are mostly Han, but you might meet some Yi if you are lucky. We know nothing about the size or condition of these temples as no one we asked had been to them.

If you want to break the long bus ride from Kunming to Dali, Chuxiong is the best place to stop, but if you are looking for Yi who have not been heavily influenced and changed by the Han Chinese, you will have to explore areas that are still officially closed. Chuxiong is a good jump-off point to areas further north. If you can reach Dayao Xian without encountering difficulties from the Gonganju, head for Dabai Caoling, a 3657-meter-high mountain at the north of the county. It is a Yi stronghold where they hold their flower festival every year on the eighth day of the second lunar month.

Lodging

Chuxiong Binguan Hotel 楚雄宾馆
Beds in this first-rate guesthouse are expensive. When we visited Chuxiong, Tibet's Panchen Lama was in town so we were not allowed beyond the front gate. A hotel representative, though he would not quote prices, informed us that the hotel has a post office, a laundry service, vehicle rentals and a CITS office. One look through the gate beyond the armed guards into the inner compound was enough to show us that the Chuxiong Binguan is more appropriate for VIPs than for budget travelers.

Chuxiong Zhaodaisuo Hotel 楚雄招待所
Located in the center of the old section of town, the Chuxiong Zhaodaisuo is the best choice for independent travelers. Beds in a five-bed room are Rmb 2 each.

Longjiang Lushe Hotel 龙江旅社
Beds in this large, dirty hotel are overpriced at Rmb 5 each. Cheaper beds exist, but the staff is reluctant to rent them to foreigners.

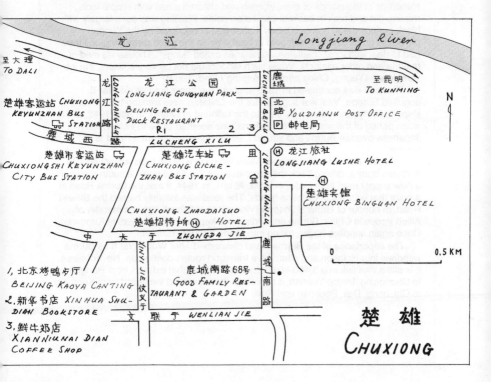

139

Transportation

Chuxiong Qichezhan Bus Station 楚雄汽车站

destination	distance (kms)	departure	cost (Rmb)
Kunming 昆明	176	07:30, 13:00	5.20
Xiaguan 下关	215	07:30, 13:00	6.00
Dayao 大姚	115	07:30, 13:00	3.40

The Burma Road

The Burma Road, that thin lifeline that linked China's besieged forces to the Allies during much of World War II, has now become legend. it crossed impenetrable jungles, precipitous mountains and bandit-infested wastelands for 1,154 kilometres, from Lashio in eastern Burma to Kunming in Southwest China. Allied soldiers and young volunteers from the West, with Chinese helpers, drove loads of medicine, food and war supplies in trucks and vehicles that quickly grew old on the Burma Road.

The Chinese began constructing the road in 1937 when war broke out against Japan. An observer at the time reported: 'The building of the road was an epic affair. To complete it in remote and jumbled high mountains and valleys in a matter of months, without benefit of modern machinery, was a marvel of work. Hundreds of thousands of men, women and children toiled with simple tools, moving dirt and rock in baskets carried on poles. Blasting was done largely with black gunpowder in bamboo tubes. Labor was conscripted by the Yunnan provincial government, which paid in food only. In the more distant regions they had to deal with local chieftains, sometimes called "kings". Thousands died of malaria and other ailments. While such labor could not be very efficient, the job was done.' (Young, *China and the Helping Hand*, 1963).

The road was completed in 1939 at about the same time World War II engulfed Europe. Vital war supplies for the Chinese were transported in Allied ships to Rangoon and then by train to the railhead at Lashio. In April 1942, at the worst period of the war when the Axis nations seemed close to victory, the Japanese overran Burma and seized Lashio, closing the Burma Road at its source.

Then the tides of war changed. Allied forces in eastern India advanced into northern Burma, driving back the Japanese. As the Allies pushed south they built a new supply road from Ledo, in India. At last, in 1944, it met the Burma Road at a point that was still in Chinese hands. The road was formally named the Stilwell Road, in honour of General Joseph (Vinegar Joe) Stilwell, the commander of Allied troops in China, Burma and India (who kept his headquarters in Kunming). Once again supplies began rolling into China through Yunnan.

The importance of the Burma Road diminished after World War II as Burma withdrew into isolation and alternative transport routes opened up. Nevertheless, it is still a vital link in a 3,400-kilometer road system that extends from Rangoon to Chongqing. Inside Yunnan, it serves as the main road westward from Kunming to Chuxiong, Dali, Baoshan and Ruili.

Chuxiong Keyunzhan Bus Station 楚雄客运站

destination	distance (kms)	departure	cost (Rmb)
Kunming 昆明	176	07:30, 08:00 14:30	5.20
Xiaguan 下关	215	07:00, 07:30	6.00
Dayao 大姚	115	13:30	3.40
Baoshan 保山 (two days)	433	07:30	11.40
Dukou 渡口	260	08:20	7.00

Chuxiong Shi Keyunzhan Bus Station 楚雄市客运站

destination	distance (kms)	departure	cost (Rmb)
Kunming 昆明	176	07:30, 13:00	5.20

The Bai

The Bai, with a population of just over one million, are the second largest minority group in Yunnan, after the Yi. They have a high cultural level, speak a language closely related to Mandarin and write with Chinese characters. In many respects they are hard to differentiate from the Han, yet their long, well-recorded and independent history clearly shows they are not Chinese.

Bai means 'white' but the origin of this name is not clear. It has nothing to do with skin color or the color of dress — Bai women wear brightly colored costumes. The Bai call themselves Speakers of the White Tongue or People of the White King, a possible reference to an early mythic ruler. The northern limit of the Dali Bai Nationality Autonomous Prefecture is a high ridge called Iron Armor Mountain (Tiejia Shan), the dividing line between the Bai and the Naxi. Common lore, often borne out by observation, states that there is a preference for all things white south of Iron Armor Mountain, while to the north black is favored. The Bai (and Pumi, another minority) both call themselves 'white', love bright colors and keep white sheep and goats. Beyond the mountain, the Naxi, Tibetans, Yi and others wear mainly black and dark blue, keep black domesticated animals and have names that derive from roots meaning 'black'. The point should not be stretched too far, however.

Dali, the ancestral home of the Bai, today has a population of †2,000. The site has been continuously inhabited since the late 8th century, when Dali was the capital of an independent kingdom named Nanzhao. At its height, Nanzhao conquered much of Burma, attacked parts of Laos and Thailand and repeatedly invaded China's Sichuan region in a border war that helped to weaken the Tang Dynasty. In 937 a Bai official usurped the throne and renamed his realm the Dali Kingdom. Although limited in size and might, this kingdom prospered and remained independent down to the middle of the 13th century.

It was then that Kublai Khan's Mongol armies conquered Yunnan in a carefully executed campaign that was part of a grand plan for the conquest of Song China. From 1253 onward, the independence of Dali, and Yunnan, was finally ended.

Patrick Booz

Dali Bai Nationality Autonomous Region
大理白族自治州

The narrow, fertile plain stretched out between the Cangshan mountain range and Erhai Lake was settled over 3,000 years ago by ancestors of the Bai people. In the eighth century, several small Bai states arose; they merged into the Kingdom of Nanzhao and, after defeating China's imperial army in 754, exerted considerable influence in Southwest China and Southeast Asia. The Kingdom of Dali replaced Nanzhao and kept its autonomy until Kublai Khan's Mongolian army defeated it in 1253. The Dali area has been under Chinese control ever since.

Taihe, the capital of Nanzhao, has virtually disappeared. Dali was established north of this site, surrounded by a city wall eight meters high with four large gates. Today, the North and South Gates remain, along with a large dirt mound on the west edge of town that was once the core of the wall.

Dali has maintained much of its ancient character. Houses are still built in traditional style: walls and floors cut from large stones, roofs decorated with stone or wooden gables, eaves and gables decorated with painted pictures. Fine masonry includes the high-quality local marble for which Dali is famous. The mild climate contributes to the beauty of the city where courtyard gardens are filled with a variety of potted plants and flowers.

The climate and beauty have attracted increasing numbers of travelers over the past three years. Dali is Southwest China's watering place: a trouble-free environment to relax and regain vitality before continuing on to other destinations. Life in Dali is convenient. A local grass-roots tourist association recognizes the need for low-cost services for independent travelers. It places English-speaking students from the Dali Number One Middle School Tourism Class in local restaurants, prints excellent bilingual maps of the area and organizes bus trips to the Shaping Market, among other things.

The budget travelers' grapevine has put Dali on the map. Recently, people have arrived for long visits, eager to take advantage of the pleasant atmosphere, low cost of living and indigenous marijuana. Once-quiet teahouse restaurants now serve a wide selection of Western food and double as discos at night. Dali appears able to absorb the influx of 'Kathmandu refugees', but many travelers lured to Dali by stories of an undiscovered paradise are angry to find this new group dominating local restaurants, the Dali Number Two Hotel and the bathhouse.

Things To Do

If you have money to spare, the streets of both Dali and Xiaguan offer interesting shopping, especially in the older neighborhoods. Walk through the lush, intensively cultivated fields east of Dali, or, in warm weather, visit the large rectangular reservoir just east of Dali for a swim and a nap. The brisk water is clean and the grass-covered levee surrounding it is surprisingly secluded.

Trekking in the Dali area is highly rewarding and brings you in contact with the traditional life of the Bai. The size of the Dali Bai Nationality Autonomous Region precludes comprehensive coverage. The following destinations are good for travelers spending a week in the area. People with more time in Dali can begin to explore the sites on the map that we did not visit.

Cangshan Mountains 苍山

This ridge of mountains shadowing Erhai Lake from the west has 19 separate peaks, with 18 streams cascading down through terraced pools to water the plain below. The mountain flowers are spectacular: camellias, cherry blossoms, lilies, azaleas, numerous kinds of cactus and many more. The highest peak, snowcapped most of the year, rises to 4,122 meters directly west of Dali and is marked by a television station at the summit.

To climb the peak, first locate a temple on a hill just west of town as your first landmark, then climb the next ridge to the north of it. Continue up this ridge, past a road, on the path to the peak. (Do not take the road, it stops far short of the peak on very steep terrain). This climb is a tough day's hike, often complicated by snow and ice on the narrow trail near the peak. There are no accommodations at the summit, but the crew at the television station sometimes allows late afternoon arrivals to stay the night. Regardless of the season, you will need food, water and warm clothing.

For an easier Cangshan hike, walk to Black Dragon Pool, a quiet mountain lake eight kilometers northwest of Dali.

Erhai Lake 洱海

Erhai, an ear-shaped lake 39.5 kilometers long and 6.3 kilometers wide, is one of the headwaters of the Mekong River. It gives prosperity to the region in irrigation water for the fertile fields nearby and a seemingly inexhaustable supply of fish. An aqueduct system built on stilts diverts lake water to high fields above the villages. We found delightful fishing villages on the northwestern shore of Erhai between Xizhou and Shaping, with sailboats, nets being repaired, boys with fishing poles and men rowing boats with their cormorants. The shoreline close to Dali is also lively and colorful.

For a boat ride on the lake, either pay a fisherman to row you out or take one of the ferryboats. The most popular ride is the 15:30 boat from Xiaguan to Dali. Spend your morning exploring the Xiaguan area on foot or by bike, then take the boat for the one-hour ride back (bikes are permitted). Tickets cost Rmb 1 each. There are boats from Dali to Xiaguan at 07:30 and 16:30, and an afternoon boat from Dali to Wase. Other boats run on an irregular schedule, such as the one from Wase to Shaping for the Monday Market. Schedules are not reliable. The 07:30 boat to Xiaguan and the 15:30 return are the only boats that seem to run consistently.

Chongsheng Si Santa Pagodas 三塔寺

These three white pagodas are among the oldest structures in Southwest China. The largest is 69.13 meters tall and was built by the Kingdom of Nanzhao in the ninth century. The other two, the North and South Pagodas, were built 200 years later and are 42.19 meters tall. All three were built using the 'earth stacking method', a construction technique using stacked earth terraces to surround a pagoda's foundation, providing a platform for further work. As the pagoda grew, the earth terraces grew with it, to be broken away only after construction was complete.

Recent renovations of the pagodas uncovered over 600 'cultural objects', the finest being a small wooden statue of Guan Yin and a Six Dynasties Period mirror engraved with supernatural beasts. Pictures of these relics hang in the small museum at the site.

View the pagodas from beyond a small reflecting pool 200 meters to the south. Several trails lead from this pool to a small village nearby where marble carvers work with ingenious cutting machines or carve the stones by hand.

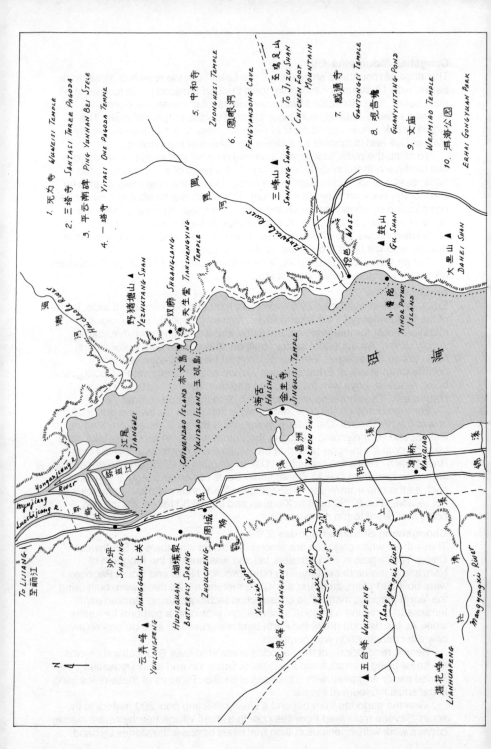

1. 无为寺 WUWEISI TEMPLE
2. 三塔寺 SANTASI THREE PAGODA
3. 平云南碑 PING YUNNAN BEI STELE
4. 一塔寺 YITASI ONE PAGODA TEMPLE
5. 中和寺 ZHONGHESI TEMPLE
6. 凤眼洞 FENGYANDONG CAVE
7. 感通寺 GANTONGSI TEMPLE
8. 观音塘 GUANYINTANG POND
9. 文庙 WENMIAO TEMPLE
10. 洱海公园 ERHAI GONGYUAN PARK

To LIJIANG 至丽江

Yonganjiang River 永安江

Myujiang 弥苴江 Luoshijiang R. 罗时江

SHAPING 沙坪

沙 SHANGGUAN 上关 SHANGGUANFENG

蝴蝶泉 HUDIEQUAN BUTTERFLY SPRING

周城 ZHOUCHENG

沧浪峰 CANGLANGFENG

Xiayige River 下义河

Wan huaxi River 万花溪

Shang yangxi River 上阳溪

五台峰 WUTAIFENG

莲花峰 LIANHUAFENG

云弄峰 YUNLONGFENG

N

Haoyu River 潮河

海 River 河 湖北

野猪塘山 YEZHUTANG SHAN

双廊 SHUANGLANG

天生营 TIANSHENGYING TEMPLE

CHIWENDAO ISLAND 赤文岛

YUKIDAO ISLAND 玉矶岛

江尾 JIANGWEI

海古 HAISHE

金圭寺 JINGKISI TEMPLE

喜洲 XIZHOU TOWN

溪

溪

阳

戊

Fengyuea River 凤雨江

凤

眼

三峰山 SANFENG SHAN

To JIZU SHAN CHICKEN FOOT MOUNTAIN

挖色 WASE

鼓山 GU SHAN

大里山 DAHEI SHAN

小普陀 MINOR PUTUO ISLAND

洱 海

湾桥 WANQIAO

溪

溪

溪

Mangyangxi River 茫洋溪

144

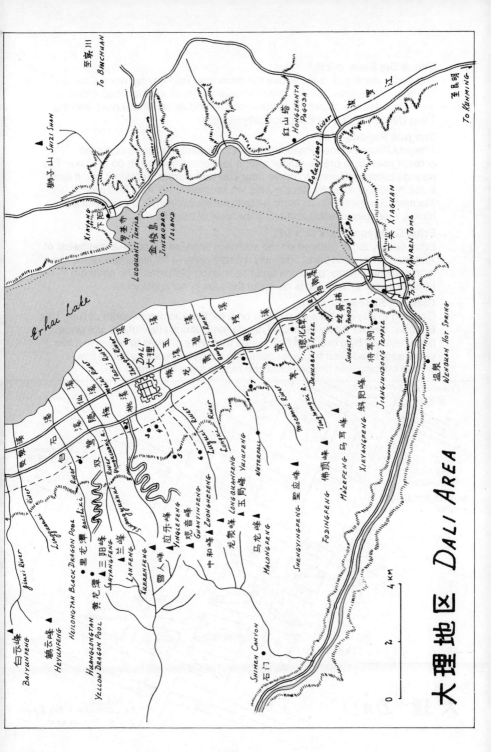

Dehua Bei Stele 德化碑

This badly damaged stele, above the main road half-way between Dali and Xiaguan, dates from 766. It marks the original site of the Nanzhao capital and once recorded the offices of its bureaucracy and its on-off alliances with the Tang Dynasty, but it is now practically illegible.

Sheguta Pagoda 蛇骨塔

Sheguta (Snake Bones Pagoda) is said to contain the bones of a giant serpent killed by a brave villager after it tormented fishermen on the lake. The pagoda is contemporary to those near Dali and stands 39 meters tall. It rests in the middle of a gently sloping field ten kilometers south of Dali near Xiaguan. Sheguta, with its large rectangular foundation, is a good place to have a quiet picnic lunch and enjoy the view of the lake.

Erhai Gongyuan Park 洱海公园

Erhai Gongyuan is situated on the southern shore of Erhai Lake southwest of Xiaguan. This public park, originally a game reserve for Nanzhao kings, has many new walkways, pavilions and observation platforms. The southern perspective of Erhai Lake is nice, but the park is not spectacular.

Gantong Si Temple 感通寺

Gantong Si sits amidst a pine grove on a hill five kilometers south of Dali. This Buddhist temple, badly damaged during the Cultural Revolution, has since been restored by a group of Bai monks who were allowed to return to it five years ago. In addition to prayer halls, the courtyard has a beautiful flower garden buzzing with the bees that the monks keep for honey.

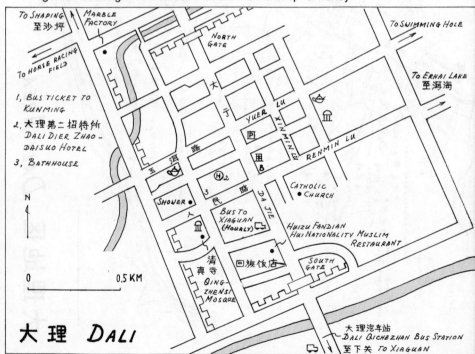

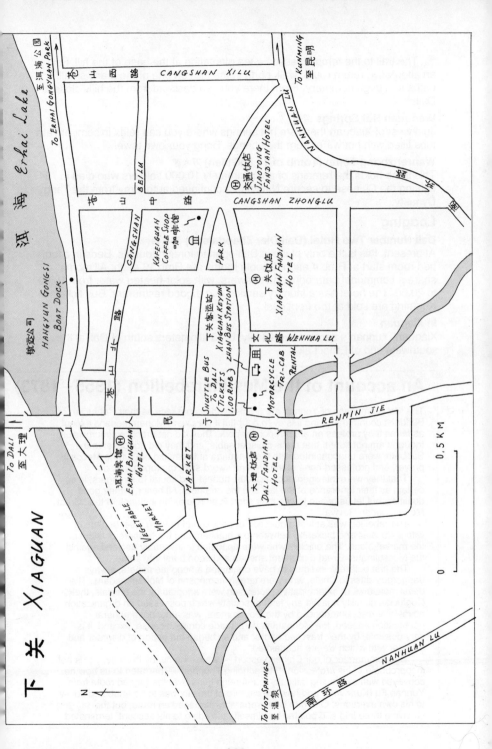

下关 XIAGUAN

洱海 Erhai Lake

To Dali 至大理

To Erhai Park 至洱海公园

To Erhai Gongyuan Park 至洱海公园

To Kunming 至昆明

CANGSHAN XILU

苍山西路

苍山中路

CANGSHAN ZHONGLU

NANHUAN LU

BEILU 苍山北路

CANGSHAN 苍山北路

铁运公司 HANGYUN GONGSI BOAT DOCK

KAFEIGUAN COFFEE SHOP 加啡馆

PARK

安通饭店 JIAOTONG FANDIAN HOTEL Ⓗ

下关饭店 XIAGUAN FANDIAN HOTEL Ⓗ

SHUTTLE BUS TO DALI (TICKETS 1.00 RMB)

下关客运站 XIAGUAN KEYUN ZHAN BUS STATION

MOTORCYCLE TRI-CAB RENTAL

WENHUA LU 文化路

洱海宾馆 Ⓗ ERHAI BINGUAN HOTEL

VEGETABLE MARKET

MARKET

RENMIN JIE 民

大理饭店 Ⓗ DALI FANDIAN HOTEL

NANHUAN LU 南环路

To Hot Springs 至温泉

N

0   0.5 KM

147

The trail to the temple passes a tea plantation at the base of the hill. For an alternative return route, walk north in the hills on one of the many small paths to a large cemetery. From there you can descend from the hills close to Dali.

Wenquan Hot Springs 温泉
Just west of Xiaguan there are hot springs where you can relax in semi-private tubs filled with hot water from the springs. Bring your own towel.

Wanrenzhong Tomb (Tomb of 10,000 Men) 万人冢
This tomb holds the remains of approximately 10,000 soldiers who died in 754 fighting the Chinese to secure Nanzhao's continued autonomy from the Tang Dynasty.

Lodging

Dali Number Two Hotel (Dali Dier Zhaodaisuo) 第二招待所
At present, this is the only place in Dali open to foreign tourists. Beds in a four-bed room start at Rmb 4 each. Double rooms are Rmb 16 each. All rooms share a communal bathroom and showers, with solar-heated water from 10:00 to 20:00. The hotel has a laundry service and a good restaurant. Bus tickets to Kunming are sold at the front desk.

In Xiaguan
Xiaguan, Yunnan's second largest city, is 15 kilometers south of Dali at the southwest end of Erhai Lake.

An account of the Muslim rebellion (1855–1873)

The Mohammedans of Yunnan are precisely the same race as their Confucian or Buddhist countrymen; and it is even doubtful if they were Mohammedans except as far as they profess an abhorrence for pork. They did not practice circumcision, though I am not sure if that rite is indispensable; and they did not observe the Sabbath, were unacquainted with the language of Islam, did not turn to Mecca in prayer, and professed none of the fire and sword spirit of propogandism.

That they were intelligent, courageous, honest and liberal to strangers, is as certain as their ignorance of the law and the prophets. All honor to their good qualities, but let us cease to cite their short-lived rule as an instance of the "Great Mohammedan Revival."

The rebellion was at first a question of pork and of nothing else, beginning with jealousies and bickering between pig butchers and the fleshers of Islam in the market place. The officials who were appealed to invariably decided against the Mussulmans. Great discontent ensued and soon burst into flame.

The first outbreak seemed to have originated among the miners, always a dangerous class in China, who were largely composed of Mohammedans. The usual measures of exterminative repression were adopted by the officials; their Confucian hostility against any faith or society which possessed an organization novel to or discountenanced by the Government, was aroused; a general persecution ensued; the Monhammedans made common cause, excited, it is very possible, by their travelled hadjis; and so began the period of disorder and disaster with which we are acquainted.

The commander of our Chinese escort — whose name, by the way, . . . is not inappropriate to his profession, "Hill-echoing Thunder" — narrated to us how he conveyed with exceeding difficulty four foreign guns over the rugged route from Yunnan Fu (Kunming), and how the capture of the city was to be attributed solely to his own exertions. One gun was irreparably damaged en route, but the surviving three laid and pointed by himself, according to his account, terminated

Erhai Binguan Guesthouse 洱海宾馆
This is the nicest place to stay in Xiaguan. Beds in this clean, comfortable hotel start at FEC 8 each in a four-bed room in the old building. The hotel has a post office and a CITS office.

Dali Fandian Hotel 大理饭店
This is the budget hotel in Xiaguan. Nothing fancy, but it is fairly clean and affordable at Rmb 2 per bed in a four-bed room.

Markets

Dali Sunday Market
Every Sunday, the streets of Dali overflow with a bountiful, active market. Old women sell cloth or hand-made clothing; young Bai girls sell traditional clothing, embroidery, or silver; old Hui men offer a selection of brass and silver pipes, Yunnan cigars and tobacco; fast-talking vendors purvey a variety of local snacks including red bean cakes and fried grasshoppers (delicious).

Shaping Monday Market
The barren hillside above Shaping, vacant six days a week, explodes with activity every fair-weather Monday. Rows of low tables line the dirt trails, displaying a range of wares equalled, as far as we know, only by the Sunday Market in Kashgar, Xinjiang Province.

In addition, livestock and poultry are commonly sold, as are hand-crafted furniture and many types of fruit. Barbers and a dentist using a pedal-powered drill solicit business from the large crowd, and owners of carts, tractors or

---

the rebellion. There seems no doubt that these guns, cast by French workmen in Kunming, were really the main cause of the Mohammedan surrender.

General Thunder told us, what was subsequently confirmed, that when the Mohammedans had surrendered and given up their arms, Tu Wen-hsiu, the so-called "sultan", and came into the camp of the besiegers, borne in a sedan chair, and inquired for Ma, the Imperialist commander. Being intoduced to his presence, he begged for a cup of water, which being given him, he said, "I have nothing to ask but this — spare the people." He then drank the water, and almost immediately expired. It appears that he had taken poison, which was suddenly brought into action by the water. His head was immediately cut off and exposed, and, heedless of his prayer — probably the most impressive and pathetic ever uttered by a dying patriot — the victors proceeded to massacre the helpless garrison and townsfolk.

The greater part of the able-bodied men, no doubt retaining some of their arms, succeeded in escaping; but a number of unresisting people, principally old men, women and children, fled from the city into the rice fields that border the lake. Hemmed in by the Imperialist pursuers, they entered the water, into which they retreated further and further; and being still pressed, were either forced out of their depth by the crush, or sought a refuge from worse ills in a voluntary death. The number of those who perished in this way has probably been greatly exaggerated. The foreign press puts it at from 3,000 to 9,000. General Thunder, undoubtedly an eye-witness, and probably a participator, told me, as we sat in the sunny verandah of the temple overlooking the scene of these horrors, that he did not think there could have been more than 500 corpses, or "the water would have stunk more." The gallant general was of opinion that Tu Wen-hsiu was a good and conscientious ruler, and respected even by his Imperialist foes; but for the Muslims generally, he professed much contempt.

Grosvenor, *Parliamentary Report: Mission Through Western Yunnan, China, No.3* (1878)

trucks earn their money by transporting goods and people to and from the market.

To get to Shaping from Dali, take the local bus that leaves on the hour from the bus stop on the main road just north of town. Several restaurants sell tickets on another bus, arranged by the Dali Tourist Association, that leaves at about 08:00. Many empty trucks pass Dali heading north, so hitching to the market is also easy. If you want a workout, rent a bike and ride the 25 kilometers to Shaping.

Festivals

Sanyuejie (Third Month Fair) 三月节
Originally a Buddhist holiday, Sanyuejie evolved into a huge fair where rare and prized goods, such as herbs or horses, were sold to both local and out-of-town customers. Tang Dynasty officials came to obtain battle horses for the imperial army. In addition to the lively and varied commerce, horse races, Bai operas, cross-bow competitions and folk dancing are held. Sanyuejie begins on the 15th day of the third lunar month and lasts for seven days.

Walking in Hills and Woods Festival (Raoshanlin Jie) 绕山林节
This celebration is to pray for an abundant harvest. Villagers form a long procession, dancing and singing their way to three local temples in their best festival attire. The procession worships gods at Shengyuan Si Temple, fairies at Jingui Si Temple and Buddhas at Chongsheng Si Temple. Raoshanlin begins on the 23rd day of the fourth lunar month and lasts for three days.

Torch Festival (Huoba Jie) 火把节
During this festival every household prepares torches, lighting them after nightfall to see out the old year. After blessing their homes and loved ones with the fire, parades of people with burning torches enter the fields to drive away harmful insects and, by association, all evils in the region. By day there are dragon boat races, then fireworks displays. The festival falls on the 24th day of the sixth lunar month.

Transportation

Xiaguan Keyunzhan Bus Station 下关客运站

destination	distance (kms)	departure	cost (Rmb)
Kunming 昆明	399	07:00	13.00, 15.00*
		19:00	15.00, 20.00*
Chuxiong 楚雄	214	07:30	6.00
Lijiang 丽江	203	07:00, 07:30, 11:00	5.70
Simao 思茅	600		16.80
(three days)			
Dukou 渡口	332	07:00	9.30
Binchuan 宾川	70		1.50
Jianchuan 剑川	128		3.60
Zhongdian 中甸	309	07:00	8.70

Buses north from Xiaguan to Lijiang, Zhongdian or Jianchuan pass through Dali 20 minutes after leaving Xiaguan. You can buy tickets for these buses at the Dali Bus Station. For destinations south or east, you must take the local bus to Xiaguan and board your bus at the Xiaguan Keyunzhan Bus Station.
* These higher prices are for Polish or Hungarian buses.

Jizushan Chickenfoot Mountain 鸡足山

During the Ming Dynasty, there were 369 shrines, 72 monasteries or temples and over 3,000 monks living and worshiping on this Buddhist holy mountain. As early as the Tang Dynasty, the Chinese monk Jia Ye visited it on his return from a pilgrimage to India. Marco Polo visited Chickenfoot Mountain 500 years later, and through the centuries representatives from Buddhist countries all over Asia came to live there.

Unfortunately, almost everything was destroyed during the Cultural Revolution. Only four temples and fewer than 40 monks and nuns remain today.

Chickenfoot Mountain, so named because its ridges look like a giant chicken's foot when viewed from the peak, is about 20 kilometers northwest of Wase, which is on the eastern shore of Erhai Lake. The entire mountain, abundant in spring-fed creeks and wildlife, is today a protected forest.

Zhusheng Si (Sacred Wish Temple) (祝圣寺) was the main complex of the mountain. It is about one hour's walk up from the bus stop at the base. This large complex of buildings, gardens, pools and shrines is where most of the monks and nuns now live. The main hall is still being restored. In small, private rooms you can see a marble bodhisattva, some Tibetan thankas and Ming-Dynasty bronze pots that survived Red Guard raids. If you get the chance, taste some of the vegetarian food the monks serve. You can stay the night here, though the accommodations at Jinding are preferable.

Zhongshan Si (中山寺) is a newly rebuilt temple half way up the mountain. Marble, fresh paint and little else can be seen here but the friendly monks might offer you tea or candy.

Huashoumen Gate (华首门) is the third surviving temple and marks the beginning of the steep climb to the top. There is nothing remarkable in this newly rebuilt temple, but the view behind it of Jinding (Golden Summit) is spectacular. A trail leading down from this site looks as if it heads back towards Erhai Lake to the southeast, but we did not try it.

Jinding (金顶), Golden Summit, is 3,240 meters high, topped by a 13-storey Tang-Dynasty pagoda which rises another 50 meters into the air. The pagoda has stairs to a balcony and rusty steel rungs inside to the top, if you trust them. From Jinding you can see Erhai Lake, Cangshan and the distant Jade Dragon range (Yulongshan) with its massive snow peak, near Lijiang to the north. The best time to be at the summit is sunrise, so it is preferable to climb the peak and spend the night at the top before descending the next day. Bring protection from gusting winds on the peak. There are two dormitories at Jinding and a restaurant serving basic food.

The trek to Chickenfoot Mountain takes four or five days.

Day 1: Take the afternoon boat from Dali to Wase, on the eastern shore of Erhai Lake. Wase has neither hotels nor restaurants, so bring your own food and camping gear. You might be able to stay at the Renminzhengfu Government Building.

Day 2: Starting early, walk east from Wase past a small village and on to Shazhi Village (沙止). Here, follow the valley northeast to its end, climb the ridge ahead and follow it, always heading towards the northeast. Eventually, you will cross a ridge crest and see the Jinding summit. We made it this far with less information. More detailed notes are available if you find our lost black notebook somewhere in this vicinity. Camp on the north side of the creek at the base of Chickenfoot Mountain.

Day 3: There is a trail behind the first village you pass which leads up the mountain. Visit the three temples and stay overnight at the peak.

Day 4: Descend to Zhusheng Si and then on to the bus station at the base of the mountain. To return to Dali by bus, you must first ride a local bus to Binchuan, 30 kilometers to the south. Once in Binchuan, buy a bus ticket to Xiaguan (the last bus leaves around 13:00). If you cannot get a ticket until the following day, stay at the hotel near the bus station or wait until the Gonganju officers arrive and escort you to another hotel.

You could try to hitchhike or take a bus from Xiaguan to Chickenfoot Mountain, but your chances are not good of getting by the Gonganju in Binchuan, where you have to board the local bus going to the mountain. If you trek to the mountain and ride the bus back, the Gonganju can do nothing but help you find a hotel and a quick ticket out of town.

Lijiang 丽江

Lijiang, a rugged and isolated town, is the center of China's Naxi minority. The town sits in a wide valley that rises steadily from lush, fertile fields at the south end to a high, lifeless desert in the north. The Naxi say that every step northward gains the height of one egg. The surrounding mountains are equally varied: low and rounded to the south and east with glaciated giants like the Yulongshan (Jade Dragon Mountain) towering 5,596 meters high to the north. Joseph Rock, an American botanist/explorer who lived in Lijiang during the 1930s, marveled at the diversity of flora and fauna in the region.

The old section of Lijiang has been the Naxi home for hundreds of years and life along its cobblestone walkways and fast-flowing canals goes on as it always has. The new, northern section of Lijiang, divided from the old city by Lion Hill, is populated mostly by Han Chinese and made up of the same dreary cement buildings and straight roads found everywhere in China.

Lijiang was once a diverse city, filled with Tibetan traders who profited from a brisk business between China and Tibet. The Naxi acted as middlemen on the trade route from Kunming to Lhasa until roads built in the 1950's bypassed the region. The local Nyingma sect (Red Hat) Tibetan monasteries, once inhabited by both Tibetan and Naxi monks, show the strong influence of Tibetan culture here. During World War II, an Allied airfield in the Lijiang valley refueled American planes flying supplies to the desperate Chinese 'over the Hump' from Burma. Much of the pidgin English spoken by older people dates from this period.

The vastness of the Lijiang valley and the grandeur of the mountains make the area a perfect destination for travelers interested in camping or trekking. In addition to Naxi settlements, there are Yi villages in the mountains. Unlike Dali, Lijiang does not yet receive a flood of travelers.

Things to do

The old Naxi section of town with its picturesque wooden buildings, three fast-flowing canals used for washing clothes, vegetables and children, and busy markets might keep you in Lijiang for days.

At the north end of town, Black Dragon Pool Park (Heilongtan Gongyuan) has a small lake (which periodically goes dry) and interesting, old temple buildings that now display exotic plants, calligraphy and paintings. The

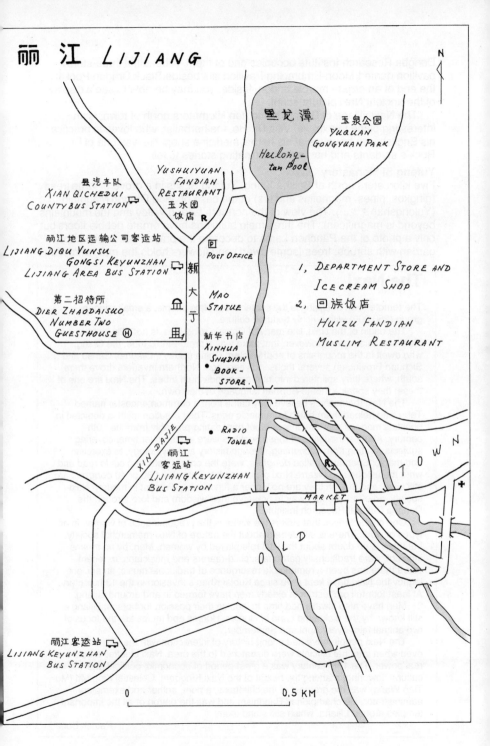

丽江 *LIJIANG*

黑龙潭

玉泉公园
YUQUAN GONGYUAN PARK

Heilong-tan Pool

县汽车队
XIAN QICHEDUI COUNTY BUS STATION

玉水园饭店
YUSHUIYUAN FANDIAN RESTAURANT
R

丽江地区运输公司客运站
LIJIANG DIQU YUNSU GONGSI KEYUNZHAN LIJIANG AREA BUS STATION

P
POST OFFICE

新大子

第二招待所
DIER ZHAODAISUO NUMBER TWO GUESTHOUSE H

MAO STATUE

新华书店
XINHUA SHUDIAN BOOK- STORE.

1, *DEPARTMENT STORE AND ICECREAM SHOP*

2, 回族饭店
HUIZU FANDIAN MUSLIM RESTAURANT

RADIO TOWER

丽江客运站
LIJIANG KEYUNZHAN BUS STATION

XIN DAJIE

R 2

MARKET

O L D   T O W N

丽江客运站
LIJIANG KEYUNZHAN BUS STATION

0   0.5 KM

N

Dongba Research Institute occupies one of them. A beautiful three-storey pavilion named Moon-Embracing Pavilion sits beside Black Dragon Pool at the end of an ornate marble bridge. Inside, you may be able to see a display of the ancient Naxi picture-script.

The Naxi village of Baisha Xiang, ten kilometers north of town, is an interesting place to explore. Visit Dr. Ho, the herbalist, who loves to practice his English with travelers at his herbal medicine shop. He was one of Dr. Rock's students and has many fascinating stories to tell.

Yufeng Si Monastery 玉峰寺

Five kilometers north of Baisha Xiang, Yufeng Si sits in a grove of large trees (gingkos, pines, magnolias and firs) at the base of Jade Dragon Mountain (Yulongshan玉龙山). The view of the northern Lijiang valley and the mountains beyond is magnificent. The three main buildings have ornate pebble floors but only a photo of the Panchen Lama to decorate the prayer hall. A well-kept garden with shrubs, trees (some dwarf) and flowers holds the main attraction

The Naxi

The remote town of Lijiang is the center of the Naxi people, a small minority group (250,000) with a richly textured culture.

The origin of the Naxi, like many of China's minorities, is not fully known. Most scholars agree, however, that there was a proto-ethnic tribe, the Qiang, who dwelt in the mountains of northwestern China (today's Qinghai, Gansu and Sichuan Provinces) several thousand years ago. Northern invaders drove them south, where they splintered into numerous individual tribes. The Naxi are one of these; they speak a Tibeto-Burman language of their own.

The Naxi themselves believe they came from a common ancestor named Tabu who helped them hatch from magic eggs. Their creation myth is depicted in booklets made of resilient, insect-proof bark dating probably from the 10th century. About a thousand of these booklets were written over time, covering subjects ranging from accounting, through history and mythology, to exorcism and magic. Shamans, called *dongbas*, were the only people who could read and write the unique and bizarre Naxi picture-script. Only about 30 or 40 *dongbas* are still alive, and though they are no longer a functioning element in modern Naxi society, an effort is under way to preserve their wisdom and lore through the Dongba Cultural Research Institute.

One characteristic that strikes the visitor is the predominance of women in all types of work. There is still debate about the nature of Naxi matriarchal society, but there is no doubt about the vital role played by women. Men, by no means indolent, were traditionally gardeners, child-rearers and musicians. In recent years there has been a remarkable resurgence of traditional music, an ancient legacy the Naxi have kept alive since Kublai Khan's invasion in the 13th century. At least four full orchestras of elderly men have formed in and around Lijiang.

Men have also always had time to indulge their passion for horses; Lijiang is still known by the nickname Land of Horses. Horses and mules are the focus of two animal fairs every April and September.

The Naxi people have had a long history of interaction with the Chinese, but even when imperial officials were dispatched to the area, Naxi chieftains held the real power. The 17th century was a great period of economic, political and cultural flowering, marking the height of the Naxi Kingdom. Celestial King Mu (Mu Tian Wang) was the greatest of the chieftains, a poet, author and exemplary administrator. He championed Buddhism and was the patron of all the important temples around Lijiang, which still stand today.

Patrick Booz

of this monastery, a 500-year-old camellia tree that blooms four months out of the year, beginning in late February or early March, producing over 4,000 blossoms. The tree, originally two small trees, is said to represent the virtuous relationship between husband and wife.

If you are hungry after your trip, a monk will serve tea, walnuts and bin-bin (locally made cornbread) with honey gathered from his bees. There is no set price; the monk prefers to accept whatever you feel is appropriate.

Getting to Yufeng Si is time-consuming any way you go. Walking takes at least three hours each way. If the wind is not too strong, a bike ride is the best solution. A visit to both the monastery and Baisha Xiang takes most of the day. If you want to speed things up, rent a *tuolaji* tractor for about Rmb 3 per hour. This way five people can see Yufeng Si, Baisha Xiang and Fuguo Si Monastery much faster than the trip would take by bike, at about the same cost. To rent a *tuolaji*, simply find one in the streets and ask the driver if he will take you.

Mandalas

If you visit any Tibetan monasteries, look for mandalas, the magical circles of Tibetan Buddhism. You will most likely find one painted on a thangka. The circular design will perhaps show a heavenly city with four squared-off entrances. If you are lucky, you may see surviving frescoes with circular designs, some quite abstract, still recognisable on the walls. Mandals are graphic, geometric representations of the cosmos — psychocosmograms — symbolizing the order and harmony achieved by a truly enlightened mind. Mandalas have great power, being seen as concentrated areas where the forces of the universe are gathered (*manda* means 'essence', while *la* means 'container').

The design is symmetrical, based on circles and squares, with a central focal point. In Tantric Buddhism, where the mandala is used to support meditation, adepts seek to absorb its power. Sometimes a mandala takes the form of an elaborate, four-gated city — a 'palace of knowledge' — which the practitioner mentally enters in order to achieve a state of mystical unity with the Buddha.

Although not created primarily to please the eye, mandalas are often works of art with great stylistic elegance and beauty. They are most frequently displayed on thangkas but some of the grandest were painted on the walls of temples and monasteries. At a few of the bigger monasteries, the monks still create magnificent mandalas made of colored sand.

Two important buildings from Fuguosi have been transfered *in toto* to Black Dragon Pool in Lijiang. They are the library and the flamboyant Wufenglou (Five Phoenix Hall).

Puji Si Monastery 普济寺
Puji Si sits in the hills five kilometers northwest of town. Founded in the 18th century, it housed 70 lamas by 1900. The monastery was reportedly razed in 1958, making it a casualty of the Tibetan conflict rather than the Cultural Revolution. There are three lamas at Puji Si today, all eager to let travelers in and show them around.

To get there, ride a bike or walk west out of town on the road in front of the Diyi Zhaodaisuo Hotel. The road will narrow and twist to the north. Two kilometers from town, the road passes a large brick prison on the left. Turn left on the dirt road just beyond the prison and follow it west past two irrigation ponds to the village of Pujicun at the base of the hills. The monastery is a 20-minute walk up a trail from the village.

Fuguo Si Monastery 福国寺

This monastery, built in the mid-1600s, was once the largest in the Lijiang area. A fort-like shell perched above the northern Lijiang valley is all that remains. The beautiful foliage in the area alone is worth the one-hour walk from Baisha Xiang.

Wenbi Si Monastery 文笔寺

This beautiful Ming-Dynasty monastery sits high above Lijiang to the southwest below a conical peak. The main hall, in a tree-lined meadow, was badly damaged in the past but locals will not say when. At its zenith, the monastery had 90 lamas, 20 of whom lived in separate houses around the main prayer halls among the old camellia trees that produced thousands of flowers annually. The forest nearby was also much larger then. The main halls remain, but they are all badly damaged. The two lamas still living at the monastery will show you around and point you to the trail further up the mountain.

Not far above the monastery, hidden by a grove of very old trees, a natural spring flows from the ground between tree roots to form small pools. The water is extremely cold and pure. The lamas protect this old grove by telling locals that the spring (which feeds the stream that waters their crops) will dry up if they cut down the trees.

Two kilometers above the spring are the ruins of an old monk's retreat. The retreat was built to honour an ascetic monk who spent his life secluded

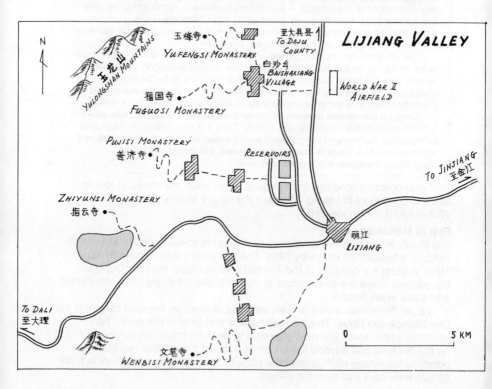

without food or clothing in a cave nearby. This monk spent his life meditating and, in old age, wrote a book describing his experiences. Young novice monks were closed into rooms alone at the retreat for three years, three months and three days to study this book. Upon completion of their studies, the novices were honored by large parties arranged by family members from Lijiang. Crumbling walls and a large foundation are all that remain of the retreat. The view of the valley from this southern perspective is quite beautiful.

To reach Wenbi Si, bike out of Lijiang on the road to Dali. Either turn left 300 meters beyond the bus station (just past a logging company) or cross the valley on the road to Dali and take the left trail nearest the hills through a collection of small villages. The ride up the mountain takes at least two hours, but the downhill ride back takes less than one.

Zhiyun Si Monastery 指云寺
We did not get to this place ourselves and our placement of it on the maps is an approximation based on what various people told us. To get there, hitchhike on the road to Dali until you see Lashi Hu Lake (Lenghai Lake), at which point you should get out and walk to Lashiba. Zhiyun Si has been converted into a school for the children of this town.

Farther Away

Jianchuan 剑川
Overlooking Jianchuan is Jinhua Shan, a mountain dotted with small temples and a single pagoda. Of note on Jinhua Shan are the figures of a Nanzhao general and a reclining Buddha carved on beautiful red stones.

To get there, take the bus to Jianchuan and walk west to the mountain which is two kilometers away across a field. Get out of town quickly as Jianchuan is not open to foreigners. If the bus station in Lijiang will not sell you tickets, hitchhike first to Baihanchang and then to Jianchuan. If you plan to visit Dali before Lijiang, take the morning bus from Dali and jump off in Jianchuan. Explore the mountain and be back on the main road by 15:00 to flag down an afternoon bus from Dali to Lijiang.

Shigu (Stone Drum Village) 石鼓
Shigu stands at the famous First Bend of the Yangzi River, where the mighty torrent turns north on itself toward the entrance to Tiger Leaping Gorge.

The village is named after a large marble tablet shaped like a drum. The work commemorates the victory of a Naxi army over 200,000 Tibetans in a bloody battle in 1548. Another marble monument, on a promontory overlooking the river, marks the place where 18,000 Red Army soldiers on the famous Long March crossed the river to escape the pursuing Nationalist army. The local citizens rose to the occasion, ceaselessly ferrying troops to the northern bank in their boats, 40–60 men per trip. The entire crossing took four days and nights and is still remembered as the greatest event in the lives of the older Naxi in Shigu.

Several buses run daily from Lijiang to Shigu and hitchhiking is also a possibility. First hitchhike to Baihanchang, walk three kilometers north to a road branching left from the main road to Tibet, and hitch the remaining 13 kilometers to Shigu.

Lodging

Lijiang Diyi Zhaodaisuo Hotel 丽江第一招待所
This hotel has been given a monopoly on foreign travelers by the local

Gonganju. Beds in four-person rooms are FEC 4.50 each. The hotel has good showers open from 19:00−22:00, a nice verandah and a beautiful garden. Avoid the restaurant and the expensive laundry service. Bikes are rented for Rmb 5.00 per day and the hotel has cars and jeeps for hire as well.

Transportation

Lijiang Qiche Keyunzhan Bus Station (two locations) 丽江汽车客运站

destination	distance (kms)	departure	cost (Rmb)
Xiaguan 下关	203	07:00	5.70
(Dali)（大理）	(190)		(5.20)
Jinjiang 金江	305	06:30	8.50
(two days)			
Kunming 昆明	603	06:30, 07:00	16.90
(two days)			
Shigu 石鼓	70	15:00	2.00
Jianchuan 剑川	75	13:30	2.10
Zhongdian 中甸	198	13:00	5.50
(two days)			

Lijiang Diqu Yunshu Gongsi Keyunzhan Bus Station 丽江地区运输公司客运站

destination	distance (kms)	departure	cost (Rmb)
Xiaguan 下关	203	07:00, 11:00	5.70
(Dali)（大理）	(190)		(5.20)
Jinjiang 金江	305	06:30, 15:30	8.50
(two days)			
Shigu 石鼓	70	07:00	2.00
Jianchuan 剑川	75	13:00	2.10
Zhongdian 中甸	198	07:00	5.50

Lijiang Xian Qichedui County Bus Station 丽江县汽车队

destination	distance (kms)	departure
Daju Xian 大具县	87	a.m., every fifth day

Jinjiang Huochezhan Train Station 金江火车站

destination	departure
Chengdu 成都	03:00, 16:30, 19:07
Kunming 昆都	06:06, 11:30

Jinjiang, a suburb of Dukou in Sichuan Province, sits on the Kunming-Chengdu rail line 305 kilometers east of Lijiang. Tickets are sold in Lijiang at the Number Two Guesthouse (Di'er Zhaodaisuo) but no sleeper tickets are available. Wait unit Jinjiang to buy tickets if you want the cheaper local price. Do not worry about availability; hard seat tickets never sell out.

Jinjiang Station holds two hard sleeper tickets for every express train passing through. If they are not sold to friends of railroad workers (a common occurrence) you might get one because they are usually not sold until an hour before departure. Additional beds might be available on the train.

If you decide to wait an extra day for a sleeper, stay at the **Jinjiang Luguan Hotel** across from the station. There are noodle shops and a tea house in the parking lot in front of the station. If you have time, catch a public bus to Dukou and explore this large industrial city.

Tiger Leaping Gorge (Hutiao Xia) 虎跳峡

Tiger Leaping Gorge ranks as one of China's great natural wonders. The Jinshajiang River, the name of the Upper Yangzi, winds its way southeast from Tibet and is already a mighty river when it flows into Yunnan Province. At Shigu, the river makes it's famous First Bend, flowing almost parallel to itself after it turns abruptly to the north. After 30 more kilometers, just beyond its confluence with the Xiaozhongdian He River, the Jinshajiang enters the great gorge. Above the south bank towers Yulongshan (Jade Dragon Mountain), its 5,596-meter ice peak shading the river for most of the day. On the north, perpetually snowbound ridges rise to a 4,701-meter summit. The river, over 2,000 meters above sea level, surges between these granite giants to create one of the world's deepest gorges.

The Jinsha Jiang rampages through 34 rapids, an unbroken stretch of white water, filling the rocky vaults with its roar. The river fills the entire floor of the gorge, which is less than 30 meters wide in places, pounding at the base of the cliffs, causing debris from high up the mountain to tumble into the cascade below. In 1986, a Chinese expedition in inner-tube barrels successfully descended this 30-kilometer set of rapids at the cost of two lives. Tiger Leaping Gorge has never been navigated by a kayak or rafting team, and an American kayaking group on a survey trip through the gorge in late 1986 doubted it could ever be done.

If you are going to trek downstream through the gorge, hitchhike or take a bus from Lijiang to Baihanchang, 46 kilometers to the southwest on the road from Kunming to Tibet. Follow the road out of Baihanchang into farmland to avoid the Gonganju before looking for a ride. Your destination is the Jinsha Daqiao Bridge, 40 kilometers north of Baihanchang. If you cannot find a truck, take one of the northbound buses that begin passing at around 10:00. There is no need to go into town and buy a ticket — just flag them down. Get out of the truck or bus a few hundred meters before the bridge and hike downstream on the south bank of the Jinsha Jiang for four kilometers until you see a small wooden ferryboat just beyond the Xiaozhongdianhe River. Cross the river to a single-lane dirt road just upstream from the gorge. If the ferryboat is not running, go back to the bridge, cross it, and hitch or walk into Hutiaojiang three kilometers further up the road. Here you can cross the Xiaozhongdianhe River on a bridge, hike back towards the Jinsha Jiang and begin the trek. Hutiaojiang is a closed town, so get across the bridge and onto the trail as quickly as you can.

For a trek upstream through the gorge, take a bus or hitchhike from Lijiang to Daju Xian via Heishui. From Daju hike to a small white pagoda and cross the river on the ferryboat to the trail leading through the gorge.

The Trail

For the most part, the trail is wide and safe, but in some places it traverses cliffs hundreds of meters high. There are no handrails, cement stairs or other safety precautions and trail surfaces are often covered with large rocks and gravel. Gusty winds, low overhangs, and frequent washout areas mandate that this trek be taken seriously. We mean not to discourage, only to stress the need for adequate footwear (hiking boots), camping equipment (including raingear) and food for a three-day trip. If you are well-prepared, mistakes resulting from haste or fatigue, which cost dearly in such a rugged and remote area, need not occur.

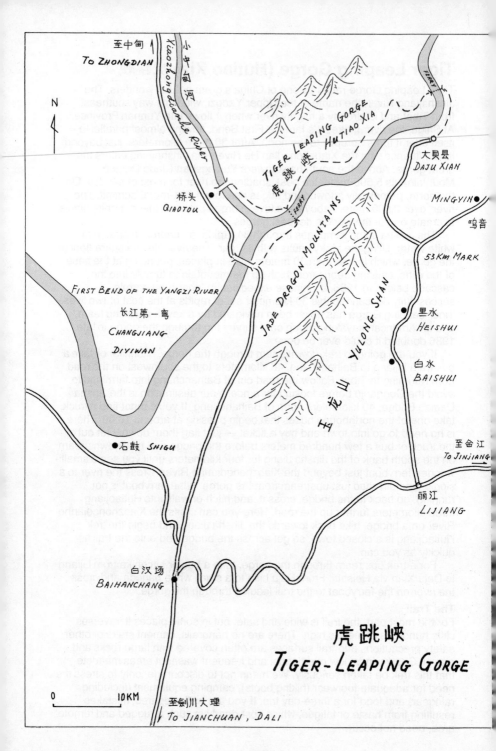

至中甸
TO ZHONGDIAN

小中甸河
Xiaozhongdianhe River

N

TIGER LEAPING GORGE
Hutiao Xia
虎跳峡

FERRY

桥头
Qiaotou

大贝县
Daju Xian

FERRY

鸣音
MINGYIN
鸣音

FIRST BEND OF THE YANGZI RIVER

长江第一弯
CHANGJIANG DIYIWAN

JADE DRAGON MOUNTAINS

玉龙山
Yulong Shan

53 KM MARK

里水
HEISHUI

白水
BAISHUI

石鼓 *SHIGU*

至金江
TO JINJIANG

丽江
LIJIANG

白汉场
BAIHANCHANG

虎跳峡
TIGER-LEAPING GORGE

0   10KM

至剑川大理
TO JIANCHUAN, DALI

Heading downstream, the first few kilometers of trail are along a single-lane road. Beside the road, the river begins to narrow and accelerate as it nears the mouth of the gorge. Above the north bank tower three giants: Black Water Snow, White Snow, and Cloud Snow Peaks. At the end of this stretch works a group of convicts, paying their debt to society by cutting a road out of marble cliffs with hammers and chisels. They appeared to be harmless and were all good-humored.

After about five kilometers on the road, the trail begins to climb and narrows to a footpath. Eight kilometers further, the trail passes Bendiwan, a small village with three large mud and timber buildings. The brown one is a small store that sells provisions. The stock is limited, so do not count on it for food. The trail is wide for several kilometers beyond the store and fresh water is plentiful making this a logical camping area. Across the gorge, the north face of Jade Dragon Mountain comes down to the river — an unbroken granite wall over 3,000 meters high. Seven spirits are believed to haunt this section of the gorge, moaning to signal the approach of storms or other dangers. Faint white outlines painted by seasonal waterfalls stripe the cliff face below the snow line. From this northern vantage point, sizes and distances are distorted. Canyon walls seem close enough to touch until dots on the far wall turn out to be full-grown trees.

A few kilometers beyond Bendiwan, the trail passes above a 90° bend in the river produced by Dayanfang, a cliff of contorted marble jutting from the north bank. This is Hutiaoxia, the Tiger Leaping Gorge, where a tiger is said to have escaped from a hunter by jumping over the mighty river.

Still further along, the trail turns away from the river, entering a deep ravine called Dashengou. From the wooden bridge deep inside the ravine you can see, high across the river, a sheer cliff fragmented into dark stone pinnacles named Black Wind Embankment (Heifengtang). Beyond the ravine the trail passes through a small village called Walnut Garden that was once inhabited by settlers from Sichuan Province. The cliff across the river from this village is named the Golden Cupboard (Jinguizi).

The most dangerous part of the trek is five kilometers beyond Walnut Garden near the end of the gorge. Here the trail is very narrow, overhangs are low and white marble dust blows constantly in the strong wind. There are no safe resting spots as the trail is cut from a vertical precipice. The last dramatic cliff face, Cock's Comb Ridge (Jiguanliang), looms opposite this narrow section of trail near the downstream entrance to the gorge.

Anyone doing the trek in two days will hit this section in the afternoon of their second day, when fatigue is the greatest. In all cases, take this section of trail slowly.

As you leave the downstream end of the gorge, the town of Daju will be visible across the river on a large plain. The ferryboat that will carry you across the river is still a three-hour walk away, past two small villages almost beyond the plain. The trail passes a field filled with logs stacked before their trip down the river to Dukou or Yibin. Stay above this field on the high trail and avoid a difficult climb up a steep slope linking the log area with the trail to the ferryboat.

The ferryboat schedule is flexible; crossings depend on the whims of the young captain. If you arrive late in the afternoon, be prepared to stay the night on a beach or in a riverside cave carved by floodwaters before crossing the river the next morning.

The entire trek is about 30 kilometers, a comfortable two-day walk allowing for ample rest time. You might want to carry extra food and set up a base camp in the gorge, allowing you to explore the higher bluffs on the northern bank before moving on.

Daju Xian 大具县

Daju is a collection of isolated Naxi villages situated on a large plain at the northern entrance to Tiger Leaping Gorge between the Jinshajiang River and Jade Dragon Mountain. Set in dramatic mountain landscape, Daju Xian is a little sanctuary amidst snow-crowned peaks, windy forests and frozen wasteland.

The dusty, gently sloping plain is used for both agriculture and grazing. Traditional farming and construction methods prevail for, despite the unpaved road linking Daju with Lijiang, the villages receive very little influence from the outside world. Asked whether she had ever seen a big city, a teenaged Naxi girl replied, 'Of course, I went to Lijiang last year'.

Except during planting and harvest times, nobody in Daju Xian has much to do. Children play in caves above the villages or ride horses bareback through the pasturelands while adults congregate to trade village gossip. Hunters who work in the nearby mountains visit the villages, flintlocks in hand, to trade furs, stock up on supplies and tell of their latest adventures.

Things to do

The prime site in the area is the downstream entrance to Tiger Leaping Gorge. From Daju it is possible to view the gorge without trekking its entire length. A trail approaching the gorge on the southern bank of the Jinsha Jiang leads to a fine observation point and camping area.

All the villages on the plain are worth visiting. At Toukuangcun Village, three kilometers south of the road, past a school, the foundations of an ancient temple overlook the entire plain. The people we met in this and other villages were interested in us and friendly and open. Travelers will probably be invited into a Naxi home for tea or a meal.

Lodging

Lijiang Xian Daju Gongxiaoshe Hotel 丽江县大具供销社
Beds in this fort-like hotel cost Rmb 0.70 each in a four-bed room. The wallpaper is made of 15-year-old newspapers filled with Mao quotes. Food in the canteen on the ground floor is good, but the selection is not.

Weinin Fuwu Fanguan Lushe Hotel 为您服务饭馆旅社
This privately managed, two-storey Naxi home-turned-hostel is run by an old man who worked with Allied fliers during World War II and speaks pidgin English. Beds are Rmb 0.70 each and the restaurant serves tasty noodles and rice dishes.

Tiger Leaping Gorge Hotel (Hutiaoxia Luguan) 虎跳峡旅馆
This newly built, freshly painted traditional building is excellent. At Rmb 1 per bed in a clean, four-bed room, this is the place to stay. We did not sample the food here ourselves, but local truck drivers think it is the best in town.

Transportation

Daju is isolated; buses to Lijiang only leave every fifth day. If you cannot wait,

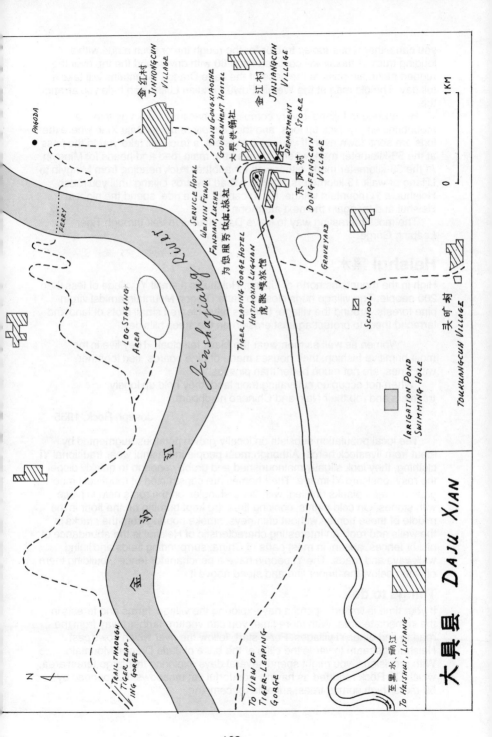

大具县 DAJU XIAN

N

1 KM

0

PAGODA

金红村 JINHONGCUN VILLAGE

金江村 JINJIANGCUN VILLAGE

DAJU GONG-XIAOSHE GOVERNMENT HOTEL 大具供销社

SERVICE HOTEL WEI NIN FUNJU FANDIAN, LXSHE 为您服务饭店.旅社

Jinshajiang River

金沙江

FERRY

LOG STAGING AREA

TIGER LEAPING GORGE HOTEL HUTIAOXIA LUGUAN 虎跳峡旅馆

TRAIL THROUGH TIGER LEAP-ING GORGE

To VIEW OF TIGER-LEAPING GORGE

至黑水，丽江
To HEISHUI, LIJIANG

DEPARTMENT STORE

东风村 DONGFENGCUN VILLAGE

GRAVEYARD

SCHOOL

IRRIGATION POND SWIMMING HOLE

头旷村 TOUKUANGCUN VILLAGE

you can either rent a *tuolaji* tractor for the rough trip or hitch a ride with a logging truck. A *tuolaji* will cost you Rmb 60 with driver, and the trip over the rugged mountain pass at the base of the Jade Dragon Mountains will take a full day. The old man at the Weinin Fuwu Fandian Lushe can help you arrange this.

Hitchhiking to Lijiang is very complicated because trucks go into the mountains empty, pick up logs, and then simply return to Daju Xian where the logs are sent down river. If you are persistent, a truck will take you to the pass at the 53-kilometer mark where it leaves the main road and heads for Mingyin. At the 53-kilometer mark, either wait for another truck heading from Mingyin to Lijiang or walk 13 kilometers along the road towards Lijiang until you reach Heishui, a Yi mountain village. If you cannot get a ride, spend the night at Heishui and try again the next afternoon.

The most interesting way to leave Daju Xian is to trek through Tiger Leaping Gorge.

Heishui 黑水

High in the mountains north of Lijiang, Heishui is a small Yi village of less than 200 people. The village hugs close to Jade Dragon Mountain amidst virgin pine forests. Around the village, farmers have cleared small plots of land and terraced them to protect against erosion on the steep hillsides.

'Women as well as men wear the black felt cloak. They live in the most primitive fashion; their houses made of pine boards, tied together with vines, are not much better than pigsties.'

'When not occupied cultivating their land, they hold up lonely travelers and rob their Naxi and Chinese neighbors.'

Joseph Rock, 1935

The local population subsists on locally-grown potatoes augmented by meat from livestock herds. Although most people in Heishui wear traditional Yi clothing, they look slightly malnourished and grubby enough to quickly dispel the rosy, postcard Yi image. Their homes are constructed of roughcut timber, gaps between planks unfilled, with large shingles on the roofs held in place with stones. On cold nights, cooking fires are kept burning on the floor in the middle of these homes without chimneys, smoke pouring from the cracks in the walls and roof. An interesting characteristic of Heishui is the abundance of picket fences, absent in most parts of China, surrounding fields and lining walkways and roads. The Yi people have a penchant for fences, building them of wood below the timber line and stone above it.

Things to do

If your time is limited, spend a day exploring the village, farms and forests in the immediate area. With more time, you can venture farther away from the road to find other Yi villages. For a start, follow the river which flows past Heishui upstream towards the cliffs at the base of Jade Dragon Mountain. With provisions, you might spend several days exploring this large forest area, which Dr. Rock reported as having wonderful flat meadows, surrounded by 50-meter-high spruce trees, suitable for camping.

Lodging

Heishui Ludian Fandian Hotel 黑水旅店饭店
This is the only building in the village that is not a Yi-style house. Beds in this rustic, dirty place will cost you Rmb 0.90. Food, mostly potatoes, is served and a small store in the courtyard sells sweets and canned food.

Transportation

Every fifth day a bus to Daju passes through, returning the next day to Lijiang. Wait for this bus or hitchhike on a truck. If you want to hitch to Daju, the empty logging trucks will take you to the 53-kilometer marker where they turn towards Mingyin. Start walking from there. A compassionate driver will stop sooner or later to pick you up. Trucks to Lijiang do not start passing through Heishui until 13:00, so spend your morning doing something more productive than waiting for a ride. You can greatly increase your chances of finding a ride by walking a kilometer out of town, where you appear more needy and drivers are more likely to stop.

Zhongdian 中甸

Zhongdian sits on a high plateau in the northwest corner of Yunnan Province very near the border with Tibet. At over 3,000 meters, the town is often bitterly cold. The surrounding mountains, once covered with lush forests, are now bare and torn by ravines. Erosion is so extreme that foreign experts have been sent to the area to help Chinese officials combat the problem. The flat countryside around town is dominated by large timber racks used to dry corn, timber or barley.

The people in Zhongdian are mostly Tibetan, and most of the buildings off the main road are built in Tibetan style. Along the main roads, private shops sell a wide selection of Tibetan goods but few Chinese goods. Han Chinese do not dominate commerce here, as they do in many Tibetan areas. Crowded street markets in both the new and old sections add color to the town. Though truck traffic to Tibet is brisk, horses are still the most common form of transportation here.

Because Zhongdian is a closed city, it is difficult to visit it for more than a day or two before getting kicked out by the Gonganju. The town is a major stopover on the road to Tibet and local authorities try their best not to let foreign travelers get near the border. During the summer, you could probably slip out of town and camp near the monastery, minimizing your chances of being discovered.

Things To Do

The daily street market near the department store on the main road is amazingly active. Goods vary from fruit trucked in from southern Yunnan Province to Tibetan clothing, religious artifacts, locally made wooden bowls and cups, tools and farm implements, fresh yak meat and live fish. For a walk, the old neighborhoods on the south side of town are a maze of dirt roads, traditional homes and interesting stores. The countryside around Zhongdian is best viewed on a walk to Jietang Songlin Si Monastery.

Jietang Songlin Si Monastery 节塘松林寺
Located an hour's walk north of Zhongdian, Jietang Songlin Si, with more than 300 monks, is one of the largest active monasteries left in Tibet. Built by the

fifth Dalai Lama 300 years ago, this Gelugpa sect (Yellow Hat) monastery had 1,300 monks in 1958. In 1959, the PLA shelled the monastery complex, which consisted of over 100 buildings, before entering it and systematically destroying every building. The monastery's gilded roof and gold, jewel-encrusted statues were taken back to China. The Chinese government justified the move as an attack on 'reactionary, feudal elements' in Tibet. Seven hundred monks were imprisoned; some were sent to Lijiang in chains to work the fields surrounding Red Hat Tibetan monasteries. Others are said still to be in prison in Xiao Zhongdian. The head lama, Gyawa Rinpoche, is actually a Mongolian who now barely walks because his legs were broken in a Chinese work camp. A few of the larger prayer halls have been rebuilt with funds raised by local Tibetans. The Chinese government has promised, but not yet delivered, Rmb 10,000 to aid reconstruction.

In 1980, the second delegation sent to Tibet by the Dalai Lama visited Zhongdian on a fact-finding tour. Reconstruction began when monks were allowed to return to the monastery in 1982. In 1986, another group from Dharamsala stayed in Zhongdian for six months to teach Buddhism, Tibetan history and Tibetan language to the remaining monks. The chorten (stupa) overlooking the monastery on the hill reputedly contains the remains of the seventh Dalai Lama, though he also has a prominent tomb inside the Potala in Lhasa.

To get to the monastery, walk north of Zhongdian to the fork in the main road. Go left and then turn right on the dirt trail 200 meters beyond the fork.

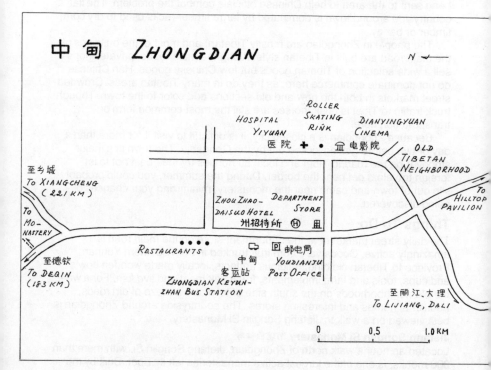

The trail leads across a large field to the monastery which is visible from the north end of town.

The Zhongdian region has always been a large Buddhist center. North of Jietang Songlin Si is a smaller affiliated complex. There are ruins of a third monastery at the south end of town. The remains of Dhondubling Monastery, which had 1,000 monks at its zenith, lie several kilometers to the west. Napiltazang, a Nyingma sect Tibetan monastery, is located seven kilometers to the northwest.

The Dalai Lamas

The Dalai Lama, as the incarnation of Chenrezi, the Bodhisattva of Compassion and Tibet's patron saint, is the spiritual and temporal ruler of Tibet. He is also the leader of the Gelugpa, or Yellow Hat sect, of Tibetan Buddhism. Fourteen Dalai Lamas have ruled in succession, each one a reincarnation of his predecessor, since the First Dalai Lama (1391−1474), who was a disciple of Tsong Khapa, the great reformer and founder of the Yellow Hats. The first Dalai Lama founded Tashilhunpo Monastery at Shigatse and was its first abbot. The title 'Dalai' or 'Broad Ocean' was given to the third incarnation by a Mongol king, and applied posthumously to the first two. The Fifth (1617−1682) was a mighty scholar, politician and architect. Aided by a Mongol prince, he unified Tibet under his rule and suppressed all rivals of the Gelugpa sect. The 13th (1876−1933) withstood a British invasion in 1904 and reaffirmed Tibet's independence in 1912 after China became a republic. An able, intelligent ruler, he tried in vain to modernise Tibet's institutions.

When a Dalai Lama dies, a search for his incarnation begins at once. Helped by state oracles, visions in the sacred lake of Lhamo Lhatso, and many other portents, search parties are sent out to find the incarnate child. Candidates are examined for eight special physical traits and the ability to correctly identify the late Dalai Lama's possessions from among similar objects. Other tests are administered to determine that the boy is indeed the right choice.

The current Dalai Lama was born to parents of humble standing in the Tibetan province of Amdo (present-day Qinghai) on July 6th, 1935. Discovered two years later to be the 14th incarnation, he was moved to Lhasa for formal religious training in preparation for assuming full governmental powers at the age of 18. Under a successive group of monk-tutors, the Dalai Lama memorized and debated thousands of texts for his Geshe Lharampa (Doctor of Divinity) examination. Secluded in the Potala Palace, he knew little of everyday life and was seen mainly on ceremonial occasions.

In 1950, three years short of the accepted age for accession, the Dalai Lama became the formal leader of Tibet in the face of political crises. From then until 1959 he tried to negotiate directly to retain independence, autonomy and religious freedom against Chinese claims that Tibet was an integral part of the Chinese Motherland. This included a nine-month trip to Beijing and meetings with Mao Zedong himself. The Dalai Lama fled Lhasa just prior to massive fighting that left tens of thousands dead and most of Tibet's holiest shrines and monasteries in ruin. Over 100,000 refugees made their way to India to help establish the Tibetan government-in-exile.

The Dalai Lama and the Chinese government have periodically held talks for his return to Tibet. In August 1979, the first fact-finding delegation, led by Lobsang Samten, the Dalai Lama's brother, returned to Tibet. Everywhere they went, unexpected crowds of ten and twenty thousand Tibetans greeted the first emissaries of their spiritual leader in 20 years. At present there is little chance of the Dalai Lama returning.

Lodging

Zhongdian Zhaodaisuo Hotel 中甸招待所

Beds at this basic hotel are Rmb 2.80 each in a double room. There is no restaurant and no showers. The toilets are across the parking lot behind the hotel.

Transportation

The Zhongdian area is policed against foreigners so thoroughly it is virtually impossible to buy bus tickets to places other than Dali or Lijiang. Hitchhiking northwest to Tibet is possible if you can find a ride and get out of town quickly. Hitchhike north following the right fork in the main road to reach Xiangcheng, 222 kilometers away in Sichuan Province. The other route to Sichuan is the Dingqu River Gorge trek, which begins in Benzilan.

Zhongdian Qichezhan Bus Station 中甸汽车站

Buses depart for Deqen, near the border with Tibet, on even days. They stop at Benzilan for the night before continuing to Deqen the second day. Daily buses run south to Dali and Lijiang. There are rumors of a bus during the summer north from Zhongdian to Xiangcheng in Sichuan.

Benzilan 奔子栏

Benzilan may be the most pleasant farming town we visited in Southwest China. Parched, cactus-covered mountains rise abruptly from the north bank of the Jinshajiang River, but a flat, narrow sliver of land rests between the south bank and the mountains. The residents of Benzilan live and work on this small plain. Most of the land is covered with randomly-shaped farms that together look like a patchwork quilt. Small streams feed an irrigation network, keeping the farmland a brilliant green even during the long dry season.

Benzilan is more a collection of small villages than one town. While new Chinese-style buildings line the road, small clusters of Tibetan homes scattered about the plain account for most of the structures. The frigid Jinsha Jiang, fresh from the Tibetan highlands, meanders past town, surprisingly slow and calm.

The sad thing about Benzilan is that obstacles, both political and geographic, make it virtually inaccessible to most travelers. Six days by bus and at least two days on foot from Chengdu, the approach from the north crosses some of the most rugged, isolated regions in China. Benzilan is only three days by bus north of Dali, but hawk-eyed Gonganju officers miss few travelers trying to sneak past Zhongdian on the road to Tibet. Once in Benzilan, however, travelers can take advantage of the close proximity of Sichuan Province to avoid trouble. If the Gonganju in Benzilan are causing difficulties, cross the Jinsha Jiang on the small ferryboat to Dongfeng (also known as Wake) and enjoy a trouble-free base in Sichuan Province.

Things to do

You could spend a week in Benzilan exploring villages, walking through brilliant green fields and resting on the banks of, or swimming in, the Jinshajiang River. There are two attractions in the large village at the center of the farmland. The first is a prayer-wheel building that always seems to be filled with Tibetan worshippers. Many people spend hours circumambulating clockwise around the hall, softly chanting prayers. The second attraction is a

Tibetan-style factory that makes delicate wooden bowls, for which Benzilan is noted. The ornery old man who runs the factory makes many of the bowls himself but seems to care little if he sells them or not. His prices start high and never come down. To find the factory, tell anyone in the village you want to buy wooden bowls (*muwan*) and they will show you the way.

Chazhuling Si Monastery 奔子栏寺

This monastery is 22 kilometers northwest of Benzilan near the pass where the road to Tibet crosses into the Mekong River (Lancangjiang) valley. The monastery itself was almost completely destroyed during the Tibetan conflict, and only recently have locally financed workers begun to restore it. There are badly damaged frescoes in the main hall that appear to be quite old. More interesting than the main hall are the dozens of small buildings clinging to the hilltop around the monastery. Most of the buildings are probably now Tibetan homes but they appear to have been a part of the vast monastery complex at one time. This monastery was the only place in Southwest China where we were sold prayer flags.

The trip to the monastery is as much fun as the actual visit. To get there, you must walk, hitchhike or hire a *tuolaji* tractor. The road climbs out of Benzilan, passing an occasional Tibetan hamlet clinging to the steep mountainside as it nears the monastery. There are numerous spectacular views of the Jinshajiang and the 6,000-meter peaks beyond its east bank in Sichuan Province. To rent a *tuolaji*, just ask anyone in town who is driving one to take you to Chazhuling. The price should be Rmb 10—15 for the round trip.

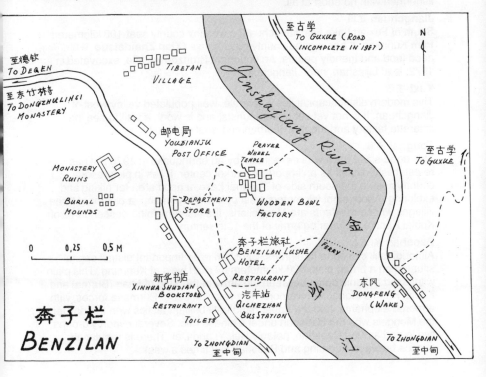

Lodging

Benzilan Lushe Hotel 奔子栏旅社

Beds in this spartan hotel are Rmb 1.70 each. There are communal toilets but no showers, so you must bathe in the river. Many Tibetan truck drivers stay here; talk to them about rides to Tibet. There are several small restaurants on the road near the hotel.

Transportation

Benzilan Qichezhan Bus Station 奔子栏汽车站

Buses to Zhongdian run on even days and buses to Deqen, on the road to Tibet, run on odd days. The quickest way out of town is to hitchhike.

The Dingqu Gorge trek begins at Dongfeng (Wake), across the river from Benzilan. (See page 249 for details).

Other Places in Yunnan Province

Fuxianhu Lake 抚仙湖

Southeast of Kunming, beyond Dianchi Lake, lies the province's deepest body of water, crystal-clear Fuxian Lake. Traditional fishing villages dot the shore. Along the lake's western edge, fishermen still practice an ancient fishing technique called 'fish ditches' (*yugou*). Stone-lined channels, or ditches, lead from the cold lake into warmer entrapment pools. The warm water proves irresistible to large, succulent fish, which are then scooped up by the fishermen with no effort at all.

Jiangchuan 江川

South of Fuxian Lake lies Jiangchuan, a wealthy county seat 100 kilometers from Kunming. It has a good county guesthouse (**Xian Zhaidaisuo** 县招待所), good food and friendly people. An important Bronze-Age site, excavated in 1972, is at Lijiashan, near Jiangchuan.

Yuxi 玉溪

This modern district capital lies in a fertile, well-populated valley west of Jiangchuan. It is not yet set up for tourists, and is worth a visit to see the cigarette factory and the mix of urban and rural prosperity.

Tonghai 通海

This good-sized town was devastated by an earthquake in 1970 but has re-established itself as an important market center. It lies in picturesque countryside on the south side of Tonghai Lake, a good area for hiking and exploring. About eight kilometers west of town is Xinmeng, a cluster of three villages whose residents are Mongolians, the last remaining descendants of Kublai Khan's conquering army of the 13th century.

Baoshan 保山

Although still closed to foreigners, Baoshan is an important district capital situated on a broad plain 600 kilometers by road west of Kunming. This plain witnessed a titanic battle between the army of the King of Mian (Burma) and Kublai Khan's Mongolian warriors. The vastly superior Burmese forces, with armored elephants, had the upper hand until brilliant tactics won the day for the Mongols who put Baoshan under Chinese rule. Several minority groups live in and around Baoshan, notably Hui, Yi and Dai. There is regular air service between Kunming and Baoshan five times a week.

Dehong 德宏

Yunnan's westernmost spur of land, known as the Dehong region, extends far into Burma and is the home of two minority groups, the Jingpo and Dai. These Dehong Dai are considered by many Chinese to be even more handsome and refined than their relatives in Xishuangbanna. The chief town of Ruili is said to be one of the most pleasing and exotic places in the entire province. Naturally, it is closed to foreigners.

The Hump

Early in 1942, Japan overran Burma in a lightning attack that cut the Burma Road, China's final land link with the Allies. Less than six months before, a lone China National Aviation Corporation (CNAC) DC3 had completed a survey flight from Kunming over an unknown region called the 'Hump' to Assam in northeast India. China's communication links had to be maintained and vital war material delivered, so freight service over the Hump began in March 1942.

Pilots respected and feared the Hump. Much of the 1,000-kilometer journey passed over mountainous regions with a base elevation of 2,500 meters. Icy peaks towered much higher; pilots pushed the planes to their maximum altitude, avoiding mountains they could not clear. Flying between 5,000 and 6,000 meters, pilots needed oxygen to combat fatigue after long hours of precision flying. The unpredictable weather was another hazard. Storms materialized quickly, producing turbulence capable of ripping the wings off a loaded aircraft, blinding pilots who relied on their vision to navigate between the tallest peaks. Many planes flew into mountains they could neither see nor fly over. Over the jungles of northern Burma mountains lower but menacing Japanese fighter patrols frequently attacked the unnamed and unescorted cargo planes. In clear weather such patrols were most effective, so Hump pilots began charting courses further north, hiding amidst the southern Himalaya.

Pilots and crews, scarce as they were during the war, were worked to exhaustion, often flying the Hump twice in a single day. Living conditions at most airfields were awful, relaxation unheard of and stress a constant problem. Pilots were issued a fifth of alcohol every other day to help them sleep.

'Losses over the route were heavy. In three years of operation the ATC (American Transport Command) was to lose 468 planes, an average of 13 a month. Sometimes the crews were able to parachute to safety and be guided out by Kachin rescue teams in Burma. Others died in the jungle or were captured by the Japanese or in some cases were caught in the treetops and their corpses found hanging long afterwards, eaten by ants.' Barbara Tuchman, *Stilwell and the American Experience in China 1911–1945*, 1970.

The Hump was but one link in what might have been the war's longest supply line; goods traveled 19,000 kilometers from the United States before reaching China. The goods came in naval convoys to the west coast of India, 2,400 kilometers across India by rail to Calcutta, 700 kilometers on the narrow-gauge Assam-Bengal Railway to airfields in Dinjam, and finally over the Hump.

Historians still debate the effectiveness of the Hump airlift. Its supporters believe the action saved China from being completely subdued by Japanese armies by giving the needed *materiel* at a critical time. Critics point out that rampant corruption, insurbordination and mismanagement of Chinese armies, rather than the lack of supplies, led to Japan's easy victories. Most historians agree that placing a higher priority on reopening the Burma Road, a possibility in 1943, would have been much more efficient, and beneficial to China, than the long, costly Hump operation.

The Geology of Southwest China

The geologic history of Southwest China is certainly one of the most fascinating, complex and scientifically important of any region in the world. By far the most significant event in shaping the major landforms of the area was the collision of the Indian subcontinent with Asia, some 40 to 50 million years ago. Driven by internal forces that are not yet fully understood, a dozen crustal fragments moved slowly across the surface of the Earth. The Indian plate traveled steadily northward at the rate of 15 to 20 centimeters per year, eventually closing the eastern arm of the ancient Sea of Tethys that once lay south of Tibet. It finally rammed into the Asian continent and caused 2,000 kilometers of crustal shortening and compression. India continues its relentless penetration into Asia, but at the slower rate of five centimeters per year.

This titanic collision created tight folds and overlapping crustal slices in the basement rocks of the Asian plate, thus forming the thickest crust (70–80 kilometers) and the highest mountains (the Himalaya) in the world. Mountain-building was not limited to the Himalaya, however, as the highlands of eastern Tibet, western Sichuan and northern Yunnan were all significantly affected. Today, signs of the rapid uplift in these areas can be seen in exceptionally deep gorges, with deposits of alluvial gravel perched several hundred meters above rivers that predated the collision. The rivers eroded downward as quickly as the mountains rose. A marvelous example of this is Tiger Leaping Gorge, where the Upper Yangzi River (Jinsha Jiang) has etched a spectacular gorge through 370 million-year-old Devonian marble, 4,000 meters beneath the ice and snow of Yulong Xue Shan, one of Yunnan's highest and most beautiful peaks.

The deformation of Asia as a result of the collision with India does not end here, however. To compensate for the continuing indentation, large blocks of China are slowly being driven outward on its unbounded sides into the basins of the South China Sea and the Pacific Ocean. The resulting horizontal movement has formed structural planes such as the Red River Fault in western Yunnan, along which the Red River now runs. This movement has caused the crust in Yunnan to pull apart and form *grabens*, extensive down-dropped areas. Some of these have filled with water to create large lakes, such as Dianchi near Kunming and Erhai near Dali.

Movement along the Red River and related faults has caused numerous high-magnitude earthquakes in Southwest China, some greater than 7.0 on the Richter scale. In addition, these faults allowed abnormally high heat flow to reach the surface of the Earth, creating the numerous hot springs in the region, and acted as conduits for the mineral-rich waters that helped deposit the well known gold reserves of Yunnan and western Sichuan. They appear, however, to have had little or no influence on the important deposits of iron, copper, lead, zinc, and tin in Yunnan, antimony in Guangxi and mercury in Guizhou.

The results of the collision with India have been superimposed on much older basement rocks that form the continental craton of Asia, the stable, relatively immobile area of the earth's crust. These deep basement rocks, as most others on the globe, do not comprise a homogeneous mass, but rather form a mixed collage of material that has increased in size over the past three billion years. Mirco-continental fragments were welded together by global tectonic forces perhaps similar to those that are now driving the Indian plate. In fact, the cratonic basement of China consists of three large and several smaller blocks of Precambrian rock (older than 600 million years), fused together along suture zones. The large Precambrian block that underlies most of southern China is known as the Yangtze Craton. Surface exposures of these rocks are rare in southwest China and are usually limited to peripheral zones. In northern

Guangxi, 2.86 billion-year-old granites can be observed along the southern cratonic border.

In contrast, the basement rocks that border the Yangtze Craton on the north and west, and which underlie Sichuan and western Yunnan, consist of folded rocks and micro-continental fragments that attached to the cratonic block, probably between 600 and 200 million years ago. An example of this, known as an accretionary fold belt, is the Sichuan Basin, formed by subsidence in an oceanic trench between 200 and 160 million years ago (Triassic-Jurassic). The basin first filled with a mixture of marine marl (clay and small organisms) and fine clastic sediments (fragments of preexisting rocks) known as flysch. Later (140 to 100 million years ago), the basin was filled with non-marine sandstone and conglomerate. These units now contain major deposits of coal and gas. The subsidence that generated these rocks in eastern Sichuan occurred long before the continental collision with India. The area was preserved as a structural basin throughout the subsequent periods of deformation because of its great distance from the point of initial collision.

A vast, shallow sea covered a major portion of the Yangtze Craton from early Cambrian through Triassic times (600 to 200 million years ago), depositing fossiliferous limestone throughout Guangxi, Guizhou and eastern Yunnan. Subsequent continental uplift and withdrawal of this sea left large areas of limestone exposed to the atmosphere. Where fractures in the limestone were numerous and rainfall abundant, acidic groundwater percolated downward and dissolved the limestone, forming caves, caverns and sinkholes. Formations such as these are common throughout Southwest China. At certain localities where the limestone was particularly well fractured and soluble, the continuous dissolution by acidic groundwater caused underground holes to widen, ceilings of caverns to collapse, and numerous sinkholes to form in adjoining patterns. In time, the surface of the limestone terrane in such areas formed a network of numerous short gullies and ravines that terminated abruptly where they discharged their waters into subterranean channels. Erosion by wind and water continually reshaped the more resistant hills, leaving a spectacular collection of elongate and odd-shaped remnants of honey-combed chambers, passageways, caves and tunnels. Known as karst topography, this type of geomorphology gets its name from the Karst Mountains of Yugoslavia where it is particularly well-developed.

Karst topography was formed in this manner at Yunnan's well-known Stone Forest, 126 kilometres southeast of Kunming. Here, elongate water channels, caves and passageways have been etched into 270 million-year-old Permian limestone. Even more spectacular perhaps, are the exotically shaped karst formations naturally sculpted from 300 million year-old Devonian limestone along the Lijiang River between Guilin and Yangshuo in Guangxi, truly a place where art and geology are one.

Robert J. Casaceli and Ilmars Gemuts

Further Reading
Molnar, P. 1986, *The geologic history and structure of the Himalaya: American Scientist, v. 74, p. 74–154.*
Tapponnier, P., Peltzer, G., Le Dain, A. Y., Armijo, R., and Cobbold, P., 1982, *Propagating extrusion tectonics in Asia: New insights from simple experiments with plasticine: Geology, v. 10, p. 611–616.*
Yang, Z., Cheng, Y., and Wang, H., 1986, *The geology of China: Oxford University Press, New York, 303 p.*
Zhang, Zh. M., Liou, J. G., and Coleman, R. G., 1984, *An outline of the plate tectonics of China: Geol. Soc. America Bulletin, v. 95, p. 295–312.*

Sichuan Province 四川

'How hard the road to Shu is!
It is as hard as the road to Heaven.'

Du Fu, eighth century

Far from China's eastern centers of power and commerce, Sichuan has traditionally dominated Southwest China with its geographic size, fertile land, huge population and wealth. Sichuan first appeared in history as the formidable State of Shu (220–280). Alternating between periods of strength and times of internal strife between competing warlords, Sichuan always remained rural in character. It stayed largely isolated from events in China's capitol until the 20th century and the Sino-Japanese War. In 1938, the Nationalist government established its new capital at Chongqing, depending on Sichuan's mountain barriers to keep the Japanese at bay. Modern industry first came into the province at this time. Entire factories, and even universities, were dismantled elsewhere in China, laboriously transported across great distances, and reassembled in Sichuan, to support the war effort.

Today Sichuan is industrialized with over 100 million inhabitants living in an area the size of France. Eighty-seven percent of the population still lives in the rich countryside that has helped make Sichuan the bread basket of China. It is easy for even a casual visitor to see that Sichuan is one of China's most affluent provinces, but also one of its most overcrowded. In 1977, for the first time in Chinese history, a Sichuanese, Deng Xiaoping, became the ruler of China.

The rugged mountains of western Sichuan and the peoples that inhabit them seem a world apart from the rest of the province. Over ten minority groups including the Tibetans, Yi, Qiang and Sifan inhabit much of this mountainous region. The Yi, who dwell in the Daliang Shan (Great Cool Mountains), withstood countless invading armies up until the 1950s when the Chinese finally took control of the area. Equally independent were the Tibetans living on the eastern portion of the Tibetan plateau, traditionally called Kham, that is now mostly included in Sichuan. Known as the Khampas, they defied control by Lhasa and were considered the scourge of Tibet and its Chinese borderlands. Chinese armies entered this area only in force and were constantly harassed by Tibetan guerrillas.

The climate in Sichuan varies dramatically between its eastern and western parts. Eastern Sichuan and the Yangzi River Valley are mountainous and relatively dry. River cities like Chongqing can reach maximum temperatures of 40°C in summer, ranking among China's hottest places.

The Sichuan Basin surrounding Chengdu has a humid sub-tropical monsoonal climate, with mild, frost-free winters, hot summers, plentiful rainfall, mist and high humidity. The average temperature in July, the hottest month, is 27°C.

Western Sichuan, with its high plateau climate, has significantly lower temperatures and rainfall than the Sichuan basin. The plateau is characterized by thin air, wide variations in daily temperature, long hours of sunshine and intense solar radiation. The northern part is much colder than the relatively temperate southern sections of the plateau.

Chengdu 成都

The ancient city of Chengdu has been the main cultural and commercial hub of Southwest China for about 2,500 years, and the capital of Sichuan for the last 600. In the second century BC, the governor of Sichuan established a school system in Chengdu that the emperor later held up as a model for all China to follow. Almost 1,000 years later, the great Tang Dynasty poet Du Fu wrote some of his best poetry while living in a little hut there for three years. Meanwhile, the city was producing famous textiles, especially silk and satin brocades, which added luxury to the refined life of the rich.

Chengdu's modern development began in 1949 and proceeded rapidly. Railways were built linking it with Chongqing, Xian and Kunming and highways were pushed through to neighboring provinces. It is now a major industrial city with a population of 2.5 million, while the entire metropolitan area boasts over eight million.

Wide avenues with modern concrete buildings cut through the city in all directions but there are still a large number of streets lined with old, half-timbered houses where craftsmen and small shopkeepers keep a fascinating street life humming along.

Things to do

Energy flows from this cosmopolitan city. The main avenues are lined with department stores, restaurants, bookstores or modern government shops, and back alleys overflow with traditional Sichuan flavor. Baihuatan Park and Renmin Gongyuan Park both have nice teahouses, as do most older neighborhoods and temples. Warm yourself with a cup of tea while watching old men play cards or Chinese chess. Join them if you know how to play.

You could spend days shopping in Chengdu. The Artists' Street Market features a wide selection of calligraphy and Chinese brush painting. A few years ago, individual artists sold their own work, but nowadays salesmen do the selling. Extremely cheap paintings can still be found. The Exhibition Hall behind the big statue of Mao has many exhibits on rotation as well as a permanent display of gift items for sale. The Renmin Shangchang Market is the place where Chengdu's citizens do their everyday shopping. Shuncheng Jie has a number of fur shops and two poorly-stocked Tibetan goods stores. An amazingly long underground shopping mall, built beneath Chengdu in its old bomb shelter system, begins near the Mao statue and goes for kilometers. Chunxi Lu has a wide variety of shops selling everything from herbal medicine to musical instruments and Japanese camera equipment. The above-mentioned shopping areas are the ones we happened to find. There are undoubtedly many more.

Baoguang Si (Divine Light Monastery) 宝光寺

This well-maintained Chinese Buddhist monastery is located in Xindu about 50 minutes by bus from Chengdu. No one should miss it. Founded 1,900 years ago, the buildings were rebuilt and enlarged many times, reaching their present proportions in the 17th century. The highlights of Baoguang Si include a 13-storey Tang-Dynasty stupa, a Tibetan Buddhist temple, a library of religious texts and a hall containing 500 clay statues of Buddhist *luohans*. Groups of Tibetan pilgrims frequent Baoguang Si, as do hordes of local Buddhists on the weekends. The vegetarian restaurant at Baoguang Si is surely one of the best in China.

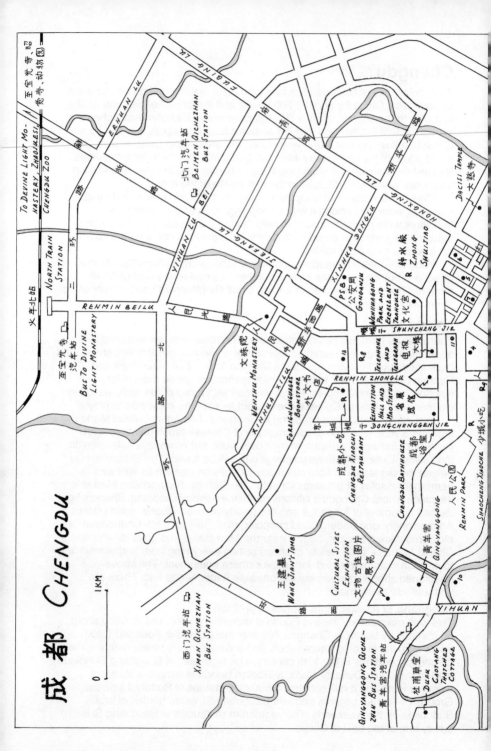

成都 CHENGDU

火车北站 North Train Station

至宝光寺 To Divine Light Monastery

至宝光寺、动物园 To Devine Light Mo-nastery, Zhaojuesi, B[?] 觉寺、动物园 Chengdu Zoo

二环路 Erhuan Lu

成绵路

北门汽车站 Beimen Qichezhan Bus Station

西二环路 Erhuan Lu

北路 Bei Lu

田田路

天星东路

新华东路

洪兴路 Hongxing

大慈寺 Dacisi Temple

驸马桥 Zhong R Shuijitiao

至宝光寺汽车站 Bus To Divine Light Monastery

一环路

北路

人民北路 Renmin Beilu

北新街 人民北路

新华西路

文殊院 Wenshu Monastery

新华书店

公安局 PSB Gonganju

文化宫 Wenhuagong Excellent Park and Teahouse 文化宫

R 8

13

电报大楼 Telephone and Telegraph

顺城街 Shuncheng Jie

外文书店 Foreign Languages Bookstore

新华西路 Xinhua Xilu

东城根 R

人民中路 Renmin Zhonglu

展览馆 Exhibition Hall and Mao Statues

备展览 Dongchenggen Jie

成都小吃 Chengdu Xiaochi Restaurant

成都浴 Chengdu Bathhouse

成都饭店 R

东城根 Dongchenggen Jie

王建墓 Wang Jian's Tomb

文物古迹展览 Cultural Sites Exhibition

人民公园 Renmin Park

少城小吃 Shaocheng Xiaochi

R 4

R 4

西门汽车站 Ximen Qichezhan Bus Station

西一环路

青羊宫汽车站 Qingyanggong-Quche-Zhan Bus Station

青羊宫 Qingyanggong

一环路 Yihuan

杜甫草堂 Dufu

杜甫草堂 Caotang Thatched Cottage

0 1KM

176

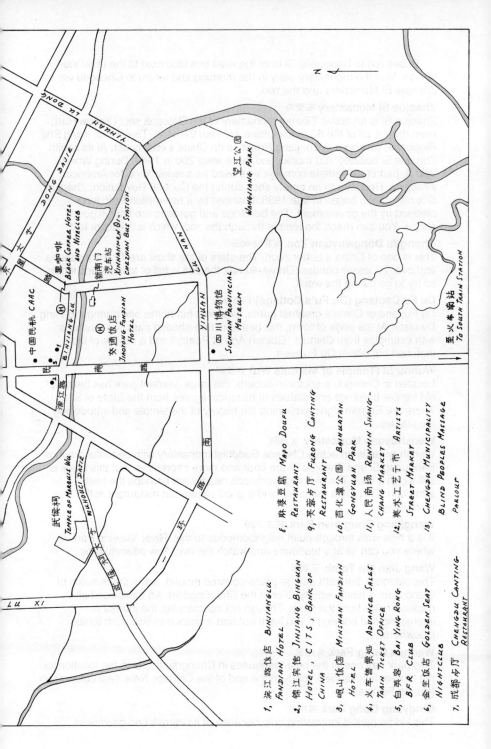

Buses run to Baoguang Si from the west bus stop next to the main train station. Visit the monastery early in the morning and return to Chengdu via Zhaojue Si Monastery and the zoo.

Zhaojue Si Monastery 昭觉寺

Zhaojue Si is an active Tibetan monastery of the Gelugpa sect (Yellow Hat), even though all of the 80 monks there are Han Chinese. The abbot, Kang Sha Rinpoche, was born in Zhejiang Province on China's east coast. At its zenith, Zhaojue Si boasted 700 monks and there were 200 in 1949. During World War II, part of the temple complex was used as a repair shop for American airplanes. Reduced to an empty shell during the Cultural Revolution, Zhaojue Si's restoration began in late 1986, financed by a two-million Rmb fund pledged by the government. The buildings and gardens are now in good shape. You can reach the temple through the zoo, which is adjacent to it.

Chengdu Dongwuyuan Zoo 成都动物园

This is one of China's better zoos. The stars of the show are 12 giant pandas and over 20 lesser pandas. On weekends the zoo is full of tourists and locals so try to go during the week.

Du Fu Caotang (Du Fu's Cottage) 杜甫草堂

Du Fu, one of China's greatest poets, lived in a hut at this site during the Tang Dynasty. At the edge of town, this peaceful tree-shaded park has pavilions with examples from China's "Golden Age of Poetry" and a replica of the thatched hut where Du Fu lived.

Wuhou Si (Temple of Marquis Wu) 武侯祠

Located in Chengdu's southern suburb, this large, verdant park has beautiful old temple buildings and statues of historical figures from the State of Shu. There are English signs explaining the history of the temple and introducing the statues.

Wenshuyuan Monastery 文殊院

Wenshuyuan is an active Chinese Buddhist monastery with beautiful grounds. Baoguang Si and Zhaojue Si are finer and more impressive, but this place is still worth a visit. The old neighborhoods nearby are perhaps the best attraction. There is a teahouse and a good vegetarian restaurant at the monastery.

Wangjiang Gongyuan Park 望江公园

It is a nice walk through quiet neighborhoods to this 'River Viewing Park' where you can sit at a teahouse and watch the river flow peacefully by.

Wang Jian Mu Tomb 王建墓

This old tomb, beneath a large grass-covered mound, holds the remains of Wang Jian, a ninth-century ruler of the Shu Kingdom. An exhibition hall displays relics from the tomb. Though not spectacular, the interior is interesting and edifying if you have not had a chance to visit such tombs elsewhere.

Wenhua Gong Park 文化宫

This park has one of the best teahouses in Chengdu. It is also the location for the lantern festival held yearly at the end of the Chinese New Year celebration (Spring Festival).

Qingyang Gong Park 青羊宫

This kiddie park is interesting only because of its unmatched gaudiness.

Chengdu Yushi Bathhouse 成都浴室
Take a book to this good bathhouse. You often have to sip tea and wait for a
while before you get a tub. Private tubs are Rmb 1.40 each.

Chengdu Municipality Blind People's Massage Parlor
Get a vigorous massage here for Rmb 0.40.

Farther away

Qingcheng Shan Mountain 青城山
Qingcheng Shan is a Daoist holy mountain 65 kilometers west of Chengdu. It
is no wonder that this beautifully forested mountain with its quiet meditative
atmosphere was chosen as a Daoist place of veneration. Before 1949, there
were 500 monks and nuns on Qingcheng Shan and 80 remain today. The
three principal Daoist shrines on the mountain, named Zhaoyang Dong,
Tianshi Dong and Shengqing Dong, were all damaged during the Cultural
Revolution but their restoration is almost complete.

The walk to the peak takes less than four hours on a wide, clearly marked
trail. The hike is much less strenuous than the climb up Emei Shan and
suitable for less-than-avid hikers and people traveling with small children. Both
Tianshi Dong and Shengqing Dong have hostels and restaurants serving
delicious vegetarian food. Try to avoid the urge to make a one-day visit from
Chengdu to Qingcheng Shan. Take the bus from Chengdu in the afternoon
and climb to Shengqing Dong for the night. Get up early the next morning,
walk for 45 minutes to the peak and check out the sunrise before descending

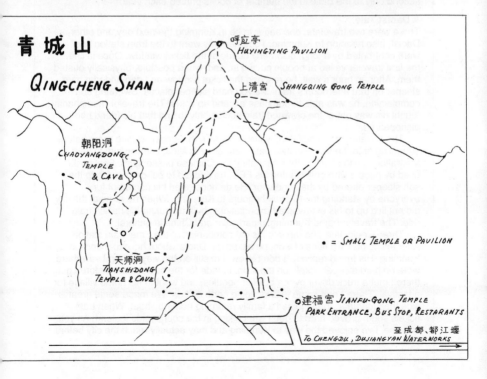

Daoism

When people lost sight of the way to live
Came codes of love and honesty
Learning came, charity came
Hipocracy took charge.
                        Dao De Jing

Daoism is the 'Path' or the 'Way', a philosophy first given form in the sixth century BC by the sage Laozi in the *Dao De Jing*, or *Book of the Virtuous Way*. A Daoist is someone who avoids conventional social obligations and leads a simple, spontaneous and patient life in close harmony with nature. Water is a truly Daoist element: the most yielding and tenuous substance, which yet, over time, can wear away the biggest mountain.

The ancient, unified symbol of *yin* (female) and *yang* (male) embodies the Daoist ideal of interaction and represents the forces of the world, embraced and contained by the joining of two parts. In its fullest flowering, the symbol stands for all of Nature's principles: dark and light, earth and sky, cool and warm, passive and active. The power of the symbol is inside each human as well.

True virtue occurs when a person interacts so harmoniously with the environment that he is without virtue. Bad behavior is due to artificial conventions and stupidity, for no one would knowingly violate the natural path. *Qing jing wu wei* — pure and calm, strive for nothing. The universal quality of Daoism has led to its incorporation into many of the world's major religions. The *Dao De Jing* is second only to the Bible in the number of books printed each year.

A Daoist Tale

There were two travelers, one eager to be in Kunming the next day, the other, a Daoist, also heading to Kunming. Together they went to the train station and were confronted by a long, disorderly queue at the ticket window. Once in line, the first traveler yelled at people cutting in, and, when possible, physically ousted them. After an hour's wait, he reached the ticket window and demanded a hard sleeper on that afternoon's train. *Meiyou* hard sleeper places. Swearing and complaining, he was able to purchase a stand up ticket. The traveler triumphantly fought his way out of the crowded train station only to find that his friend had disappeared.

The traveler, much agitated, waited angrily in the smoky waiting room before struggling onto the train. All the seats were already filled, causing him to vent his frustration in a loud voice, thus alienating the Chinese passengers. Feeling ill-used by people who only wanted his FEC, he refused to eat or upgrade to the soft sleeper offered by the conductor. He demonstrated his contempt for everyone by standing for 18 straight hours to Kunming. When he arrived, the city did not live up to his extravagant expectations, built up during his hellish train ride. The traveler hated Kunming in particular and China in general.

Three weeks later, he ran into his old companion at the Emei train station. After telling his own tales of woe, he asked the Daoist about his experience in Kunming. His friend replied, "I don't know, I'm still on the way. When I saw there were no hard sleeper tickets on the train, I made for the bus station. Before I got there I met a truck driver over a bowl of noodles, and went to his home village for a festival. There I met some fellows going north by bus. We made some great side trips together, then I joined a family returning home by boat. When train tickets south proved hard to get, I went hiking in the countryside instead. As you can see, I've enjoyed the way to Kunming and may actually reach the city before I leave this country."

the mountain. Spend the afternoon at the nearby Dujiang Waterworks or in Guanxian before returning to Chengdu.

Buses from the Xin Nanmen Chezhan Bus Station in Chengdu run to Qingcheng Shan frequently. Buses between the mountain and Guanxian run hourly from 07.00–16.00. Tickets are Rmb 0.50.

Dujiang Waterworks 都江堰

China's most ancient and successful water system is located on the Minjiang River 57 kilometers west of Chengdu. This giant flood control project, begun in 221 BC, irrigated the fertile Sichuan plain, allowing it to support the densest agricultural population anywhere in the world. The project diverts water from the fast-flowing Min Jiang into an intricate network of canals. The nearby Two King Temple (Erwang Si) was built to commemorate the scholar Li Bing and his son who designed the waterworks. Though historically important, many tourists find the site visually uninteresting. If it sounds appealing to you, combine it with a visit to Qingcheng Shan. The bus ride from Chengdu to the waterworks takes about two hours. The nearby town of Guanxian looks interesting and worth exploring for a day.

Lodging

The Black Coffee (Hei Kafei) 黑咖啡

In a country filled with whitewashed concrete hotels, the Black Coffee is a welcome sight. The hotel occupies a large, underground bomb shelter built on Mao's orders 20 years ago to protect people from a Russian nuclear attack.

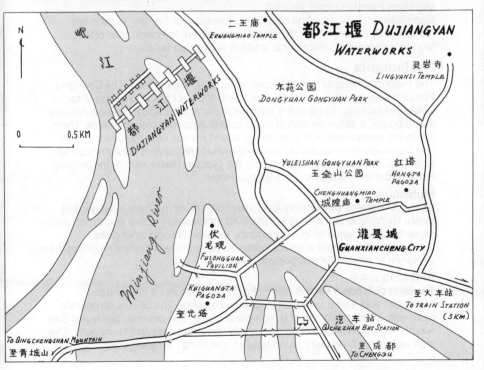

The long hallways, decorated with Occidental prints (mostly Renaissance), copies of Greek statues, plastic plants and strings of beads, hold two restaurants, a bar, a bakery, a nightclub and many rooms. Beds in a four-person room are Rmb 5 each and double rooms cost Rmb 16. The rooms are clean, but you can hear the occasional footfalls of rats in the ventilation system. Although the Black Coffee is a bit musty and noisy, it is a great place to write home about.

Binjiang Lu Fandian Hotel 宾江路饭店

This hotel is a favorite of Hong Kong Chinese tourists. Beds with mattresses in a four-bed room are FEC 10 and double rooms with private bathroom are FEC 40. There is a restaurant plus taxi and tour bus services here.

Jiaotong Fandian Hotel 交通饭店

Known as the Traffic Hotel, the Jiaotong Fandian is the newest budget hotel in Chengdu. It is conveniently located next to the south bus station. Beds in a four-bed room are FEC 8 each and all guests share communal toilets and showers.

Jinjiang Fandian Hotel 金江饭店

Chengdu's best hotel, the Jinjiang offers a full range of services including laundry and dry cleaning, a bar, a coffee shop, several restaurants, a beauty parlor, a post office and a Friendship Store. Unfortunately, the dorms were removed when the hotel was renovated in 1985. The cheapest bed is now FEC 24 in a triple room that shares communal toilets and showers.

Minshan Fandian Hotel 岷山饭店

Completed in 1987, this first class hotel towers over the city. Rooms are probably too expensive for the budget traveler but the bank, post office, laundry service, bar, restaurants and gift shops can be used.

Restaurants

The Furong, Chengdu's best known restaurant, is overrated. The Chengdu Fandian Restaurant is better, but we found the best place to be the Mapo Doufu Restaurant. To no one's surprise, it serves the spicy Sichuan delicacy *mapo doufu*, a delicious dish of bean curd in a special piquant sauce. There are many restaurants with English signs and menus near the Jinjiang Hotel, and hundreds of inexpensive, privately-owned restaurants exist throughout Chengdu. For good Western food, try the Garden Restaurant at the Jinjiang Hotel or the restaurants in the Minshan Hotel.

Nightclubs

Chengdu vibrates with activity long after most cities in China have gone to sleep. Nightclubs and discos entertain an increasingly active young population eager to spend some of their new-found wealth. Though most clubs discourage Westerners from attending, several will let travelers in, giving them a chance to enjoy Chinese popular culture.

BFR Club 白英容

The BFR club has a Rmb 6 cover charge and features a house band, a restaurant and a vast selection of Chinese alcohol. The BFR is an upscale club, with all the trappings of a high-class place. The patrons, displaying their wealth in a surprisingly conspicuous way, wear dresses and fancy suits. The staff welcomes foreigners as do English-speaking Chinese guests.

Golden Seat Cafe (Jinzuo Kafei Ting) 金坐咖啡厅

The Golden Seat nightclub has a Rmb 5 cover charge and features a house band, snacks and beer. Lots of mirrors, chrome and plastic — not terribly classy, but fun nonetheless.

Black Coffee 黑咖啡

The Black Coffee was a pioneer club in Chengdu, the 'in' place in 1985. It has long since lost its most interesting customers and musicians to other clubs, but a visit to this bomb shelter complex is still enjoyable.

Transportation

Chengdu Huochezhan Train Station 成都火车站

destination	departure
Chongqing 重庆	07:20, 19:25, 21:55, 22:10, 22:53
Jiachuan 嘉川	07:25
Kunming 昆明	07:42, 16:15
Beijing 北京	08:40, 12:20, 17:55
Yibin 宜宾	09:27
Shanghai 上海	12:55
Xi'an 西安	15:08
Taiyuan 太原	15:30
Mianyang 绵阳	16:00
Wuchang 武昌	17:30
Dukou 渡口	19:35
Jinjiang 金江	19:33
Lanzhou 兰州	20:25
Xi'an 西安	21:00

Xin Nanmen Qichezhan Bus Station 新南门汽车站

destination	departure	cost (Rmb)
Leshan 乐山	07:00–15:00 10 buses daily	6.30
Emei Shan 峨嵋山	07:00, 08:00, 13:30	6.00
Qingcheng Shan 青城山	07:00	
Kangding 康定	07:00, several buses every day	17.10
	08:00	14.60
Ya'an 雅安	06:30–14:00 8 buses daily	5.70
Dazu 大足	06:30	7.60
Neijiang 內江	07:30	6.00
Zigong 自贡	07:00	7.50
Yajiang 雅江	3rd and 7th of every month	24.10
Daowu 道孚	2nd and 8th of every month	27.40
Danba 丹巴	07:50, odd days	20.80
Ganzi 甘孜	6th and 10th of every month	35.20

Ximen Chezhan Bus Station 西门车站

destination	departure	cost (Rmb)
Erwang Si 二王寺 (Dujiang Waterworks)	8:30	2.00
Guanxian 灌县	08:00–18:00 9 buses daily	1.80
Heishui 黑水	08:00	14.90
Maowen 茂文	08:00	9.10
Aba 阿坝	07:30	24.00
Nanping 南坪	07:00, odd days	16.70
Songpan 松潘	07:00, odd days	15.70
Barkam (Ma'erkang) 马尔康	07:00, odd days	18.00

Qingyang Gong Qichezhan Bus Station 青羊宫汽车站

destination	departure	cost (Rmb)
Leshan 乐山	08:30, 08:50, 12:00	6.30
Ya'an 雅安	07:30, 08:20	5.70
Guanxian 灌县	09:10, 16:40	1.80
Daba 大巴	07:00–17:00 12 buses daily	1.80

Beimen Qichezhan Bus Station 北门汽车站

destination	departure	cost (Rmb)
Emei Shan 峨嵋山 (Baoguo Si)	07:40, 09:50	5.20
Leshan 乐山	06:50	5.50
Ya'an 雅安	06:00, 09:40	5.10
Mianyang 绵阳	07:20, 10:20	4.50
Jiangyou 江由	08:30, 12:50	5.80
Nanbu 南部	06:00	10.40

Chengdu Local Bus Routes

bus #1: From Beimen Qichezhan Bus Station to Wuhou Si Temple.

bus #4: From Daci Si Temple past the Exhibition Hall to Ximen Qichezhan Bus Station.

bus #9, 15: From Beimen Qichezhan Bus Station to the zoo.

bus #16: From Beizhan North Train Station to Nanzhan South Train Station.

bus #35: Travels the length of Binjiang Lu (near the Jiaotong Hotel, Black Coffee and the Jinjiang Hotel) all the way to Qingyang Gong.

Emei Town 峨嵋

Emei Town, resting between the Chengdu-Kunming rail line and Emei Shan Mountain, is a typical farming town of the Sichuan plain. The rich variety of fruits and vegetables available at the local street markets attests to the fertility of the land.

Things to do

Chinese tourists use Emei Town as a base from which to climb Emei Shan. Spend a day here exploring local markets and eating spicy Sichuan food at the numerous local restaurants.

Restaurants

Many of the small restaurants along Yujiadian Jie are good, several serving steamed dumplings (*jiaozi*). Try the coffee shop next to the Emei Xian Binguan Hotel for a snack, a cup of coffee or some hot milk.

Lodging

Emei Xian Binguan Hotel 峨嵋县宾馆

This guesthouse offers a range of accommodations. The cheapest is a bed in a four-bed room for Rmb 4. Nice double rooms, with TVs and private bathrooms with large tubs, go for Rmb 20. The hotel restaurant is said to be quite good.

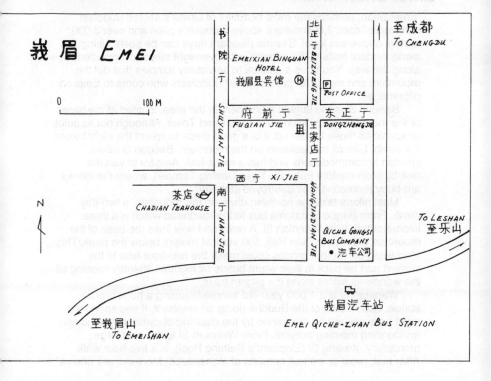

Transportation

Emei Shan Luyou Chuzu Qiche Gongsi Travel Bus Company
峨嵋山旅游出租汽车公司

destination	departure	cost (Rmb)
Chengdu 成都	8 buses daily	5.30
Leshan 乐山	8 buses daily	1.10
Emei Shan 峨嵋山	several buses daily	8.00 (going up)
(Jieyin Dian) 接引殿		6.00 (coming down)

Emei Qichezhan Bus Station 峨嵋汽车站

destination	departure	cost (Rmb)
Chengdu 成都南站	06:30, 08:30	5.20
(South Train Station)	10:30, 13:40	
Chengdu 成都火车站	09:30	5.20
(Main Train Station)		
Leshan 乐山	06:20–17:30	1.10
	12 buses daily	
Ya'an 雅安	07:30, 14:00	
Emei Shan 峨嵋山	07:00, 09:10	0.30
(Baoguo Si) 报国寺	12:30	

Emei Shan 峨嵋山

'Emei Shan, perhaps the most beautiful of China's sacred Buddhist mountains, rises 2,000 meters above Sichuan's plain and over 3,000 meters above sea level. Several pleasant days can be spent hiking along verdant trails to the summit, with overnight stops at monasteries along the way. You have a chance to see many temples that dot the mountain, and meet Tibetan and other Buddhists who come to Emei on pilgrimages.

'Baoguo Si is the largest monastery in the area, located at the base of the mountain a few kilometers from Emei Town. Although not as quiet or scenic as those farther up, it is a good place to spend the night before the climb. Like all monasteries on the mountain, Baoguo Si offers spartan accommodations and has a mess-hall. Also try to visit the nearby sixth-century Fuhu Si (Tiger Taming Temple), where the monks are busy recreating their destroyed statuary.

'Most hikers take the northern route up the mountain, a two-day climb. From Baguo Si catch a bus to the roadhead which is a three-kilometer trek from Wannian Si. A new road now links the base of the mountain with Jinyin Dian Hall, 500 vertical meters below the peak. This road was built so tour groups could make the two-hour hike to the summit and be back in their warm hotels by nightfall, thereby missing all the wonderful sights along the pilgrim trails.

'Wannian Si is a 1,000-year-old temple featuring a huge bronze statue, cast in 980, of the Buddha riding an elephant. If you spend the night here you will be awakened by the clashing of cymbals and gongs announcing morning prayers. From Wannian Si to the next large monastery, Xixiang Si (Elephant's Bathing Pool), is a five-hour walk. After that, most of the trail consists of stone steps. Monkeys are often a

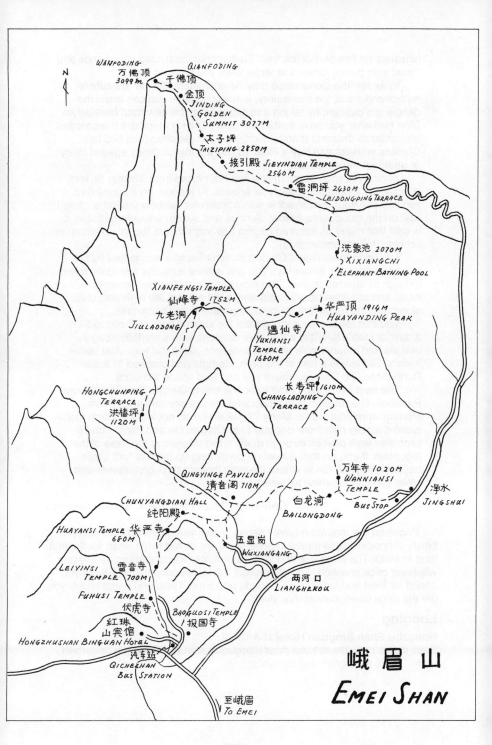

WANFODING
万佛顶
3099 M

QIANFODING
千佛顶
金顶
JINDING
GOLDEN
SUMMIT 3077M

太子坪
TAIZIPING 2850M

接引殿 JIEYINDIAN TEMPLE
2540M

雷洞坪 2430M
LEIDONGPING TERRACE

洗象池 2070M
XIXIANGCHI
'ELEPHANT BATHING POOL

XIANFENGSI TEMPLE
仙峰寺 1752M

九老洞
JIULAODONG

华严顶 1914M
HUAYANDING PEAK

遇仙寺
YUKIANSI
TEMPLE
1680M

HONGCHUNPING
TERRACE
洪椿坪
1120M

长老坪 1610M
CHANGLAOPING
TERRACE

QINGYINGE PAVILION
清音阁 710M

万年寺 1020M
WANNIANSI
TEMPLE

净水
JINGSHUI

CHUNYANGDIAN HALL
纯阳殿

白龙洞
BAILONGDONG

BUS STOP

HUAYANSI TEMPLE 华严寺
680M

五显岗
WUXIANGANG

LEIYINSI 雷音寺
TEMPLE 700M

FUHUSI TEMPLE
伏虎寺

两河口
LIANGHEKOU

红珠
山宾馆
HONGZHUSHAN BINGUAN HOTEL

BAOGUOSI TEMPLE
报国寺

汽车站
QICHEZHAN
BUS STATION

至峨眉
To EMEI

峨眉山
EMEI SHAN

N

nuisance on this part of the trail. To disperse them, clap your hands and thrust your palms forward to show them you have no food.

'In winter, the stone steps may be encrusted with ice. Be sure to rent crampons at the monastery. In icy conditions you can avoid the dangerous descent by taking a minibus down the new road from Jieyin Dian Hall after you have visited the peak. The icy steps are treacherous, far harder to descend than to climb, and people often take bad falls. Chinese workers can buy a Rmb 10,000 insurance policy against injury or death on the mountain.

'Jinding (Golden Summit) is a five-hour climb from Xixiang Si, with spectacular mountain scenery all around. At the top, on a sunny day, you can see your own shadow within a circular rainbow (called a 'glory') cast on the cloudbanks below. Sunrise and sunset are unforgettable. It is said that many an inspired pilgrim has leaped from the mountaintop in ecstasy (not recommended).

'The once-magnificent Golden Summit Temple was gutted by fire several years ago. Nowadays you can admire a nearby television tower through its charred arches. The monastery guesthouse, however, is intact and provides heavy coats and quilts against the nighttime chill along with the usual fare for both vegetarians and carnivores.

'You can retrace your steps from the summit back to Baoguo Si in a day, or take a two-day alternative descent, with waterfalls, dragon bridges and innumerable stone inscriptions along the way. Just below Xixiang Si there is a fork in the path. Go right and proceed to Jiulao Dong (Nine Old Caves), where you can also spend the night.

'The next place you come to on the trail is Qingyin Ge (Clear Sound Pavilion). The pavilion is in a beautiful area of streams and forests, offering wonderful walks. Many Chinese who do not want to climb to the summit simply hike from Baoguo Si to Qingyin Ge and back. The 16-kilometer walk passes through many small villages at the base of the mountain. If you do this, it is worth continuing up the trail half a mile beyond Qingying Ge to where the path threads through a ravine with steep cliffs and rushing torrents'.

China Off The Beaten Track, Brian Schwartz

Prices on the mountain have risen in recent years. Dorm beds, fruit and bowls of noodles have tripled in price since we visited Emei Shan for the first time in 1983. The price rise is due to the influx of tourists who routinely pay whatever price is asked. To help protect the local economy, note what you spend for food and lodging in Chengdu and Emei Town and bargain until you get the price down to near that level.

Lodging

Hongzhu Shan Binguan Hotel 红珠山宾馆
Beds in this new, clean hotel near Baoguo Si start at FEC 7 in a three-bed room. There are communal showers.

Transportation

Baoguo Si Qichezhan Bus Station 报国寺汽车站

destination	departure	cost (Rmb)
Chengdu 成都	06:50−15:30 11 buses daily	5.50
Leshan 乐山	07:00−18:00 16 buses daily	1.30
Emei Town 峨嵋	frequent buses	0.30

Minibuses take passengers from the Baoguo Si parking lot to Emei Town or the train station (Rmb 1), Wannian Si (Rmb 2), Jieyin Dian (Rmb 8) or to Leshan (Rmb 3).

From Jieyin Dian, minibuses run to Baoguo Si (Rmb 6), Emei Town (Rmb 6), or the train station (Rmb 6.50). These fill up quickly and stop running before 17:00.

Leshan 乐山

Leshan has been settled for over 3,000 years at the place where three mighty rivers converge, the Dadu He, the Qingyi Jiang and the Min Jiang. Since ancient times, rich and influential travelers have flocked to see Leshan's natural and man-made wonders.

Leshan lies 165 kilometers south of Chengdu and 31 kilometers southeast of Emei Shan Mountain. Steep, jungle-covered mountains surround Leshan's historical sites, which date from six of China's greatest dynasties. The prime attraction of the region is Dafo, the Big Buddha, the largest Buddha statue in the world.

Things to do

Leshan is one of the most colorful towns in Sichuan. Markets near the river wharf are the liveliest, showing the town's prosperity in the wide range of goods and the large crowds. Every restaurant we visited in this area was good. Even late at night, vendors cluster around the movie theater serving local snacks.

Walk along the banks of the Min Jiang or the Dadu He rivers to see the fishing, freight and passenger boats. On warm days, sit in the sun at the junction of these two rivers and watch the fishermen secure their nets to bamboo frames in the river.

Dafo Si Temple 大佛寺

Dafo Si is the site of Dafo, the 71-meter-high sitting Buddha that was carved out of a mountain during the Tang Dynasty. The grandeur of the statue is best seen from the ferry boat that passes below it on the Min Jiang, and from a teahouse built close to the statue's head. A long stairway descends the cliffs beside the Big Buddha so tourists can have their pictures taken sitting on his big toe. Nearby, small grottoes have 2,000-year-old stone carvings.

To reach Dafo Si, take a ferryboat past it to Wuyou Si Temple further down the Min Jiang. In their haste to see the statue, many tourists miss the hilltop gardens and temple halls of Wuyou Si. This well-cared-for site has pleasant teashops, no crowds, and all the splendor of Dafo Si. Follow the trail down the hill behind Wuyou Si and cross a small river on a suspension bridge to enter

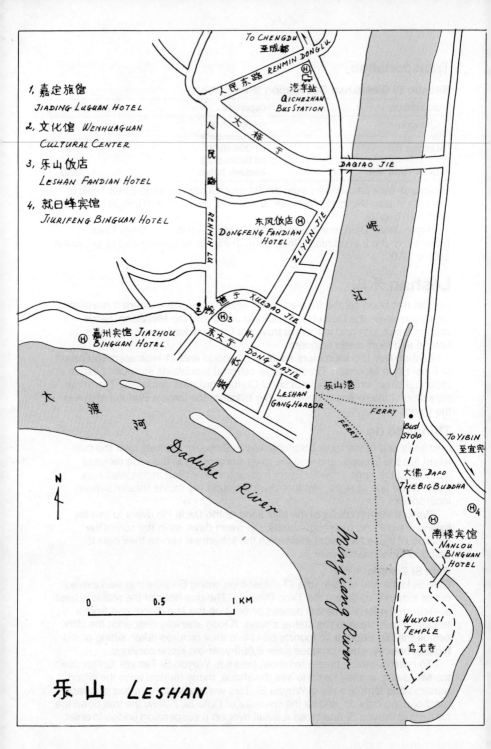

1. 嘉定旅馆
   JIADING LÜGUAN HOTEL
2. 文化馆 WENHUAGUAN
   CULTURAL CENTER
3. 乐山饭店
   LESHAN FANDIAN HOTEL
4. 就日峰宾馆
   JIURIFENG BINGUAN HOTEL

To CHENGDU
至成都
RENMIN DONGLU 人民东路
汽车站
QICHEZHAN
BUS STATION

人民路 DAGIAO JIE

大桥子

岷

东风饭店
DONGFENG
FANDIAN
HOTEL

ZIYUN JIE

江

RENMIN LU

嘉州宾馆 JIAZHOU
BINGUAN HOTEL

XUEDAO JIE 学道子

DONG DAJIE 东大子

乐山港
LESHAN
GANG HARBOR

FERRY

大

渡

河

Daduhe River

FERRY

Busi
Stop

To YIBIN
至宜宾

大佛 DAFO
THE BIG BUDDHA

南楼宾馆
NANLOU
BINGUAN
HOTEL

Minjiang River

N

0   0.5   1 KM

WUYOUSI
TEMPLE
乌尤寺

乐山 LESHAN

Dafo Si. Many private restaurants at the bridge serve lunch, though prices are high.

The manicured gardens at Dafo Si offer a peaceful resting place. After a visit to the Big Buddha, explore the hill behind him to find a crumbling Tang Dynasty pagoda. Near Dafo Si is the Zangjinglou Buddhist temple. Though inactive, it features well-restored gold statues, small wooden images and shrines. Nearby, two hotels look quiet and comfortable. Follow the large trail north past Dafo along the river until it reaches the road and the bus stop. Here you can take a bus to Emei Town or Chengdu, or cross the river by ferry back to Leshan. The walk up the river to the bridge and into town takes about an hour.

Farther Away

Qianfo Yan Thousand Buddha Cliffs 千佛岩
This famous Buddhist site contains two thousand images that were carved during the Sui, Tang, Ming and Qing Dynasties. We did not visit it ourselves, but it is said to contain some of the best carvings in Sichuan Province. To get there, take a local bus to Jiajiang from either Emei or Leshan.

Meishan 眉山
Halfway between Chengdu and Leshan sits Meishan, a small Sichuanese town. According to a local tourist brochure, it is famous for the Temple of the Three Sus. This former residence of three Northern Song Dynasty scholars surnamed Su has been converted into a Sichuan-style temple and park. Several locals we talked to said it was worth a visit.

Lodging

Jiazhou Binguan Hotel 嘉州宾馆
This expensive, first-rate hotel, at FEC 40 per bed in the cheapest double room, is far outside the budget of most independent travelers.

Dongfeng Fandian Hotel 东风饭店
This cheap, fairly clean hotel is in the center of Leshan. Double rooms with television and a balcony cost Rmb 8. Communal showers have hot water every night.

Jiading Luguan Hotel 嘉定旅馆
This grubby hotel has improved since 1983. It is next to the bus station, convenient for early morning departures. Beds are Rmb 3.50 each in a double, Rmb 2.90 each in a triple and Rmb 2.45 each in a four-bed room.

At Dafo
Scenic and relaxing accommodations can be found at two hotels on the hill behind Dafo but they are inconvenient for visits to Leshan and far from transportation centers. The nearest buses are at the stop on the road near Dafo.

Nanlou Binguan Hotel 南楼宾馆
This beautiful little guesthouse is attached to a temple just behind Dafo and is a frequent convention site. Nice double rooms start at Rmb 21.20.

Jiurifeng Binguan Hotel 就日峰宾馆
This guesthouse is about half a kilometer away from Dafo, away from the nearest road, a quiet, peaceful place to stay. Beds start at Rmb 7 each in a four-bed room and double rooms with private bath are Rmb 24.

Transportation

Leshan Qichezhan Bus Station 乐山汽车站

destination	distance (kms)	departure	cost (Rmb)
Chongqing 重庆 (2 days)	438	06:20	21.00
Yibin 宜宾	264	06:40	9.20
Emei Town 峨嵋	31	06:40 – 17:30 12 buses daily	1.10
Emei Shan 峨嵋山 (Baoguo Si) 报国寺	39	07:00 – 16:30 8 buses daily	1.40
Chengdu 成都	169	06:10 – 15:00 9 buses daily	5.60
Huochezhan 火车站 (train station)	14	07:40 – 18:10	1.10

(Leshan Qichezhan Bus Station sells train tickets, too).

Lunchuan Qiche Shoupiao Wai (bus stop below Dafo)

Eight daily buses run to Chengdu from 09:20 – 16:40. Many vehicles, both public and private, go to Emei Town, Emei Shan and the train station.

Emei Huochezhan Train Station 峨嵋火车站

The Emei Huochezhan Train Station is 21 kilometers from Leshan and can be reached by bus from the Leshan Qichezhan Bus Station.

destination	departure
Chengdu 成都	13:00, 16:00
Kunming 昆明	09:50, 18:42

Xichang and the Liangshan Yi Region
凉山彝族自治州

Xichang (西昌) is the capital of the Liangshan Yi Nationality Autonomous Region, which occupies the southernmost portion of Sichuan Province. Xichang's 150,000 inhabitants, a majority of whom are Han Chinese, live either in the old, walled town or in new neighborhoods extending south towards the train station. The old city has narrow cobblestone streets flanked by stone and timber houses. Here vendors and shopowners sell their wares outdoors on the roadside. The dry, sunny climate encourages much public, open-air town life. In the new section of town, markets encroach on wide, paved avenues where the occasional passing truck looks incongruous among horse-drawn carts and farmers toting goods to market on shoulder poles.

Xichang is surrounded by diverse landscapes. North and west of town, dry mountains covered in scrub brush or cactus crowd the horizon. South and east of town, green mountains watered by underground springs overlook fertile fields and Qionghai Lake. While interesting to visit for itself, Xichang is also the best jump-off point for the remote Yi and Tibetan regions of southern Sichuan Province.

Things to do

Xichang's ancient city wall is still three-quarters intact and can be seen well from the South, East and North Gates. Inside the wall, Han, Yi, Hui and an

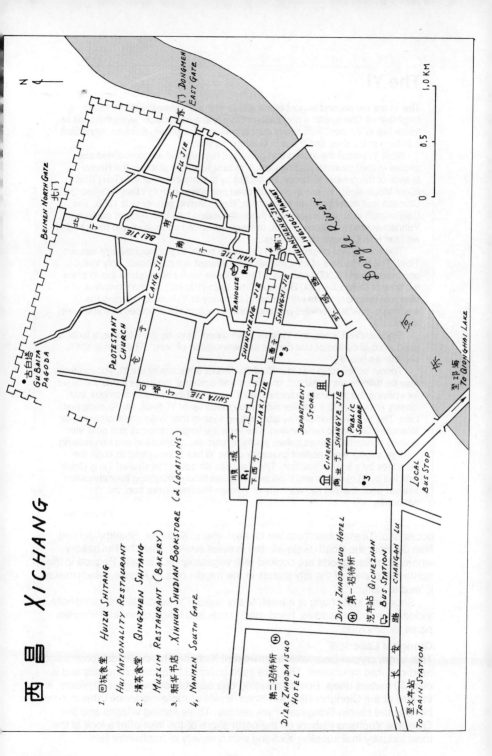

西昌 XICHANG

1. 回族食堂 HUIZU SHITANG
   HUI NATIONALITY RESTAURANT
2. 清真食堂 QINGZHEN SHITANG
   MUSLIM RESTAURANT (BAKERY)
3. 新华书店 XINHUA SHUDIAN BOOKSTORE (2 LOCATIONS)
4. 南门 NANMEN SOUTH GATE

古白塔 GUBAITA PAGODA

北门 BEIMEN NORTH GATE

东门 DONGMEN EAST GATE

PROTESTANT CHURCH

北宁 BEINING JIE

南宁 NAN JIE

仓宁 CANG JIE

石宁 SHITA JIE

顺城宁 SHUNCHENG JIE

茶宁 TEAHOUSE Rd.

上西子 SHANGXI JIE

环城市场 HUANCHENG JIE LIVESTOCK MARKET

东河 Donghe River

至邛海 To QIONGHAI LAKE

川 Fu JIE

上西子 XIAXI JIE

川哭城宁 R₁

下西子 XIAXI JIE

DEPARTMENT STORE 商业田

CINEMA 商业宁 SHANGYE JIE

PUBLIC SQUARE

3

3

LOCAL BUS STOP

第一招待所 H DIYI ZHAODAISUO HOTEL

汽车站 QICHEZHAN BUS STATION

长安路 CHANGAN LU

第二招待所 H DIER ZHAODAISUO HOTEL

至火车站 To TRAIN STATION

1.0 KM
0.5
0

193

The Yi

The Yi are the second largest ethnic group in the Southwest and the fourth largest in all China, with a population of five and a half million. More than half of these live in Yunnan, with heavy concentrations in southern Sichuan, significant numbers in Guizhou and a few in Guangxi as well.

Most Yi inhabit the slopes and gorges of high upland areas, isolated and secure in their mountain fastnesses. The best example of this is the Nuosu branch of the greater Yi family. Protected by the immensity of the Liang Shan (Cool Mountains), 'where even birds need permisssion to fly', they repelled the Chinese and maintained an aristocratic, slave-owning society until 1958. The Sani branch is an exception; they live in the rolling hills and fields of eastern Yunnan around the Stone Forest, practice advanced agriculture and have traded with the Han Chinese for centuries.

The source and origin of the Yi lies to the north, in the mountains of eastern Tibet. The particulars of their migration southward are not known, only that it occurred around 3,000 years ago. The Chinese have known about the Yi since the time of Confucius (500 BC) and Sima Qian (100 BC), China's greatest classical historian, wrote with amazing accuracy of Yi habits, including the wearing of hair in a forward-pointing horn, a custom still practiced in some areas today.

Since earliest times, the Yi have been called 'Lolo' by the Chinese, a loosely-used word of contempt that carries the connotation of 'wog'. The term is still sometimes heard.

Today, scholarship has identified 30 distinct branches of the Yi. Though there may be differences in habitat, costumes and customs, language forms the basis for unifying the disparate branches. All Yi speak a Tibeto-Burman tongue that closely links them to a smaller sub-group made up of Yi, Naxi, Nu, Kucong and Lisu. The Yi have their own syllabic writing system that looks remarkably similar to ancient Germanic runic writing. The texts are largely religious and deal with animist concerns such as nature spirits, excorcism, propitiation and rain-making.

The strong, independent character of the Yi has been upheld through the centuries by a warrior tradition. The Nanzhao Kingdom that rivalled Tang China was led by Yi generals and in recent times, as though mirroring their ancestors' exalted past, the last two warlords of Yunnan Province were from the Yi nationality.

Patrick Booz

occasional Tibetan merchant vie for customers. Xiaxi Jie, Shangxi Jie and Nan Jie near the South Gate are the liveliest streets. Visit the Hui bakery, where all baked goods are cooked with vegetable oil. Gubaita Pagoda in the northwest corner of the city stands in the middle of a PLA base, which makes it hard to visit.

Shopping in Xichang is a treat. Many special Yi products are found here, including wooden saddles, hand-made rings and long copper and wooden pipes for smoking.

Qionghai Lake 邛海
This large, crystal-clear lake southwest of Xichang stands amidst forests and reed-covered mountains. The lake itself covers 31 square kilometers and is over 30 meters deep. Boats, including one capable of towing water-skiers, are for hire at the Qionghai Binguan Hotel. Boats at more moderate rates can be hired at the Haibin Gongyuan Park nearby. Three fishing villages and the Qionghai Yuchang Fishery on the north shore of the lake offer a look at the local industry that supplies Xichang with a variety of freshwater fish.

Lushan Reed Mountain 芦山

Lushan has been a Buddhist holy site since the Tang Dynasty. Today, a temple, a library and six nunneries dot the trail leading from the Liangshan Yi Nationality Museum to the peak. The entire region is a protected forest. Many of the trees are labeled and dated (in Chinese only), and the oldest cypress trees date back to the Eastern Han Dynasty (206 BC−8 AD). The walk to the top of the mountain takes no longer than four hours, and you can reach the radio towers on the ridge above the temples in under three hours.

The following sites are listed in order, from the bottom of the mountain to to the peak.

Liangshan Yi Nationality Museum (Liangshan Yizu Bowuguan) In contrast to many musty provincial museums, this clean, well-organized complex displays an interesting mixture of artifacts, maps and photos depicting the economic, cultural and political history of the Yi people. The display of Yi ceremonial clothing is magnificent. All captions are in Chinese, but most displays speak for themselves. Admission for foreigners is Rmb 2 but bargain for the local price which is Rmb 0.20.

Guangfu Si Nunnery The halls are nice, but most of the statuary is new. Some of the oldest cypress trees on the mountain are in and around the courtyard area.

Gusanan This nunnery houses the Lushan Zhaodaisuo Hostel (芦山招待所). Beds are Rmb 1 each and good vegetarian food is served.

Guzu Shidian Library One lone monk works here transcribing religious texts. Rough stone statues of generals from the Three Kingdoms Period decorate the main hall.

Guanyin Ge The statues and wall hangings here appear significantly older than those elsewhere on the mountain. Out front sits an ornate stele with text and a picture of Guanyin, the Goddess of Mercy.

Yaochi Gong Fine old maps of Chickenfoot Mountain and the Dali area of Yunnan hang on the walls. The elderly nuns here are as lively as teenagers. In the back is a small shrine in honor of the recently deceased abbess.

Guwang Huangdian Unusual free-standing statues adorn this small nunnery, which is now being restored.

Qingyang Gong Old unrestored frescoes, beautiful despite their poor condition, cover the walls of the main hall. People here like to congregate in the small, smoky courtyard.

Zushi Dian This temple was razed to the ground during the Cultural Revolution. Very little remains.

Radio Towers On the crest of a ridge north of the peak, the flat ground around the radio towers is an ideal camping or picnic spot with a view of the lake below, the mountain and Xichang to the north. Dozens of eagles nest nearby and boldly duel overhead, indifferent to the watchers below. The peak is an hour's walk beyond these towers.

Qinglong Si Monastery 青龙寺

Locals told us that Qinglong Si, in the hills above the southeastern shore of Qionghai Lake, is comparable to the nunneries on Lushan. Its prime attraction is the lush forest surrounding the monastery. According to local belief, the trees there are unusually tall because the water from nearby springs is especially potent. To get there from Xichang, take bus #6 to its eastern terminus and walk south to Dayucun Village on the shore of Qionghai Lake.

Follow the shoreline to the monastery. Alternatively, you can arrange for a fishing boat to take you across the lake to the monastery from Haibin Gongyuan Park.

Lodging

Qionghai Binguan Hotel 邛海宾馆

This luxurious, lakeside hotel complex is popular for government conferences. The cheapest double room, which goes for Rmb 16, is spotlessly clean, large and has a bathroom with a tub and hot water. The hotel food is tolerable, but the Lushan Fandian, 50 meters outside the main gate to the left, has delicious dumplings (shuijiao).

In Xichang, try the **Diyi Zhaodaisuo Hotel** or the **Dier Zhaodaisuo Hotel**. Both are cheap and near the bus station.

Transportation

Xichang Qichezhan Bus Station 西昌汽车站

destination	distance (kms)	departure	cost (Rmb)
Chengdu 成都 (2 days)	552	06:30	19.00
Xide 喜德	82	10:30, 12:30	2.70
Xinshizhen 新市镇 (two days)	337	07:20	11.30
Muli 木里 (2 days)	253	07:00, 08:00	11.90
Yanyuan 盐源	150	07:00, 08:00	5.30
Leibo 雷波 (2 days)	317	13:00	11.20
Jinyang 金阳 (2 days)	215	07:30	10.10

The bus station sells plane tickets for the Monday and Thursday flights to Chengdu departing at 09:10.

Xichang Huochezhan Train Station 西昌火车站

destination	departure
Chengdu 成都	00:53, 07:00, 20:08
Kunming 昆明	02:54, 19:50
Jinjiang 金江	07:11

Farther away

Luoji Shan Mountain 螺髻山

Luoji Shan, 50 kilometers south of Xichang, is a remote mountain region notable for its vast, mature forests, its 'five-color' lakes, meadows bursting with wildflowers and rugged upland terrain. Chinese film companies love it. Many movies have been filmed here, including the dramatic true story of an American pilot who was captured by Yi people in World War II and forced to work as a slave until 1949.

There are no hotels or restaurants in the area, so food and camping gear are essential. Students regularly camp out for at least two nights and they report that the most spectacular lakes, connected by a series of waterfalls, are quite a distance from the road. The climb to the top, said one local teacher, is equal to a hike up Emei Shan with no monasteries, walkways, restaurants or other forms of support. To get there, take the daily bus to Puge and get off at the mountain as the bus passes it.

Xilou Village

Xilou in Puge county is the site of the annual July Torch Festival. *China Tourism* says 'the Torch Festival in July at Xilou Village is a "feast for the eyes" for it offers to visitors such entertainment as bull fights, horse races and wrestling as well as a "Torch Girl" pageant.'

To get there, take the bus to Puge and then another bus (or walk) to Xilou.

Muli 木里

Muli is a Tibetan Autonomous County two days west by bus from Xichang. Historically, Tibetans from this area periodically raided territories to the south, sometimes marauding as far as Lijiang where they earned a reputation as ferocious fighters. We know nothing about this area except that the surrounding mountains are very high and there is a monastery in the town.

Zhaojue 昭觉

Zhaojue, lying in a broad valley 3,200 meters above sea level, looks like a modern Chinese town until you see the people. *National Geographic* (Vol. 168, no. 3) estimates the population to be 93% Yi. The poorer people live in the hills around town, coming to Zhaojue only to trade for supplies. They spend the cold nights huddled under their black capes sleeping on the road.

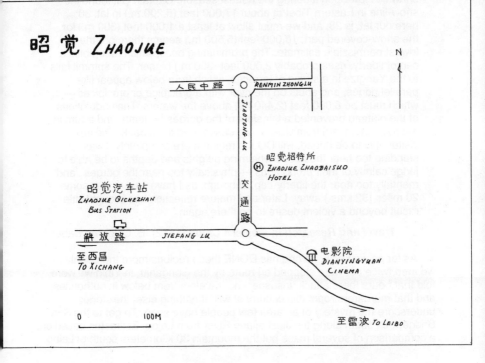

The bus from Xichang to Leibo stops for the night at Zhaojue and the Gonganju will most likely send any foreigner they find back to Xichang. We believe the officials in Zhaojue have little tolerance for stray travellers because of the obvious poverty here.

Leibo 雷波

Leibo is a small town on the banks of the Jinshajiang River, 317 kilometers from Xichang. The main place of interest near Leibo is Ma Hu (Horse Lake), 40 kilometers along the road north of town. A monastery occupies a small island in the middle of the lake. Reports about this monastary vary. Some say monks live there and welcome guests; others say that a burned-out shell is all that remains. Everyone agrees that there is a place nearby to buy food and stay the night. To get to Mahu, take the bus from Leibo at 07:30 or trek on the trail, said to be 10 kilometers shorter than the road. To get to Leibo from Xichang, hitchhike or take the two-day bus which passes through Zhaojue. From Yibin, take a boat to Xinshizhen and a bus for one day from there.

Taiyang Qiao (Sun Bridge) 太阳桥

'. . . As we turned a knoll, one of those discoveries which so seldom fall to the fortune of the modern tourist flashed upon me. About 20 miles (32 kms.) distant to the north-west, in a cloudless sky, rose a stupendous boss (outcrop), the culminating point, and the terminal, of a snowy ridge some 15 miles (24 kms.) long. The height of the ridge can only be estimated, as I possessed no means of measuring low angles conveniently. An approximation may however be easily made since the snow lies low upon it during the hottest season. Captain Gill found the snow-line in Eastern Tibet at about 17,000 feet (5,200 m.) in lat. 30; here our lat. is 28, and we must allow at least a 1,000 feet (300 m.) for the snow-covered part; 18,000 feet (5,500 m.) seems therefore the lowest permissible estimate. The prominating boss, which resembles a cap of liberty, rises probably 2,000 feet (600 m.) higher. The summit falls to the Yangtze in a series of terraces, which from below appear like parallel ridges, and abuts on the river with a precipice or precipices — which must be 8,000 feet (2,440 m.) above the waters. The undulations of the plateau prevented a fair sight of the gorges beneath, and a turn in the river shut them from view as we descended to its bank. The next visitor, it is to be hoped, will DO the region more completely. I was standing too near those overwhelming heights and depths to be able to judge calmly of their proportions — physically too near the gorges , and mentally too near the liberty-cap, although, as I have said, it was some 20 miles (32 kms.) away. Later and mature reflection has brought little result beyond a violent desire to go there again.'

Travel and Research in Western China (1882), E. Colborne Baber

As far as we know, no one has DONE these regions more thoroughly — we tried twice but were stopped en route by the Gonganju. In Yibin we were told that bears there attack unsuspecting travelers from below in outhouses, and that murderers roam this country at will. If nothing else, the stories underscore the mystery of an area few people have seen. To get to the Sun Bridgé, trek south along the Jinshajiang River from Leibo. Estimates based on a comparison of several maps put the mountain 30 kilometers south of Leibo.

Yibin 宜宾

Yibin, known as the First Port on the Yangzi, is a small city at the point where the Min Jiang and Jinsha Jiang join to form the Yangzi River. Evidence of a rich history is everywhere, including Xuanzu Dian, a Three Kingdoms-period pavilion, Daguan Lou, a Ming Dynasty hall built with no nails, and the Black and White Pagodas.

Yibin is an important market city with long, cobblestoned streets filled with shoppers looking over the large selection of fruits, vegetables and other commodities.

Things to do

Markets are most active around Daguan Lou. The best examples of traditional Sichuan architecture are found along the alleys near the wharf. There are three city parks, a Three Kingdoms-period park nearby (with the pavilion), beautiful riverfront areas to explore and two pagodas.

Townsfolk told us the story of the Black and White Pagodas. Very long ago (probably during the Tang Dynasty) the two pagodas were built simultaneously, identical except for their opposite color. Much later, but still long ago, a high government official decided to switch the tops of the two pagodas to fulfill a perverse whim. This was done with great care, the job taking several years, and since then the top of the White Pagoda has been black, the top of the Black Pagoda white.

The best rest spot we found was the teahouse just above the intersection of the two rivers. Drink tea (Rmb 0.15) while watching the active First Port on the Yangzi just below. There are actually five small ports further up the Jinsha Jiang, but these are considered to be above the Yangzi River, not on it.

Farther away

Liubei Chi Pools 流杯池
We do not know where this site is or what it is, nor did anyone we asked, but it was on an all-Sichuan tourist map and might be worth the adventure to find it.

Zhuhai (Bamboo Sea) 竹海
Not far from Jiang'an, Zhuhai is a large government-protected bamboo forest reputed to extend as far as the eye can see. In older groves the largest trees grow to half a meter or more in diameter, extending 40 to 50 meters into the air. One Gonganju official said that guests frequently wander off the trails, lose their sense of direction in the thickets and become lost. To get there from Yibin or Chongqing, take a bus to Jiang'an. The Bamboo Sea is nearby. It is also possible to hitchhike into the region from northern Guizhou Province.

Xingwen 兴文
Xingwen is a city reputed to have large caves and a Stone Forest much like the one near Kunming. From Xingwen, you can bus or hitchhike south into northern Guizhou Province.

Changning 长宁
Changning, 34 kilometers southwest of Jiang'an, is the site of Xuanluo Dian (Spiral Snail Hall). We could find no information on either the town or the site, but the government must recognize some tourist potential since Changning was officially opened to foreign tourists in November 1986. Buses to Changning run daily from Yibin.

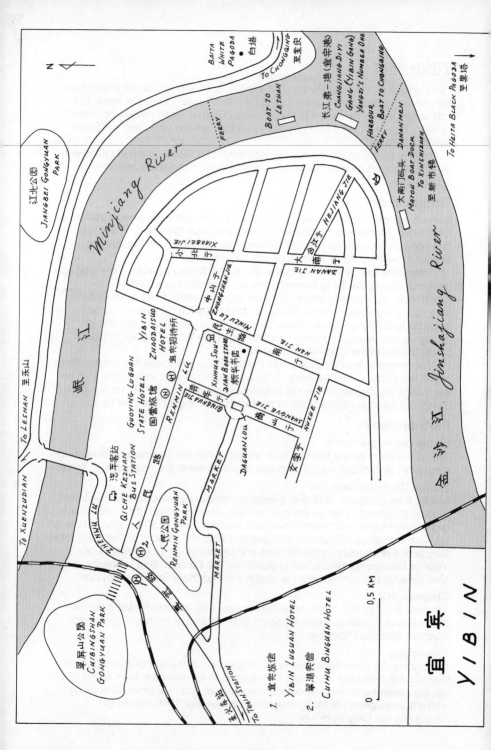

YIBIN 宜宾

1. 宜宾旅馆 Yibin Luguan Hotel
2. 翠湖宾馆 Cuihu Binguan Hotel

Minjiang River 岷江

Jinshajiang River 金沙江

To Leshan 至乐山
To Xuenzudian 至序族店

江北公园 Jiangbei Gongyuan Park

BAITA WHITE PAGODA 白塔

TO CHONGQING 至重庆

长江第一港(宜宾港) Changjiang-Diyi Gang (Yibin Gang) Yangzi's Number One Harbour

FERRY

BOAT TO LESHAN

BOAT TO CHONGQING

FERRY

大南门码头 Matou Boat Dock

大南门 Dananmen

To Kinshizhen 至新市镇

To Heita Black Pagoda 至黑塔

汽车客站 Qiche Kezhan Bus Station

Guoying Luguan State Hotel 国营旅馆

Yibin Zhaodaisuo Hotel 宜宾招待所

Xinhua Shu Dian Bookstore 新华书店

人民公园 Renmin Gongyuan Park

Cuibingshan Gongyuan Park 翠屏山公园

To Train Station 至火车站

Zhenwu Lu 真武路

Renmin Lu 人民路

Qinghua Jie 青华街

Zhongshan Jie 中山街

Xiaobei Jie 小北街

Hejiang Jie 合江街

Minzu Lu 民族路

Nan Jie 南街

Danan Jie 大南街

Market 市

Daguanlou 大观楼

Shangye Jie 商业街

Nuoxe Jie 挪学街

Wenzixi 文字于

0 0,5 KM

N

Gongxian 珙县

Gongxian, 63 kilometers south of Yibin, is the site of Renxuan Guan,（人悬棺）a collection of ancient burial mounds.

Luzhou 泸州

Luzhou, 143 kilometers east of Yibin, sits at the confluence of the Yangzi and the Tuo Jiang rivers. The main attraction in Lushan is Yunfeng Si (Cloud Peak Temple),（云峰寺）which is said to be large and beautiful. Luzhou is accessible by bus from Yibin and by boat from both Yibin and Chongqing.

Lodging

Yibin Zhaodaisuo Hotel 宜宾招待所

The Gonganju requests that all foreign travelers stay here. Cheap beds go for Rmb 2 in a four-person room. Double rooms start at Rmb 9. A detailed map of Yibin stands in in the lobby.

Guoying Luguan Hotel 国营旅馆

Next to the Yibin Zhaodaisuo, this place looks much the same. Boat, bus and plane tickets (Chengdu airport) are sold here. All buses depart from the bus station, regardless of where tickets are sold.

Cuihu Binguan Hotel and the Yibin Luguan Hotel are both near the bus station and should be cheap.

Transportation

Changjiang Diyi Gang (First Port on the Yangzi) 长江第一港

Boat tickets are sold at an office near the wharf on Hejiang Jie, but workers might refuse to sell them to you. If so, go to the correct dock a few minutes before departure and buy your ticket after boarding the boat.

destination	departure	cost (Rmb)
Xinshizhen 新市镇 (via Pingshan)	07:00 (even days)	8.70
Leshan 乐山	daily	
Chongqing 重庆 (hovercraft)（飞船）	06:30 (varies by season; arrives same day)	

Yibin Huochezhan Train Station 宜宾火车站

destination	departure
Chengdu 成都	08:47 (express) 11:17 (slow)
Chongqing 重庆	05:58
Zigong 自贡	05:58, 08:47, 11:17
Neijiang 內江	05:58, 08:47, 11:47

Qiche Kezhan Bus Station 汽车客站

destination	departure	cost (Rmb)
Chongqing 重庆	05:50 06:20 (Japanese bus) 重庆日本车	10.50 13.70
Leshan 乐山	06:30	9.10
Pingshan 屏山	06:50	2.80
Xingwen 兴文	07:20	5.00
Jiang'an 江安	check at the station	

Dazu 大足

The name Dazu means Big Foot, but it is of no relation to the mythical *yeti*. Dazu is famous as one of China's most important centers for Buddhist art. Its grottoes, constructed between the ninth and 13th centuries, have been under national protection as historical relics since 1961. This is probably the best of the hundreds of sites in Southwest China at which to see sculpture and bas-relief images.

The town itself, 163 kilometers from Chongqing and 34 kilometers from the rail line at Youting, sits on the vast Sichuan farm plain. Dazu is sometimes included in tour group itineraries, but its limited facilities and the remoteness of the area keep their numbers down. A visit to Dazu is a good way to break up the long trip by bus from Leshan to Chongqing and an attractive alternative to a long wait in Chongqing for the cruise down the Yangzi River.

Things to do

This is a delightful town for strolling around, and its friendly inhabitants leave tourists in peace. There may be more tea houses per capita in Dazu than anywhere in China. Bring a book or a deck of cards and spend an afternoon sipping tea in a quaint, Sichuanese *chaguan*.

Beishan (Northern Hill) 北山

Beishan, called Longgang in ancient times, is two kilometers north of Dazu. At some point in the ninth century, the governor, Wei Junjing, began carving

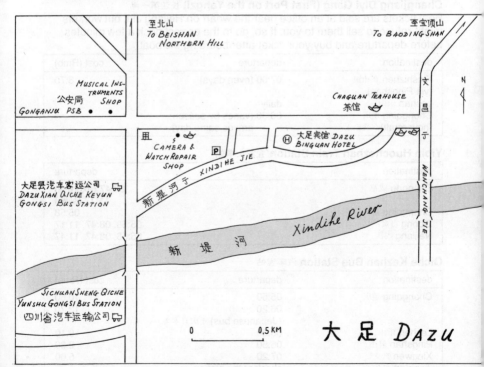

Buddhist images here. Over the next 250 years nearly 10,000 images were carved, often with Confucian, Daoist or historical themes. Many of the sculptures have weathered over the years, but some are still in fine condition. Off in the distance you will see a pagoda that contains many Buddhist carvings, as well as two 10-meter-high stone Buddhas carved into the cliff at its base. The pleasant walk from town includes a long flight of steps. A road is under construction to give easier access for tour groups.

Baoding Shan Hill 宝顶山
Baoding Shan, 15 kilometers northeast of Dazu, was the center of Tantric Buddhism's Chengdu Yoga sect. Monk Zhao Zhifeng spent 70 years (1179 to 1249) collecting funds and commissioning more than 10,000 Buddhist images to be carved along a 500-meter face of the hill. Unlike most sculpture groups in China, the Baoding Shan carvings were done under the direction of one man according to an overall plan. The highlights include a huge reclining Buddha and an astonishing Guanyin (Avalokitesvara) with 1,007 distinct hands, each containing an eye on its palm, occupying a 100-square-metre place of honour.

The active Buddhist temple at Baoding Shan was founded over 700 years ago. It was closed by the Cultural Revolution, when its 30 monks disappeared. The government has only recently allowed six monks and five acolytes to come from Chengdu and reopen the temple.

Buses from Dazu run from 08:00—16:30. Tickets cost Rmb 0.50. Buses from Youting run from 09:00—15:20. Foreigners are not allowed to stay in the hotels at Baoding Shan, but if you happen to miss the last bus. . .

Hualong Shuiku Reservoir 化龙水库
Hire a local fisherman to row you around on this man-made lake or make use of the bathhouse and the pool filled with lake water. The surrounding area looks inviting for exploration and camping. Buses run from Dazu to Hualong Shuiku in summer. In winter, take the Baoding Shan bus to Hualong and walk for one kilometer to the lake.

Shiyang and Shimen 石羊，石门
The Buddhist carvings at these sites are in poor condition. CITS runs tours to the sites if you are interested.

Lodging

Dazu Binguan Hotel 大足宾馆
This comfortable hotel is the only one in town allowed to accept foreign travelers. Beds are Rmb 3.50 each in a four-person room and double rooms are Rmb 28. These rooms share communal toilets and showers. Double rooms with private bathrooms in the new building are Rmb 53. The Dazu Binguan has a restaurant, a gift shop and a bar with a wide selection of reasonably priced drinks. The bartender is a friendly gentleman who likes to listen to Western music.

The hotel sells tickets for a Japanese bus to Kunming. Tickets cost Rmb 8.90 each and the bus leaves at 08:00.

Transportation

Sichuan Sheng Qiche Yunshu Gongsi Bus Company 四川省汽车运输公司

destination	departure	cost (Rmb)
Chongqing 重庆	05:40—13:30 6 buses daily	5.70
Chengdu 成都	06:40	9.30
Youting 邮亭	07:30-18:00	1.20
Zhibing 直宾	07:30	7.00
Zigong 自贡	07:15	5.80
Luzhou 泸州	05:40—13:30	4.30

Dazu Xian Qiche Keyun Gongsi Bus Company 大足县汽车客运公司

destination	departure	cost (Rmb)
Youting 邮亭	06:20—17:10	1.20
Xiangshan 香山 (Baoding)	07:10—15:30	0.50
Longshuihu 龙水湖	09:00, 17:30	0.40

Chongqing (Chungking) 重庆

Chongqing, perched on a rocky promontory at the confluence of the Yangzi and Jialing rivers, is known as 'Mountain City' (Shancheng), and is probably the only city in China without hordes of bicyclists. Although it is a great modern city, central Chongqing has kept its old character, including numerous food stalls and private markets.

The city of Chongqing was established during the Song Dynasty on a site that had already been settled for almost 2,000 years. Until this century, Chongqing was a large Yangzi River trading town surrounded by ancient walls. Rapid modernization began in the 1920s and accelerated when Japan's invasion of the coast drove the ruling Nationalists inland in the 1930s. In 1938, Chiang Kai-Shek made Chongqing the Nationalist capital, relying on the rugged terrain of eastern Sichuan Province for protection against advancing Japanese armies. Defenseless against air attack, Chongqing suffered four years of relentless Japanese bombing, making it one of the most bombed cities of World War II.

Modern Chongqing, the center of both light and heavy industry for Southwest China, has a huge urban area. A million people live in the old city, and at least another five million live in the surrounding suburbs.

Things to do

Pipa Shan Gongyuan Park and City Museum 枇杷山公园，博物馆
Many gardens, with an aviary and a teahouse, occupy a lookout on the highest hill in the old city. This park seems to be the favorite rendezvous for couples. The Chongqing Museum, located on the grounds, is worth seeing. Displays include newly excavated dinosaur fossils from Zigong.

Eling Gongyuan Park 鹅岭公园
Open from 08:00—18:00, this verdant park, with the best tea garden in Chongqing, provides a splendid view of the city under a bamboo canopy. The six-storey pagoda on the peak dates from the 1970's and looks much better

from a distance.

Renmin Gongyuan Park 人民公园

The outstanding feature of this park is the informal Sichuan opera held here every Saturday evening.

Luohan Si Temple 罗汉寺

Founded over 1,000 years ago, the Luohan Si had more than 70 masters at its height. Today there are 18 masters and some 30 students. The temple suffered massive damage from Japanese bombing and from Red Guards during the Cultural Revolution. A row of small Buddhist grotto shrines lines the entrance and three large gold Buddhas from the Ming Dynasty sit at the rear. The main hall contains 500 painted gold figures of *luohans* (saints, demigods and holy men) from the Qing Dynasty and the side temple has 500 highly individual *luohans* made of clay.

The monks run an excellent vegetarian restaurant. Lunchtime is always crowded. We ate three wonderful dishes and rice for under Rmb 3. Tea and noodles are served all day.

Luohan

Luohan is the Chinese rendering of the Sanskrit word *arhat*, a name that describes a person within the Buddhist faith who has overcome worldly desires and extinguished within himself the three poisons of greed, hate and delusion.

In short, before the concept of the Bodhisattva appeared around the time of Christ, *arhats* embodied the highest ideal of sainthood and were considered personal disciples of the Buddha.

In China, many extravagant stories grew up around the supernatural powers of these guardians of Buddhism. Early depictions presented just 18 *luohans*, but in time the number grew to 500 to allow for the larger family of disciples and holy men. The pictures and sculptures of *luohans* we see today are mainly derived from the works of Tang Dynasty painters.

Wenhua Gong Cultural Palace 文化宫

The program of cultural events offered here changes frequently. Drop by when you arrive in town to see if anything of interest is scheduled during your visit.

Sichuan Fine Arts Institute 四川省美术学院

This institute, in wooded grounds overlooking the city, moved to Chongqing from Shaanxi Province in 1953. Some of China's most promising artists are trained here and works of art from all over China are on display.

Liberation Monument 解放碑

The monument is actually nothing more than a clock tower located in the center of town. Nearby you will find a large department store containing Chongqing's first escalator, a good Foreign Language Bookstore (Waiwen Shudian), many restaurants, most featuring Sichuan firepot, street markets and some old neighborhoods.

Chiang Kai-Shek's Chongqing Residence 桂园

We tried to visit this site, but it was closed. We hear the displays inside recreate the decadence in which Chiang Kai-shek lived at a time when his country was on the verge of capitulating to Japanese armies and millions of people were starving. Most travelers feel a visit is not worth the trip.

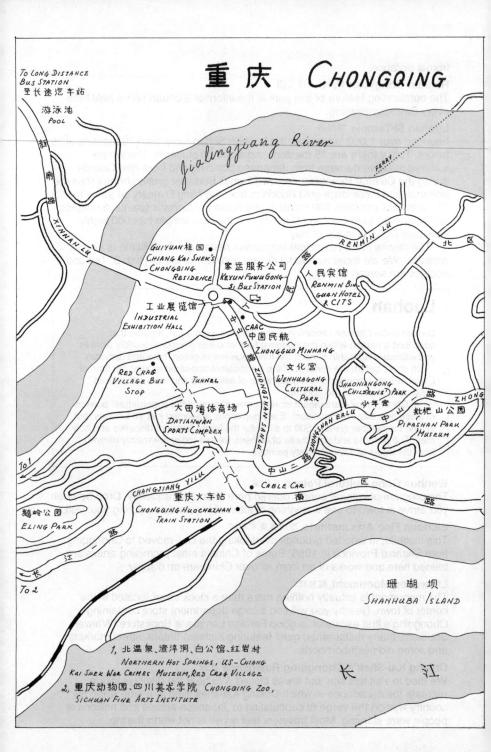

重庆 CHONGQING

To Long Distance
Bus Station
至长途汽车站

游泳池
Pool

Jialingjiang River

FERRY

新南路
XINNAN LU

RENMIN LU
人民路 北区

GUIYUAN 桂园
CHIANG KAI SHEK'S
CHONGQING
RESIDENCE

客运服务公司
KEYUN FUWU GONG-
SI BUS STATION

人民宾馆
RENMIN BIN-
GUAN HOTEL
& CITS

工业展览馆
INDUSTRIAL
EXHIBITION HALL

CAAC
中国民航
ZHONGGUO MINHANG

文化宫
WENHUAGONG
CULTURAL
PARK

SHAONIANGONG
CHILDRENS' PARK

中山三路 ZHONGSHAN SANLU

RED CRAG
VILLAGE BUS
STOP

TUNNEL

大田湾体育场
DATIANWAN
SPORTS COMPLEX

少年宫

枇杷山公园
PIPASHAN PARK
MUSEUM

中山 路 ZHONG

CHANGJIANG YILU

ZHONGSHAN ERLU

中山二路 ZHONGSHAN ERLU

CABLE CAR

南区路

重庆火车站
CHONGQING HUOCHEZHAN
TRAIN STATION

鹅岭公园
ELING PARK

To 1

To 2

长江

SHANHUBA ISLAND
珊瑚坝
SHANHUBA ISLAND

长 江

1, 北温泉、渣滓洞、白公馆、红岩村
  NORTHERN HOT SPRINGS, US-CHIANG
  KAI SHEK WAR CRIMES MUSEUM, RED CRAG VILLAGE
2, 重庆动物园、四川美术学院 CHONGQING ZOO,
  SICHUAN FINE ARTS INSTITUTE

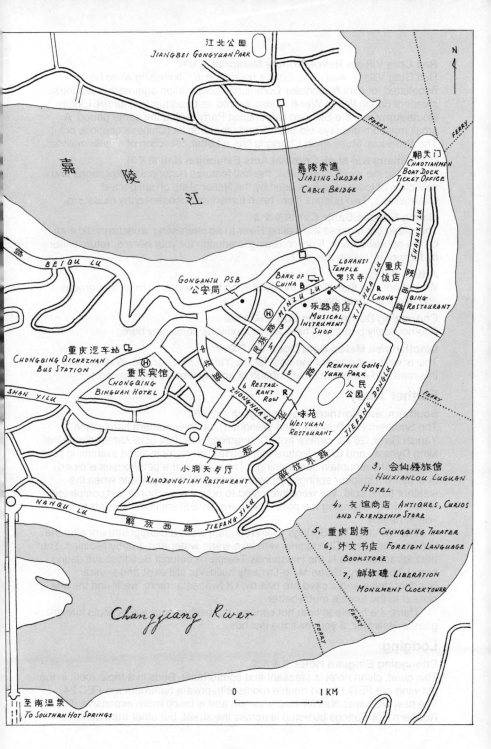

江北公园
JIANGBEI GONGYUAN PARK

嘉陵索道
JIALING SUODAO
CABLE BRIDGE

嘉 陵 江

BEIQU LU

朝天门
CHAOTIANMEN
BOAT DOCK
TICKET OFFICE

FERRY

FERRY

陕西路
SHAANXI LU

GONGANJU PSB
公安局

BANK OF
CHINA
B

MINZU LU
民族路

罗汉寺
LOHANSI
TEMPLE

重庆饭店
R CHONG
QING
RESTAURANT

新华路 XINHUA LU

乐器商店
MUSICAL
INSTRUMENT
SHOP

H

重庆汽车站
CHONGQING QICHEZHAN
BUS STATION

H
重庆宾馆
CHONGQING
BINGUAN HOTEL

SHAN YILU

7

6 RESTAURANT ROW
R

味苑
WEIYUAN
RESTAURANT

中华路 ZHONGHUA LU

3

4

5

人民公园
RENMIN GONG-
YUAN PARK
人民
公园

解放东路 JIEFANG DONGLU

FERRY

R

小洞天夕厅
XIAODONGTIAN RESTAURANT

解放东 JIEFANG

NANQU LU

解放西路 JIEFANG XILU

Changjiang River

FERRY

3. 会仙楼旅馆
HUIXIANLOU LUGUAN
HOTEL

4. 友谊商店 ANTIQUES, CURIOS
AND FRIENDSHIP STORE

5. 重庆剧场 CHONGQING THEATER

6. 外文书店 FOREIGN LANGUAGE
BOOKSTORE

7. 解放碑 LIBERATION
MONUMENT CLOCKTOWER

0   1 KM

至南温泉
To SOUTHERN HOT SPRINGS

N

Red Crag Village Revolutionary Memorial 红岩村
Red Crag Village was Zhou Enlai's residence in Chongqing while he negotiated for joint Nationalist-Communist cooperation against the Japanese invaders during World War II. It also served as headquarters for the Eighth Route Army and the Sichuan Communist Party during the same period. A small museum displays old photos and memorabilia (Chinese captions only). The Provincial Museum in Chengdu has a better collection of similar material.

U.S.-Chiang Kai-shek Criminal Acts Exhibition Hall 渣滓洞
Located in the western suburbs, the hall features historical photographs and a collection of torture devices used by the Nationalists on suspected Communists. Two prisons have been turned into unnoteworthy museums.

Jialing Suodao Cable Car 嘉陵索道
This cable car crosses the Jialing River to an interesting, anachronistic area on the opposite bank. If one crossing is enough for your nerves, return either by ferry or by taking bus #11.

Artists Village
We did not visit this village, though it is on the itinerery of most tour groups and might be quite interesting.

Chongqing Dongwuyuan Zoo 重庆动物园
Another really bad zoo. There are four pandas on display here.

Qiaotianmen Matou Boat Dock 朝天门码头
This is where you board the boat for the Yangzi River cruise. Walk around this area and experience the hubbub of activity around the busy port.

Farther Away

Southern and Northern Hot Springs 南，北温泉
The Southern Hot Springs (Nan Wenquan), on the southern bank of the Yangzi River, 26 kilometers from Chongqing, were first established during the Ming Dynasty and today feature bathhouses, an olympic-sized swimming pool and beautiful mountain surroundings. The water in the bathhouses is piped directly from sulphur springs just warm enough to be enjoyable when the weather turns cold. We were interested to note a new church just completed on the street encircling the park. There are several small restaurants in the village nearby.

The Northern Hot Springs (Bei Wenquan) were a disappointment after the two-hour ride from Chongqing, with luke-warm water and grubby facilities. The best attraction here is the Hotsprings Temple, a defunct Buddhist site dating from 12th century. Some Ming-Dynasty buildings still exist and several Buddhis steles and a cave are nearby. Of two restaurants, we found the one closest to the temple much better.

There are hotels at both hot springs, but neither normally accepts foreign guests. However, if you miss the last bus . . .

Lodging

Chongqing Binguan Hotel 重庆宾馆
This quiet, clean hotel is pleasant and comfortable. Beds in a triple room in the old wing are FEC 10 and double rooms with private bathroom are FEC 24. The new wing was built for businessmen and is much more expensive. The Northern Hot Springs bus stop is across the street, but other transport and

sites are farther away.

Huixianlou Luguan Hotel 会仙楼旅馆
The Huixian Binguan is located in the most interesting and convenient part of Chongqing. Dorms on the 12th floor have beds for Rmb 7, each with a good view of the city. Double rooms with private bathroom cost Rmb 63.

Renmin Binguan Hotel 人民宾馆
This huge structure, modeled after the Temple of Heaven in Beijing, is quite a sight. It contains an enormous domed theater flanked on both sides by four storeys of hotel rooms and poor restaurants. The dorm rooms were once located in a dressing room behind the stage. On a return visit we discovered that they had disappeared completely. It is possible that they will be re-opened or moved to another part of this massive hotel. At present, the cheapest bed is FEC 14 in a four-bed room with bathroom. There are three restaurants, a bar, a gift shop, and an art gallery within the complex. The hotel is convenient for both the train and bus stations, although beyond walking distance of the train. It is several kilometers from the Liberation Monument area.

Restaurants
Sichuan firepot (*huoguo*) or hotpot is world famous and Chongqing has the best firepot cuisine in Sichuan. Eating from the firepot is easy. Order the meat or vegetables you want by pointing, toss them into the boiling, spicy broth, allowing the meat to cook at least three minutes, then eat what you have cooked and quickly try to put out the fire in your mouth with beer or any other cold drink. Firepot is served by most restaurants along the two 'restaurant rows' shown on the map.

Good vegetarian lunches are served at the Luohan Si Temple from 11:30–13:30 . Go early as the place is always crowded.

Chongqing's good restaurants include the Weiyuan Fandian, Lao Sichuan Fandian and the Chongqing Fandian. We found the hotel restaurants to be mediocre and overpriced.

Transportation

Changtu Qichezhan Long Distance Bus Station 长途汽车站

destination	departure	cost (Rmb)
Dazu 大足	08:00	5.70
Leshan 乐山	07:00	19.00
Daxian 大县	07:00	7.50
Liangping 梁平	07:00	6.50
Wanxian 万县	07:00	11.00
Zhongxian 忠县	08:00	9.40

Chongqing Qichezhan Bus Station 重庆汽车站

destination	distance (kms)	departure	cost (Rmb)
Bei Wenquan 北温泉 (Northern Hot Springs)	58	07:40, 08:20	2.30
Leshan 乐山	422	06:45	22:10

Keyun Fuwubu Gongsi Bus Company 客运服务部公司

destination	distance (kms)	departure	cost (Rmb)
Dazu 大足	160	08:10	10.50
Hechuan 合川	80	08:10, 15:10	5.20
Wansheng 万盛	125	07:10, 13:40	7.30

Chongqing Huochezhan Train Station 重庆火车站

destination	departure
Wuchang 武昌	05:35, 21:15
Guiyang 贵阳	06:00, 18:32
Chengdu 成都	07:08, 18:12, 18:56
	19:37, 20:35, 22:20
Guangzhou 广州	07:58
Daxian 大县	08:50
Anbian 安边	10:40
Zhengzhou 郑州	14:34
Kunming 昆明	15:30
Beijing 北京	16:31, 21:55
Wansheng 万盛	17:30
Shanghai 上海	23:40

Boats

There is a special ticket office inside the boat station specifically for the Yangzi River boats to Wuhan. Just follow the English signs. Ticket office hours are 14:00−15:30 and 18:30−21:00. You can board these boats between 20:00−22:00 the night before your departure. See the Yangzi River section for price and time schedules.

To go upriver on the Yangzi, purchase tickets at the other windows in the boat ticket office. A boat departs on even days only to Hechuan, Luzhou, Yibin and Leshan. Third class tickets to Leshan cost Rmb 35.10. The boat departs at 04:00 and you can board the night before.

Chongqing Local Bus Routes

There are three kinds of local buses. The articulated buses are the cheapest, slowest and most crowded. Smaller, single-section buses are faster, less crowded, and only slightly more expensive. Private minibuses also follow many of the bus routes, usually toward the Liberation Monument, stealing passengers from the crowds waiting for the big buses. For double the price, they offer a fast, relaxing air-conditioned ride.

bus #3: Begins at the 'Zoo and Sichuan Fine Arts Institute bus stop' and terminates near the zoo. Bus #26 carries on to the zoo; bus #23 goes to the Institute.

bus #12: From Qiaotianmen Boat Dock to the Chongqing Huochezhan Railway Station.

bus #13: From the Industrial Exhibition Hall past the Renmin Binguan Hotel to Luohan Si Temple.

bus #15: Circular route from the Liberation Monument past the Renmin Binguan Hotel, past the Jialing Suodao Cable Car to near the Children's Park and back to the Liberation Monument.

bus #16: Begins at the 'Red Crag Village bus stop' and goes to Red Crag Village.

bus #17: Begins at the 'Red Crag Village bus stop' and goes past the U.S.-Chiang Kai-Shek War Crimes Museum.

bus #41: Begins at the 'Nan Wenquan Southern Hot Springs bus stop' and terminates at the Southern Hot Springs.

The Yangzi River 长江

The Yangzi River, known in China as the Chang Jiang (Long River), is the third longest river in the world. For thousands of years its treacherous waters were the main trade and travel route between Sichuan and the rest of China. In recent times, the Upper Yangzi has at last been made safe for navigation thanks to extensive rock removal and construction of the Gezhouba Dam near Yichang.

The three famous Yangzi River Gorges are located on a stretch of river roughly 200 kilometers long between the towns of Fengjie and Yichang. The best way to see the gorges is aboard one of the passenger boats that run a regular service between Chongqing and Wuhan, in both directions. The journey takes three days and two nights, one day of which is spent in the gorges.

Though quite beautiful, the sheer cliffs and high peaks disappoint many travelers who overanticipate their splendor. The journey is worth making at any time of year, but the summer months are preferable when the water is high and the weather clear. The drawback is the heat which can reach 40°C. In the late autumn, we found it a bit foggy.

Daily boats depart early in the morning from both Chongqing and Wuhan so you may want to board the night before and sleep on the boat. There are four different classes on the large boats (second through fifth) and three on the smaller boats (third through fifth). Second class double rooms are at the front of the boat, allowing a better view. Third class ranges from berths in a four-bed room with a television on the smaller boats to big cabins with six to 12 beds on the larger boats. Fourth class ranges from 12 to 24 berths per cabin. Sometimes the cheaper berths are hard bunks. Fifth class berths are below deck with large crowds and poor ventilation. On small boats, fifth class may only provide hard seats. For the budget traveler we recommend third or fourth class. For privacy and a better view, go for second class.

Often you can only buy fourth or fifth class tickets at the dock. To upgrade a ticket, take it to the ticket window on the boat. Sometimes a foreigner can get on board without a ticket and then purchase one. Whether upgrading or purchasing tickets on board, a single receipt will be your ticket.

When you board, the steward takes your ticket in return for a numbered bed tag. Before you disembark, he returns it in exchange for the tag. Keep your ticket to show the security man on the dock.

The second class dining room has a varied (and expensive) menu, but in general shipboard food is poor. Bring fruit, nuts, candy and dried noodles with you. If you want to eat in a dining room you need to buy a meal ticket at the ticket window ahead of time in order to be served.

Boats from Chongqing to Wuhan stop in several towns along the way. Different boats stop in different places so decide what you want to see and then buy your boat ticket to that point.

The following places are listed in order, traveling downstream from Chongqing. Every rock, peak, or feature of the river has a name and a legend attached to it, but we will limit ourselves to mentioning only the most obvious sites.

Shibaozhai 石宝寨
The first notable sight is a startling, red, 12-storey pagoda clinging to the side of a high hill on the north bank of the Yangzi. Originally, it was just a temple at the top of the hill, built in the reign of Emperor Qianlong (1736–1796). It could only be reached by an iron chain attached to the cliff so in 1819 a nine-storey wooden pavilion was added on below to spare visitors the discomforts of climbing the chain. In 1956 three more storeys were added, making the whole structure 56 meters high. Each floor is dedicated to an ancient general, local scholar or renowned Chinese poet. To visit Shibaozhai, disembark at the small town of Xitouzhen on the south bank and cross the river on a local ferry.

Wanxian 万县
About two hours beyond Shibaozhai the boat reaches Wanxian, a big town on the north bank known as the Gateway to East Sichuan. Half way between Chongqing and Yichang, Wanxian was historically the main port for East Sichuan merchandise. Boats usually stop here for several hours, or overnight, in order to pass through the gorges by daylight. Upriver boats also make a long stop. The town is built high above the river, safe from all but the worst floods, with long flights of steps down to the water. There is a lively night market on Shengli Lu specializing in cane and rattan ware such as baskets, bed mats, hats and straw shoes. Roadside food stalls serve spicy noodles and fresh fruit and the town has some good restaurants.

Yunyang 云阳
This town is on the north bank but its main tourist site, the Zhang Fei Miao Temple, is opposite on the south bank, requiring a local ferry ride. The temple was swept away in the flood of 1870, so the present buildings date from the late 19th century. More than half of the temple's collections of paintings, tablets and inscriptions were lost during the Cultural Revolution, but much restoration has taken place in the past few years. The temple stands amidst tranquil gardens, waterfalls and pools.

Fengjie 奉节
The most pleasant town we found was Fengjie, which stands at the western entrance to Qutang, the First Gorge. A one-hour walk east or a 20-minute ferry ride takes you to Baidicheng Temple on the crag which forms the actual gateway to the gorge. The temple is not spectacular but the view into the gorge on a clear day more than rewards the walk. When the second stage of the Gezhouba dam is completed, the water level will rise and Baidi Mountain will become an island.

Fengjie itself is a friendly city with busy street markets and good restaurants. For a cheap place to stay, we recommend a room at any regular Chinese hotel. If the manager does not want the responsibility of having you in his establishment, he will point you towards a place that will. We spent Rmb 5 each for a double room and never found the more expensive hotel officially approved for foreigners.

Qutang, the First Gorge 瞿塘峡
Qutang is the shortest but grandest of the three gorges, only eight kilometers long and 150 meters at its widest point, with lofty limestone peaks almost 1,200 meters high soaring above. It was known to early Western travelers as

Chongqing to Shanghai: Distance and Price List 重庆至上海里程票价表

Port Name	kms	2nd Class	3rd Class	4th Class	5th Class	Seat
Fuling 涪陵	120	15.90	6.60	4.70	3.90	3.30
Fengdu 丰都	172	23.20	9.70	6.90	5.80	4.80
Gaozhen 高镇	191	25.80	10.70	7.70	6.40	5.30
Zhongxian 忠县	239	30.50	12.70	9.10	7.60	6.30
Xituo 西沱	278	35.10	14.60	10.50	8.70	7.30
Wanxian 万县	327	40.80	17.00	12.10	10.10	8.40
Yunyang 云阳	382	47.40	19.80	14.10	11.80	9.80
Fengjie 奉节	446	53.80	22.40	16.00	13.40	11.10
Wushan 巫山	481	58.10	24.20	17.30	14.40	12.00
Badong 巴东	533	63.10	26.30	18.80	15.70	13.10
Yichang 宜昌	648	73.90	30.80	22.00	18.30	15.30
Zhicheng 枝城	704	78.10	32.50	23.20	19.10	16.10
Shashi 沙市	796	84.20	35.10	25.10	20.90	17.40
Chenglingfan 城陵矶	1043	99.80	41.60	29.70	24.70	20.60
Hankou 汉口 (Wuhan)	1274	112.40	46.80	33.50	27.90	23.20
Huangshi 黄石	1417	121.90	50.70	36.30	30.30	25.20
Jiujiang 九江	1543	128.60	53.60	38.30	31.90	26.60
Anqing 安庆	1707	137.40	57.20	41.00	34.10	28.40
Wuhu 芜湖	1911	146.90	61.20	43.80	36.50	30.30
Nanjing 南京	2007	150.80	62.80	44.90	37.40	31.20
Shanghai 上海	2399	167.30	69.70	49.80	41.50	34.60

Add the following extra ticket service charges:

(Rmb)
Second class 8
Third class 6
Fourth class 4
Fifth class 2

'Wind Box Gorge'. Early in the morning the boat passes through Kui Men, the gorge's entrance below Baidi Temple, while morning mists swirl among the crags. Up until a hundred years ago, this gorge was virtually impassable for boats coming upstream. Passengers had to leave their boats and climb over the peaks while the boats waited, sometimes for weeks, for a favorable east wind. In 1889, local people hewed a towpath by hand which ran the whole way from Baidi to Wushan, so that boats could be hauled through the gorge by manpower. The path can still be seen high up on the northern face. The town of Daixi marks the eastern end of Qutang. Here the Yangzi widens out and flows calmly for about 25 kilometers.

Chongqing to Hankou (Wuhan) 重庆至汉口

Port Name	Arrival	Departure	Arrival	Departure
Chongqing 重庆	↑ Water level above 9 meters 07:00		↓ Water level below 9 meter 07:00	
Fuling 涪陵	11:30	12:00	11:20	11:45
Zhongxian 忠县	15:15	15:30	15:30	16:00
Wanxian 万县	18:00	04:35	18:25	02:30
Fengjie 奉节	0:00	08:20	06:55	07:15
Badong 巴东	11:20	12:45	10:45	11:30
Yichang 宜昌	17:00	17:30	15:30	17:00
Zhicheng 枝城	19:30	20:30	20:00	20:20
Shashi 沙市	23:00	23:30	23:00	23:30
Chenglingfan 城陵矶	07:30	08:00	09:45	10:20
Hankou (Wuhan) 汉口	16.00		18:00	

Wushan 巫山

The Daning River meets the Yangzi at the little town of Wushan on the north bank. This town is only important because the Daning River has recently been opened to foreign tourism and trips originate here. A trip up the Daning takes you 33 kilometers through gorges that many consider more beautiful than those on the Yangzi. If you make the excursion in one of the long, low, wooden, motorized sampans that can be hired by a group for Rmb 160, the round trip can be done in one day. A county guesthouse provides basic lodging in Wushan. Cheaper local ferries take longer and require an overnight stop at Dachang a town with fine farmhouse architecture and the remains of a Qing-Dynasty city gate.

Wu Xia , the Second Gorge 巫峡

Below Wushan, the river approaches the entrance to the 40-kilometer-long Wu Xia (Witches Gorge). The middle Yangzi gorge straddles the border between Sichuan and Hubei provinces, marked by the little trading town of Peishi on the south bank. Near the east end of the gorge, the stretch of water just above the north-bank town of Guandukou used to be the most dangerous point of Wu Xia. Here limestone rocks jutted out into the river like huge stone gates, causing rapids and whirlpools. These were finally blown up in the 1950s, along with dangerous rocks in the shipping channel. Now the Yangzi leaves the gorge safely and flows past the coal mining town of Badong and the agricultural market town of Zigui in western Hubei.

Xiling, the Third Gorge 西陵峡

The last gorge starts at the village of Xiangxi and zigzags for 76 kilometers down to Yichang. It is the longest and historically the most dangerous of the Yangzi gorges. Before the passage was made safe in the 1950s, passengers would leave their boat and rejoin it beyond the rapids after walking along a winding mountain path past the White Bone Pagoda, a giant pile of bleached bones belonging to the thousands who had lost their lives at this frightening place.

Yangzi River Trackers

'The traffic is now carried on by junks of an average capacity of 20 tons, the largest being of 80 tons. They are hauled up by the force of trackers, as many as 300 sometimes to one junk. There are a good many wrecks ... but practically all the cargo that leaves Ich'ang (Yichang) arrives at Ch'ung-king (Chongqing) someday — condition very uncertain.

'At K'uei Fu (Fengjie) the worst of the tracking is over, and very glad we were, for it is most inhuman work. From early dawn to dark the trackers are tearing through the water, often swimming over sharp rocks, often falling and cutting themselves. No slaves ever did such work. The wonder is that they are not brutalized by such a life; it will scarcely by believed that these men are the most merry, good-natured creatures, with a quick sense of humor and of the ridiculous. They have one advantage — they are not pent up in rooms. They sleep under a mat in the front of the boat and live in the open air, summer and winter. But the work is inhumanly hard; there are splendidly made men among them, but they are exceptions.'

F.S.A. Bourne, *Trade of Central and Southern China*, 1898

Xiling comprises seven small gorges and formerly had two of the fiercest rapids in the entire 648-kilometer stretch of the Yangzi between Chongqing and Yichang. The boat leaves the last gorge at the strategic Southern Crossing Pass where the river suddenly widens dramatically. Ahead lies the new Gezhouba Dam and the city of Yichang.

Gezhouba Dam

The massive, 70-meter-high dam stops the Yangzi's flow and forces all shipping up and down the gorges to pass through one of its three locks. The first stage of the dam was completed in 1981, making it the biggest dam in China. The second stage will produce 14 billion kilowatt hours of electricity a year. You can arrange to visit the dam in Yichang.

Yichang is a middle-sized, drab, industrial port city, guardian of the eastern entrance to the gorges. It engages in chemical and steel production and oversees the work on the dam. From here it is less than 24 hours by boat to Wuhan.

Much of this information is either quoted or paraphrased from Judy Bonavia's *A Guide to the Yangzi River*. Supplementary information was provided by Dave Econome and Dave Thompson.

Northern Sichuan Province

The open areas of Sichuan north of Chengdu comprise an off-the-beaten-track paradise matched by few other places in China. The circular route described in the sections below passes through the spectacular mountainous country of the Tibetans, remote Qiang villages and Hui (Muslim) communities. High passes and huge forests, panda reserves and national parks, mosques and monasteries, all combine to make this an exceptional area.

The traveler in a hurry will have an unforgettable week here, but those with more time can easily lose themselves for a month or two and return knowing they have lived the backpacker's dream.

Wenchuan 汶川

Wenchuan, a town in the Maowen Qiang Nationality Autonomous County, is a stop on the bus ride from Chengdu to Songpan. The main street has an active daily market full of Qiang people in their brightly colored traditional clothing. We only passed through on the bus, but those interested in exploring a rare Qiang area might consider spending a day or two here.

Maowen 茂文

Maowen is the center of a Qiang Nationality Autonomous County. The Qiang people are among the earliest settlers of western China and perhaps the first to engage in farming. They pioneered the domestication of animals and the cultivation of wheat. Their animist religion dictated that everything in nature has a soul and should be worshipped. The Qiang are distant relatives of the Tibetans, although their wildly colorful clothes more closely resemble those of Southeast Asians. All Qiang women learn embroidery at a young age. In warm weather it would be rewarding to spend several days in Maowen exploring the surrounding mountains. In winter snow makes such journeys too difficult.

Things to do

The Qiang are the main attraction. Except for a market near the old city gate, the town itself is uninteresting. The mountains, rugged as they are, are crisscrossed with trails to Qiang settlements. In a nearby village named Heihu

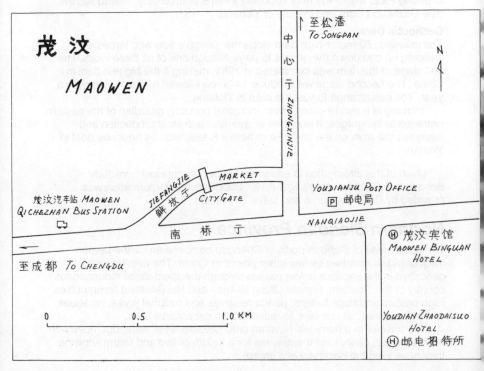

there are ancient Qiang blockhouses that look like castles clinging to the mountainside.

Lodging

Maowen Binguan Hotel 茂文宾馆
This new hotel was built to accommodate foreign guests.

Youdian Zhaodaisuo Hotel 邮电招待所
Double rooms cost Rmb 5. There are communal toilets but no showers.

Restaurants

There is a restaurant with English signs across from the bus station and several other restaurants nearby.

Transportation

Maowen Qichezhan Bus Station 茂文汽车站

destination	departure
Barkam (Ma'erkang) 马尔康	07:30
Mianyang 绵阳	07:30
Guanxian 灌县	10:00
Wenchuan 汶川	15:00

Songpan 松潘

The old, walled town of Songpan is in the Aba Tibetan Autonomous Region. Its mixed population is 40% Hui, 35% Tibetan and 25% Han Chinese. Three gates and much of the old city wall of this former garrison still stand. Perched over 3,000 meters high, Songpan is blanketed in snow from November to April. Most visitors pass through Songpan heading towards Jiuzhaigou and Huanglong Si. Songpan is both an enjoyable city to explore and a convenient jump-off point for these two famous national parks.

Things to do

Qingzhen Gu Si Mosque is the focal point of Songpan's Muslim community. Repairs to this interesting building, damaged during the Cultural Revolution, are almost complete.

The first village south of town along the main road is primarily a Hui settlement and it, too, has a mosque.

Zaga Pubu Waterfall 大瀑布
Locals talk about a waterfall 30 kilometers west of Songpan that they claim is bigger and more beautiful than Huangguoshu in Guizhou Province (officially China's biggest waterfall). There is said to be a hotspring near the falls. Specifics about this site are not available. A bus service to the falls may begin in 1988.

Farther away

Chuanzhu Si Monastery 川主寺
Chuanzhu Si (Gamisi in Tibetan), with over 50 monks, is the largest monastery in the Songpan area. Located about 40 kilometers from Songpan on the road to Nanping, Chuanzhu Si is almost inaccessible except during the summer months when tour buses are plentiful. There are two Tibetan festivals

held here annually. The first is a New Year Festival held on the fifth day of the first lunar month. The second is a summer festival held on the 15th day of the sixth lunar month.

Lodging

Songpan Xian Songzhou Luxingshe Hotel 松潘县松州旅行社
Beds here start at Rmb 2.50 in four-bed rooms. Double rooms are Rmb 9. All rooms are basic, but the large, well-padded wooden beds are quite comfortable. All rooms share communal toilets and showers (when there are enough guests to warrant opening them).

Renmin Zhaodaisuo Hotel 人民招待所
Beds in a four-person room are Rmb 2.50 and in a three-bed room cost Rmb 3. Double rooms are Rmb 9 and singles are Rmb 7. The double and single rooms feature king-size beds. All rooms share communal toilets and showers.

Songpan Xian Lushe Hotel 松潘县旅社
Beds in four-bed rooms are Rmb 1−2. Triple rooms are Rmb 9 and double rooms are Rmb 5. All rooms share communal toilets and showers.

Transportation

Minibuses to Huanglong Si or other destinations can be arranged at the Tourist Bureau in the Government Office. There might be vehicles to Zaga Pubu Waterfall as well.

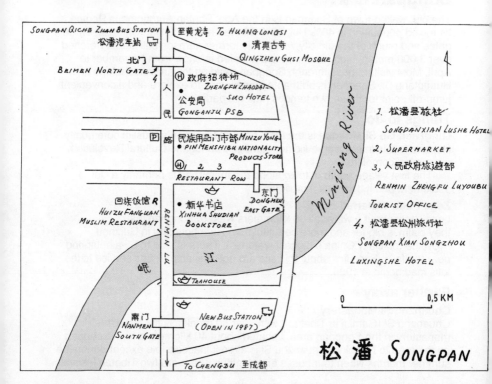

Songpan Qichezhan Bus Station 松潘汽车站

destination	departure	cost (Rmb)
Chengdu 成都 (via Hongyuan, Lixian and Wenchuan. This route will stop once the Maowen road opens)	07:00, even days	23.50
Chengdu 成都 (via Maowen)		11.60
Maowen 茂文		5.00
Nanping 南平	07:00, odd days	5.10
Jiuzhaigou 九寨沟	07:00, odd days	3.60
Ruo'ergai 若尔盖 (Zoige)	2nd, 8th, 12th, 18th, 22nd and 28th each month.	7.00
Barkam (Ma'erkang) 马尔康	check at the station for departures.	

Huanglong Si National Park 黄龙寺

Huanglong Si, a national park and protected area established in 1983, is set in a deep valley surrounded by glacial peaks. The narrow road leading to it crosses a 4,100-meter pass with a glorious view of snowbound crags rising to 5,588 meters.

Before the pass you can see a large monastery, and in the actual valley of Huanglong Si, which means Yellow Dragon Monastery, there are two small Tibetan monasteries.

The strange geology of the area makes Huanglong Si an intriguing place to visit. The valley is covered with over 3,000 karst-formed pools, the largest of which is over an acre in size and the smallest only one meter across. The pools are filled with yellow, sapphire blue, green and white mineral-tinted water. Some of the most beautiful pools descend in a series of steps linked by long cascades. The mountains around the valley are forested with fine, big trees of many varieties, some of them labeled with their Chinese and Latin names. The dark rock and snowfields of the high peaks framing the rainbow colors of the pools, plants and trees leave you with an unforgettable impression.

Things to do

The Chinese government is to be commended for the four-kilometer pathway, dotted with well-placed pavilions, that threads its way up the pool-filled valley without harming the natural beauty of the area. The walk up the trail and back to the base takes three to four hours.

We visited Huanglong Si in the middle of November, only a few days before the entire valley was isolated for the winter by a heavy snowfall. Our exploration was brief and confined exclusively to the valley floor. In summer, Tibetan settlements high in the mountains are accessible on foot, opening the possibility of extended treks.

Lodging

There is a small village in the valley with a few small, simple guesthouses.

Thangkas

Thangka is the name for the scroll-banners seen hanging in almost every monastery or family shrine in regions peopled by Tibetans. They carry painted or embroidered pictures inside a broad, colored border and they can vary greatly in size. A thangka could be as small as the page of a book, while an important monastery may possess a thangka big enough to cover the facade of an entire building for special religious festivals. On ordinary thangkas, the picture is usually made on paper or cotton canvas which is protected by a thin dust-cover and the mounting is of colorful silk. A heavy wooden stick at the base allows a thangka to be rolled up like a scroll for storage or transportation, or to hang securely without flapping.

Thangkas first appeared in Tibet around the 10th century. The scroll form seems to have been borrowed from China; the style of painting probably came from Nepal and Kashmir. Apprentice thangka painters studied under experienced lamas and their works were consecrated before they could be hung.

Thangkas are widely used in monasteries as teaching tools because of their convenient movability. Common folk hang them in homes as protection against evil spirits, which are believed to abound in wild places like Kham. At the highest level of religious practice, mystics in a state of meditation seek to become one with the deity portrayed.

Thangkas can be simple in design or very complicated. They can deal with a great number of subjects of which a few are Tibetan theology, astrology, pharmacology, lives of Buddhas, saints and deities, and mandalas.

The village also has a small restaurant.

Transportation

Except during the winter when the passes are closed, minibuses make the round trip to Huanglong Si from Songpan and Jiuzhaigou. The number of tourists determines the frequency of buses.

Jiuzhaigou National Park 九寨沟

The national park at Jiuzhaigou is set aside as a natural protected area and panda reserve. You first enter a little valley that appears fairly unimpressive, but as the bus follows the road further into the Y-shaped valley, closer to its terminus 30 kilometers away, the scenery becomes more and more spectacular. From behind small mountains spring great snowcapped peaks, most of them between 4,000 and 5,000 meters high. Spur valleys climb abruptly to dead ends and hundreds of prayer flags flutter over little villages. Ahead lie the bamboo haunts of the giant panda.

Farmers steer their animal-drawn plows beside a series of clear turquoise-colored lakes that are linked by magnificent waterfalls. At the end of the valley, the deep blue water of Long Lake mirrors snowy peaks and glaciers. According to legend, the goddess Worusemo dropped her magic mirror while fighting a demon and the slivers of broken glass were transformed into the lakes of the Jiuzhaigou valley. Geologists claim that the area evolved from the limestone bed of a vast sea that lay here some 200 to 400 million years ago. When Earth's colliding tectonic plates forced the seabed up into mountain ranges, fractures and erosion created the string of barrier lakes. The high mineral content of the water causes the beautiful turquoise color.

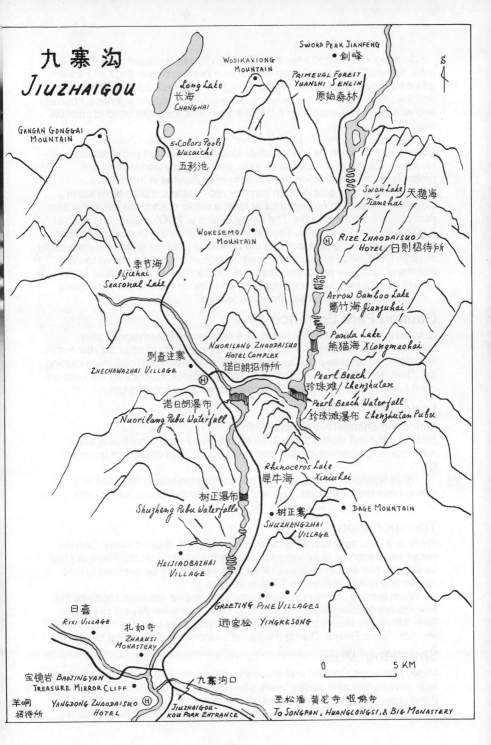

九寨沟
JIUZHAIGOU

GANGAN GONGGAI MOUNTAIN

Long Lake
长海
CHANGHAI

5-Colors Pools
Wucaichi
五彩池

WOSIKAXIONG MOUNTAIN

SWORD PEAK JIANFENG
剑峰

PRIMEVAL FOREST
YUANSHI SENLIN
原始森林

Swan Lake
Tianehai
天鹅海

RIZE ZHAODAISUO HOTEL 日则招待所

季节海
Jijiehai
Seasonal Lake

WOKESEMO MOUNTAIN

Arrow Bamboo Lake
箭竹海 Jianzuhai

Panda Lake
熊猫海 Xiongmaohai

NUORILANG ZHAODAISUO HOTEL COMPLEX
诺日朗招待所

则查洼寨
ZHECHAWAZHAI VILLAGE

Pearl Beach
珍珠滩 Zhenzhutan

Pearl Beach Waterfall
珍珠滩瀑布 Zhenzhutan Pubu

诺日朗瀑布
Nuorilang Pubu Waterfall

Rhinoceros Lake
犀牛海 Xiniuhai

树正瀑布
Shuzheng Pubu Waterfalls

树正寨
SHUZHENGZHAI VILLAGE

DAGE MOUNTAIN

HEIJIAOBAZHAI VILLAGE

GREETING PINE VILLAGES
迎客松 YINGKESONG

日喜
RIXI VILLAGE

扎如寺
ZHARUSI MONASTERY

宝镜岩 BAOJINGYAN
TREASURE MIRROR CLIFF

羊峒
招待所
YANGDONG ZHAODAISUO HOTEL

九寨沟口
JIUZHAIGOU-KOU PARK ENTRANCE

0   5 KM

至松潘 黄龙寺 啦嘛寺
TO SONGPAN, HUANGLONGSI, & BIG MONASTERY

Jiuzhaigou is named after nine Tibetan villages scattered throughout the area. Signs of Tibetan religious life are everywhere; prayer flags and water-powered prayer wheels, many *chortens*, the reconstructed Zharu Monastery, and the small shrines in every home. Men dress in traditional jerkins, *chubas* and woollen boots, women in full robes wear their long hair braided into 108 plaits.

Jiuzhaigou is a nature photographer's dream, and the Chinese government is taking its first tentative steps towards good conservation. However, the influx of careless tourists, both Chinese and foreign, will probably doom to extinction the ten remaining pandas in the reserve.

Jiuzhaigou gets cold even in summer, so travelers should have warm clothes. In winter, be prepared for at least a meter of snow on the valley floor. Also prepare for the altitude. The valley begins at 2,000 meters and rises to 3,000 meters at Long Lake. The best times to visit are in June and October when the weather is pleasant and the hordes of Chinese tourists are mercifully absent. The food available in the area outside of the peak summer tourist months is basic but adequate. Standard Tibetan fare of *tsampa* and butter tea, as well as a potato dumpling soup, can be found in the villages year-round.

Jiuzhaigou has four main areas, as follows.

Goukou Park Entrance 沟口

Goukou is the first settlement along the road into the Jiuzhaigou valley. Because the nicest areas of the park are accessible from other locations, this was our least favorite place to stay. Some good hiking destinations, including the Zharu Monastery, are within easy range of Goukou. It is also the jump-off point for the large monastery 12 kilometers west towards Songpan.

Lodging

Yangdong Zhaodalsuo Hotel 羊峒招待所
Beds in this hotel start at Rmb 3. All rooms share communal toilets and washrooms. Luxury cabins are also available for high officials or guests of CITS.

Other hotels in Goukou and the nearby Tibetan village are used only during peak tourist periods. Two restaurants and two stores selling gifts, a few basic necessities and food are in the area.

Transportation

There is a bus route to both ends of Jiuzhaigou's Y-shaped valley. Service varies and becomes quite irregular outside the tourist season. There are few vehicles to hire and even fewer for hitchhiking. It might be possible to rent horses and hire guides in the Tibetan villages.

When leaving Jiuzhaigou, wait at the entrance on the main road and flag down buses to Songpan between 08:30 – 09:00 on even days. Tickets are Rmb 3.60 each. Buses to Nanping leave on odd days between 10:30 – 11:00 and tickets are Rmb 2. During the tourist season many additional buses run.

Shuzheng 树正

Midway between Goukou and Nuorilang, Shuzheng is a small Tibetan village near several beautiful barrier lakes. The Shuzheng Pubu Falls are visible from the village. Crossing Shuzheng lake to the opposite side offers a new and dramatic perspective of the area. Round trip hikes to other Tibetan villages away from the road can be completed in one day.

Lodging

Zhongxincan Luguan Hotel 中心餐旅馆
This hotel has a superior staff and the manager is a good cook. He will try to locate whatever food you want and allow you to try your hand at the wok. He also serves *tsampa* and yak butter tea. If you ask, he will try to arrange a meal for you in a Tibetan house. Dorm beds cost Rmb 3 and double rooms are Rmb 8.

Shuzheng Luguan Hotel 树正旅馆
Beds are Rmb 3 each in this small hotel. All rooms share communal toilets. There is a small restaurant in the hotel.

Nuorilang 诺日朗

Set at the Y-intersection of the valley, Nuorilang is the tourist center of Jiuzhaigou. Zechawa village, Nuorilang Falls, Rhinoceros Lake, Mirror Lake and Pearl Beach Falls are all within easy walking distance. Renting boots is a must for wading above Pearl Beach Falls. You can take a bus or walk the spectacular 18 kilometers up the eastern fork of the valley which ends at the indescribably blue Long Lake. Along the way visit Seasonal Lake and the transparent Multicolored Pool. The mountains beyond this road are the highest and most rugged in the region.

Lodging

Minzu Lou Lushe Tibetan Guesthouse 民族楼旅社
This fine, wooden Tibetan structure is managed by a friendly Tibetan family. There is no insulation so it is noisy in summer and cold in winter. Beds are Rmb 2.50 each and additional blankets cost Rmb 0.20 each if the two provided with the bed should prove inadequate.

Dage Lushe Hotel 达戈旅社
This one-storey cement building has beds in triple rooms for Rmb 3 each. All rooms share communal toilets and showers.

Nuorilang Binguan Hotel 诺日朗宾馆
Though nothing special, this is the best place to stay in the area. All beds are Rmb 8 and share communal toilets and showers. The tourist office is located in front of this hotel.

Rizegou 日则沟

Rizegou is a solitary, rugged place located near the end of the western fork of the Jiuzhaigou valley. The area is perfect for seclusion and contemplation and is an excellent base camp for trips into the mountains beyond. This place, 3,000 meters high, was once the haunt of pandas and their large bamboo groves still stand nearby. There are several picturesque lakes in the area and a waterfall that drops several hundred meters into the valley.

Lodging

Rizi Binguan Hotel 日则宾馆
This cement structure looks like an old army barrack. All beds are Rmb 4 and everyone shares communal toilets. There is a restaurant at the hotel and a small shop.

Nanping 南坪

Nanping is a pleasant town in the Aba Tibetan Autonomous Region, lying in a broad valley surrounded by high mountains. The town seems typically Chinese, though official signs are in both Tibetan and Chinese script and lots of Tibetans in native dress walk the streets. Other Tibetan features like yak butter tea, prayer flags and monasteries are conspicuously absent. Judging from the many construction projects now under way, Nanping will grow rapidly in the near future.

The road into Nanping traverses a mountain pass over 3,000 meters high. Snow on this pass, and in Nanping, usually starts to fall in December and lasts for two or three months.

Things to do

Nanping is good to walk around in, though there are no real sites in town. Make friends with the Tibetans, who certainly enjoy looking at you. There is a pagoda under construction on a hill overlooking the town.

Lodging

Nanping Xian Zhaodaisuo Hotel 南平县招待所

The Nanping Zhaodaisuo is the only hotel in town that takes foreigners. We found the place clean and comfortable. The cheapest beds are Rmb 2 each and double rooms are Rmb 9.

All rooms share communal toilets and the showers have hot water after 18:30. There is a restaurant here, although you can do much better elsewhere.

Restaurants

Chengguan Xiao Shidian Restaurant 成关小食店

The cooks here will try to cook food the way you want them to. They will even shop specially for food to be served at a later meal. This is a friendly, clean place.

Transportation

Nanping Qichezhan Bus Station 南坪汽车站

destination	departure	cost (Rmb)
Songpan 松潘	07:00	5.10
Wenxian 文县	10:00	2.00
Zhaohua 昭化	06:30	9.10
Chengdu 成都	07:00	16.70

Minibuses to Jiuzhaigou leave between 07:00−08:00 from the bus station gate. During the peak tourist season, tickets may be sold at the bus station. At other times tickets can be purchased from the driver. The Gulou Fandian Hotel also sells tickets to Jiuzhaigou for Rmb 2. The bus departs at 07:30 from the bus station gate and takes two hours.

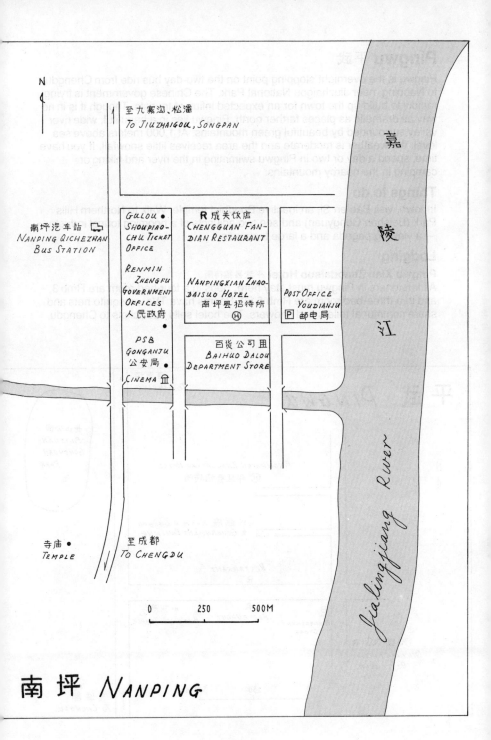

Pingwu 平武

Pingwu is the overnight stopping point on the two-day bus ride from Chengdu to Nanping, near Jiuzhaigou National Park. The Chinese government is trying rapidly to build up the town for an expected influx of tourists. Though it is in no way as dramatic as places farther north, Pingwu lies in a beautiful, wide river valley surrounded by beautiful green mountains. At 1,000 meters above sea level, the weather is moderate and the area receives little snowfall. If you have time, spend a day or two in Pingwu swimming in the river and hiking or camping in the nearby mountains.

Things to do

In town, visit Bao'en Si, an inactive Buddhist temple. Walk to Northern Hills Park (Beishan Gongyuan) and see two adjuncts of a booming tourist industry — a viewing pagoda and a large teahouse.

Lodging

Pingwu Xian Zhaodaisuo Hotel 平武县招待所
All foreigners in Pingwu must stay here. Beds in a four-bed room are Rmb 3, and in a three-bed room are Rmb 5.50. Rooms have TVs, mosquito nets and share communal toilets and showers. The hotel sells bus tickets to Chengdu.

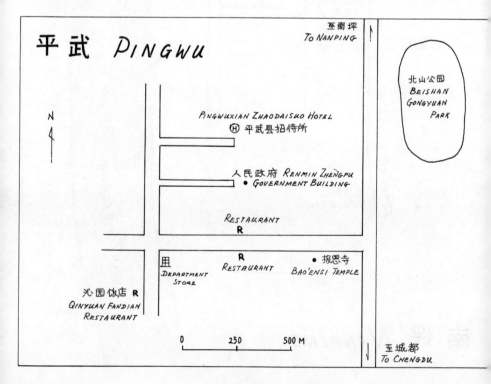

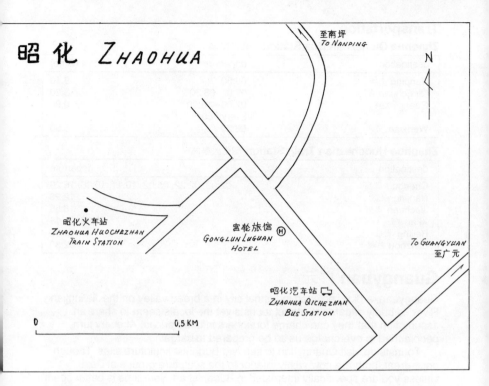

昭化 ZHAOHUA

至南坪
To Nanping

N

昭化火车站
ZHAOHUA HUOCHEZHAN
TRAIN STATION

宫轮旅馆
GONGLUN LUGUAN
HOTEL
(H)

To Guangyuan
至广元

昭化汽车站
ZHAOHUA QICHEZHAN
BUS STATION

0   0,5 KM

Transportation

Pingwu Qichezhan Bus Station 平武汽车站

destination	departure
Mianyang 绵阳	06:30, 09:00, 10:30, 12:00
Jiangyou 江由	08:00, 13:00
Shuijing 水晶	07:00, 10:30, 12:30, 15:00

Zhaohua 昭化

Zhaohua, one of the most polluted cities in Southwest China, is of interest to travelers only because it is here that you can break from the Chengdu-Xian rail line and travel by bus to Nanping en route to Jiuzaigou. The bus trip takes twelve hours.

Lodging

Baolun Luguan Hotel 宝轮旅馆

The staff at this basic hotel make a special effort to give foreign travelers the best accommodations available. Beds in a four-bed room are Rmb 2 and double rooms range from Rmb 9−77. All rooms share communal toilets and showers. For eating, try one of the restaurants between the train station and the bus station.

227

Transportation

Zhaohua Qichezhan Bus Station 昭化汽车站

destination	departure	cost (Rmb)
Nanping 南坪	06:30	9.10
Qingchuan 青川	07:00, 08:30	3.20
Guangyuan 广元	07:00–18:00 every hour	0.90
Wenxian 文县	06:20	5.50

Zhaohua Huochezhan Train Station 昭化火车站

destination	departure
Chengdu 成都	02:03, 02:32, 05:02, 10:11, 10:36, 16:29
Nanjing 南京	12:20
Jiachuan 嘉川	16:55
Xi'an 西安	05:05, 21:18
Beijing 北京	23:36
Lanzhou 兰州	02:30

Guangyuan 广元

Guangyuan, a dirty, polluted industrial city in a broad valley on the Jialingjiang River, is badly situated to attract tourists yet the locals seem to share an assumption that they can charge foreigners inflated prices. At every turn, people tried to overcharge us so be prepared to bargain.

Tourists do visit Guangyuan to see two Buddhist sculpture sites. Though once great, both are now vastly inferior to the sculpture groups at Dazu. Unless you are specifically interested in Buddhist art, your time is better spent elsewhere.

Travelers bound for Jiuzaigou have sometimes mistakenly gotten off the train here. The quickest way to Jiuzhaigou is to disembark at Zhaohua.

Things to do

A walk along the river, especially away from town, can be pleasant. Look for large rafts made of logs lashed together, a result of logging that has deforested many of Sichuan's mountains.

Huangze Si Temple 皇泽寺

Just above the railroad tracks, Huangze Si (Imperial Flavor Temple) features six caves and 28 niches. The carvings are all badly weathered. Beware of the gatekeeper, who might try to charge you Rmb 3 to enter.

Qianfo Yan (Thousand Buddha Cave) 千佛崖

Over 17,000 statues originally graced Thousand Buddha Cave. Destruction caused by the building of the Sichuan-Shaanxi Highway in 1932 has left only 400 intact today. The Rmb 5 admission fee includes a book in Chinese explaining the carvings. We protested and were allowed to view the site free of charge.

Lodging

Guangyuan Fandian Hotel 广元饭店

Conveniently located across from the bus station, the Guangyuan Fandian has beds starting at Rmb 1.10 in a six-person room. Beds in a triple are Rmb 3.80 each. All rooms share communal toilets and showers.

Transportation

Guangyuan Qichezhan Bus Station 广元汽车站

destination	departure	cost (Rmb)
Zhaohua 昭化	08:00 – 18:00 every hour	0.90
Nanchong 南充	06:40	10.10
Bazhong 巴中	06:40, 07:00 07:20, 10:30	6.30
Hanzhong 汉中	07:00	6.00
Mianyang 绵阳	07:00	7.80
Yilong 义龙	06:40	8.10

Guangyuan Huochezhan Train Station 广元火车站

destination	departure
Chengdu 成都	01:38, 02:01, 04:34, 09:48 10:07, 11:10, 16:06
Beijing 北京	0:16, 14:20, 18:20
Chongqing 重庆	17:06
Nanjing 南京	12:55
Lanzhou 兰州	03:07
Shanghai 上海	19:30
Xi'an 西安	05:55, 22:05
Jiachuan 嘉川	17:45

Western Sichuan Province

All places in Sichuan west of Chengdu are officially closed to foreign friends. This edict is haphazardly enforced by the various Gonganju offices of the region and a general rule of thumb states that the farther away you get from Chengdu, the less likelihood you have of running into trouble.

The 1,000-kilometer journey from Chengdu to the border of present-day Tibet passes through the heartland of Kham, traditionally Tibet's eastern province, but now largely subsumed under and administered by Sichuan. If you venture this way you will cross high passes, drop into deep valleys, be dwarfed by outrageous mountain ranges, pass frozen rivers, see lone nomads and rub shoulders with robust Khampas. You may also suffer altitude sickness, freeze to death, wait days for bridges to be repaired, eat detestable food, suffer hideous sunburn and lose your fillings on bad roads. It is all part of the joy and exhilaration of this wild country.

A straight burn along the quickest route from Chengdu to Tibet passes through Kangding, Daofu, Luhuo, Ganzi, Dege, Qamdo, Baqen and Nagqu before finally arriving in Lhasa, at least two weeks after embarking. Many say this route traverses the most beautiful scenery in the world. Accordingly, take your time and enjoy the friendly Khampas and their land rather than spending 14 of 15 days bouncing along a road. Once off the main highway you are guaranteed of visiting wondrous places that have never seen foreigners.

Prepare yourself thoroughly for the harsh conditions that exist in the Land of Snows.

Ya'an 雅安

This nice little city is a complete contrast to Chengdu. In a broad valley of the Qingyi River between forested hills, its 90,000 residents live at a leisurely pace in uncrowded neighborhoods by the riverbanks. Ya'an is a refreshing mixture of Han Chinese tradition and modern Chinese peasant culture, with a dash of Tibetan influence. Although new concrete buildings are sprouting up, the city's style is still small two-storey wooden houses and shops.

Near Ya'an a monument once marked the traditional border between China and Tibet. This was an important trading post where Tibetans would exchange furs for guns and bricks of Chinese tea and today it still has the feel of a border town.

The weather in Ya'an is relatively mild, but be prepared for an occasional snowstorm during the winter.

Things to do

People who enjoy walking love Ya'an. The narrow, tree-lined streets bustle with business around small, open-front shops while old men smoke pipes or sip tea in roadside tea houses and young people play pool on makeshift tables. Streets on the south side of the river near the athletic field include a market and crowds of kids playing games in carnival booths like those at an American county fair. Buy a live fish in the market and have it cooked in a nearby restaurant. Set the price beforehand. Be on the lookout for *congming yu*, a type of fish that is supposed to increase the intelligence of its diner — a

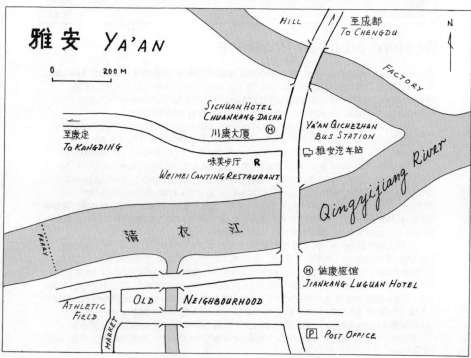

230

modest claim, accompanied by a Rmb 35 price tag.

The streets leading east from this market towards the main road are all worth exploring. For a more vigorous hike, the hill north of town on the road back to Chengdu has several footpaths. All of Ya'an is visible from the top. Most notable is the light brown sludge pouring from the factories below the hill directly into the river.

Lodging

Chuankang Dasha Hotel 川康大厦
Double rooms are Rmb 4.80 and beds in four-bed rooms are cheaper still. All rooms share communal toilets and showers. There is a large restaurant-disco on the third floor and a rooftop lookout offering the best view in town.

Ya'an Shi Jiankang Luguan Hotel 雅安市健康旅馆
Beds in a triple room are Rmb 2.40 and double rooms are Rmb 7. All rooms share communal toilets and a bathhouse. Most buses from Chengdu to Kangding stop here for the night.

Restaurants

Weimei Canting Restaurant 味美餐厅
This large restaurant opposite the Chuankang Dalou Hotel serves large meals for Rmb 2–3 per person.

Yinyue Chating Tea and Snack Shop 音乐茶厅
This shop occupies the second and third floors above the Weimei Canting. Buy a cup of coffee and enjoy it out on the deck overlooking the streets. Simple meals and cakes are also served.

Transportation

Ya'an Qichezhan Bus Station 雅安汽车站
There are early morning buses every day to Kangding, Luding, Emei, Leshan and Chengdu.

Luding 沪定

Luding's fame rests on its 250-year-old chain link suspension bridge spanning the Daduhe River. During the Long March in 1935, the Communists were being pursued northward through southwest Sichuan by Nationalist troops who hoped for a final slaughter on the west bank of the Dadu He. The bridge proved the salvation of the Red Army.

Decisive battles were not new to this region. Conquering Mongol armies crushed the Song Dynasty's forces here, and later, at this same spot, Qing-Dynasty troops demolished the last remaining Taiping army. The Communists' only hope of escaping annihilation was to capture the Luding bridge. During a two-day forced march that covered over 200 kilometers, a Communist regiment under Yang Chengwu beat a Nationalist army to Luding, captured the bridge and held it until the bulk of the Communist armies arrived to cross the river. This action is considered the most courageous of the entire Long March.

Other than the bridge, there is not much to see in Luding. To get to western Sichuan or Tibet you have to stop in Kangding to make connections. If the view of Gongga Shan (7,556 meters high) from the road to Luding arouses your curiosity, take the bus from Luding to Xinxing and start the two-

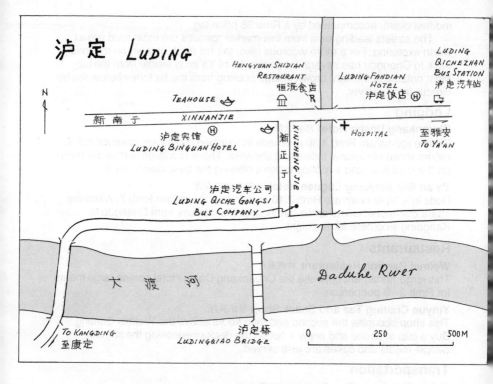

day trek to the base camp.

Things to do

Walk across the bridge and keep walking until you reach one of the unspoiled hamlets along the river. If you like to hike, the 55-kilometer road to Xinxing is a beautiful two-day trek.

Lodging

Luding Binguan Hotel 沪定宾馆
Triple rooms cost Rmb 7.50. Single beds are also available. A double room with a private bathroom is Rmb 20. There is a restaurant and a small store in the hotel.

Luding Fandian Hotel 沪定饭店
Double rooms in this small, noisy hotel next to the bus station are Rmb 6 each. There are no showers and the toilets are 50 meters up a hill.

Restaurants

Hengyuan Shidian Restaurant 恒源食店
This might be the best restaurant in town. It serves good vegetables covered in delicious sauces and the cook will make an effort to prepare food the way you want.

Transportation

Luding Qiche Gongsi Bus Company 泸定汽车公司
The daily bus to Moxi and Xinxing leaves at 07:20.

Luding Changtu Qichezhan Bus Station 泸定长途汽车站
Few buses originate at this station. You must wait for a bus from either Ya'an or Kangding.

Gongga Shan 贡嘎山

'. . . And then suddenly, like a white promontory of clouds, we beheld the long-hidden Minya Konka rising 25,600 feet (7,556 meters) in sublime majesty.

'I could not help exclaiming my joy. I marveled at the scenery which I, the first white man ever to stand here, was privileged to see.

'An immense snowy range extended from north to south, and peerless Minya Konka rose high above its sister peaks into a turquoise-blue sky. A truncated pyramid it is, with immense lateral buttresses flanked by an enormous glacier many miles in length. This glacier, in turn, is joined by another coming directly from Minya Konka itself.'

Joseph F. Rock, "The Glories of the Minya Konka,"
National Geographic Magazine, Vol. LVIII. No.4, 1930.

Minya Konka, as the Tibetans call Gongga Shan, towers above the eastern

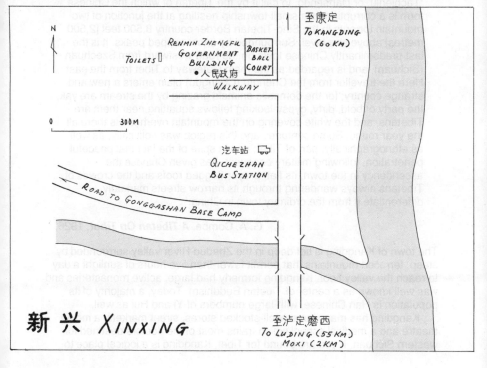

extension of the Tibetan Plateau. When Joseph Rock first gazed at this peak, he was so carried away by elation that he reported the discovery of the world's highest mountain, over 30,000 feet (9,144 metres) high. Though Gongga Shan is not the world's tallest peak, it is one of the most difficult to climb. There have been only two successful attempts, one in 1939 by two Americans and another in 1957 by six Chinese climbers. In 1981 a team of 13 Japanese climbers was thwarted when eight climbers were killed by an avalanche only 300 meters from the summit.

Xinxing is a small Yi mountain village on the road from Luding, a two-day trek below the base camp used by climbers. Local authorities realize that the area is closed so get out of town after disembarking from the bus to avoid problems. If you have to spend the night in Xinxing, the Government Building has a few beds. A long, steep hike to the top of the hill, directly behind this building, offers a spectacular view of Gongga Shan and its sister peaks, provided that the usual cloud cover has lifted.

The scenery is spectacular in Xinxing, but there is little reason to visit unless you have camping equipment and intend to trek to the base camp. Bring food with you as there are no restaurants. A daily bus leaves Xinxing for Luding at 10:00. You can probably get a seat on this usually crowded bus by walking a few kilometers down to Moxi where the bus first stops to pick up passengers.

Kangding 康定

'Tachienlu, or Dartsendo, to call it by the Tibetan of which the Chinese form is a corruption, is a small township nestling at the junction of two mountain torrents in the Sino-Tibetan Border country 8,500 feet [2,500 metres] above sea-level. Surrounded by snow-capped peaks, it is the last predominantly Chinese town on the road westward from Szechuan (Sichuan), and is regarded as the main Gateway to Tibet from the east. Here the traveller from the Chengtu (Chengdu) plain enters a new and strange country; for the domestic animals grazing by the stream are yak, the party of bold, dirty, gypsy-looking fellows squatting near them are Tibetans, and the white covering on the mountain overhead is there all the year round. Some centuries ago this region was politically, as well as ethnographically, part of Tibet; and in spite of the fact that peaceful penetration, following military conquest, has given Chinese the ascendency in the town, its flat, prayer-flagged roofs and the crowds of Tibetans always wandering through its narrow streets markedly differentiate it from the ordinary town in China.'

G. A. Combe, *A Tibetan On Tibet*, 1926.

The town of Kangding is set deep in the Zheduo River valley surrounded by steep, terraced mountains that permit fewer than five hours of sunlight a day to reach the valley floor. Kangding formerly had large, active monasteries and was well known as a center of Tibetan Buddhism. Today, a majority of its population is Han Chinese, with large numbers of Yi and Hui as well.

Kangding has many large, well-stocked stores, street markets, a movie theatre and a medical school which trains most of the doctors destined for western Sichuan. If you are bound for Tibet, Kangding is a logical place to stop for several days to acclimatize before heading into the high mountains.

Things to do

Wander through the market along the river and observe Kangding's multi-ethnic population. For day hikes, explore the terraced fields and small villages above the town.

Nanwu Si Monastery 南戊寺

Founded over 400 years ago, Nanwu Si was the second largest monastery in Kangding and had over 100 monks before 1950. Today the monks, including one Han Chinese and several mischievous boys, number fewer than 20. The abbot here spent 17 years studying in Lhasa and knew the Dalai Lama as a child. Nanwu Si is the central and most active temple in town.

Kangding Lama Si Monastery 康定喇嘛寺

This monastery, located in the center of the old town, dates back at least 500 years. Badly damaged and looted during the Tibetan Conflict of 1959, it was used as a warehouse for storing and refinishing furniture during the Cultural Revolution and only recently reopened as a place of worship. The delapidated, walled complex, visible from a distance above small, run-down hovels, has not yet been restored. The workers who still live in the monks' quarters and the small restaurant conspicuously placed at the entrance of the complex are, no doubt, holdovers from the Cultural Revolution. The two prayer halls tell the same story, one restored and the other still housing furniture. The restored hall, lacking the ornamentation usually found in halls of its size, is like

The Panchen Lamas

The Panchen Lamas, abbots of Tashilhunpo Monastery in Shigatse, came into existence in the 17th century when the Fifth Dalai Lama gave this title to his beloved and learned tutor. 'Panchen' means 'Great Scholar', and he is believed to be the incarnation of Amitabha, the Buddha of Infinite Light. As Tibet's second holiest figure, he was in theory free of involvement with politics. From the 17th century onward, the Panchen and Dalai Lamas initiated one another as divine leaders and the elder one served as tutor to the younger. When a Panchen Lama died, a search began at once for the infant reincarnation, in much the same manner as the Dalai Lamas.

The current Panchen Lama, born in 1938, was one of several child candidates under final testing for the title when the Chinese government proclaimed him to be the tenth Panchen Lama. There is still some debate over his selection, but in most places in Tibet he is revered as the true incarnation. Like the Dalai Lama, he also negotiated with the Chinese government for Tibet to retain some autonomy. After the Dalai Lama fled Tibet, the Chinese attempted to elevate the Panchen Lama's status and use him as the leader of Tibet's government. He is lauded for his attempts to work with the Chinese administrators and to save some of Tibet's greatest religious treasures.

His relationship with the Chinese became stormy and he eventually spent 14 years as a political prisoner in Qincheng Prison Number One near Beijing. Speaking on his incarceration, as reported by the New China News Agency, the Panchen Lama stated, "For a period of time I discarded the banner of patriotism and committed a crime. Guided by Chairman Mao's revolutionary line, I have corrected my errors."

Now he holds a job in Beijing and has revisited Lhasa and Tashilhunpo Monastery twice, each time drawing huge and enthusiastic crowds of pilgrims. In the autumn of 1986, he visited parts of Kham, including Kangding, Daofu and Ganzi.

a new home ready to be decorated. The other hall, dark, its frescoes defaced, is still used as a warehouse, locked up most of the time because the lamas fear repercussions if they are caught opening it for foreigners.

Kangding Da Lama Si Monastery 康定大喇嘛寺

The present structure, opened in 1982, was built 500 meters above Kangding on the foundation of a 600-year-old building that was burned to the ground during the Tibetan Conflict. Reconstruction is not yet complete, but mural sketches, unfinished statuary and unpainted, half-carved pillars are of interest. The monk who has undertaken the restoration might escort you into his small prayer hall and serve tea.

A large white stupa and a new amphitheatre sit just above the monastery. Three pavilion lookouts are being built on the mountain, two below the monastery and one above it. The lower two are already favorite hangouts for local adolescents who go there to smoke. The upper pavilion offers a spectacular view over the river, the terraced fields and the snowcapped peaks. Branch off any of the higher trails for a secluded walk in the forest. There are level spots suitable for camping, with abundant water for drinking.

Maofangchang Wenquan Hot Springs 温泉

The bus trip to this local bathing spot takes less than an hour. We did not have the pleasure of visiting the springs ourselves, but locals assured us the trip is well worth it. Catch the bus to the springs on the street in front of the government complex.

Qingzhen Luguan Di'er Canting Hui Restaurant and Mosque
清眞旅馆第二餐厅

This is the center of the Muslim community. The mosque is little more than a wall with pictures of Mecca and Kashgar, but the restaurant serves delicious food and has an amiable Hui clientele.

Festivals

Si Yue Si Festival 四月四

Tibetans gather on Kangding's Horse Race Hill (Saima Shan 赛马山) for horse races, folk dances, tug-of-war and wrestling matches on the fourth day of the fourth lunar month.

Stupas

One of the most ubiquitous structures throughout the Buddhist world is the stupa: a round dome or cylinder on a (usually) square base, with a shaft or spike emerging upwards. The stupa is as fundamental a symbol to Buddhists as the cross is to Christians.

Stupas probably evolved in India from prehistoric times as burial mounds for local rulers and heroes. Legend says that in the 5th century BC Sakyamuni, the historical Buddha, asked to have his ashes interred in a stupa. With the launching of the new religion, stupas became formalized objects of worship. King Ashoka of India (273–232 BC) built innumerable stupas as an act of piety and to gain religious merit.

In early Buddhist art, Sakyamuni was never portrayed in human form, since the state of Buddhahood was considered indescribable. Instead, a stupa became the Buddha's symbol, a reminder of his earthly existence and a place of devotion. Stupas were erected by pilgrims in places where the main events of his life took place. Stupas became the main cult objects in monasteries where they were often used to hold the mummified bodies or ashes of saints, or to hold sacred objects, relics or scriptures. They were built to mark the place where a deity or a saint was said to have lived, or perhaps to commemorate events, like the founding of a monastery or, nowadays, a restoration.

The shape of stupas was adapted to local architecture wherever they spread and came to include a huge variety of types. The slender pagodas of China and Japan evolved from earlier, squat stupas. Sizes could range from tiny, ritual altar stupas to ceremonial gate-stupas big enough to straddle a thoroughfare. Yet all kept the same basic components.

The different parts are associated with the elements. The base stands for earth, the dome for water and the shaft for fire, topped by a half-moon for air and a sun for infinite space. The shaft is usually formed of 13 rings, which represent the 13 steps to enlightenment. Decorated stupa-tombs have one side of open grill-work on the dome if a mummified body lies inside. These are only found in major monasteries of Tibet. Stupas containing scriptures, charms or treasures are closed, but may have a niche for a statue.

Chorten is the Tibetan word for a stupa. It refers not only to recognizable stupas but also to any sacred protuberance — a rock, a cairn or a pile of carved *mani* stones, or a jumble of stones and prayer flag staves erected on a mountain pass. These objects are all to be worshipped by circumambulation, clockwise, with the sacred object always on the pilgrim's right.

Elisabeth Booz

Lodging

Ganzijun Fenqu Di'er Zhaodaisuo Hotel 甘孜军分区第二招待所

Foreign travelers are usually directed to this hotel. Beds in a triple room are Rmb 3 and double rooms are Rmb 10. All rooms share communal toilets and there are no showers. The restaurant on the first floor is poor. Better food can be found on the streets. Many truck drivers bound for Tibet stop at this hotel, so if you want a ride westward, begin here.

Luguan Hotels 旅馆

Try one of the dozen or so *luguan* hotels found on both sides of Yaheqiao Lu between the bus station and the Zhaodaisuo Hotel. These small, Sichuan-style hotels are very old and lean on one another like a house of cards ready to fall. Inside, rooms are small and often partitioned by only thin newpaper-covered walls. Needless to say, facilities are either archaic or nonexistent.

Transportation

Kangding Qichezhan Bus Station 康定汽车站

Buses leave early every morning to Daowu, Ganzi, Xiaojin, Luding, Jiu Long, Chengdu, Emei Shan and Leshan. On alternating days there is a bus to Xiang Cheng, which reaches Yajiang the first day and passes through Litang the second. Buses to Derong depart on the 9th, 19th and 29th of each month for the three-day trip. Buses to Dege run on the 2nd, 7th, 21st, and 27th of every month.

Daofu 道孚

Daofu, known as Dawu in Tibetan, is an overnight stop on the bus trip from Kangding to Ganzi. The town sits in a broad valley at an elevation of 3,000 meters and is larger than most in the Ganzi Tibetan Autonomous Region but looks more Chinese than Tibetan.

Things to do

A market lines the main road north of the bus station. Furs, musk, Tibetan knives, money belts, herbs and medicines can be found here. The restaurants in this market area are the best in town.

Daofu Si Monastery 道孚寺

Surprisingly, this monastery is located close to the bus station, not perched miles away. It is currently undergoing restoration, which is largely complete. The many monks in residence carry on a colorful and lively existence. Photography is permitted. The Dalai Lama stayed here in 1954 and his room is kept in perfect condition in case he ever returns. There is also a room for the Panchen Lama.

Lodging

Daofu Xian Zhaodaisuo Hotel 道孚县招待所

Foreign travelers are usually turned away from the hotel at the bus station and sent here. Beds in rustic, but clean, four-bed rooms are Rmb 1.40 each. The hotel restaurant serves a fine bowl of noodles.

Transportation

Daily buses go to both Ganzi and Kangding.

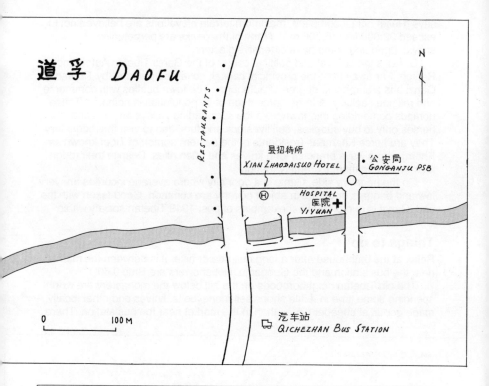

道孚 *DAOFU*

RESTAURANTS

县招待所
XIAN ZHAODAISUO HOTEL

公安局
GONGANJU PSB

HOSPITAL
医院
YIYUAN

汽车站
QICHEZHAN BUS STATION

0   100 M

N

Letter from the Road: Luhuo

'If you take the bus from Xinduqiao to Ganzi, the first night is a stop in Luhuo. All travelers will be guided to a hotel across the street from the bus stop. Rmb 4 gets you a bed and an electric light in a four-bed room. Foreigners are usually separated from Chinese. A number of restaurants are on the right after leaving the hotel. Don't expect anything beyond sustenance.

'Down the road from these restaurants you will see the Tibetan part of town and a monastery on a hillside opposite the river. There is no clear path to the monastery so improvise. The building appears huge from a distance, but up close you see that it is being rebuilt. The mud walls and some interior framework are in place. Huge, carved, unpainted wooden columns lie on the ground. There are no monks in residence but the rebuilding effort is a remarkable testimony to the Tibetan spirit.'

Scott Klimo

Ganzi 甘孜

Ganzi is situated on a high valley floor 3,800 meters above sea level, at the base of the Chola Shan Mountains whose snow-covered peaks tower 3,000 meters higher still. The Ganzi region is so remote and inaccessible that the altitude of many peaks is uncertain. A current United States Air Force map says 'Relief data incomplete, maximum terrain elevations are believed not to exceed 22,000 feet (6,706 m.)'. Many of the peaks are perpetually snowcapped and some have extensive glaciers.

Ganzi is the cultural and political center of the Ganzi Tibetan Autonomous Region. Far away from the provincial capital, governed primarily by Tibetans, Ganzi has a surprising degree of autonomy. The town bustles with commerce and religious activity. A large percentage of its population is nomadic. These nomads come riding into town from the surrounding valleys on yaks and horses only to buy supplies, sell livestock and furs, and to visit the monastery. They are fierce Khampas (residents of the eastern portion of Tibet known as Kham) who always brandish long knives and often rifles. Despite their rough look, we found them extremely friendly.

On the negative side, Ganzi is a poor city where average incomes are very low and beggars or others in abject poverty are common. Good taken with the bad, Ganzi is one of the best examples of post-1949 Tibetan society within China.

Things to do

Relax at the bathhouse after a long bus ride or hike. It is between the market near the bus station and the Gonganju. Hot showers are Rmb 0.60.

The old Tibetan neighborhoods on the hill below the monastery are worth spending some time in. Little shops sell moneybelts, knives and other locally made goods at cheaper prices than in the market near the bus station. There

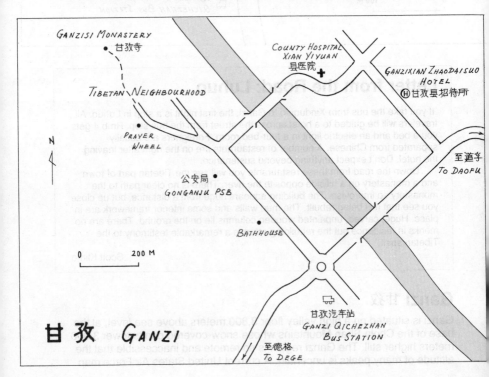

Letter from the Road: Ganzi Si Monastery

The head lama of Ganzi Si, a friend of the Dalai Lama, arrived from India a few years ago. He lives in an apartment at the top of the monastery and will allow you to take his photograph once he has struck a suitable pose. You can recognize him by his huge build and handsome handlebar moustache.

From the roof, prayer flags are visible on a hill a few kilometers away. A strenuous hike of two and a half hours will bring you to this spot, where you can enjoy a spectacular view of Ganzi, the river valley and the Chola Shan Range stretching in both directions. If you face the Chola Shan and look left, the ruins of another monastery appear. Carry on to this site. Although much of the structure has been destroyed, rebuilding is going on and one part of the monastery houses numerous examples of old, original Tibetan religious painting.

Several white tents, similar to Mongolian yurts, sometimes stand across the river from Ganzi. These belong to Tibetan nomads who are extremely friendly and hospitable; they will almost certainly invite you inside for tea and *tsampa*. A ferry, in fact a simple dugout canoe with a man and a pole, will take you across the river for Rmb 1.

Behind the nomad camp to the right is a small Tibetan village with a temple. The temple is locked, but if you show up the man with the key will soon appear to let you in.

Scott Klimo

is a small shrine with a prayer wheel on the main path. Locals welcome you inside to watch or even help turn the wheel.

Ganzi Si Monastery 甘孜寺
Even at a distance, the village atmosphere around Ganzi Si is striking. Tibetan homes, dirt alleyways, people and livestock all huddle together below the massive religious complex while vultures circle observantly overhead. The monastery was completely destroyed during the Tibetan Conflict and reconstruction work is not yet complete. The lowest levels contain prayer rooms and thousands of old Tibetan texts, the middle levels have smaller prayer rooms and the upper level is a large prayer hall with five statues. One room at the monastery has been specially prepared for the Dalai Lama. From the roof of the monastery you can view the Ganzi valley spread below and the icy peaks beyond. Bring a snack from town and eat it on the roof.

Farther away

Dajin Si Monastery 大金寺
This monastery, 30 kilometers farther along the road to Dege, is reputed to be several times larger than Ganzi Si with many more monks. The monastery is set in a beautiful meadow below magnificent peaks. To get there, hitchhike on the main road from Ganzi. Start early so you have time to hitch a ride back into town. We hear the Dajin Si area is ideal for camping.

Lodging

Ganzi Xian Zhaodaisuo Hotel 甘孜县招待所
Double rooms are Rmb 7, with cheaper beds in four-bed rooms. All rooms share communal toilets and there are no showers. This hotel gets our highest recommendation for its friendly, helpful staff and excellent canteen that serves hearty meals. Rustic rooms, like those in a mountain lodge, are clean and

cozy. Plenty of hot water is available for drinking and washing. The staff will lend you a coal burner on cold winter nights.

Camping
If you visit Ganzi during the summer, consider camping on the outskirts of town with a group of Tibetan nomads. Several Americans we know said this was the best time they had in China.

Transportation

Ganzi Qichezhan Bus Station 甘孜汽车站
Buses to Daowu and Kangding depart daily. On the 4th, 9th, 16th, 23rd and 29th of each month buses to Dege pass through Ganzi.

Hitchhiking
If you are patient, hitchhiking is no problem in either direction. Convoys of trucks leave town very early, so if you are out on the road by sunrise you can probably get a ride quickly.

Kham

Tibet is made up of three regions. To the east lies Kham, now divided into the Ganzi, Deqen and Muli Tibetan Autonomous Prefectures in addition to the eastern section of what the Chinese call 'Tibet'. Kham has always been considered the most rugged and inaccessible region of Tibet, with endless ranges of huge mountains and terrifying gorges formed by the headwaters and tributaries of three mighty Asian rivers, the Salween, Mekong and Yangzi. Vast forests, now largely depleted, were once home to large numbers of giant pandas, lesser pandas, bears, wolves, leopards, eagles and other creatures.

The human inhabitants are called Khampas, a people as proud, fierce and independent as their land. Divided into clans and tiny kingdoms only loosely controlled by Lhasa, Khampas were once feared throughout Tibet and the Chinese border regions as merciless bandits. Today they remain imposing figures, big, stocky and fearless, with enormous sheepskin coats worn with the right shoulder bare even in the coldest weather. To complete the image of toughness, they wear fur hats, leather and wool boots and always carry long, sword-like knives tucked into their belts. Despite their fierce looks, Khampas frequently greet travelers with a big, friendly smile and a pat on the back. They put a high value on honesty and can dispense rough justice.

The basic diet in Kham, similar to that in most parts of Tibet, consists of tsampa (roasted barley flour), butter tea and yak meat. By Tibetan standards it is a rich agricultural area.

Today, most Khampas are settled, yet large numbers of nomads still wander across Kham's rugged landscape, occasionally going into scattered towns to trade, their lives little changed over the last thousand years.

During the 1950s, Khampas strongly resisted 'liberation', 'democratic reforms' and collectivization movements forced on them by the Chinese government. Groups from Dege and Litang spread out across the whole of Tibet to organize resistance, while those remaining in Kham successfully waged guerrilla warfare for several years. In 1959, many groups fought their way through Tibet to India and Nepal. An uneasy peace with periodic outbreaks of violence has existed in Kham since then.

Dege 德格

Dege is the last city on the Chengdu-Lhasa highway before it leaves the Ganzi Tibetan Autonomous Region of Sichuan Province and enters Tibet. Dege is five days by bus from Chengdu and at least nine days by truck from Lhasa. The main attraction in Dege is the Bakong Scripture Printing House. Founded 250 years ago, it now houses over 200,000 wooden printing blocks including Buddhist classics, interpretations of the scriptures, early Tibetan medical and pharmaceutical works and the only surviving woodblock copy of *The Origins Of Indian Buddhism*.

Festivals

Monlam Festival

Monlam Chenmo (Great Prayer Festival) commemorates the Buddha and strengthens Tibetan Buddhism. The festival is celebrated in Dege on the 15th day of the seventh lunar month.

Yajiang 雅江

Yajiang, on a hill above the Yalongjiang River, is little more than a wide spot in the road serving as the stop-over on the two-day bus ride from Kangding to Litang, Batang or Xiangcheng. Yajiang exists primarily to provide services to the drivers and vehicles that ply the road to Tibet.

Just below the town, the main road crosses a new, modern bridge.

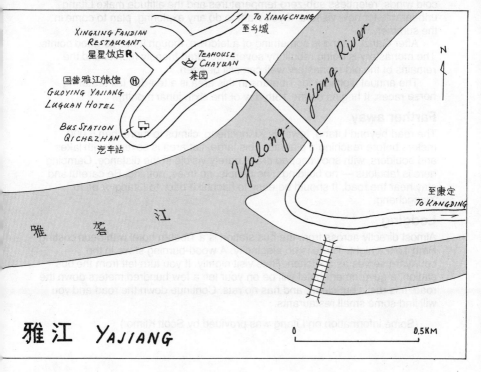

Photographing it is strictly forbidden and signs to this effect are posted all over town.

Things to do

There is nothing special here, but Yajiang is an interesting town to browse in nonetheless. Though it is a Tibetan town, we found no monasteries in the vicinity. The teahouse near the hotel is popular and often full of card players. For a good bowl of noodles or other tasty dishes, try the Xingxing Fandian Restaurant.

Lodging

Guoying Luguan Hotel 国营旅馆
Beds in a four-bed room are Rmb 1.50 each. All guests share a common toilet and there are no showers.

Transportation

Buses run every other day to Xiangcheng and back to Kangding. Daily buses go to Litang, and there are frequent trucks going in both directions.

Litang 理塘

Litang, set at 4,000 meters on the Kangba Plateau, ranks among the highest settlements in the world. Tough, weather-worn Tibetans struggle endlessly to scrape out a living from the unforgiving surroundings. In winter months, bitterly cold winds, relentless sub-zero temperatures and the altitude make Litang unbearable for new visitors. If you want to do any exploring, plan to come in the summer.

After Ganzi, Litang is something of a letdown, though it has its good points. The monastery is being rebuilt by several hundred friendly monks and the remains of the old monastery wall can still be seen.

The annual highlight for Tibetans in this area is a ten-day fair featuring horse races. It begins on the 13th day of the sixth lunar month.

Farther away

The road beyond Litang, towards Xiangcheng, climbs to more than 5,000 meters before reaching a plateau. This large, flat area is covered with lakes and boulders, with snowcapped crags barely visible in the distance. Camping here is fabulous — no buildings, no people, no trees, nothing. Be careful and stay near the road. It should be easy to hitchhike back to Litang or on to Xiangcheng.

Lodging

Almost directly across from the bus station is a Tibetan hotel with beds costing Rmb 1.70 a night. There is no electricity. A wood-burning stove in the courtyard serves as a kitchen. Rats visit nightly. If you turn left from the bus station, a government hotel will be on your left a few hundred meters down the road. It is rustic but clean, and has no rats. Continue down the road and you will find some small restaurants.

(Some information on Litang was provided by Scott Klimo.)

A Tale from Kham

Once upon a time there was a little bird which had built its nest upon the ground. One day a herd of elephants came along the way. "Do not tread on my nest," said the little bird, and the kind elephants passed by. But an old elephant came up a long way behind. "Do not tread on my nest," said the little bird. "! will," said the old elephant. "Am I not the king of beasts?" and set his great foot on it. Then the little bird cried "I will be revenged!" but the old elephant laughed, and said, "Am I not the king of beasts?" So, away flew the little bird for revenge to the crows, who came and pecked the old elephant's eyelids and made them very sore; and away flew the little bird to the bees, who came and stung the sore places and blinded the old elephant. Then said the little bird to the old elephant, "My heart is sad for you, so old and blind. Unless I help you, you will soon die of hunger, poor old elephant. I know a rich pasture of long grass. Follow the sound of my voice and I will guide you thither." So the old elephant followed the little bird, and she led him over the brink of a precipice, and down he fell, and was killed. In this manner the little bird was revenged.

The Djriung Yi, the Story Book is a classic epic of Kham. Several excerpts from the text were provided by a high lama of Tibet to E.C. Baber, and published in his book *Travels and Researches in Western China (1882)*.

Xiangcheng 乡城

Xiangcheng, in the southwestern section of the Ganzi Tibetan Autonomous Region, displays characteristics drawn from both north and south. The population is largely Tibetan and the local religion is Tibetan Buddhism. But unlike other towns in western Sichuan, this population is comprised largely of farmers. Xiangcheng sits on a broad, fertile floodplain where arable land is plentiful. At an altitude of 2,000 meters, snow and freezing temperatures are rare so crops are cultivated year round. While culturally Tibetan, Xiangcheng lies in a geographic region similar to much of northern Yunnan Province.

Things to do

Explore the farming villages near Xiangcheng. There are two north of town on the flat plain near the river.

Xiangcheng Si Monastery 乡城寺

Everyone who visits Xiangcheng should see Xiangcheng Si. The murals and statues are new but beautiful. The main hall overflows with small statues, *thangkas* and cloth wall hangings, all of which appear ancient.

As you leave the monastery courtyard, turn right on the street and right again at the first alleyway. Enter the large stable to your left. This is what remains of the old monastery. The walls of the large hall are still covered with faint traces of once-magnificent murals. On the ground amongst the hay you will find broken tablets or hand-carved tiles. The lamas still regularly pray in this large stable, sitting with the livestock to worship below the crumbling frescoes.

The Xiangcheng Monastery was large and politically powerful until the late 1950s. The monks, labeled renegades by the Chinese government, were active in resisting the advance of the People's Liberation Army in the area. In 1957, the monastery was classified as a military target and bombed from the air. Many monks were killed, but most of those who survived resisted PLA

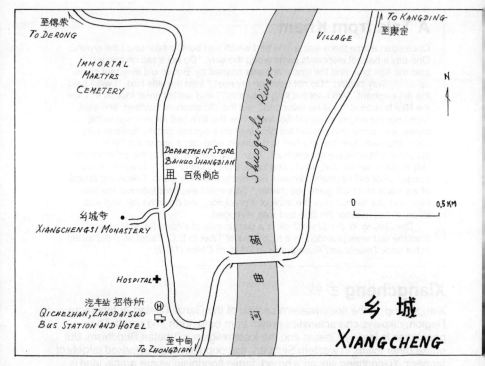

至得荣
TO DERONG

IMMORTAL
MARTYRS
CEMETERY

DEPARTMENT STORE
BAIHUO SHANGDIAN
⊞ 百货商店

乡城寺 ●
XIANGCHENGSI MONASTERY

HOSPITAL ✚

汽车站 招待所
QICHEZHAN, ZHAODAISUO
BUS STATION AND HOTEL

至中甸
TO ZHONGDIAN

硕曲河 Shuoquhe River

VILLAGE

至康定
TO KANGDING

N

0   0.5 KM

乡城
XIANGCHENG

advances until late 1958 when they fled west to Lhasa to kindle resistance
there.

Immortal Martyr Cemetery 墓地
Crowning the hill north of town, the cemetery and monument are worth a visit
though the gates will probably be locked and foreigners are not allowed in.
The graves, which number in the hundreds, are for PLA soldiers who died
while 'liberating' Xiangcheng in two battles, both held on October 17, 1958.
Tibetan dead were buried elsewhere.

Farther away

The road from Litang to Xiangcheng descends through a narrow, vertical
canyon before it meets the Yanghe River 35 kilometers north of Xiangcheng.
Coming from Litang, you will catch a glimpse of this canyon. Hitchhike back to
it and camp, exploring the canyon by either hiking up the road or along the
stream at the canyon floor. You might meet lumberjacks who, unfortunately,
have begun working in the canyon. You could easily camp for a week here if
you bring enough food from Xiangcheng. Water and firewood are plentiful, as
are large fish in the stream.

Lodging

Sichuan Qiche Yunshu Gongsi Kangding Gongsi Zhaodaisuo Hotel
四川省汽车招待所
This hotel is conveniently located behind the bus station. Beds in a four-
person room are Rmb 2, but the management may try to charge you for the

whole room. The restaurant at the hotel is good, and the cook is willing to let travelers use his kitchen. Hotel staff will help you buy a bus ticket or arrange a ride with a truck.

Transportation

Buses to Zhongdian in Yunnan Province do not run during the winter, but occasionally make the trip in summer. Buses bound for Derong arrive on the 10th, 20th and 30th of each month and depart early the next day. Buses to Litang, Kangding and Chengdu leave every other day. Traffic on these remote mountain roads is light, but hitchhiking is still an alternative if you are patient.

Derong 得荣

Derong, a bumpy one-day bus ride to the southwest of Xiangcheng, vibrates with activity like no other town in the region. Located at the southern terminus of the unfinished Xiangcheng-Benzilan road, Derong is one of China's modern boomtowns, with crews working round-the-clock to raise a town from isolated wilderness. Buildings go up overnight, as temporary generators illuminate lattice shacks housing off-duty road crews back from blasting areas. There is a frontier feeling to this town that never sleeps.

Things to do

Derong is really nothing more than a large village and seeing it takes no time. You do not have to go out to visit the town, the town will come to visit you.

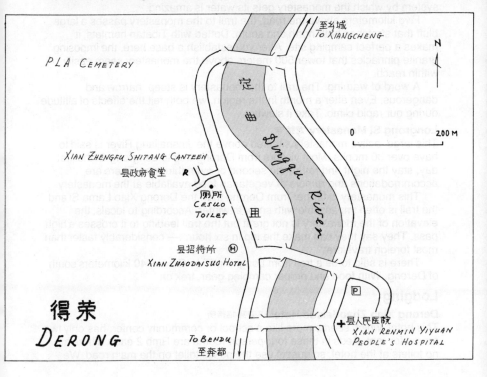

247

Derong gets no tourist traffic, so every foreign traveler causes a stir. The attention you get in Derong is quite different from the 'staring circles' common in China. Here people seek real contact, often bringing you eggs or cooked food, whether they speak English, Chinese or Tibetan.

A cemetery filled primarily with dead PLA soldiers is on the hill just above town. The gates were firmly locked when we tried to enter, and no one in town could (or would) tell us how many soldiers were buried there or when most of them died.

Derong Xiao Lama Si Monastery 待荣小喇嘛寺

The four-hour hike to this monastery is tough, but there is great beauty in the rugged canyon along the way. The trail, which breaks from the road 10 kilometers north of town at the rope bridge, leads from the valley floor up an increasingly narrow canyon skirting waterfalls and sheer cliffs through a scrub landscape into the pine forests that enfold the monastery. The further you progress up the mountainside, the more mystical the journey becomes. Large sentry-like prayer flags guard the entrances to narrow canyon passageways. Wind whistles through the trees in the canyons as hawks soar overhead, and the sonorous note of temple trumpets draws you closer.

The monastery itself, which in the past fulfilled all expectations of a weary climber, is a bit of a let down today. Razed during the Tibetan Conflict, smoke-stained outlines of the old building on the walls of its protecting cave are the only reminder of its former glory. The present structure, rebuilt entirely by local Tibetans does, however, radiate the energy of an active monastery. The drip system by which the monastery gets its water is amazing.

Five kilometers above the road, the trail to the monastery passes a large bluff that stretches both north and south. Dotted with Tibetan hamlets, it makes a perfect camping site. After you establish a base here, the imposing granite pinnacles that tower 500 meters above the monastery seem easily within reach.

A word of warning. The trail to the monastery is steep, narrow and dangerous. Even after a month in the region, we both felt the effects of altitude during our rapid climb. Take it slowly.

Longrong Si Monastery 龙绒寺

This large, active monastery situated above the Jinshajiang River is said to have over 30 monks. Most visitors from Derong trek to Longrong Si the first day, stay the night and return the second or even third day. There are accommodations and rumors of vegetarian food available at the monastery.

This monastery is farther from Derong than the Derong Xiao Lama Si and the trail is often impassable with snow in winter. According to locals, the elevation of the monastery is not great but the trail leading to it crosses a high pass. They say they can make the trip in six hours — considerably faster than most foreign travelers.

There is said to be a trail from Longrong Si to Guxue, 40 kilometers south of Derong. With food and proper camping gear, trek on.

Lodging

Derong Xian Zhaodaisuo Hotel 得荣县招待所

This hotel, which seems more like a school or community center, has only two rooms for rent. Beds in these four-person rooms are Rmb 2 each. There are no toilets at the hotel, so guests use the public toilet on the main road. We think this toilet is the only one in town because everyone seems to use it. The hotel's lack of curtains is a bother because local children, often accompanied by curious parents, flock to the window to catch what may be their first glimpse of a foreigner.

Transportation

There are three buses a month to Xiangcheng, on the 2nd, 12th, and 22nd. You can also try hitching. There will be no reliable transportation south of Derong until the road to Benzilan in Yunnan Province is completed in 1988. At present, the road extends 30 kilometers southward.

Dingquhe River Gorge Trek 定曲河

The Dingquhe River Gorge trek consists of an 80-kilometer walk south from Derong in Sichuan Province to Benzilan in Yunnan Province. The road south stops at the Yanquhe River, so walking is the only way to get from Derong to the road network in Yunnan.

Walk (or hitch a ride with road crews if you can) south from Derong on the road to Bendu, a small Tibetan hamlet with 100 inhabitants. At Bendu, a smaller river joins the Dingqu He and the canyon above this river looks excellent for camping. Both rivers flow extremely fast through rapids and waterfalls. Picturesque, but keep your distance.

At Bendu, the main road crosses to the east bank of the Dingqu He and a trail continues south along the west bank, so you can walk on either side. The road is complete as far as the north bank of the Yanqu He, 15 kilometers south of Bendu. Here, all southbound travelers must cross the Yanqu He strapped to a pulley on a cable bridge. This heart-stopping method of crossing rivers was once common, but is becoming rare as remote areas become more developed. If you choose to walk along the west bank of the Dingqu He, cross to the east bank one kilometer above the river intersection in order to use the cable crossing, or go just beyond the river intersection to find a footbridge.

The Guxue trailhead is just south of the cable crossing. Here, the trail leaves the canyon floor, climbing 500 meters before reaching Guxue 10 kilometers away. If you have walked from Derong, consider camping where the rivers meet. Water is abundant and the rivers are well stocked with fish. Climb to Guxue the following morning.

Guxue 古学

South of Derong, the Dingqu He valley gives way to a rugged and sometimes vertically-walled gorge. During the rainy season, streams turn into cascades that spray the canyon floor. On the western bank of the river unbroken canyon walls are striped by tilted sedimentary deposits. On the eastern bank, the precipice is broken 700 meters above the river by a long, narrow shelf with cliffs rising above. Guxue is the first in a string of Tibetan villages scratching their subsistence from this bluff. Linked to the 20th century by a single telephone line, Guxue has neither electricity nor running water. Howling winds and the booming report of an occasional dynamite blast from roadcrews at work far below are all that break the absolute wilderness silence.

Things to do

Guxue, a rare product of geographic isolation, is the most untouched Tibetan community we found in Southwest China. Explore the dirt trails of the village,

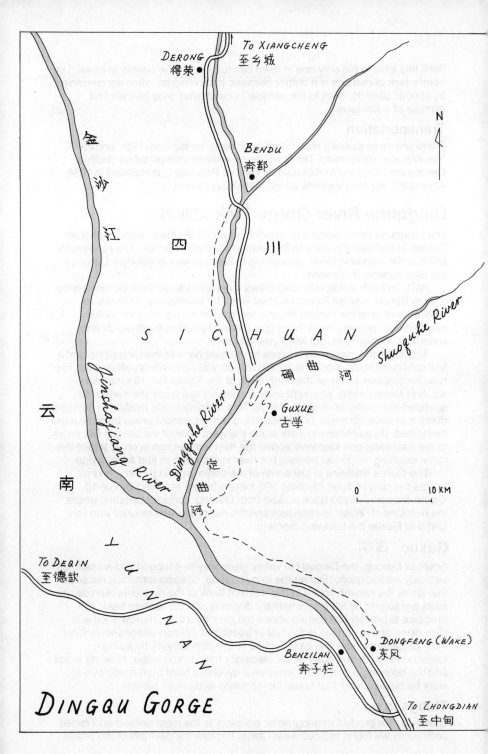

DERONG
得荣

TO XIANGCHENG
至乡城

BENDU
奔都

N

金
沙
江

四 川

S I C H U A N

硕 曲 河   Shuoquhe River

古学
GUXUE

定

曲

河

Jinshajiang River

Dingquhe River

云

南

TO DEQIN
至德钦

Y U N N A N

DONGFENG (WAKE)
东风

BENZILAN
奔子栏

TO ZHONGDIAN
至中甸

DINGQU GORGE

0   10 KM

the fields that surround it and visit Tibetan homes. Traditional dances and singing contests are common here, and most of the people in town participate in the festivities, held around a bonfire outside the village.

Xinchu Si Monastery 新于寺

This monastery is the focal point of life in Guxue. On the ground level the rooms and hallways are used for subsistence activities: women kneading dough and frying bread, men and boys chopping up meat, older men sharpening knives. Higher up within the building, work gives way to religious activities. At one end of the top level, a prayer room has seats for 30 monks, a large drum, a gong and hundreds of religious texts. At the opposite end lives the head lama. An open patio in the center serves as a village meeting place.

The head lama, who is under 40 years of age, studied at a Nationalities Institute in western Sichuan. Having gone on extended pilgrimages through Yunnan, Sichuan and Tibet, he is both well-learned and experienced. He speaks a little English and is eager to learn more. He is likely to invite a passing traveler to dinner.

Like most monasteries in Tibet, Xinchu Si suffered during the Tibetan Conflict. Locals told how PLA soldiers destroyed the building by collapsing the support beams with dynamite. Certainly the role of religion has changed since 1949, but the role Xinchu Si plays in local economics, politics and cultural activities makes it hard to imagine that religious influence is disappearing.

Two other monasteries, Degong Si and Huajiao Si, are said to be within a day's hike of Guxue.

Longrong Si Monastery outside Derong is accessible by trail from Guxue as well as from Derong. It should be possible to trek from Derong to Longrong Si and then on to Guxue, eliminating a time-consuming backtrack.

Lodging

Renmin Zhengfu Government Building 人民政府大厦

This place has a few beds for Rmb 1 each. There is no restaurant of any kind in town, so stock up on supplies in Derong.

Trail to Yunnan

A wide trail leading south from Guxue to Dongfeng (also known in Tibetan as Wake) traverses the narrow bluff and sometimes rises over 1,000 meters above the river. The first 12-kilometer stretch of this trail parallels the Dingquhe River southward towards its junction with the Jinshajiang River. It passes through two small Tibetan villages before scaling a steep cliff directly above the river junction. Fill up your canteens at either of these two villages; the next water source we found was a village five hours to the south. With the exception of the trail section just above the river junction, this part of the walk is easy.

Past the junction, the trail climbs higher up the canyon wall, exposed to gusting winds. 13 kilometers south of the river junction, the trail arrives at a small Tibetan hamlet with fewer than 20 buildings. The locals have water and bread if you need them. The herdsmen in this area are very poor, so insist on paying for everything you take from them. If you are tired, there are suitable camp sites nearby, although the whole area is on a ridge exposed to the wind. An hour south of the village, the trail descends into a protected canyon and crosses a small stream to a flat, sheltered site ideal for camping. Notice the intricate irrigation system suspended high above the stream.

The trail continues southward for the remaining 15 kilometers to Dongfeng (Wake) and Benzilan. Five kilometers south of the stream, you will see the unfinished road 500 meters below the trail beside the river. We learned the hard way that getting down to this road is a problem. The promising trail we decided to take led us part way down the mountain before ending far short of the road in a cactus patch. We had to climb over several brush fences farmers had erected to keep livestock off their fields before we reached the road, tired and scraped up. The trail, which climbs in places before reaching Dongfeng, is difficult, but may be the wiser choice considering the awful descent to the road. If you choose to go by the road, be sure there are people on it before you go down. An empty road usually signifies a broken bridge or imminent blasting.

Dongfeng (Wake)
This small, boring village is nothing more than a single road lined with shacks. The only reason to stay on the Sichuan side of the river is if you have difficulties with the Yunnan Gonganju, in which case the convenient provincial border allows you to visit Benzilan by day and retreat to your dull but safe sanctuary in Sichuan by night. There is a hotel in Dongfeng on the main road. Cross the Jinsha Jiang on the rowboat ferry to Benzilan (see page 168), a more interesting place. The ferry costs Rmb 1 and makes the crossing every 30 minutes.

Other Places In Sichuan Province

Zigong 自贡
120 kilometers southeast of Leshan, Zigong is the site of China's richest source of Stone Dragon Bones, otherwise known as dinosaur fossils. A large museum in town contains exhibits of the best finds. It is an agreeable old town with red timbered buildings overlooking a small river. All local buses are powered by natural gas held in giant bags on the roof.

Neijiang 内江
Neijiang is located midway between Chengdu and Chongqing on the rail line. The view from the train presents a large, ugly, industrial town in the middle of Sichuan's Red Basin.

Barkam (Ma'erkang) 马尔康
Barkam (Ma'erkang) is a Tibetan town in the Aba Tibetan Autonomous Region, located two days by bus from Chengdu and one day from Songpan. Barkam has six Buddhist monasteries and is set in a beautiful river valley. This is a highly recommended town.

Deyang 德阳
Less than 70 kilometers north of Chengdu on the Chengdu-Xi'an rail line, Deyang is close to Chong Tong Mu, the Tomb of Chong Tong.

Mianyang 绵阳
Mianyang, about 150 kilometers north of Chengdu on the Chengdu-Xi'an rail line, has a number of historical sites worth visiting, notably Tai Bai Guju, the former residence of Tai Bai, Jiang Wan Mu, the tomb of Jiang Wan, Pingyangfu Junque Watchtower and Yunuquan, Jade Woman Springs.

Nanchong 南充
Nanchong is a port on the Jialingjiang River less than 200 kilometers north of Chongqing. Nearby is the Bai Ta Pagoda.

A Guide to Pronouncing Chinese Names

The official system of romanization used in China, which the visitor will find on maps, road signs and city shopfronts, is known as *Pinyin*. It is now almost universally adopted by the Western media.

Non-Chinese may initially encounter some difficulty in pronouncing romanized Chinese words. In fact many of the sounds correspond to the usual pronunciation of the letters in English. The exceptions are:

Initials

c	is like the *ts* in '*its*'
q	is like the *ch* in '*cheese*'
x	has no English equivalent, and can best be described as a hissing consonant that lies somewhere between *sh* and *s*. The sound was rendered as *hs* under an earlier transcription system.
z	is like the *ds* in 'fa*ds*'
zh	is unaspirated, and sounds like the *j* in '*j*ug'

Finals

a	sounds like 'ah'
e	is pronounced as in 'her'
i	is pronounced as in 'sk*i*' (written as *yi* when not preceded by an initial consonant). However, in *ci, chi, ri, shi, zi* and *zhi*, the sound represented by the *i* final is quite different and is similar to the *ir* in '*sir*', but without much stressing of the *r* syllable.
o	sounds like the *aw* in '*law*'
u	sounds like the *oo* in '*ooze*'
ü	is pronounced as the German *ü* (written as *yu* when not preceded by an initial consonant)

Finals in Combination

When two or more finals are combined, such as in *hao*, *jiao* and *liu*, each letter retains its sound value as indicated in the list above, but note the following:

ai	is like the *ie* in '*tie*'
ei	is like the *ay* in '*bay*'
ian	is like the *ien* in '*Vienna*'
ie	similar to 'ear'
ou	is like the *o* in '*code*'
uai	sounds like 'why'
uan	is like the *uan* in '*iguana*' (except when preceded by *j*, *q*, *x* and *y*; in these cases a *u* following any of these four consonants is in fact *ü* and *uan* is similar to *uen*.)
ue	is like the *ue* in '*duet*'
ui	sounds like 'way'

Examples

A few Chinese names are shown below with English phonetic spelling beside them:

Beijing	Bay-jing	Kangxi	Kahn-shi
Cixi	Tsi-shi	Qianlong	Chien-lawng
Guilin	Gway-lin	Tiantai	Tien-tie
Hangzhou	hahng-jo	Xi'an	Shi-ahn

An apostrophe is used to separate syllables in certain compound-character words to preclude confusion. For example, *Changan* (which can be *chang-an* or *chan-gan*) is sometimes written as *Chang'an*.

Tones

A Chinese syllable consists of not only an initial and a final or finals, but also a tone or pitch of the voice when the words are spoken. In *Pinyin* the four basic tones are marked ˉ, ´, ˇ and ` . These marks are almost never shown in printed form except in language texts.

Prepared by May Holdsworth

Chinese Phrasebook

by K. Mark Stevens

Food and drink

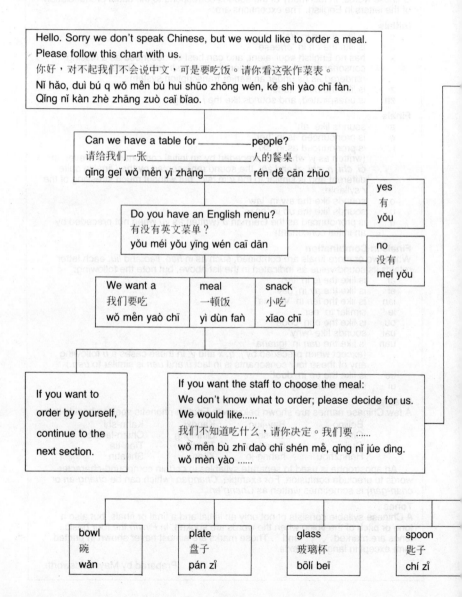

Hello. Sorry we don't speak Chinese, but we would like to order a meal.
Please follow this chart with us.
你好，对不起我们不会说中文，可是要吃饭。请你看这张作菜表。
Nǐ hǎo, duì bú q wǒ mền bú huì shūo zhōng wén, kě shì yào chī fàn.
Qǐng nǐ kàn zhè zhāng zuò caǐ bǐao.

Can we have a table for _____ people?
请给我们一张_____人的餐桌
qǐng geǐ wǒ mền yī zhāng _____ rén dě cān zhūo

Do you have an English menu?
有没有英文菜单？
yǒu méi yǒu yīng wén caī dān

yes
有
yǒu

no
没有
meí yǒu

We want a
我们要吃
wǒ mền yaò chī

meal
一顿饭
yì dùn faǹ

snack
小吃
xǐao chī

If you want to
order by yourself,
continue to the
next section.

If you want the staff to choose the meal:
We don't know what to order; please decide for us.
We would like......
我们不知道吃什么，请你决定。我们要......
wǒ mền bù zhī daò chī shén mě, qǐng nǐ júe dìng.
wǒ mèn yào ......

bowl
碗
wǎn

plate
盘子
pán zǐ

glass
玻璃杯
bōlí beī

spoon
匙子
chí zǐ

254

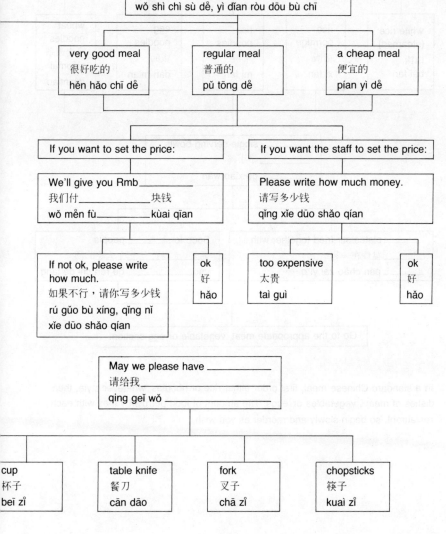

I am a vegetarian and do not want any meat
我是吃素的，一点肉都不吃
wǒ shì chì sù dě, yì dǐan ròu dōu bù chī

very good meal
很好吃的
hěn hǎo chī dě

regular meal
普通的
pǔ tōng dě

a cheap meal
便宜的
pían yì dě

If you want to set the price:

If you want the staff to set the price:

We'll give you Rmb_____
我们付_____块钱
wǒ měn fù_____kùai qīan

Please write how much money.
请写多少钱
qǐng xiě dūo shǎo qían

If not ok, please write how much.
如果不行，请你写多少钱
rú gǔo bù xíng, qǐng nǐ xiě dūo shǎo qían

ok
好
hǎo

too expensive
太贵
taì guì

ok
好
hǎo

May we please have _____
请给我_____
qǐng geǐ wǒ _____

cup
杯子
beī zǐ

table knife
餐刀
cān dāo

fork
叉子
chā zǐ

chopsticks
筷子
kuaì zǐ

255

Rice and Noodles

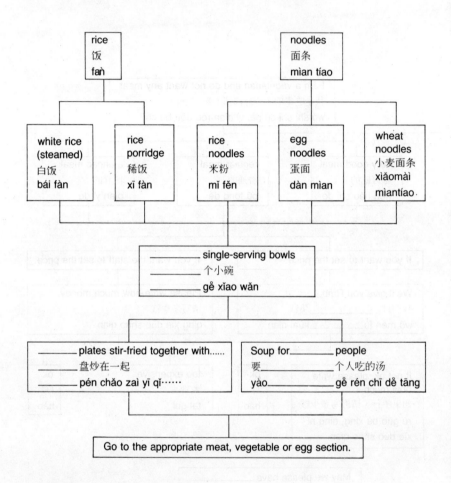

In a standard Chinese meal, first order either rice or noodles, whatever style, then dishes of meat , vegetables or eggs. The amount of food per dish varies with each restaurant, so begin slowly and reorder as you wish.

Meat

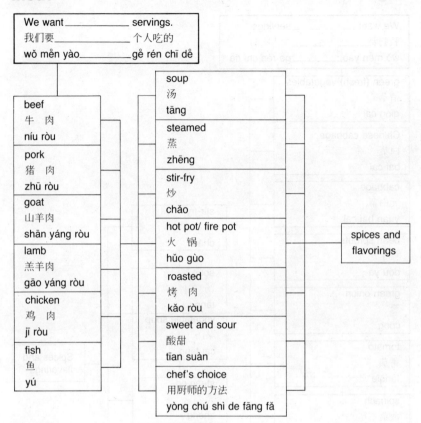

We want _____ servings.
我们要_____ 个人吃的
wǒ mén yào_____ gě rén chī dě

beef 牛 肉 níu ròu	soup 汤 tāng	
pork 猪 肉 zhū ròu	steamed 蒸 zhēng	
goat 山羊肉 shān yáng ròu	stir-fry 炒 chǎo	
lamb 羔羊肉 gāo yáng ròu	hot pot/ fire pot 火 锅 hǔo gùo	spices and flavorings
chicken 鸡 肉 jī ròu	roasted 烤 肉 kǎo ròu	
fish 鱼 yú	sweet and sour 酸甜 tīan suàn	
	chef's choice 用厨师的方法 yòng chú shì de fāng fǎ	

Eggs

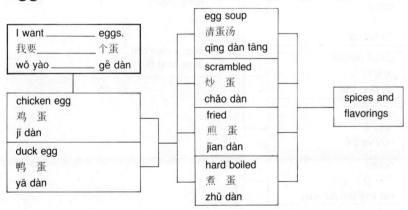

I want _____ eggs.
我要_____ 个蛋
wǒ yào _____ gě dàn

chicken egg 鸡 蛋 jī dàn	egg soup 清蛋汤 qīng dàn tāng	
duck egg 鸭 蛋 yā dàn	scrambled 炒 蛋 chǎo dàn	spices and flavorings
	fried 煎 蛋 jīan dàn	
	hard boiled 煮 蛋 zhǔ dàn	

Vegetables

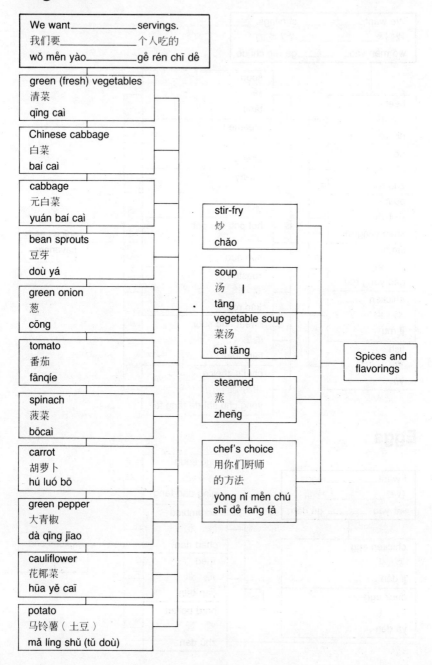

We want_____ servings.
我们要_____个人吃的
wǒ mén yào_____ gě rén chī dě

green (fresh) vegetables
清菜
qīng cài

Chinese cabbage
白菜
baí caì

cabbage
元白菜
yuán baí caì

bean sprouts
豆芽
doù yá

green onion
葱
cōng

tomato
番茄
fānqíe

spinach
菠菜
bōcaì

carrot
胡萝卜
hú luó bō

green pepper
大青椒
dà qīng jīao

cauliflower
花椰菜
hūa yě caī

potato
马铃薯（土豆）
mǎ líng shǔ (tǔ doù)

stir-fry
炒
chǎo

soup
汤
tāng
vegetable soup
菜汤
caì tāng

steamed
蒸
zheñg

chef's choice
用你们厨师
的方法
yòng nǐ mén chú
shī dě fañg fǎ

Spices and flavorings

Spices and Flavoring

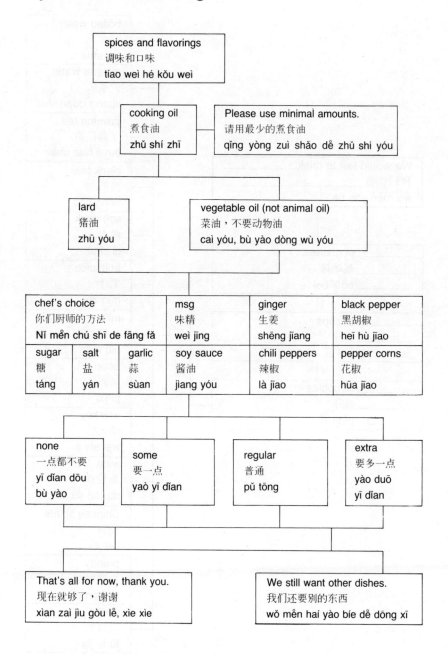

spices and flavorings
调味和口味
tíao weì hé kǒu weì

cooking oil
煮食油
zhǔ shí zhī

Please use minimal amounts.
请用最少的煮食油
qǐng yòng zuì shǎo dě zhǔ shi yóu

lard
猪油
zhū yóu

vegetable oil (not animal oil)
菜油，不要动物油
caì yóu, bù yào dòng wù yóu

chef's choice	msg	ginger	black pepper
你们厨师的方法	味精	生姜	黑胡椒
Nǐ měn chú shī de fāng fǎ	weì jīng	shēng jīang	heī hù jīao

sugar	salt	garlic	soy sauce	chili peppers	pepper corns
糖	盐	蒜	酱油	辣椒	花椒
táng	yán	sùan	jiang yóu	là jīao	hūa jīao

none
一点都不要
yī dían dōu
bù yào

some
要一点
yaò yī dían

regular
普通
pǔ tōng

extra
要多一点
yào duō
yī dían

That's all for now, thank you.
现在就够了，谢谢
xìan zaì jìu gòu lě, xìe xìe

We still want other dishes.
我们还要别的东西
wǒ měn haí yào bíe dě dōng xī

259

Drinks

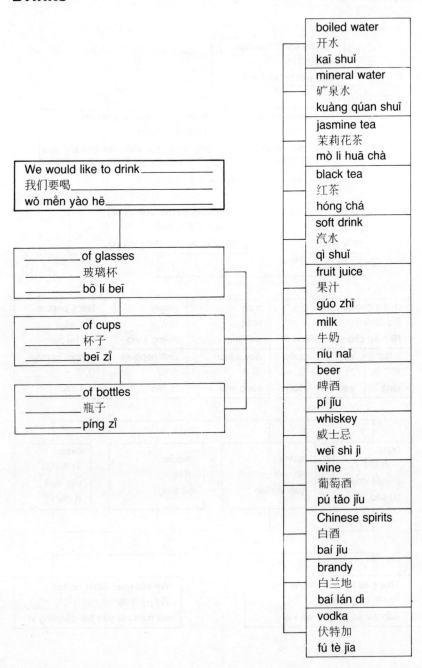

We would like to drink _____
我们要喝_____
wǒ mén yào hē_____

_____ of glasses
_____ 玻璃杯
_____ bō lí beī

_____ of cups
_____ 杯子
_____ beī zǐ

_____ of bottles
_____ 瓶子
_____ píng zǐ

boiled water
开水
kaī shuǐ

mineral water
矿泉水
kuàng qúan shuǐ

jasmine tea
茉莉花茶
mò li huā chà

black tea
红茶
hóng ćhá

soft drink
汽水
qì shuǐ

fruit juice
果汁
gúo zhī

milk
牛奶
níu naǐ

beer
啤酒
pí jǐu

whiskey
威士忌
weī shì jì

wine
葡萄酒
pú tǎo jǐu

Chinese spirits
白酒
baí jǐu

brandy
白兰地
baí lán dì

vodka
伏特加
fú tè jīa

Lodging

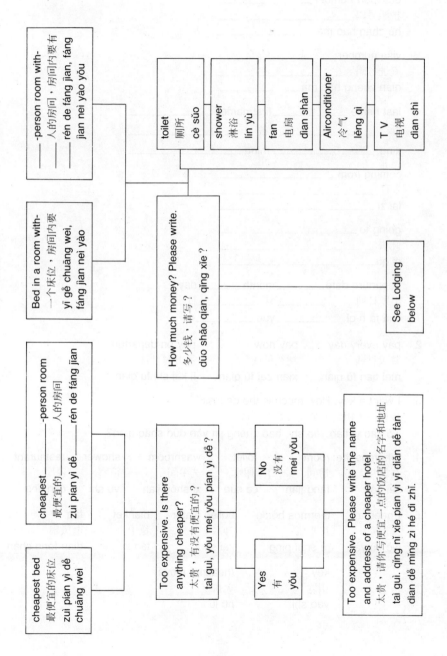

——-person room with-
人的房间，房间内要有
rén de fáng jiān, fáng
jiān nei yào yǒu

toilet
厕所
cè suǒ

shower
淋浴
lín yù

fan
电扇
dian shàn

Airconditioner
冷气
lěng qì

T V
电视
dian shì

Bed in a room with-
一个床位，房间内要
yi gě chuáng wei,
fáng jiān nei yào

How much money? Please write.
多少钱，请写？
duo shǎo qián, qǐng xiě ?

See Lodging
below

cheapest _____-person room
最便宜的 _____ 人的房间
zuì pian yì dě _____ rén de fáng jian

cheapest bed
最便宜的床位
zuì pian yì dě
chuáng wei

Too expensive. Is there
anything cheaper?
太贵，有没有便宜的？
tai gui, yǒu mei yǒu pian yì dě ?

No
没有
mei yǒu

Yes
有
yǒu

Too expensive. Please write the name
and address of a cheaper hotel.
太贵，请你写便宜一点的饭店的名字和地址
tai gui. qǐng nǐ xiě pian yì yǐ dian dě fàn
dian dě míng zì hé di zhǐ.

1. The following information is required for Chinese hotel registration.

    passport number _____
    护照号码 _____
    hù zhào haò mǎ _____

    visa number _____
    签证号码 _____
    qìan zhèng haò mǎ _____

    last name _____ first name _____
    姓 _____ 名 _____
    xìng, _____ míng _____

    coming from _____
    来自 _____
    laí zì _____

    going to _____
    此去 _____
    cǐ qù _____

    departure date _____ month _____ day
    出发日期 _____ 月 _____ 日
    chū fā ři qǐ _____ yue _____ ri

2. pay every day   pay now   pay on departure
   每天付钱   现在付钱   离开时付钱
   meǐ tīan fù qían   xìan zaì fù qían   lí kāi shí fù qían

3. I want a key. How much is the deposit?
   我要一条钥匙，保证金要多少钱？
   wǒ yào yī tiáo yào shǐ, bǎo zhèng jīn yào dūo shǎo qían?

4. Where is the: room   toilet   washroom   ·shower   restaurant
   在那儿：   房间   厕所   洗手间   浴室   餐厅
   zaì nǎr: fáng jían   cè sǔo   xi shǒu jīan   yù shì   cān tīng

5. I need a: thermos bottle   boiled water   blanket   fan
   我需要：   热水瓶   开水   毯子   电风扇
   wǒ xū yào   rè shuǐ ping   kaī shuǐ   tǎn zǐ°   dìan fēng shàn

                 key   (heating) stove
                 钥匙   火炉
                 yào shi   hǔ lù

262

6. Please turn on the electricity.
请你开电
qǐng nǐ kaī dìan

7. When is there hot water for washing? Please write.
From_____hours,_____ minutes to_____hours, _____minutes
什么时候有热水可以洗澡，请写。
从_____时_____分到_____时_____分
shén mě shí hoù yǒu rè shuǐ kě yǐ xǐ zǎo. Qǐng xǐe?

8. Do you have a clothes washing service?   yes   no
你们洗衣服吗？   洗   不洗
nǐ měn xǐ yī fù ma?   xǐ   bú xǐ

Transportation

Trains

1. I want to buy train tickets to _____
   我要买火车票去_____
   wǒ yaò maǐ huǒ chē pìao qù _____

2. that leaves on _____ month, _____ day, _____ hour, _____ minute
   (note: you may not know the departure time and can leave it blank)
   _____ 月 _____ 日 _____ 时 _____ 分开车
   _____ yuè, _____ rì, _____ shí, _____ feñ kāi chē

3. Do you have?
   有没有
   yǒ méi yǒu

hard sleeper	yes	no	price ? yuan		
硬卧	有	没有	多少钱？_____	块	
yìng wò	yǒu	meí yǒu	dūo shǎo qían? _____kuai		
soft sleeper					
软卧	有	没有	多少钱？_____	块	
rǔan wò	yǒu	meí yǒu	dūo shǎo qían? _____kuai		
hard seat					
硬座	有	没有	多少钱？_____	块	
yìng zùo	yǒu	meí yǒu	dūo shǎo qían? _____kuaì		
soft seat					
软座	有	没有	多少钱？_____	块	
rǔan zùo	yǒu	meí yǒu	dūo shǎo qían? _____kuaì		

4. I want _____ of _____(class) train tickets
   我要买_____张_____等的火车票。
   wǒ yào maǐ _____zhāng _____ deňg de hǒu chē pìao.

5. Train number____ departs at ____ hrs____min, from platform number____
   火车号码_____，_____时___分开车，_____月台。
   hǒu chē hào mǎ _____, ____shí ___ fēn kaī chē, _____ yùe taí.

6. When does the train arrive?
   火车什么时候到？
   huǒ chē shén mè shí hoù dào ?

   _____ month _____ day _____ hour _____ minutes.
   _____ 月 _____ 日 _____ 时 _____ 分到
   _____ yùe _____ rì _____ shí _____ fēn dào.

264

Upgrading Train Tickets

Go to the conductor's desk in
the hard seat car nearest the
dining car.

I would like to upgrade my ticket to:	hard sleeper	soft sleeper	soft seat
我要换票	硬卧	软卧	软座
wǒ yaò huàn pìao	yìng wò	rǔan wò	rǔan zùo

Where is the ticket conductor's desk?
车长卖票处在哪里？
chē zhǎng maǐ pìao chù zaì nǎ lǐ?

Are there any tickets?		Yes	No
有没有空位子？		有	没有
yǒu meí yǒu kòng weì zì?		yǒu	meí yǒu

I will wait here until you can sell me a ticket.
我在这里等你卖票。
wǒ zaì zhè lǐ děng nǐ maì pìao.

Buses

1. I want to buy bus tickets to _____.
   我要买公共汽车票去 _____。
   wǒ yào maǐ gōng gòng qì chē pìao qù_____.

2. that leaves on_____month,_____day
   _____月_____日开
   _____yuè, _____rì kāi

3. (If a bus is sold out, you may still be able to buy stand-up tickets, and
   the first availible seat will be given to you.)
   Please sell me stand up tickets.
   请卖给我站票
   qǐng maǐ geǐ wǒ zhàn pīao.

4. If there is no bus on that date, when does the next bus leave?
   Please write the date.
   如果那天没有车，下一班公共汽车什么时候开？请写。
   rú gǔo nà tīan meí yǒu chē, xìa yī bān gōng gòng qì chē shén mě
   shí hòu kai? Qǐng xǐe.

5. How much is one ticket? Please write the price.
一张车票多少钱？请写。
yī zhāng chē piào dūo shǎo qían? Qǐng xīe.

6. I want to buy＿＿＿＿＿ tickets.
我要买'＿＿＿＿＿＿张车票。
wǒ yào maǐ ＿＿＿＿＿＿ zhāng chē pìao

7. What time does the bus leave?
这班公共汽车什么时候开？
zhè bān gōng gòng qì chē shén mě shí hòu kai?

＿＿＿＿＿hours＿＿＿＿minutes
＿＿＿＿＿时＿＿＿＿分开
＿＿＿＿＿shí＿＿＿＿fēn kāi

8. What time can I load luggage on top of the bus?
我什么时候可以放行李？
wǒ shén mě shí hòu kě yǐ fàng xíng lǐ?

＿＿＿＿＿hours＿＿＿＿minute
＿＿＿＿＿时＿＿＿＿分
＿＿＿＿＿shí＿＿＿＿fēn

9. When does the bus arrive?
什么时候到？
shén mě shí hòu dào?

＿＿＿＿month＿＿＿day＿＿＿hours＿＿＿minutes
＿＿＿＿月＿＿＿日＿＿＿时＿＿＿分到
＿＿＿＿yùe＿＿＿rì＿＿＿shí＿＿＿fēn dào

10. Please show me where to board the bus.
请你带我去上车的地方。
qǐng nǐ daì wǒ qù shàng chē dě dì fāng.

Boats

1. I want to buy boat tickets to＿＿＿＿.
我要买船票去＿＿＿＿＿＿＿
wǒ yào maǐ chúan pìao qù＿＿＿＿.

2. that leaves on＿＿＿month,＿＿＿day,＿＿＿hrs＿＿＿min
＿＿＿月＿＿＿日＿＿＿时＿＿＿分开船
＿＿＿yùe,＿＿＿rì,＿＿＿shí,＿＿＿feñ kāi chúan

3. Do you have

	yes	no
special class 特等 tè děng	有 yǒu	没有 meí yǒu
first class 头等 tou děng	有 yǒu	没有 meí yǒu
second class 二等 èr děng	有 yǒu	没有 meí yǒu
third class 三等 sān děng	有 yǒu	没有 meí yǒu
fourth class 四等 sì děng	有 yǒu	没有 meí yǒu
fifth class 五等 wǔ děng	有 yǒu	没有 meí yǒu

number of people per room
每间房有多少人_____。
meǐ jīan fáng yǒu dūo shǎo rén.

price per person
多少钱一个人_____
dūo shǎo qían yī gě rén

4. I want_____tickets, _____class
我要买_____张 _____等船票
wǒ yaò maǐ _____zhāng _____děng chúan pìao

5. Boat number_____departs at____hrs____min from gate number_____.
船号码_____, _____时_____分开，在什么闸口_____。
chúan haò mǎ _____, _____shí_____ fēn kaī, zaì shén mě
zhá kǒu _____?

6. When can I board the boat?
   什么时候上船
   Shén mě shí hòu shàng chúan

   _____month_____day _____hrs _____min
   _____月_____日_____时_____分
   _____yuè _____rì_____shí_____fēn

7. When does the boat arrive?
   什么时候到
   Shén me shí hòu dào

   _____month_____day_____hrs _____min
   _____月_____日_____时_____分到
   _____yuè_____rì_____shí_____fēn dào

8. I want to upgrade my ticket to (see #3)
   我要换票
   Wǒ yào huàn pìao

Planes

1. I want to buy plane tickets to_____.
   我要买飞机票去_____。
   wǒ yào maǐ feī jī pìao qù_____.

2. leaving on _____ month,_____day
   _____月_____日起飞
   _____yuè, _____rì qǐ fēi

3. flight number _____
   飞机号码_____
   feī jī hào mǎ_____

4. If there is no flight that day, when is the next available flight? Please write.
   如果那天没有飞机，下一班飞机什么时候？请写
   rú gǔo nà tīan meí yǒu feī jī, xìa yī bān feī jī shén mě shí hòu？Qǐng xiě.

5. I want to buy_____tickets.
   我要买_____张票。
   wǒ yào maǐ _____zhāng pìao.

268

6. What time does the bus depart the CAAC office?.
   从民航办公室去飞机场，汽车什么时候开？
   cóng mín háng bàn gōng shì qù feī jī chǎng, qì chē shén mě shí hòu kāi?

   _____ hrs _____ min
   _____时_____分起飞
   _____shí_____fēn fei?

7. What time does the flight take-off ? _____ hrs _____ min
                                          _____时_____分起飞
                                          _____ shí _____fēn ǒi fei

8. What time does the flight arrive? _____ hrs _____ min
   什么时候到？   _____时_____分到
   shén mě shí hoù dào?   _____ shí _____fēn dao

Hitchhiking

1. Where are you going?
   你去什么地方？
   nǐ qù shén mě dì fāng?

2. Can you take me to_____?   Yes   No
   你可不可以带我去_____?   可以   不可以
   nǐ ké bù ké yǐ daì wǒ qù _____?   ke yi bù ke yi

3. If not, can you take me part way towards_____?   Yes   No
   如果不能，能不能带我往_____   可以   不可以
   rú gǔo bú néng, néng bù néng daì wǒ wǎng _____.   ke yi bù ke yi

4. What time do you leave
   我们什么时候走？
   wǒ mén shén mě shí hòu zǒu

   Today_____hrs :_____min or tomorrow _____hrs _____min
   今天_____时_____分开；明天_____时_____分开
   jīn tīan _____ shí_____ fēn kaī;míng tīan_____shí_____ fēn kaī

5. What time will we arrive?   _____hrs _____min
   什么时候到？   _____时_____分到
   shén mě shí hòu dào?   _____ shí_____fēn daò

6. How many kilometers to_____?
   去_____多少公里？
   qù_____ dūo shǎo gōng lǐ ?

269

7. I need to use the toilet.
   我要用厕所
   wǒ yào yòng cè sǔo.

8. Where can I wash up?
   在哪里洗手？
   zaì nǎ lǐ xǐ shǒu?

9. I'm hungry, do you want to eat?   Yes   No
   我饿了，吃饭吗？   好   不好
   wǒ è le, chī fàn mǎ?   hǎo   bù hǎo

10. Can we stop for a few minutes to take photos?   Yes   No
    请你停车，我要拍照片   好   不好
    qǐng nǐ tíng chē, wǒ yào paī zhāo pìan.   hǎo   bù hǎo

11. If you write your address, I will mail photos to you.   Okay   Not okay
    写你的地址给我，我会寄照片给你，好不好？   好   不好
    xǐe ni de dì zhǐ géi wǒ, wǒ hui jì zhāo pìan geǐ nǐ,   hǎo   bù hǎo
    hǎo bú hǎo.

12. I want to stay in the same hotel as you.   Okay   Not okay
    我要跟你住同一间旅社   好   不好
    wǒ yào gēn nǐ zhù toǹg yi jīan lǔ shè.   hǎo   bù hǎo

Useful Words and Phrases

1. Numbers

one	一	yī
two	二	èr
three	三	sān
four	四	sì
five	五	wǔ
six	六	líu
seven	七	qī
eight	八	bā
nine	九	jǐu
ten	十	shí
hundred	百	baǐ
thousand	千	qīan
ten thousand	万	wán
twentyfive(two＋ten＋five)	二十五	er shí wǔ

2. Money

How much money?	多少钱	duō shǎo qían?
too expensive	太贵	taì guì
Chinese dollar	块(元)	kuaì (yuàn)
10 cent denomination	毛(角)	máo (jǐao)
1 cent denomination	分	fēn
$24.37 (two＋ten＋four＋kuai＋	二十四元	èr shí sì kuaì sañ
three＋mao＋seven＋fen)	三角七分	máo qī fēn

3. Time

today	今天	jīn tīan
tomorrow	明天	míng tīan
yesterday	昨天	zúo tīan
day	天	tīan
month	月	yùe
year	年	nían
morning	上午/早上	shàng wǔ/zǎo shàng
noon	中午	zhōng wǔ
afternoon	下午	xìa wǔ
night	晚上	wǎn shàng
Sunday	星期天	xīng qī tīan
Monday	星期一	xīng qī yī

Tuesday	星期二	xīng qī èr
Wednesday	星期三	xīng qī šan
Thursday	星期四	xīng qī sì
Friday	星期五	xīng qī wǔ
Saturday	星期六	xīng qī líu

4. Useful expressions

How are you?	你好吗	nǐ haǒ mǎ
Thank you	谢谢	xìe xìe
Please	请	qǐng
I'm sorry	对不起	duì bù qǐ
Excuse me		
(sorry to trouble you)	麻烦你	má fán nǐ
I don't smoke	不会抽烟	bù huì chōu yān
Okay/good	好	hǎo
Not okay/bad	不好	bù hǎo
To want	要	yào
Don't want	不要	bù yào

5. Where is the _____ ?

	在那里	_____ zaì nǎ lǐ
Bank of China	中国银行	zhōng gúo yín háng
barber shop	理发店	lǐ fā dian
bath house	浴室	yù shì
bicycle rental	出租自行车	chū zū zì xíng chē
boat dock	码头	mǎ tóu
bus station	汽车站	qì chē zhàn
CAAC	中国民航	zhōng gúo mín háng
CITS	中国旅行社	zhōng gúo lǚ xíng shè
city bus stop	公共汽车站	gōng gòng qì chē zhàn
post/communications office	邮电局	yóu dìan jú
Foreign Affairs Bureau	外事局	waì shì jú
GongAnJu(PSB)	公安局	gōng ān jú
hospital	医院	yī yùan
hotel	宾馆，饭店，	bīn gǔan, fàn dìan,
	招待所	zhāo daì sǔo
mountain	山	shān
park	公园	gōng yuán
philatelic bureau	集邮局	jí yóu jú
post office	邮局	yóu jú
restaurant	餐厅/饭店	cān tīng/fàn dìan
taxi	出租汽车	chū zū qì chē
toilet	厕所	cè sǔo

| train station | 火车站 | hǔo chē zhàn |
| washroom | 洗手间 | xǐ shǒu jiàn |

6. I want to buy _____ 　我要买 　wǒ yaò maǐ_____

map	地图	dì tǔ
toilet paper	卫生纸	weì shēng zhǐ
soap	肥皂	feí zào
shampoo	洗发剂	xī fā jì
sanitary napkins	卫生巾	weì sheńg jīn
battery	电池	diàn chí
flashlight/torch	手电筒	shǒu dìan tǒng
candle	蜡烛	là zhú
lighter	打火机	dǎ hǔo jī
stamps	邮票	yóu pìao
envelope	信封	xìn fēng
post cards	明信片	míng xìn pìan
beer	啤酒	pí jǐu
cigarette	香烟	xīang yān
toothpaste	牙膏	yá gāo
condom	避孕套	bì yùn tào

Health and Medicine

English	Chinese	Pinyin
abdominal pain	腹痛	fù tòng
allergy	敏感	mǐn gǎn
altitude sickness	高度症	gāo dù zhèng
antibiotic	抗生素	kàng shèng sù
antiseptic	消毒剂	xìao dú jì
aspirin	阿斯匹林	ā sī pī lìn
bite	咬	yǎo
blood/bleeding	流血	līu xùe
broken(bone)	断(骨)	dùan(gǔ)
bruise	伤痕	shāng hén
burn	烧伤	shāo shāng
cold	感冒	gǎn mào
cough	咳嗽	ké sōu
cut	伤口	shāng kǒu
diarrhoea	拉肚子	lā dù zì
doctor	医生	yī shēng
eye	眼睛	yǎn jìng
fever/temperature	发烧	fā shāo
headache	头痛	tóu tóng
heart	心脏	xīn zàng
injection	打针	dǎ zhēn
insulin	胰岛素	yí dǎo sù
itch	发痒	fā yǎng
kidney	肾脏	shèn zàng
lungs	肺脏	feì zàng
lip balm	润唇膏	rùn chún gāo
liver	肝脏	gàn zàng
nauseous	恶心	ě xīn
oxygen	氧气	yǎng qì
pain	疼痛	téng tòng
penicillin	盆尼西林	pén ni xī lin
rabies	狂犬病	kuáng qǔan bìng
sick	生病	shēng bīng
sinus	慢性鼻窦炎	màn xìng bí dōu yān
sore	痛	tòng
sprain	扭伤	nǐu shāng
throat	咽喉	yān hóu
tired	累	leì
toothache	牙痛	yá tòng

Tibetan Glossary

by Milan M. Melvin

The following list of Tibetan words and phrases is all too brief but sufficient for you to acquire the basic necessities and, depending on your inclination, to get out of or into trouble. Tibetans are wonderful, fun-loving people and even this small snatch of their language can launch you into some unforgettable relationships.

Pronunciation

The vowel 'a' must be pronounced like the 'a' in 'father' — soft and long, unless it appears as -ay, in which case it is pronounced as in 'say' or 'day'. A slash through a letter indicates the neutral vowel sound uh.

Word Order

Simple Tibetan sentences are constructed as follows:

Noun (or pronoun)	Object	Verb
I	mountains	going
Nga	kang ree la	dro ge ray

The verb is always last.

Verb Tenses

Tibetan verbs are composed of two parts: the root, which carries the meaning of the verb, and the ending, which indicates the tense (past, present, or future). The simplest and most common verb form, consisting of the root plus the ending -ge ray, can be used for the present and future tenses. The root is strongly accented in speech. In order to form the past tense, substitute the ending -song.

'nyo ge ray' means, loosely, 'buying, going to buy'
'nyo song' means 'bought'

Only the verb roots are given in this glossary; remember to add the appropriate endings.

Pronouns

I Nga
you (singular) kirang
he, she, it korang, ko
we nga-tso
you (plural) kirang-tso
they korong-tso
this dee la
my, mine nge, ngay, narang kee
your, yours (singular) kirang kee
his, hers, its korang kee
our, ours narang-tso yee
your, yours (plural) kirang-tso yee
their, theirs korong-tso yee

Relations

name ming la
child poo goo
boy poo
girl po mo
man, husband cho ga
woman, wife kyee men
brother poon dya
sister poon kya, ah jee la

275

father   pa ba, pa la
mother   ah ma

Time

minute   ka ma
hour   tchø zø
day   nyee ma, shak ma
week   døn ta
month   da wa
year   lo
day before yesterday   ke nyee ma
yesterday   ke sang
last night   dang gong
today   ta ring
tomorrow   sang nyee, sang
day after tomorrow   nang nyee
now   tanda, ta ta
always   tak par
morning   sho kay
afternoon   nyeen goon

Numbers

one   cheek
two   nee
three   soom
four   shee
five   nga
six   trook
seven   døn
eight   gye, kay
nine   koo, goo
ten   tchoo
eleven   tchoop cheek
twelve   tchoog nee
thirteen   tchook soom
fourteen   tchoop shee
fifteen   tchoo nga
sixteen   tchoo trook
seventeen   tchoop don
eighteen   tchup kyay
nineteen   tchur koo
twenty   nee shoo tamba
twenty-one   nee shoo sak cheek
twenty-two   nee shoo sak nee
twenty-three   nee shoo sak soom
twenty-four   nee shoo sup shee
twenty-five   nee shoo say nga
twenty-six   nee shoo sar trook
twenty-seven   nee shoo sub døn
twenty-eight   nee shoo sap kay
twenty-nine   nee sar koo

thirty   soom tchoo tamba
forty   sheep joo tamba
fifty   ngup tchoo tamba
sixty   trook tchoo tamba
seventy   døn tchoo tamba
eighty   kyah joo tamba
ninety   koop tchoo tamba
one hundred   gyah tamba
two hundred   nee gyah
three hundred   soom gyah

Food

barley   droo, nay
roasted barley flour   tsampa
beef   lang sha
breakfast   sho kay ka lak
butter   mar
cheese   choo ra
chicken meat   cha cha
chili peppers   mar tsa
cigarette   ta mak
corn   droo
egg   go nga
flour   to sheep, pak pay
food   ka lak
fruit   shing dong
lunch   nyeen goong ka lak
dinner   kong dak ka lak
meat   sha
milk   o ma
millet   ko do
onion   tsong
potato   sho ko
rice   dray
sugar   chee ma ka ra
tea   cha
vegetables   ngup tsay, tsay
wheat   tro, dro
delicious   shimbo

Other Nouns

bag   gye mo, gye wa
blanket   nya tee, gam lo, nye zen
book (common)   teb
book (religious)   pay zya
boots   som ba, lam
bridge   sam ba
candle   yang la
cave   trak poo, poo goo
cup   mok, cha gar
dog   kee, kyee

276

donkey poon goo
fire may
house kang ba
hill ree
kerosene sa noom
kettle tib lee
knife tee, tree
lake tso
matches moo see, tsak ta
medicine men
   pill ree poo
moon da wa
mountain kang ree
mountain pass la
cooking pot hai yoom, rak sang
rain char pa
river tsang po, tchoo, chu
rock do
room kang mee
snow kang, ka
spoon tur ma, too ma
star kar ma
stomach tro ko
sun nyee ma
thread koo ba
Tibet Pø la
Tibetan people Pø pa
Tibetan language Pø kay
trail lam ga
umbrella nyee doo
water tchoo, chu
Westerner in gee, pee ling
wind loong bo chem bo
wood shing

Verbs

arrive lep
bring kay sho
buy nyo
carry kay
feel cold cha
come yong
cook ka lak so
drink toong
eat shay sa
forget jay, chay
get up lang
give tay, nang
be hungry tro ko tok
learn lap
look meek tang

make, fix so
see ton
sell tsong
be sick na
sit, stay day, shook
teach lap
go dro, do
wait goo
work le ka chee

Adjectives

lost lak song
thirsty ka kam
good yak po
bad yak po min doo
big chem bo
small choon choon
weak shook choon choon
strong shyook chem bo
empty tong ba
full kang
beautiful dzay bo
expensive gong chem bo
cold trang mo
hot tsa bo
different kye per, cheek be ma ray
same nang shing
few tet see tet see
much, many mang bo
light yang bo, yang
heavy jee po, jee ba tsa po

Adverbs

up ya la
down ma la
near nye bo
far ta ring bo, gyang bo
here deh roo
there pa roo, pa ge
left yom ba
right yay ba
slow ka lee
quickly dyok po, dyok po
really, very she ta, she tai

Miscellaneous

and tang, ta
another yang ya
how much, how many ka tzø
maybe cheek chay na
sometimes tsam tsam

277

other   shem ba, shen da, yem ba
what   ka ray
where from   ka ne

where to   ka ba, ka par, ka roo
who   soo
why   ka ray chay nay

Phrases

hello!, greetings!   tashi delay
enough!, stop!   deek song
finished   tsar song, deek song
I do not understand   ha ko ma song
I understand, I know   ha ko gee doo, ha ko song
right!, really!, yes   ray, la ray
very important   kay chembo, ne ka chem bo
what is this called?   dee ming la ka ray see ge ray?   dee ka ra ray?
how much is (this)?   (dee la) gong ka tzø ray?
it doesn't matter   kay kay chee ge ma ray, kay kay so ge ma ray
be careful, slowly   ka lee ka lee
I am hungry   nge tro ko to kee doo
are/is there any (onions)   (tsong) doo-ay, (tsong) doog-ay?
please bring (onions)   (tsong) kay sho ah
o.k., thanks   la so
goodnight   sim jam, sim jam nang ro
how far is (Lhasa)?   (Lhasa la) gyan lø yø ray?
how are you?   kirang sook po day bo yeen bay?, kirang ko sook day be yeen
   bay?
I am fine   sook po day bo yeen, day bo doo

Chronology of Periods in Chinese History

Palaeolithic	c.600,000–7000 BC
Neolithic	c.7000–1600 BC
Shang	c.1600–1027 BC
Western Zhou	1027–771 BC
Eastern Zhou	770–256 BC
Spring and Autumn Annals	770–476 BC
Warring States	475–221 BC
Qin	221–207 BC
Western (Former) Han	206 BC–8 AD
Xin	9–24
Eastern (Later) Han	25–220
Three Kingdoms	220–265
Western Jin	265–316
Northern and Southern Dynasties	317–589
Sixteen Kingdoms	317–439
☐Former Zhao	304–329
☐Former Qin	351–383
☐Later Qin	384–417
Northern Wei	386–534
Western Wei	535–556
Northern Zhou	557–581
Sui	581–618
Tang	618–907
Five Dynasties	907–960
Northern Song	960–1127
Southern Song	1127–1279
Jin (Jurchen)	1115–1234
Yuan (Mongol)	1279–1368
Ming	1368–1644
Qing (Manchu)	1644–1911
Republic	1911–1949
People's Republic	1949–
Cultural Revolution	1966–1976

Festivals and the Lunar Calendar

Nature has provided the earth with two obvious time markers — the sun and the moon. The huge majority of Chinese festivals, including minority festivals, are dated by the traditional lunar calendar. Lunar time, being linked to the regular appearance of the full moon, had certain clear advantages for the organization of social activities before the invention of modern artificial light. However, because the sun regulates the seasons, any agricultural civilization needed to reckon its working year by solar time. The Gregorian calendar, used everywhere in the modern world, is a solar calendar. Ancient China had a solar calendar as well, which is still used to regulate the agricultural year.

But how has the lunar calendar coexisted with the solar, and how have common, simple people guided their farming by the sun while determining nearly everything else by the moon?

This astronomical puzzle was solved at least three thousand years ago:

Given that one lunar month = 29½ days
then 12 lunar months = 354 days
and given that one solar year = 365 days

then the question is: what about the odd 11 days? Or, how can the two calendars be adjusted in such a way as to bring sun and moon reckoning into harmony?

Simply speaking, the solution can be explained in terms of two discoveries and two practical steps.

Discovery One: The 11 days left over between the end of a 354-day lunar year and a 365-day solar year can be partly 'mopped up' by adding extra months now and then, thus making some lunar years 13 months long instead of 12. For example, if one extra moon month is added in three solar years, the discrepancy between the solar calendar (3 × 365 = 1095 days) and the lunar calendar (12 + 12 + 13 moon months = 1091½ days) is reduced to 3½ days.

Step One: The practice of adding extra (intercalary) months began very early, probably before 1,000 BC.

Discovery Two: Before the eighth century BC, it was discovered that 19 complete years of solar time contain almost exactly the same number of days as 235 complete months of lunar time. In other words, the movements of sun and moon, which are naturally out of step if considered over the period of one year, fall naturally into step over a period of 19 years. With this knowledge, the two calendars obtained a remarkably good fit by simply adding seven extra moon months every 19 years.

Step Two: Seven intercalary months were indeed added to the lunar calendar every 19 years, most at three-year but some at two-year intervals.

Today, practically speaking, the lunar calendar lags approximately four to six weeks behind the solar calendar. For example, lunar First Month usually falls in February, the Fifth Month in June or early July and the Eighth Month in September.

The Lunar New Year Festival, also known as Spring Festival (*chunjie*), is the most important celebration of all, a time of universal happiness and family reunions.

Below are the dates of Lunar New Year's Day that correspond to the solar (Gregorian) calendar.

1988   February 17
1989   February 6
1990   January 27
1991   February 15
1992   February 4
1993   January 23
1994   February 10
1995   January 31

Joan Law and Barbara E. Ward

China's Endangered Species

The list of endangered species in China is long and includes animals as varied as the Beibu Gulf sea cow, Yangzi River crocodile, Xinjiang wild ass and Chinese paddlefish. Among hundreds, only 80 endangered species are protected by the United Nations Convention on International Trade in Endangered Species (CITES), a convention designed to halt international trade in threatened wildlife. China has signed and ratified CITES, though no nationwide effort to curtail the exploitation of endangered animals has yet been made. In many cases, hunters and trappers are unaware that the animals they hunt face extinction or that they work in violation of Chinese law. In some instances, police officials or game wardens have used their positions to exploit these animals for their own profit.

As a foreigner traveling in China, you will almost certainly see rare animals being sold and may even be approached by local merchants who view you as a potential customer for their exotic prizes. During our travels we came across many rare birds, pangolins, civet cats, a snow leopard pelt, and were even told by smugglers of an available panda skin. Rather than curse hunters and traders in China for their cruelty, use the attention you attract in a market to spread vital information about the status of the animals you see. Wildlife experts acknowledge that hunters and trappers in remote areas of China (the people who supply smugglers with their animals) are probably unaware of the endangered status of the animals they prey upon. When you encounter a rare animal in a market, dead or alive present the following paragraph to the merchant:

By signing the Convention on International Trade in Endangered Species, China has shown a commitment to protect wildlife threatened with extinction. The hunting and sale of this animal is against both Chinese and international law.

签名加入了国际稀有生物交易公约之后，中国表现了愿保护濒临绝种野生动物的决心。这类野生动物在中国及其他国家一律禁猎及售。

We have included a short description of threatened animals most commonly exploited for economic gain in China to give you a better chance of identifying them in the markets. There are, of course, many others on the road to oblivion that you should keep an eye out for.

Animals classified as endangered will probably not survive if present conditions continue. Those classified as vulnerable will become endangered in the near future.

Snow leopard (xuebao) 雪豹
Status – endangered
This elusive big cat roams the high mountain regions of Central Asia. It has a milky-white coat covered in dark spots, with a long, magnificently full tail. Snow leopards are still found in the mountains of western Sichuan and northern Yunnan, though most travelers are far more likely to see one (or parts of one) being sold by fur traders in Chengdu, Lhasa or Kashgar. Prized

for their coats and paws, they are still hunted extensively, even though they now number only in the hundreds.

Cloud leopard (yunbao) 云豹
Status – endangered
The nocturnal cloud leopard, native to the jungles of south China and Southeast Asia, is an exotic delicacy in Hong Kong and Canton. Intensive hunting, encouraged by high prices for live specimens, has driven this cat close to extinction. Cloud leopard pelts are also in demand and quite valuable. Only several hundred cloud leopards remain on earth.

Pangolin (chuanshan jia) 穿山甲
Status – vulnerable
Pangolins, or scaly anteaters, live in the forests of Nepal, Burma, India, southern China and Southeast Asia. The commercial demand for them is so great that their numbers are being depleted rapidly. Their flesh, including tongue, blood and internal organs, is a Cantonese delicacy; their shell-like armor and soft leather underbellies make valuable shoes, boots and leather accessories. Live pangolins, caged and ready for shipment to Hong Kong, are a common sight on the streets of Guangzhou, Wuzhou and Nanning, despite Chinese laws strictly prohibiting their exploitation.

Muntjac (ji) 麂
Status – vulnerable
Muntjacs are small, nocturnal deer, sometimes known as Barking Deer. Males are characterized by a set of long, tusklike upper canine teeth used for defense. Muntjacs are hunted widely in China to satisfy both local and international consumers. Their treatment in captivity is especially cruel because cooks believe it is important that muntjac be served as freshly as possible. At cooking time, one hind leg is chopped off a live muntjac and the animal is left, suffering but not dead, until more flesh is needed for cooking. Though muntjacs are threatened, they are still unprotected by Chinese law.

Civet cat (lingmao) 灵猫
Status – vulunerable
Civet cats are long bodied, short legged carnivores that live throughout Asia. There are many varieties, though all have a cat-like appearance, with some characteristics of racoons. It is not common knowledge in China that their numbers are dwindling rapidly; they will become extinct if present hunting practices continue. Civets are desired both for their meat, popular in China and Hong Kong, and for a secretion of their anal gland used to manufacture perfume. Civet cats are common in the markets of Southwest China.

Slow loris (lanhou) 懒猴
Status – endangered
The slow loris is a primate that inhabits the forests of southern China and Southeast Asia. Lorises are covered in grey or brown fur and have large eyes characteristically circled by dark patches. As their name implies, they move slowly with great deliberation, often crawling through trees in slow motion. Lorises are hunted both for their fur and for their meat, which is a Cantonese delicacy. They are often found in the markets of Guangzhou, Wuzhou and Nanning, in violation of Chinese law. They are coming close to extinction.

Tiger (laohu) 老虎
Status – endangered

Tigers were once found throughout the forests of southern Asia. It is little wonder that tigers are a popular target for poachers and smugglers. Everything from their pelts to their blood, hearts gall bladders, eyes, teeth, paws and bones are of value. Tiger blood is said to increase sexual virility in human males and teeth, paws and eyes are powerful symbols of good luck. Many tigers are captured and killed in China or smuggled live through China on their way to Hong Kong, Taiwan or other overseas markets. This trade is in violation of both Chinese and international law. Tiger skins are common in the fur markets of Chengdu, Lhasa and Kashgar, and some are found elsewhere. The tigers that remain in China are so widely dispersed and relentlessly hunted that experts fear they are headed for extinction.

Giant panda (da xiongmao) 大熊猫
Status – endangered

The giant panda, found in northwest Sichuan and southern Gansu, is said by experts to number under 1,000. Human encroachment upon their natural habitat, cyclical decline in their food supply of bamboo, and an extremely short breeding period have contributed to a decline in their numbers in recent years. International attention has brought foreign capital and scientific expertise to help the panda, and there has been progress in captive breeding. In spite of this increased awareness, pandas are still hunted and their skins periodically surface in China or Hong Kong, en route to lucrative Western markets.

Birds
Many rare birds are exploited in China for economic gain. Markets throughout the Southwest boast a wide selection of owls, eagles, hawks and falcons, as well as many more exotic specimens. Birds are either sought as pets or for their feathers, meat, eyes and bones. Birds in China, numerous as they are in the marketplace, fare badly, perhaps more so than other rare animals. Dozens of species are approaching extinction.

Recommended Reading

General Background

Bonavia, David. *The Chinese* (London: Penguin Books, 1981)

Fairbank, John King. *The United States and China* (Cambridge: Harvard University Press, 1985)

Fairbank, John King et al. *East Asia: Tradition and Transformation* (London: George Allen & Unwin, 1973)

Leys, Simon. *Chinese Shadows* (London: Penguin Books, 1974)

Leys, Simon. *The Burning Forest* (New York: Henry Holt and Co., Inc., 1986)

Liang, Heng and Shapiro, Judith. *Son of the Revolution* (New York: Vintage Books, 1984)

Polo, Marco; trans. R.E. Lathan. *The Travels of Marco Polo* (London: Penguin Books, 1958)

Spence, Jonathan. *The Gate of Heavenly Peace: The Chinese and Their Revolution* (London: Faber and Faber, 1982)

Tuchman, Barbara. *Stilwell and the American Experience in China* (New York: The Macmillan Company, 1970)

Wilson, Dick. *The Long March* (London: Penguin Books, 1971)

Literature

Barme, Geremie and Minford, John, eds. *Seeds of Fire* (Hong Kong: Far Eastern Economic Review, 1986)

Chen, Ruoxi. *The Old Man and Other Stories* (Hong Kong: Renditions Paperbacks, 1986)

Xixi. *A Girl Like Me and Other Stories* (Hong Kong: Renditions Paperbacks, 1986)

Southwest China

Baber, E. Colborne. *Travels and Researches in Western China* (Taipei: Ch'eng Wen Publishing Co., 1971)

Backus, Charles. *The Nan-chao Kingdom and Tang China's Southwestern Frontier* (Cambridge: Cambridge University Press, 1981)

Davies, Major H.R. *Yun-nan — The Link Between India and the Yangtze* (London: Cambridge University Press, 1909)

de Beauclair, Inez. *Ethnographic Studies: the Collected Papers of Inez de Beauclair* (Taipei: Southern Materials Center, Inc., 1986)

Fitzgerald, C.P. *The Tower of Five Glories: A Study of the Min Chia of Ta Li* (Connecticut: Hyperion Press Inc., 1973)

Goullart, Peter. *Forgotten Kingdom* (London: John Murray, 1957)

Hsu, Francis. *Under the Ancestor's Shadow* (Stanford: Stanford University Press, 1975)

Rock, Joseph F. *The Ancient Na-Khi Kingdom of Southwest China* (Cambridge: Harvard University Press, 1947)

Rock, Joseph F. *Through the Great River Trenches of Asia* (Washington, D.C.: National Geographic Society, 1926)

Sutton, S.B. *In China's Border Provinces: The Turbulent Career of Joseph Rock, Botanist/Explorer* (New York: Hastings House, 1974)

Ward, F. Kingdon. *Plant Hunting on the Edge of the World* (London: Cadogan Books, 1986)

Wilson, E.H. *A Naturalist in Western China* (London: Cadogan Books, 1986)

Zhong, Xiu. *Yunnan Travelogue: 100 Days in Southwest China* (Beijing: New World Press, 1983)

Tibet

Avedon, John F. *In Exile from the Land of Snows* (London: Wisdom Publications, 1984)

Dalai Lama. *My Land and My People* (New York: Potala Corp., 1983)

Snellgrove, David and Richardson, Hugh. *A Cultural History of Tibet* (Boulder: Prajna Press, 1980)

Stein, R.A. *Tibetan Civilization* (Stanford: Stanford University Press, 1972)

Tucci, Giuseppe. *The Religions of Tibet* (London: Routledge & Kegan Paul, 1980)

Health

Hackett, Peter H. *Mountain Sickness — Prevention, Recognition and Treatment* (New York: The American Alpine Club, 1980)

Weights and Measures

Length

1 m = 100 cm = 3.28 ft = 1.09 yd
1 ft = 0.30 m
1 km = 1,000 m = 0.62 mile
1 mile = 1,760 yd = 1.60 km

Area

1 ha = 2.50 acres
1 km^2 = 0.38 mile^2
1 mile^2 = 2.60 km^2

Volume

1 l = 0.26 gal
1 gal = 3.78 l

Weight

1 kg = 1,000 gm = 2.20 lb
1 lb = 0.45 kg
1 oz = 28 gm

Temperature

Celsius: $C = \frac{5}{9}(F-32)$
Fahrenheit: $F = \frac{9}{5}C + 32$

Index of Places

287